OFFICE FOR NATIONAL STATISTICS

Ethnicity in the

windon
ollege

mped
other

1 and
ill be

Volume Three
Social geography and ethnicity in
Britain: geographical spread, spatial
concentration and internal migration.

Edited by Peter Ratcliffe

London: HMSO

Notice
On 1st April 1996 the Office of Population Censuses and Surveys (OPCS) and the
Central Statistical Office (CSO) merged to form the Office for National Statistics.
The Office for National Statistics will be responsible for the full range of
functions carried out by OPCS and CSO.

The views expressed in this publication are not necessarily those of the Office for
National Statistics.

Front cover photograph: © Crispin Hughes/Photofusion

OFFICE FOR NATIONAL STATISTICS

ETHNICITY IN THE 1991 CENSUS
Volume 3 Social geography and ethnicity in Britain: geographical spread, spatial concentration and internal migration

ISBN 0 11 691657 5

CORRECTIONS

page viii   The following biographical note should be included.

Philip Rees is Professor of Population Geography at the University of Leeds. Over the 1992-96 period he has worked as Coordinator of the ESRC/JISC 1991 Census of Population programme. This programme has purchased Census data from the UK Census Offices and made it available in machine readable form to all UK academic researchers via easy-to-use access software. All the authors of these ethnic volumes will have used this resource. His interests cover population matters in Europe as well as the United Kingdom, and he has recently completed an edited volume *Population Migration in the European Union* (John Wiley, 1996).

page 147   Table 4.4. The final data column (migration within regions, %) should read:

All	7.6
White	7.5
All ethnic minorities	8.3
Black-total	9.4
Caribbean	6.8
African	14.9
Other	10.9
South Asian	6.5
Indian	6.1
Pakistani	6.6
Bangladeshi	8.3
Chinese and Other	11.1
Chinese	10.9
Other-Asian	11.3
Other-Other	11.0

London: HMSO
September 1996

Contents

Foreword

1991 was an important landmark in British census taking; a question on ethnic group was included for the first time.

ONS invited over 40 academic experts on ethnicity from a number of fields – including demography, social statistics, geography and sociology – to contribute chapters to four volumes of analyses of 1991 Census ethnic group data. Amongst these authors, five also acted as editors.

I am particularly grateful to the editors and the authors for their excellent work, and also to John Haskey who acted as the series coordinator.

JOHN FOX
Group Director
Census, Population and Health Group
ONS

Preface

This is the third volume in the series commissioned by the Office of Population Censuses and Surveys (now the Office for National Statistics) to analyse the ethnic group question in the 1991 Census. The 1991 Census was the first in Great Britain in which such a question had been posed. The other volumes in the series are:

Volume 1 Demographic characteristics of the ethnic minority populations. Edited by David Coleman and John Salt.

Volume 2 The ethnic minority populations of Great Britain. Edited by Ceri Peach.

Volume 4 Employment, education and housing among the ethnic minority populations of Britain. Edited by Valerie Karn.

Acknowledgements

Grateful acknowledgement is made to the Economic and Social Research Council for the purchase of the computer files of the 1991 Census and to the University of Manchester Computer Centre and to the University of Manchester Census Microdata Unit through which these files were made available to the academic community.

Notes on contributors

Tony Champion is reader in population geography at the University of Newcastle upon Tyne. His principal interests lie in the monitoring and analysis of population change in Britain, particularly their regional and local dimensions. Publications include *Counterurbanization* (Arnold, 1989); *People in the Countryside* (Paul Chapman, 1991); *Migration Processes and Patterns: Research Progress and Prospects* (Belhaven, 1992) and *Population Matters: The Local Dimension* (Paul Chapman).

Mark Johnson is a senior research fellow at the Centre for Research in Ethnic Relations, University of Warwick. His research interests include appropriate research methods and the delivery of social welfare services and 'public goods' in societies of diversity. He is joint author of *Surveying Service Users in Multi-Racism Areas* (1984); *Ethnic minority Community Needs in Dacorum* (1995) and a number of other studies of health service delivery. He has recently been working with the European Commission against Racism and Intolerance at the Council of Europe.

Rob Lewis is director of demographic and statistical studies at the London Research Centre. He is chair of the British Urban and Regional Information Systems Association. He has a long-standing interest in race issues and is currently chair of GLARE (Greater London Action for Racial Equality).

David Owen is a senior research fellow at the Centre for Research in Ethnic Relations, University of Warwick. His research interests are in the analysis of the social and economic circumstances of minority ethnic groups in Britain, together with the study of internal migration and population change and local labour market analysis. He has recently published a major research report, *Ethnic Minority Women and the Labour Market: analysis of the 1991 Census*, for the Equal Opportunities Commission. He is joint author of *Changing Places* (1987, with Champion, Green, Ellin, and Coombes).

Ceri Peach is professor of social geography at Oxford University and a fellow of St Catherine's College. He has held visiting fellowships at ANU, Berkeley and Yale. His research interests are in patterns of migration, settlement and segregation. Books include: *West Indian Migration to Britain: A Social Geography* (Oxford: Oxford University Press, 1968); *Urban Social Segregation* (Longman, 1975); with Susan Smith and Vaughan Robinson, *Ethnic Segregation in Cities* (Croom Helm, 1981); with Colin Clarke and David Levy, *Geography and Ethnic Pluralism* (Allen and Unwin, 1984); with Colin Clarke and Steven Vertovec, *South Asians Overseas: Migration and Ethnicity* (Cambridge: Cambridge University Press, 1990).

Deborah Phillips is a lecturer in the Department of Geography at the University of Leeds. She has researched widely in the field of 'race' and ethnicity, with particular reference to housing. Her publications include, *What Price Equality?* (1987) and she is co-author of *Ethnic Minority Housing: Explanations and Policies* (1989) with Sarre and Skellington) and Race and Housing in a Property Owning Democracy, *New Community*, (with Karn, 1992).

Peter Ratcliffe is a senior lecturer in sociology in the Department of Sociology, University of Warwick. A statistician by training, he has written widely in and at the interface between the disciplines of sociology, social statistics, social policy and social geography. Since the mid-1970s, his work has principally focused on issues of 'race' and ethnicity. His main publications are (co-authored) *Colonial Immigrants in a British City: A Class Analysis* (1979); *Racism and Reaction: A Profile of Handsworth* (1981); (co-edited) *Ethnic Discrimination: Comparative Perspectives* (1992) and (edited) *'Race', Ethnicity and Nation: International Perspectives on Social Conflict* (1994).

Vaughan Robinson is director of the University of Wales Migration Unit and a senior lecturer in the geography department at the University of Wales, Swansea. His main research interests are in migration studies, ethnic relations and refugee studies. His books include: with Susan Smith and Ceri Peach, *Ethnic Segregation in Cities* (Croom Helm, 1981); *Transients, Settlers and Refugees* (Clarendon, 1986); *The International Refugee Crisis* (Macmillan, 1991); with Richard Black, *Geography and Refugees* (Belhaven, 1992); *Geography and Migration* (Elgar, 1995).

David Rossiter is a senior computing officer at Oxford University Computing Service. He received his doctorate in geography at the University of Sheffield for research into the use of census data to estimate inter-war patterns of electoral behaviour in the British coalfields. He provides advice on the use of statistical and mapping software and is responsible for supporting users of census data at Oxford. He has also published papers on electoral redistricting and is currently working on a research project funded by the Leverhulme Trust into the operations of the Parliamentary Boundary Commissions.

Marian Storkey is a senior research officer at the London Research Centre with responsibility for the statistics and demography of different ethnic groups. She obtained an MSc in demography from the London School of Economics. Recent work includes completing the first phase in the development of a new model to project the numbers of different ethnic populations of London. She is the author of the Census report *London's ethnic minorities – one city, many communities*.

Chapter 1
Social geography and ethnicity: a theoretical, conceptual and substantive overview

Peter Ratcliffe

1.1 Introduction

This is the third volume in a series specifically commissioned to illustrate the salience of ethnicity to analyses of social characteristics in Britain as we approach the next millennium. This has been facilitated by the addition in the 1991 Census of Population of a question on 'ethnic group'. The current book aims to cast light on issues which are of immense significance not only to the social scientist but also to the policy analyst concerned to assess the nature and source of urban inequalities, and the general reader who wishes to understand both the changing ethnic geography of contemporary Britain and its wider implications. One cannot achieve any of this, however, without a discussion first of what is meant by 'ethnicity', and secondly of how spatial patterns can be studied, and change over time assessed.

For these reasons the current chapter begins with a consideration of what is normally meant by the term ethnicity. It will be seen that this involves a (brief) theoretical excursus into not only the various interpretations of ethnicity, but also an analysis of the relation between 'ethnicity' and 'race', not to mention its relation to birthplace and nationality. It is also necessary to consider the 'politics of ethnicity' as both the self-definition of ethnic identity and the (external) ascription of ethnic labels and 'racialised' discourse are of immense importance, in that they have impacted in various ways on material social reality.

Having explored its theoretical complexity, we have to ask how we measure it. As Bulmer (1986, 1996) has argued, many different conceptual schema, and systems of labelling, have been used in the literature. It was felt to be of sufficient importance to be included in the 1991 Census for the first time, and a great deal of research was undertaken to ensure that the measure produced data with high levels of reliability and validity. We assess how successful the resulting ethnic group question was in practice.

Its success was always going to depend, at least in part, on its acceptability to those whose ethnicity it sought to 'measure'. Given the widespread evidence of continuing inequalities in access to employment and the basic citizenship rights involving good quality education, housing, social welfare and health services (Jones, 1993; Mason, 1995), and the fact that discriminatory behaviour, at an individual or institutional level, on the basis of perceived 'ethnic' or 'racial' difference is at the root of these, the asking of such a question was always going to be controversial. Its unacceptability to some people, and in particular possible variations in acceptability levels to different sectors of the population, threaten both the validity of responses and the response rate itself. The potential impact on our analyses, and measures taken to improve data quality in the light of these problems, are therefore assessed.

Given an appropriate level of data quality, and a sufficiently fine spatial scale, mapping the ethnic geography of Britain in 1991 and measuring levels of concentration/segregation is relatively straightforward. Rather less easy is the assessment of patterns of change over time. This is so essentially because of inter-censal shifts in areal boundaries and (much more significantly) the fact that there was no ethnic group question prior to the 1991 Census. The latter problem led initially to a reliance on surrogate measures such as country of birth or country of birth of head of household (itself a problematic concept). This introductory chapter addresses this issue with reference to later sections of the volume.

The book is divided into three principal sections; the ethnic geography of Britain at a national scale, a detailed analysis of the three major areas of minority ethnic settlement, and a concluding section containing amongst other things a brief appraisal of the policy implications of spatial segregation/concentration on the basis of ethnicity or race, or both. The present chapter seeks to assist the reader by spelling out the essential aims and objectives of each section, and points to some of the more significant findings. It also gives an indication of the issues which may prove difficult to follow for the general reader: as is the general convention in this series of volumes, such issues are separated from the main text and placed in boxes.

1.2 Ethnicity and the 1991 Census

There are a myriad of questions which come to mind when the concept of ethnicity is raised. First, there is the obvious issue of definition: what exactly is it? In particular, how does it relate (if at all) to the concept of 'race', which retains a significant place within popular, everyday discourse? Second, there is the question of whether it is measurable, and specifically whether it is measurable in the context of a self completion document such as the census form. Third, assuming we can measure it, should we? Why should 'we' (i.e. social scientists, government, civil servants, and other interested parties) wish to know about the ethnic composition of the British population? Fourth, given that such a question was asked in 1991, how successful was it (in producing reliable and valid data)? Fifth, we need to ask whether the related problems of under-enumeration/undercount and data imputation pose a significant threat to the validity of our findings. And finally, there is the issue, briefly alluded to in the previous section, of how one can assess the changing ethnic geography of Britain when there is no census data on ethnic group prior to 1991.

Ethnicity and ethnic group: defining the indefinable?

Ethnicity is one of those terms, like race, which because of its central position in contemporary discourse often goes unquestioned. We 'know' it is important because we hear daily on the TV news bulletins and read in the newspapers that there is ethnic conflict in various parts of the world, there is ethnic cleansing in the former Yugoslavia, there are problems faced by ethnic minorities in countries such as Britain, and so on. But, do we really 'know' what 'ethnic' actually means?

The truth is that we usually do not, or if we do, our definition (insofar as it is consistent) probably does not accord with the usage of many others. At the risk of oversimplifying an extremely complex field of study one could suggest three major interpretations; the first sees ethnicity as essentially primordial; the second sees it in a more dynamic, and explicitly contemporary, sense as involving attachment to co-ethnics but embodying a sense of continual change. Both of these imply a concern with 'boundary maintenance', the marking off of 'cultural territory'. The third interpretation sees ethnicity as essentially 'situational', i.e. dependent on social context (see Jenkins, 1986; Ratcliffe, 1994: especially Chapter 1).

If ethnicity is primordial it involves a sense of communal attachment to the past, sometimes expressed as 'memories of a shared past' (Bulmer 1986: 54). It also involves common ancestry 'and aspects of group identity based on "kinship, religion, language, shared territory, nationality or physical appearance"' (Ratcliffe, 1994: 6). Under our second definition, we have a continually evolving entity (perhaps with vestiges of the primordial) where the essential elements of ethnic identity and ethnic group membership (and nomenclature) shift over time. Ethnic categories are therefore in no sense fixed, and might prove elusive empirically, in that they may change radically (say) over the decade between successive censuses. The 'situational' view of ethnicity presents even more problems in empirical terms, in that there may be no single, unambiguous 'true answer' to a question about one's ethnic identity.

Ethnicity, and by implication ethnic group, is clearly not strictly amenable to static categorisation (however sophisticated), but despite its complexity it could at least be argued that it represents one possible way of conceptualising social divisions and cleavages. The ontological status of 'race' is, however, much less secure. There is now almost universal agreement in the literature that the biological notion of race should be rejected in favour of a view which sees the term as essentially merely a social construct, but one which nevertheless has attained, and continues to represent and exert, a powerful ideological presence (Miles, 1993; Ratcliffe, 1991, 1994 – especially Chapter 6; Mason, 1995). As argued above, its use in popular discourse gives it a certain common sense quality, i.e. many, perhaps most, people clearly believe that 'races' exist. Furthermore, this belief is underpinned by the widespread institutional use of the term, as evidenced, for example, by the Commission for Racial Equality (CRE) and, of course, the Race Relations Acts. One way out of the conceptual dilemma is to talk about 'racialisation' and 'racialised discourse', in other words arguing at least implicitly that although 'races' do not exist, there are those who in thought, speech and actions behave as if they do.

The point is that in much contemporary analysis, race and ethnicity are either seen as synonymous or the latter is used as a euphemism for the former. Ultimately, the issue for those of us who attempt to write about the material experiences of various groups in a multi-cultural, polyethnic society such as Britain becomes one of making pragmatic decisions about the definition, form and boundaries of major groupings. These groups are ones which both see themselves, and are seen by others, as culturally distinct from other groups. It is also recognised that, irrespective of concerns about the ontological status of race, perceived phenotypic differences (and especially skin colour) are central to the material experiences of certain groups because of the continued presence of racism. So, when we use the terms 'ethnicity', 'ethnic group' or 'ethnic origin' we are in effect employing a simplified pragmatic interpretation of the term 'ethnic', combined with an acceptance that the process of racialisation is part of the allocative equation. In a sense, we are effectively fusing ethnicisation and racialisation. How then do we code ethnic group in practice?

Ethnic group: measuring the unmeasurable?

As implied in the previous paragraph, ethnicity is a matter of ongoing debate in the academic literature. Even if one decided on an acceptable theoretical definition, it would not be operationalisable in the context of a census document which is intended as a simple self-completion form, by necessity rather brief and already concerned with many key issues ranging from housing and employment, to education qualifications and health status. As we shall see in the next section, the central concern behind the collection of data on ethnic group, is relative material disadvantage, and not the exploration of cultural and religious differentiation.

As will be argued below, pressure from social scientists along with other interested parties such as government departments, local authorities and the CRE, were in large part responsible for the introduction of the ethnic group question. Their representations to government were principally to the effect that research evidence showed that certain groups in society, and in particular those of South Asian and Caribbean origin, were being systematically denied their full citizenship rights thanks to discriminatory practices. Any question would in the first instance need to isolate these groups, in a statistical sense. More broadly it would need to address the position of minorities; i.e. those variously described in the literature as 'ethnic minorities', 'ethnic minority groups' or 'minority ethnic groups'.

The important thing to note is that these groups are not simply minorities in a statistical sense: they are both relatively small in number and are in some way oppressed or subjected to inferior treatment on account of their ethnic or racial identity (Giddens, 1993: 254). Having said this, in labelling groups in general, the convention in this volume will be to use the term 'minority ethnic groups', thereby explicitly placing the emphasis on the question of population size. This is done so as to make it clear that we recognise that all individuals in all groups have an ethnic identity; it is simply that these groups vary in size, and those which form the focal point of the analysis are both small and are usually socially and/or economically disadvantaged in some way(s). Where one of the alternative labels has been used in the text this is invariably because an author has felt the need to vary the wording for stylistic reasons.

A great deal of research was undertaken to devise a question which would (a) provide reliable and valid data, and (b) prove acceptable to potential respondents (Sillitoe, 1978,1987; Sillitoe and White, 1992; Bulmer, 1996). This revealed a certain level of suspicion, particularly among urban residents of African and Caribbean origin, of the motives behind asking the question. Other groups wished to be listed separately in any coding scheme (for example, there were representations on behalf of the Irish community), many complaining that their ethnicity was being obscured in the various forms of question being piloted. The final version used in the 1991 Census, which is presented in Figure 1.1 along with the associated question on country of birth, was almost inevitably going to be a compromise of one form or another.

Figure 1.1 ***1991 Census of Population questions on country of birth and ethnic group***

10 Country of birth

Please tick the appropriate box.

If the 'Elsewhere' box is ticked, please write in the present name of the country in which the birthplace is now situated.

England	☐	1
Scotland	☐	2
Wales	☐	3
Northern Ireland	☐	4
Irish Republic	☐	5
Elsewhere	☐	

If elsewhere, please write in the present name of the country

11 Ethnic group

Please tick the appropriate box.

If the person is descended from more than one ethnic or racial group, please tick the group to which the person considers he/she belongs, or tick the 'Any other ethnic group' box and describe the person's ancestry in the space provided.

White	☐	0
Black-Caribbean	☐	1
Black-African	☐	2
Black-Other *please describe*	☐	
Indian	☐	3
Pakistani	☐	4
Bangladeshi	☐	5
Chinese	☐	6
Any other ethnic group *please describe*	☐	

Source: 1991 Census of Population, H enumeration form for private households, reproduced in Dale and Marsh (1993), p.367.

What is clear about the census ethnic group question is that the one thing it does not measure is ethnicity; at least in any of the forms outlined in section 1.2. 'White' cannot in any sense be regarded as an ethnic group label: as can be seen in Figure 1.2, it conflates an enormous number of groups with quite distinct cultural, spatial and religious heritages; for example, a variety of northern European groups, including the indigenous British and, significantly, the Irish and those of Greek or Turkish origin (including Cypriots of both national origins).

Figure 1.2   The 1991 Census of Population ethnic classification

4-fold classification	10-fold classification	Full listing
White	White	White
		Irish
		Greek/Greek Cypriot
		Turkish/Turkish Cypriot
		Mixed White
Black groups	Black Caribbean	Black–Caribbean
		Caribbean Island
		West Indies
		Guyana
	Black African	Black–African
		Africa south of the Sahara
	Black Other	Black–other
		Black–British
		Black–Mixed Black/White
		Black–Mixed Other
Indian/Pakistani/ Bangladeshi	Indian	Indian
	Pakistani	Pakistani
	Bangladeshi	Bangladeshi
Chinese & Others	Chinese	Chinese
	Other–Asian	East African Asian
		Indo-Caribbean
		Black-Indian sub-continent
		Black-other Asian
	Other–Other	North Africa/Arab/Iranian
		Mixed Asian/White
		British ethnic minority (other)
		British (no indication)
		Other Mixed Black/White
		Other Mixed Asian/White
		Other Mixed–Other

Source: D. W. Owen (1992) Appendix 2, in *Ethnic Minorities in Britain: Settlement Patterns.* Statistical Paper No. 1, ESRC Centre for Research in Ethnic Relations, University of Warwick.

'Black' (like 'White') is ostensibly grounded in the phenotype paradigm, though in practice has become much more, in that it has acquired a political dimension, embodying a transformation of the historical negativity as a race category (Lawrence, 1982) into a positive symbolic expression of resistance to racial oppression. As to the division of the Black population enshrined in the fixed-choice categories, Pan-Africanists with direct familial roots in the Caribbean might still (with obvious justification) describe their ethnic group as Black–African and not Black–Caribbean. Those of Indo–Caribbean origin may or may not highlight their distinct ethnic heritage. The bottom line is that 'Black' (as with its hyphenated variants) is not an ethnic group label.

Indian, Pakistani and Bangladeshi are essentially reflections of geography and/or nationality. Lest one was tempted to think of 'Indian' as an ethnic group one only has to reflect for a moment on the fierce, ongoing ethno-nationalist struggles in

Kashmir, the Khalistan movement amongst Punjabi Sikhs, and the continuing tensions between Hindus and Moslems in Indian towns and cities. Parallel fault lines appear in the form of social divisions and ethnic politics in Britain. In contrast, those of Pakistani and Bangladeshi origin are principally, though by no means exclusively, Moslem and so might be thought of as slightly more homogenous: but it should be stressed that this is largely a question of degree.

The Chinese, as Peach (1996) argues, are in effect a conflation of disparate groups with their roots in Hong Kong, Singapore, Vietnam and Taiwan as well as the People's Republic itself. And the 'Other' category, by definition, contains a wide variety of peoples with vastly different histories, cultures and religious traditions.

The question addressed later in this section is whether, given this critique, the ethnic group question worked, in the sense of producing reliable and valid data. The natural response might be, 'how could it, if it wasn't measuring ethnicity?' A more considered response would be one which first asked (a) why the data were required, and (b) how the data were intended to be used by those who sponsored their collection – in other words reliability and validity should be viewed in the context of a particular underlying research agenda.

Why collect census data on ethnic group?

There were two principal arguments behind the introduction of a question on ethnic group. First, policy analysts, certain pressure groups and statutory bodies such as the CRE, argued that hard data at a national scale on the material disadvantage of minority groups, were desperately needed. The CRE indeed felt that without such data there was no way of assessing the success or failure of the existing (1976) Race Relations Act (Sillitoe, 1978). Second, primary data on ethnic group would be required because it was no longer viable to rely on the existing country of birth question as a means of producing surrogate measures (e.g. an individual's country of birth, or that of the household head). Even in the early post war years birthplace was unreliable as a proxy for ethnicity given, for example, the migration to Britain of the Indian-born offspring of colonial households.

In the 1990s the principal problem is somewhat different. As Peach (1996) points out, over half (54 per cent) of Black–Caribbeans enumerated in 1991 were born in the UK, along with 50 per cent of Pakistanis, 43 per cent of Indians and 37 per cent of Bangladeshis. For those in the Black–Other category the figure rose to no less than 85 per cent. To use birthplace (or even birthplace of head of household) in these circumstances would then be unwise in the extreme.

For the social scientist, as we have seen, ethnicity and the associated idea of ethnic group are complex entities which are not amenable to investigation in essentially fact gathering exercises, such as the decennial census. But, crucially, if it is the case that material disadvantage applying to broadly defined groups is the key issue, then it follows that rather cruder divisions of the population will suffice (hence the remarks at the end of the previous section). Interestingly, the compression of ethnic group data into the four-fold classification used in the Small Area Statistics and

Special Migration Statistics (shown in Figure 1.2) illustrates both the underlying aims of the question, and at the same time some of the attendant concerns.

There is a rather obvious parallel between this list of categories and the explicitly racial coding scheme of the form which largely disappeared from academic discourse in the 1960s: namely 'White', 'Black', 'Coloured' and 'Other'. The fact that those who described themselves as Black, but who also indicated (say) a part South Asian heritage, were to be excluded from the Black groups, underlines the 'racialisation' critique. This partly explains the increased hostility to the question on the part of some academic commentators who were already inclined to the view that the collection of such data, especially in a document which people are required by law to complete, was indefensible. Also of this view were many Black residents who feared the political consequences of the ready availability on computer of such data (an issue to which we will return later in this section). For them, assurances about anonymity and confidentiality were unconvincing. This combined with sections of the political Right which appeared to favour the concealment of inequality, and some 'liberal' opinion which argued that even if inequalities could be proven, the political will to rectify them was absent.

Although the 'no lobby', with its rather curious set of political bedfellows, won the day in 1981, in that plans to include an ethnic question were dropped (at a very late stage), this simply delayed its introduction by a decade. The next two sections are concerned in different ways with the question of how good these new data are. First, there are the critical questions of reliability (whether the measurement process is replicable and consistent) and validity (whether the question measures what one wants it to measure).

The reliability and validity of 1991 Census data on 'ethnic group'

Although we have already cast doubt on the validity of the ethnic group data, by demonstrating a lack of fit between the theoretical interpretation of ethnicity and the form of the question actually used, it has been suggested that a more pragmatic stance should be adopted. The question gives respondents the opportunity to define their own ethnic identity. In the context of a self-completion questionnaire covering the entire British population (and a question which was to be coded 100 per cent), an open ended format would have been impracticable. But then, as every good textbook tells the intending researcher, a pre-coded approach (even with a few 'other – please specify' options) tends to structure responses and lead to a degree of distortion.

It is quite feasible for those of East African Asian origin, for example, to opt (say) for Indian (as a reflection of their ethnic heritage) rather than describing their identity more fully; thereby leading to an entry (in the 10-fold classification) as Other–Asian. (For the UK-born we would have no way of identifying the former group.) This, then, suggests that data reliability may have been a problem, if not necessarily a major one, in that the same person could be coded in two quite different ways. Similarly Indo–Caribbeans could have opted for the label Black–Caribbean either as being the 'nearest' category, or alternatively because they wished to embrace the label Black for reasons such as those discussed earlier. Were they to opt for Black–Other and describe their background as Asian, however, a quite different scenario ensues. In this case it could be argued that the subjective sense of ethnic group identity becomes contaminated with the objectification implicit within the coding procedure; and this applies to anyone of South Asian origin who asserts a Black identity for whatever reasons (cultural, religious, political, and so on). The coding process simply negates the adopted identity by imposing an Asian label; in other words one is not permitted to be both Asian and Black.

A quite different distortion of the subjective can occur within households. This is where the person completing the census form imposes his or her perceptions of identity on other household members. One obvious example would be where (say) a Jamaican-born adult may define an offspring as Black–Caribbean when the individual concerned might wish to adopt a quite different ethnic group label, for example Black–British (i.e. Black–Other). This is an empirically very common outcome given that, as Owen (1996) argues, those opting for the Black–British label formed 32.5 per cent of the Black–Other total. This again casts some doubt on data quality in the context of reliability.

On the positive side, as Owen also notes, the 1991 Census appears to have produced a higher figure for the total minority ethnic population than estimates based on either the Labour Force Survey (LFS) or country of birth data. This suggests that the exercise has been a success in discriminating (in a statistical sense) more effectively between those with different ethnic identities; in particular, it may be that some of those who would have been described as White have been given more 'precise' labels. Overall, Owen (1996) and Ballard and Kalra (1994) concur that the ethnic group question was 'broadly successful'.

Bulmer (1996) presents two further arguments which should lead us to be more confident about data quality, despite the above concerns and those dealt with in the following section. First, the Post Enumeration Survey to the 1989 Census Test suggested that the question was (at 7 per cent) only marginally less popular than the (also newly introduced) question on limiting long term illness. A mere 0.5 per cent claimed to have refused to complete the form (which was voluntary) directly as a result of the ethnic group question, and the accuracy of the ethnic group data was estimated at between 85 and 90 per cent. Second, for the 1991 Census itself, an elaborate procedure was introduced to ensure high data quality at the coding stage. Bulmer admits that some coder error is inevitable, particularly in the case of the more heterogeneous categories such as Black–Other and Other–Other, but concludes that the likely scale of the problem is small.

This leaves only one area where major concerns about the integrity of the data have been voiced: under-enumeration and the adopted solution (where feasible), data imputation.

The impact of under-enumeration and data imputation on 'ethnic group' analyses

The problem of under-enumeration has two components: missing data on returned census forms, and failure to return a census form. As Bulmer (1996) and Mills and Teague (1991) argue, the Census Office has well established procedures for dealing with the former problem. It essentially works by imputing responses on the basis of the relationship between census variables in continually updated data sets formed by valid responses. In the case of the 1991 Census, some 1.2 per cent of forms were subjected to this imputation procedure on the grounds of invalid or missing items.

This cannot, of course, provide a solution in the situation where a household, for whatever reason, withholds information on the whole array of questions for a particular individual; i.e. where one or more of the household members simply 'disappears'. The likelihood of this occurring had grown enormously given the possible desire of many to remain invisible to officialdom in the era of the Poll Tax. This was believed to be associated with an even more worrying problem for the Census Office; the non-return of census forms.

The problem would not have been quite so serious had the incidence of non-response been effectively a random process. One could then simply assume that the achieved returns represented a random subsample of the total, and an extremely high one at that. The problem was that the undercount was proportionately much more severe in poorer urban neighbourhoods, and in areas with significant minority ethnic group settlement. Simply to ignore the undercount would therefore have been to risk seriously distorting the position of minority ethnic groups: by underestimating their presence in certain urban locations, for example, inferences about changes in ethnic differentials could have been rendered unsound. This would have constituted a particular problem for the current volume given that temporal shifts in spatial patterns and levels of segregation are core themes.

A system of data imputation for whole households was used for the first time in the 1991 Census. In cases where no form had been returned and the census enumerator had evidence of a household being present at a particular address, imputed records for the missing household (and its resident members) were generated. This was done 'by copying them from other forms which had been returned, using four key items: the type of area in which the household was located, the number of people and the number of rooms noted or guessed by the enumerator while in the field, and whether the accommodation was self-contained or not' (Bulmer, 1996 (page 52, Volume 1)). The records of no less than 869,098 persons were created in this way. Particularly important in the context of the current volume is the fact that 114,065 of these records were coded as applying to a person whose ethnic group was other than 'White'. This illustrates clearly the point that the data relating to those from minority ethnic groups has been subject to a much higher level of imputation than that for the 'White' majority (as would have been predicted from earlier comments about differential undercount).

The areas with the highest level of data imputation for minority groups are shown in Table 1.1. From this we can draw two important conclusions. First, all of the areas where the incidence of data imputation for minorities is 10 per cent or more (and indeed all of the top 10 listed) were inner London boroughs. Secondly, nine of the top thirteen were areas where those of Black–Caribbean origin constituted the largest minority ethnic group. Both of these findings are consistent with those of the OPCS research leading up to the inclusion of the ethnic group question; namely that the greatest areas of resistance to its inclusion were inner urban locations with significant Black populations, and especially those in the Metropolis. This source of resistance is then widely believed to have been compounded by the Poll Tax factor noted earlier. Quite apart from refusal to complete a census form, higher levels of undercount would in any case be expected in what tend to be more densely populated areas with young mobile populations.

Table 1.1 *Districts with highest incidence of imputation for minority ethnic groups*

Local authority	Minority ethnic group	percent of popn	No. imputed	Percent of minorities imputed	Largest minority ethnic group
Lambeth	74,079	30.3	8,090	10.9	Black–Caribbean
Southwark	53,386	24.4	5,759	10.8	Black–Caribbean
Kensington & Chelsea	21,603	15.6	2,327	10.8	Other–Other
Westminster	37,439	21.4	3,753	10.0	Other–Other
Hackney	60,839	33.6	6,074	10.0	Black–Caribbean
Hammersmith & Fulham	25,989	17.5	2,031	7.8	Black–Caribbean
Haringey	58,667	29.0	4,551	7.8	Black–Caribbean
Islington	31,085	18.9	2,408	7.8	Black–Caribbean
Lewisham	50,749	22.0	3,839	7.6	Black–Caribbean
Camden	30,418	17.8	2,199	7.2	Bangladeshi
Manchester	51,183	12.6	2,987	5.8	Pakistani
Wandsworth	50,604	20.0	2,931	5.8	Black–Caribbean
Bristol	19,281	5.1	1,108	5.8	Black–Caribbean
Liverpool	17,046	3.8	928	5.4	Other–Other
Brighton	4,432	3.1	241	5.4	Other–Other
Brent	108,869	44.8	5,792	5.3	Indian
Leeds	39,725	5.8	2,005	5.1	Indian

Source: Compiled by David Owen, CRER, University of Warwick, from 1991 Census Local Base, and reproduced in Bulmer (1996).
Statistics Crown Copyright, showing top 17 districts with number of cases imputed in 1991 Census exceeding 240.

In sum, the problem is three-fold: missing persons in enumerated households; missing households known to the enumerator; and finally, households who are missed completely because the enumerator is unaware of their existence. (The Census Validation Survey (CVS) provides further details of the sources and scale of possible errors associated with 'undercount'.)

As Bulmer (ibid.) argues, our knowledge of the demographic structure of the various minority populations suggests that they would in general have been more affected by the undercount than 'Whites'. Although they have different migration patterns (see Chapter 5) all the minority groups tend to have younger populations, with higher proportions of infants and young adults and, as will become increasingly evident through a reading of later chapters, they tend to be relatively heavily concentrated in urban locations. Ballard and Kalra (1994) endorse these arguments in their analysis of 'Black' groups, suggesting a higher undercount among Black–Caribbean and Black–Other groups, and Bulmer reports indirect evidence from the study of electoral registration undertaken as part of the CVS, suggesting higher levels of non-registration amongst minority ethnic groups in general (as compared with White residents) but (barring the effects of sampling error) substantially higher levels amongst the Black groups. Rees and Phillips (see Chapter 2) give approximate weighting factors which can be applied to minority ethnic groups, as a way of attempting to minimise the undercount problem.

In conclusion, it could be argued that, but for certain concerns about the effects of under-enumeration and undercount and about reliability and validity, the latter partly to do with the objective and subjective dimensions of the process by which ethnic identity is determined (which by definition are inevitably difficult to reconcile), one can use the ethnic group data with confidence. The 1991 Census did not, and could not, produce data which would totally satisfy the requirements of the academic sociologist and social anthropologist. It did, however, succeed in producing data of very high quality, especially given the inbuilt constraints of the census methodology.

Assessing the changing ethnic geography of Britain

One of the key aims of the present volume is to assess the way in which the ethnic geography of Britain is changing over time, now that primary immigration has been dwarfed in significance by the development of the resident minority population. Data problems stemming from under-enumeration and a lack of reliability and validity present one type of threat to this enterprise. Others arise from non-comparability of data at various points in time, and such issues as sampling error.

Three distinct types of change analysis are attempted here. The first aims to explore changes in spatial patterns over (principally) the decade leading up to the 1991 Census. The second involves analysis of the one-year migration data from the 1991 Census, in order to compare levels of mobility between the various population groups. The third takes a rather different tack, by attempting to see what present data can tell us about likely changes in the future ethnic geography of Britain. This is achieved by comparing, for example, the position of immigrant members of minority populations with that of their UK-born offspring. The inherent problems of each of these approaches are now discussed in turn.

The central problems with the analysis of change during the intercensal period 1981–91, have already been noted. In order to assess change effectively one needs a stable geographical base: this implies in the British case a spatially comparable network of enumeration districts and wards. As this patently does not exist thanks to population shifts, one needs to resort to the use of digitised boundary datasets which permit the marrying of boundaries; either 1991 data to the 1981 boundaries or 1981 data to 1991 boundaries.

As these datafiles have now been made available thanks to work at the University of Manchester, the principal problem lies in the unavailability of ethnic group data prior to the 1991 Census. The problems raised by relying on country of birth data have already been discussed. To use country of birth data for both 1981 and 1991 (as Peach and Rossiter do at one point in Chapter 3) solves the problem of comparability, but is clearly geared to addressing a particular question, namely changes in *immigrant* settlement patterns (and does still, of course, entail the implicit assumption that birthplace equates with ethnicity). The only way of assessing changes in ethnic group patterns is to attempt to convert 1981 birthplace data to ethnic group data. 1991 ethnic group by birthplace matrices, clearly cannot be used directly to convert data from the earlier decade as the proportion of UK-born is considerably higher in 1991. To use LFS data from the early to mid-1980s also invokes problems, due to sampling error and the lack of a sufficiently fine spatial scale. In an important development, Rees and Phillips (see Chapter 2) have designed a complex algorithm which enables estimates of 1981 ethnic group populations to be generated.

There are no such problems of data comparability in the second area of change; one year migration, given that the data are contained on the 1991 Census form. The only real drawback with the data, assuming that there are no recall errors, is the fact that they only measure location at two discrete points in time. This means, as pointed out by Champion (see Chapter 4), that any additional moves which have taken place between the two nominated dates will not be recorded. The level of mobility may therefore be underestimated. The same problem, only more serious given the larger time span, occurs when one uses the Longitudinal Study (LS) to study intercensal movement. There are two very useful points in favour of this type of analysis, however. First, as ethnic group appears on the 1991 data file and one is dealing with linked files, it is possible to look at gross flows by ethnic group over the 10-year period. Secondly, whilst one-year flows can be misleading if the year in question is unusual in some way (for example, in the event of deep recession and an extremely stagnant housing market) 10-year flows with their broader grain approach are potentially capable of yielding much more useful information.

The third approach to social change is that which takes cross-sectional data, and looks at people and households at different stages of the life/housing career cycle. In the case of data on ethnicity, one way of gaining a glimpse into the future is to compare the positions of the first generation (i.e. immigrants to Britain) and their offspring, who may or may not have reached the family building stage of the life cycle. The obvious comparator groups here would be equivalent age cohorts in the White population, given the problems in comparing (say) middle-aged and elderly minorities with their much younger offspring. Admittedly, the latter difficulty is a common feature of all cross-sectional comparative work: and remains so in the current case, even if one was to introduce into the equation the experiences of immigrants in earlier decades. But the problem is compounded in this case by small sample sizes in certain key groups, such as adult UK-born Bangladeshis (see Robinson, Chapter 5).

Having considered problems associated with the determination of ethnic group and the analysis of changing spatial patterns, we move on to look at how these various issues are tackled in the chapters which follow. In the interests of clarity, each of the three sections is taken in turn, beginning with the attempt to describe the ethnic geography of Britain, principally in terms of spread, concentration/segregation and (internal) migration.

1.3 Geography and ethnicity in Britain: the national picture

The central aim of the first two substantive chapters of the book (Chapters 2 and 3) is to sketch out the broad national patterns of ethnic settlement: the rest of Part 1 looks at migration (a) for ethnic groups as a whole (Chapter 4) and (b) for first generation migrants as against the second (and successive) generations (Chapter 5). The focus at this stage is very much on geographical patterns rather than ethnic differentials (say) in housing, employment, and education. (The latter are in any case the subject of volume 4 in the current series, edited by Valerie Karn.) Where the question of substantive disadvantage does emerge, however, is in Part 2, in that such issues are central to the discussion about why residential patterns in specific urban locations are significant. We would argue, for example, that high levels of concentration and segregation *per se* are not a problem; they only become so when locality is taken into account.

Chapter 2 describes in considerable detail the geographical spread of the groups specified in the 10-fold ethnic group classification, and shows that, although most of Britain's minority population (92 per cent) is concentrated in a number of what the authors call 'ethnic core' regions (South East, East Midlands, West Midlands, Yorkshire and Humberside, and the North West) and, in particular, in larger urban districts within them, there is considerable variation in the ethnic mix in different localities. What the chapter adds to the existing literature in particular, however, is a sophisticated methodology for estimating ethnic group composition in 1981 from raw birthplace data. The results of applying this algorithm to the 459 districts in Great Britain, are quoted in full (in Appendix 2.2) alongside the 1991 district data (adjusted for undercount), enabling the reader to undertake a 1981–1991 change analysis for selected districts.

This constitutes an enormously useful research resource in itself. It is also however, complemented by a spatial redistribution analysis which concludes that the amount of redistribution (between 4 and 10 per cent), was surprisingly small given the rapid growth in minority ethnic populations (of between 24 and 95 per cent). The outcome was a greater degree of metropolitan concentration in 1991 (compared with a decade earlier), accompanied by an increased share of the group population in the core areas. Rees and Phillips conclude that this is largely explainable in terms of the outflow of Whites, the growth of households *in situ* following the birth of children, new households tending to locate close to existing areas of concentration, and in-migrants (from outside the UK) joining existing communities in such areas. They also argue that much more research is required to understand the patterns which they describe, and conclude by providing a challenging agenda for future research.

Central to all debates about race and ethnicity in Britain (and elsewhere) are the concepts of concentration and segregation. Common in the academic literature, even if only implicitly, is the view that a high degree of spatial integration is indicative of social integration in the sense of assimilation, and perhaps even acculturation. Physical separation, as measured by high levels of segregation and spatial isolation, on the other hand, is indicative of social pluralism. Neither of these conclusions follows from its premise, however, and as Peach and Rossiter (in Chapter 3) point out, concepts such as segregation are much more complex and elusive than they are commonly thought to be. To complicate the picture still further there are also competing measures of segregation/concentration/isolation, all of which in varying degrees lack robustness in the face of changing spatial scale and areal boundary definition.

The key point is that whichever of the conventional segregation measures one uses (and at whatever spatial scale), there remain massive differentials between the levels of segregation experienced by minority ethnic groups in Britain and those routinely observed in the USA, at least in the case of African Americans. To those who would ask therefore whether Britain is moving towards an American future (persistently high levels of ethnic segregation in the worst urban neighbourhoods) the answer is very clearly in the negative. This is so despite the fact that, as we have just seen, Rees and Phillips found a tendency towards increased concentration in the 'ethnic core areas'. Bangladeshis tend to be the group with the highest level of segregation from Whites and from other minority groups, except where they shared urban territory with fellow Moslems of Pakistani origin. Their extremely high level of segregation in Tower Hamlets in east London is in some ways a special case in that a predominantly poor migrant group settling in a high housing cost area is bound to be dependent on social housing; that which was available in this case tended to be in hard-to-let flatted accommodation in relatively small, clearly defined areas within the borough. And concentration was enhanced as a direct consequence of a local council policy which responded to racial attacks on Bangladeshis by moving such families 'for their own safety' into blocks of poor quality flats and maisonettes with co-ethnics, thereby effectively punishing the victims rather than the perpetrators (Phillips, 1986).

The Chinese, despite the popular stereotype of Chinatowns which suggests high levels of segregation, tend in practice (at ward level) to be the least segregated (of the minority groups considered in this volume), with small clusters of households spread across many towns and cities. This is explained in large part by their distinct socio-economic profile, being more dependent than most on the restaurant/take-away trade (perhaps even more so than Bangladeshis outside the capital).

A particularly significant feature of Peach's work over the years has been his avoidance of the popular fallacy of seeing segregation in ethnically mixed areas solely in terms of ethnicity or race based explanations. Whilst it is clearly tempting when looking at clusters of people sharing a common cultural and religious heritage to suggest that they live in close proximity either because they wish to (for reasons to do with their ethnicity), because they are forced to (as a result of discriminatory practices or as a defence against racist attacks, or some combination of both), it could be that they live in those areas because they share quite different characteristics; poverty, low status work, unemployment, and so on. Peach and Rossiter's analysis therefore asks how far a class-based explanation goes in accounting for observed differentials in segregation patterns.

As noted earlier, Chapter 2 makes a number of suggestions as to the ways in which geographical mobility has impinged on ethnic spatial patterns between 1981 and 1991; adding that further research was needed into the precise nature of these (internal) migration flows. Chapter 4 goes a long way towards filling this void. In his highly detailed analysis, which also includes an appraisal of the various methodological problems associated with the study of migration flows, Champion first of all calls upon the Local Base Statistics and National Migration (100 per cent) statistics, based on the census one-year change-of-address data, to examine overall migration propensities by ethnic group. Whilst not strictly migration rates, given that the population on which such figures are based, is that resident in 1991 (and not 1990), this does provide interesting insights into ethnic differentials in the propensity to move address over the short term. It reveals, for example, that although migration *levels* are highest among the Indian population, their migration 'rate' is one of only two amongst minority groups which is lower than that for Whites (Black–Caribbeans being the other). At the other extreme, no less than a quarter of Black–Africans were found to have changed their address over this one-year period; possibly a reflection of the high proportion of students amongst this group. In fact, a more sophisticated analysis based on age-specific rates changed the overall picture somewhat, and when allowance was made for those who had been living outside Britain a year before census night and those classified as 'origin not stated' the overall difference (between 'White' and 'non-White') evaporated.

The chapter then develops a much more detailed analysis of the nature of migration flows, starting with inter- and intra-regional movement and going on to look at within district, between district within county and between county within region levels. It is then possible to develop the analysis further by controlling for age and, by using the two per cent Sample of Anonymised Records (SAR), Champion discusses differentials in the distance of moves undertaken by individuals from the 10 ethnic groups identified in the Census. This shows that migration rates and proportion of long-distance moves are highest amongst the Chinese and Others, yet Blacks who have the next highest migration rate have the lowest proportion of long distance movers.

The small numbers problem and the attendant suppression of migration flows, inevitably became more of a problem when finer grain analyses were attempted, and this problem was compounded by the low overall level of migration associated with recession and the sluggishness of the housing market in the year in question (1990/1). There was, however, intriguing evidence of suburbanisation (and even exurbanisation) amongst some minority groups in London; specifically movement from Inner to Outer London boroughs, and from London to Essex and Surrey. Whether in the case of intra-Greater London moves this is merely spillover into contiguous boroughs is not clear, but it may be indicative of a general, gradual improvement in living standards, if perhaps only for those who have secured relatively high status, well paid employment.

The LS, as argued above, permits an analysis of movement between successive censuses. As with the one–year change-of-address data it only records a person's address at two discrete points; in this case two days 10 years apart. It therefore cannot pick up any moves which occurred in the intervening period, but does open up the possibility of tracing overall movement over a 20–year period, i.e. 1971–1981–1991. As Champion argues, it also permits a reworking of earlier migration analyses (for 1971 and 1981), which had to rely on birthplace data in the absence of an ethnic group measure. If one adheres to a conventional absolute (rather than situational) conception of ethnicity, i.e. one that relates to heritage and is therefore time invariant, the three linked files can be allocated to an ethnic group on the basis of the 1991 Census question. Unfortunately, at the time the final version of this chapter was written (Spring 1995), the 1991 LS data entry had not been completed. Chapter 5, which was written slightly more recently, makes some use of this new data source, and further extends the discussion of migration to cover intercensal movement.

These first three substantive chapters taken together provide a detailed national summary and mapping of changes in minority settlement patterns, over the last decade in particular. They have not, however, attempted to differentiate the spatial patterns or migratory profiles of immigrant members of those communities and their UK-born offspring. Chapter 5 aims to correct this omission, at least in the case of the Black–Caribbean, Indian and Pakistani groups (Bangladeshis are excluded on the grounds that sample sizes relating to the UK-born were too small to produce stable estimates). In recognition of the fact that varying migration histories (by ethnic group) have produced migrant cohorts of radically different age profiles, Robinson controls for this factor, and also investigates whether (following Peach and Rossiter, in Chapter 3) social class provides at least a partial explanation for differences in settlement patterns and internal migration propensities between the various ethnic groups.

In terms of spatial patterns, the British-born minorities tend to be over-represented in the conurbations and under-represented in the South East and Outer London (as compared with their immigrant counterparts). More pertinently, British-born heads of household tend to live in areas of sparse ethnic settlement. This is particularly the case for those of Indian origin, with 52 per cent of the British-born (as against 26 per cent of the ethnic group as a whole) living in areas where Indians form less than 1 per cent of all household heads. Accordingly, Robinson describes British-born Indians as 'social and spatial pioneers'.

An investigation of 10-year (1981–1991) migration via the LS underlines some of the conclusions reached by Champion in his one year change-of-address analysis in the previous chapter; in particular the evidence of decentralising in London and outward movement to the South East. There are, however, interesting disparities between the migration profiles of the British-born from the different groups, as well as disparities which are intra-ethnic, inter-generational in nature. For example, the second generation of Caribbean origin (or, at least those who have not described themselves as Black–British and hence effectively opted for the label Black–Other) were seen to be more mobile than the immigrant generation and less rooted to the traditional settlement areas. They were rather more likely to move to London from the provinces, and decentralise from inner to outer London (a parallel being drawn with Whites of a similar age). Within the Indian population, Robinson notes, the roles were reversed to a point, and suggested the emergence of a 'new geography' built on a more general decentralisation. His overall conclusion was that inter-generational differences, although in some cases not particularly large, nevertheless suggested clearly divergent trajectories rather then simply being a reflection of the obvious non-comparability of the groups through being at different stages of the life-cycle.

1.4 Spatial patterns and ethnicity: the local dimension

The second section of the volume takes a detailed look at the three areas where the vast majority of Britain's minority ethnic groups are located: London, the (East and West) Midlands, and the Pennine towns and cities. At this scale it is now possible to undertake a much more in-depth analysis of the nature of these populations, to show their internal differentiation and examine their position in relation to the material deprivation thesis advanced earlier. The question to ask of all areas is whether the census provided convincing evidence to suggest the continuation of racial or ethnic disadvantage; specifically in terms of housing, (un)employment, education and health. If there was indeed such evidence, was it universal (i.e. applying to all minority groups) or particularistic, in the sense of applying only to certain groups, and/or certain subgroups?

The importance of London as a focal point for immigration and settlement over the centuries and the fact that in 1991 it contained approaching a half (44.6 per cent) of Britain's minority population means, as the authors of Chapter 6 say, that it would be unthinkable not to devote a chapter to it. They remind us importantly that the ethnic group question does not tell the whole story in terms of the ethnic mosaic of a major cosmopolitan city. Accordingly, Storkey and Lewis use detailed birthplace data from the census, in conjunction with that on ethnic group, to demonstrate the massive variety of its population. This also serves to remind us that the boundaries of disadvantage are unlikely to be coterminous with those of ethnic groups, however carefully we define them.

Mapping the residential patterns of the major ethnic groups highlights interesting differences, and complements very effectively the statistical analysis of differentials in levels of concentration and segregation undertaken by Peach and Rossiter in Chapter 3. It demonstrates very effectively the nonsense perpetrated in some sections of the research literature that South Asians constitute a meaningful group for purposes of analysis. Their settlement patterns are markedly different, their migration histories in terms of volume, nature and timing vary significantly and, of particular importance to the current argument, their social class profiles and general economic and material well-being are radically at variance.

Analysis of the census data on health (via the question on limiting long term illness – llti) showed that Bangladeshi adults and the elderly from all South Asian groups suffered particularly in this respect, as did young Black people in certain boroughs such as Lambeth and Hackney. Pakistani and Bangladeshi households were especially likely to be living in overcrowded conditions, and of the Black groups, those of African origin fared worst. With the exception of the Indian group whose class profile, significantly, is closest (of all principal minority groups) to that of Whites, and the Chinese, who are heavily concentrated in a particular segment of the labour market, unemployment rates for both males and females are between roughly twice and three times as high for minority groups as for the White group. The chapter therefore concludes that, despite the undoubted successes of many of minority origin, there remains much evidence of severe material disadvantage.

Similar evidence abounds in the case study of the Midlands, which conflates the East and West regions to produce the next most significant area of minority settlement, accounting for 20.3 per cent of the British total. In this chapter, Owen and Johnson use a number of sophisticated statistical techniques to assess the material disadvantage thesis. Rather than relying, for example, on a tabular analysis of census variables they use a cluster analysis to generate a typology of areas, and then look at the social composition of these areas (in particular their ethnic mix). This confirms the findings of earlier research that, but for some notable exceptions (once again usually the Indian and East African Asian middle class), minorities tended to be concentrated in poorer residential areas. Nearly two minority residents in five lived in deprived inner urban areas, with older poor quality (largely terraced) housing, low rates of car availability/ownership, low levels of higher education qualifications, relatively few white collar workers and extremely high levels of unemployment. A further quarter were located in 'depressed council estates', with relatively high levels of flatted accommodation, low economic activity rates and, once again, high levels of unemployment.

They also trace the background, growth and development of the various minority groups in different parts of the Midlands in some detail and, as with Chapter 2, estimate shifts in population over 1981–1991 (in this case for the 12 Midland districts with the largest minority ethnic presence). Indeed, with the complete listing of district populations in 1981 and 1991 in Appendix 2 of Chapter 2, the reader will be in a position to compare estimates of population change over the intercensal period under different assumptions. Owen and Johnson conclude that segregation levels appear to have declined a little over this period, though much may depend on the technical problems discussed earlier, namely the lack of a comparable ethnic group measure in 1981. Overall, they see 'continuity and surprisingly little change'.

The Pennine towns and cities provide the final case study. In comparison with London and the Midlands, little has been written about patterns of ethnic settlement in the North. Chapter 8 seeks to rectify this omission by providing a detailed account of the many disparate communities from towns and cities such as Bradford and Leeds in West Yorkshire and Oldham and Rochdale in Lancashire with their historical association with textiles, to the major cities of Manchester and Liverpool through which much of this produce passed on its way by sea to foreign markets.

Once again periodisation of migration flows and sources highlights major differences between these locations; with the growth of the minority population in a major port such as Liverpool taking place much earlier than in the inland mill towns, and being principally Black rather than South Asian in origin. Riots in Liverpool as early as 1919, and in other British ports simultaneously, provide ample testimony to the historic salience of race and ethnic inequality (May and Cohen, 1974), and also to the social and political significance attached to the issue of segregation. Many debates at the time (1919) raised the aura of the 'enemy within', as symbolised by the concentration of the Black population in small well defined areas of the city.

As with the other two case studies, Rees and Phillips describe and account for the current spatial patterns of the various minority ethnic groups, and focus on evidence of material disparities between these groups and the majority White population. 1991 Census data on housing, car availability, economic activity and (un)employment revealed parallels with the position of minorities elsewhere. Levels of segregation from Whites and other minority ethnic groups were again highest in general for the Bangladeshis and Pakistanis, and relatively low between these two groups.

1.5   Ethnic segregation and concentration: research and policy implications

This volume describes in some detail the changing patterns of residence of Britain's minority ethnic groups, both first generation and their offspring, examines the impact of internal migration on these patterns, and goes as far as the census data permit in assessing material disadvantage. Insofar as the latter highlights a continuing problem, the analysis serves an extremely useful function. But simply measuring ethnic disadvantage is arguably not enough: it is incumbent on the analyst to take the debate into the policy sphere. Two questions come to mind: first, 'What impact has urban policy had on the markedly inferior position of large sections of these minority groups?' and second 'What direction might future policy take, assuming an agreed aim to tackle any remaining disparities in material position?' Chapter 9 addresses both of these.

To answer the first question, one needs essentially to investigate whether areas with high concentrations of minority residents have been targeted for policy intervention of various kinds, and then to assess whether minority communities have received their 'fair share' of this investment, i.e. one which is commensurate with their relatively disadvantaged status. The problem as with all such work is that, in the absence of widespread ethnic monitoring it is very difficult, if not impossible, to assess exactly where money has been spent. All one can usually do in practice is to match money with areas; potentially inducing an analytical problem equivalent to that of the ecological correlation fallacy. In other words, even if investment is earmarked for an area with a high concentration of minority residents it does not preclude the possibility that it is White residents who actually benefit.

A consistent argument in the urban policy arena, apart perhaps from specific initiatives such as Section 11 funding, has been that poverty and lack of economic infrastructural development are the key to rectifying inequalities at an individual level. So arises the theory of the 'trickle down' effect. Investment goes to areas where the poor are concentrated: Black people in these areas are poor, therefore Black people benefit from such investment. The problem is that the theory has frequently been disproved in practice. Urban politics, largely through the racialisation of decision-making procedures, often see to it that funds are diverted away from minorities and minority-run projects (Ratcliffe, 1992; CRE, 1994). Furthermore, a recent study for the DoE by Robson et al. (1994), in analysing investment in the 57 UPA districts, showed that few districts achieving positive outcomes had significant concentrations of minority residents. As to the direction of current policy, most analysts now agree that the spatial focus has begun to shift. It has arguably moved away from tackling the consequences of deprivation and disadvantage *per se*, and in so doing has tended to shift away from areas where minorities are concentrated.

This leads us to the second question. Chapter 9 argues that for material disadvantage to be adequately addressed, some of the current concerns of the CRE would need to be met. Specifically, greater powers, involving the stengthening of existing anti-discrimination legislation (which has now been on the Statute Book for two decades), and a greater commitment to making codes of practice in matters of (say) housing, employment and education effective (or even mandatory), in both theory and practice. More widespread ethnic monitoring would be part and parcel of this process. It may also be that some resort to race/ethnicity-specific policy making may be necessary to redress the sort of material inequalities evidenced by the current volume.

This volume has aimed not only to provide an appraisal of current geographical patterns and current inequalities. It has also attempted to stimulate interest in future work on these issues by developing a possible future research agenda. To this end, the final chapter suggests a number of potentially fruitful lines of inquiry. It also looks forward to the 2001 Census and assesses the sort of issues which are deserving of some consideration if this exercise is to provide data of an even higher quality than that produced in 1991. Central to this are questions about the future form of the ethnic group question, and the nature of the census agenda; both of which are currently the subject of ongoing discussions between ONS, government departments, local authorities, academics and other interested parties.

In sum, the book aims to enhance debate on a number of fronts. It raises conceptual issues, such as those associated with the operationalisation of ethnic identity or ethnic group. It raises technical and/or methodological issues such as the measurement of levels of segregation and isolation, and the assessment of intercensal change given the non-comparability of data/geographical boundaries. It presents a detailed analysis of shifts in the ethnic geography of Britain. It raises important social issues relating to ethnic differentials in material well-being. And finally, it investigates the extent to which urban policy has thus far addressed these differentials. We assess what these debates mean for future policy debates and also for future research into both policy issues and the more theoretical matters of particular interest to the sociologist and social geographer.

References

Ballard, R. and Kalra, V.S. (1994) *The Ethnic Dimension of the 1991 Census: a preliminary report.* Manchester: University of Manchester Census Group.

Bulmer, M. (1986) Race and Ethnicity. In Burgess, R. G.(ed.) *Key Variables in Social Investigation* London: Routledge and Kegan Paul.

Bulmer, M. (1996) The Ethnic Question in the 1991 Census of Population. In Coleman, D. and Salt, J. (eds.) *Demographic Characteristics of the Ethnic Minority Populations.* Ethnicity in the 1991 Census series, Volume 1. London: HMSO.

Commission for Racial Equality (1994) Environmental Health and Racial Equality. London: CRE.

Giddens, A. (1993) *Sociology.* Cambridge: Polity Press.

Jenkins, R. (1986) Social Anthropological Models of Ethnic Relations. In Rex, J. and Mason, D. (eds.) *Theories of Race and Ethnic Relations.* Cambridge: Cambridge University Press.

Jones, T. (1993) *Britain's Ethnic Minorities.* London: PSI.

Lawrence, E. (1982) Just Plain Common Sense: the 'roots' of racism. In Centre for Contemporary Cultural Studies (ed.) *The Empire Strikes Back: race and racism in 70s Britain,* 47–94 London: Hutchinson/Routledge.

Mason, D. (1995) *Race and Ethnicity in Modern Britain.* London: Oxford University Press.

May, R. and Cohen, R. (1974) The Interaction Between Race and Colonialism: A Case Study of the Liverpool Race Riots of 1919. *Race and Class,* XVI(2), 111–26.

Miles, R. (1993) *Racism after 'Race Relations'.* London: Routledge.

Mills, I. and Teague, A. (1991) Editing and imputing data for the 1991 Census. *Population Trends,* 64, 30–7

Owen, D. (1996) Size, structure and growth of the ethnic minority populations. In Coleman, D. and Salt, J. (eds.) *Demographic Characteristics of the Ethnic Minority Populations.* Ethnicity in the 1991 Census series, Volume 1. London: HMSO.

Peach, C. (1996) Introduction. In Peach, C. (ed.) *The Ethnic Minority Populations of Great Britain.* Ethnicity in the 1991 Census series, Volume 2. London: HMSO.

Phillips, D. (1986) *What Price Equality?: a report on the allocation of GLC housing in Tower Hamlets.* London: Greater London Council.

Ratcliffe, P. (1981) *Racism and Reaction: a profile of Handsworth.* London: Routledge and Kegan Paul.

Ratcliffe, P. (1992) Renewal, regeneration and 'race': issues in urban policy. *New Community* 18(3), 387–400.

Ratcliffe, P. (ed.) (1994) *'Race', Ethnicity and Nation: International Perspectives on Social Conflict.* London: UCL Press.

Robson, B. et al. (1994) *Assessing the impact of urban policy* (DoE Inner Cities Research Programme). London: HMSO

Sillitoe, K. (1978) Ethnic Origins: the search for a question. *Population Trends,* 13, 25–30.

Sillitoe, K. (1987) Questions on race/ethnicity and related topics for the Census. *Population Trends,* 49, 5–11.

Sillitoe, K. and White, P.H. (1992) Ethnic Group and the British Census: the search for a question. *Journal of the Royal Statistical Society (Series A)* 155, part 1, 141–163.

Chapter 2
Geographical spread: the national picture

Philip Rees and Deborah Phillips

2.1 Introduction

The 1991 Census of Great Britain provides, for the first time, statistics on the numbers of people in the different ethnic groups living in all the cities, towns, villages and hamlets of the country through a self-assessment question (OPCS and GRO(S), 1992; 1993; 1994). In previous censuses, reliance has had to be placed on surrogate measures, namely the country of birth of a person (from 1841), the country of birth of parents (1971) or of the 'head of household' (1981). These statistics gave reasonable pictures of the geographical distribution of minority ethnic groups who had recently arrived in this country, but have become increasingly misleading as greater and greater proportions of the main non-White groups have been born in the United Kingdom.

Several detailed reports have already been prepared on the overall geography of ethnicity revealed by the 1991 Census. Owen (1992a; 1992b) produced a comprehensive account of the national picture, regional patterns and selected local authority concentrations. He also reviewed what could be learned from the sequence of country of birth and ethnic origin statistics over the period 1971–91, while recognising the difficulties of making exact statements about the extent of change. Teague (1993) has summarised the first results from the 1991 Census, including a map of local authority districts in Great Britain showing residents from minority ethnic groups as a percentage of the total population. Owen (1994a; 1994b, Chapter 2) has extended this analysis with a detailed review of ward level and enumeration district clustering of ethnic minority groups and the levels of segregation and isolation experienced. This work has shown that minorities are concentrated in large and medium-sized cities in England in a belt stretching from London in the South East to the textile towns of Lancashire in the North West. It also identifies a core set of regions in which most of Britain's minority ethnic population is to be found. The South East, East Midlands, West Midlands, Yorkshire and Humberside, and the North West together contain some 92 per cent of Britain's minority ethnic population, but only 66.8 per cent of its White population. Within these 'ethnic core' regions, minority groups are concentrated in the larger urban districts, particularly London.

So what does this chapter offer to supplement and build on previous accounts? First, it attempts to reconstruct the likely evolution of minority ethnic group populations over the decade 1981–91 in order that any changes to the pattern of ethnic concentration can be detected. Second, it considers the detailed changing geographies of the nine individual non-White groups identified in the 1991 Census, comparing and contrasting the patterns revealed. Any one census provides only a snapshot in time of the geographical distributions of populations that are undergoing continuous evolution. Hence, the present geography needs to be interpreted in the light of what has gone before.

Two requirements have normally to be satisfied when constructing and analysing a time series for geographically located populations. The first is that the geographical units remain constant in terms of their boundaries, and the second is that the same population groups can be identified at the different points in time. The first requirement is largely met when we use the 459 local government districts of Great Britain as our geographical net: only minor shifts of population in a few places are necessary to convert 1981 Census population statistics into statistics for the 1991 Census districts.

The second requirement is not met because the ethnic group question was asked for the first time in 1991. Comparable ethnicity data are available in both the 1981 and 1991 Censuses in the form of country of birth tables. However, the relationship between counts of the population by country of birth and by ethnicity has changed profoundly over the decade. Specifically, far more members of minority ethnic groups were born in the UK in 1991 than in 1981. It is still useful to compare country of birth groups between successive censuses but this provides only a picture of the non-native members of a minority ethnic group. The relationship between ethnicity and country of birth has also been changing. Specifically, the proportion of Whites born in New Commonwealth countries (largely during the colonial era) has been declining as these (mainly elderly) people die. A fresh approach to the problem of measuring the changing geographical spread, of minority ethnic populations, is therefore needed.

Section 2.2 of the chapter sets out the method adopted for estimating the mid-1981 district populations for the 10 ethnic groups used in the 1991 Census. This builds on earlier work by Haskey (1991). No claim for perfection can be made but we have sufficient confidence in the estimates to make it useful for them to be available in full as Appendix 2.2. Section 2.3 uses estimates that are linked closely to the 1991 Census counts, to review the geographical spread of minority ethnic groups in mid-1991. This supplements the descriptions already provided by Teague (1993) and Owen (1994a; 1994b). Section 2.4 then looks in some detail at the patterns of growth and redistribution of minority ethnic group populations over the decade 1981–91. This analysis makes use of a summary of the district statistics for 20 regions in Great Britain, the full details of which are provided in Appendix 2.1. The concluding section of the chapter evaluates the robustness of the change estimates, summarises the geographical patterns and geographical change that has occurred and makes suggestions about ways in which the 1981 estimates (and hence the analysis of change) can be improved.

2.2   Estimation method

The problem of estimating minority ethnic populations in the years prior to the 1991 Census was tackled by Haskey (1991), who produced estimates by county and metropolitan district. The essence of the method was to draw on information contained in the Labour Force Survey (LFS), which asks questions about both ethnic group and country of birth. From the LFS, tabulations of individuals in the sampled households were produced, cross-classified by country of birth and ethnic group for 1981 and for 1986–88. The conditional probabilities of ethnic group given country of birth for control areas (metropolitan 'counties' and region remainders) were then calculated from the LFS tables. These were then applied to the country of birth counts from the 1981 Census for local districts, so as to yield country of birth by ethnic group tables. The 1981 tables were adjusted to tables based on 1986–88 to yield estimates for that latter set of years.

The crucial assumption involved in the Haskey method is that the LFS conditional probabilities for control areas apply to all the districts within those areas. In practice, where metropolitan counties or region remainders contained districts with and without substantial minority ethnic populations, the underlying district probabilities were very different. Use of the control matrix resulted in overestimation of the minority ethnic population in districts with low numbers and underestimation in those with higher concentrations. For example, persons born in India in a small shire district reported in the 1981 Census were more likely to be White (elderly residents born in India to parents associated with the Imperial regime), while those in areas of ethnic concentration were far more likely to be of Indian ethnicity.

The 1991 Census provides information classifying populations by country of birth and ethnic group membership that is much more locally specific (LBS, Table L51), and these data can be used to compute conditional probabilities of ethnic group given country of birth for each of the 459 local authorities. The 1991 Census conditional probabilities can be applied to the 1981 Census country of birth counts for the districts (as in Haskey's method), but this assumes that the probabilities found in 1991 apply equally in 1981. As noted above, it is likely that the probabilities of persons born in the UK being non-White were higher in 1991 than in 1981, so that the method is likely to lead to an overestimate. This can be rectified by adjusting the resulting minority ethnic group estimates to minority ethnic estimates for control areas derived from the 1979–1981–1983 Labour Force Surveys, in the same way as Haskey adjusted his 1981 estimates to the 1986–1987–1988 Labour Force Surveys. In addition, the minority ethnic group estimates in 1981 and 1991 were both adjusted to sum to the revised mid-year population estimate series based on backcasting from the 1991 mid-year final revised rebased population estimates for districts, with an allowance in 1991 for differential under-enumeration of the different ethnic groups. Box 2.1 sets out the sequence of steps in the algorithm for the estimation of 1981 and 1991 minority ethnic group populations while Box 2.2 gives the detailed equations employed.

Further improvement of this method could be made through the additional use of age-classified country of birth by ethnic group cross-tabulations for control areas. Such tables could be derived either from the individual Sample of Anonymised Records (SAR) or from the Longitudinal Study (LS). The conditional probabilities would then be derived from the population who were aged 10 or over in 1991, eliminating those born in the decade 1981–91. Use of such probabilities from the individual SAR would continue the assumption that the 1991 probabilities applied in 1981 or, in other words, that the population had remained geographically

Box 2.1   *Steps in estimating 1991 and 1981 ethnic populations*

Step

1   The 1991 and 1981 populations of districts are input.
The 1981 district populations are adjusted in a couple of dozen cases by the addition/subtraction of populations so that they correspond with the 1991 boundaries.

2   The 1991 Census Table L51 counts are input.
The table rows are aggregated to the 18 country of birth groups used in the 1981 Census.
The counts are multiplied by undercount factors from OPCS and GRO(S) (1994) specific to each ethnic group:

White	1.02	Pakistani	1.03
Black–Caribbean	1.03	Bangladeshi	1.03
Black–African	1.05	Chinese	1.03
Black–Other	1.04	OtherAsian	1.03
Indian	1.03	Other–Other	1.03

3   The inflated Table L51 counts are adjusted to sum to the mid-1991 district populations.

4   The conditional probabilities of ethnic group given country of birth group are computed.

5   The 1981 Census Small Area Statistics Table 4 counts of persons by country of birth are input.

6   The 1981 country of birth counts are multiplied by the 1991 conditional probabilities to yield a country of birth by ethnic group matrix.

7   The matrix counts are adjusted to sum to the 1981 mid-year populations from step (1).

8   The Labour Force Survey counts of Whites and non-Whites are input from the pooled 1979, 1981 and 1983 LFS.
The LFS counts are adjusted to sum to the 1981 mid-year populations from step (1).

9   The 1981 district counts are adjusted so that they sum to the 1979–81–83 LFS estimates of Whites and non-Whites for 20 metropolitan county and region remainder areas.

10   The 1981 and 1991 matrices are summed to yield ethnic group and country of birth estimates.

Box 2.2   *Technical specification of the estimation models*

Step 1

Definitions:

P^d (91)   = mid-1991 population estimate for district d

P^d (81i)   = initial mid-1981 population estimate for district d

D^d = population transferred into/out of district d as a result of boundary changes between 1981 and 1991

Method:

$P^d(81)$ = $P^d(81i) + D^d$

Step 2

Definitions:

$C_{ea}^d(91)$ = 1991 Census count of persons of ethnicity e and country of birth a (1991 grouping), resident in district d

$C_{eb}^d(91)$ = 1991 Census count of persons of ethnicity e and country of birth b (1981 grouping), resident in district d

$f_e(91)$ = undercount factor specific to group e at the 1991 Census

C' = 1991 Census count adjusted for the undercount

Method:

$C_{eb}^d(91)$ = $\underset{a \supset b}{E} C_{ea}^d(91)$

$C_{eb}^{'d}(91)$ = $f_e(91) \, C_{eb}^d(91)$

Step 3

Definition:

$P_{eb}^d(91)$ = mid-1991 population estimate for persons of ethnicity e and country of birth b for district d

Method:

$P_{eb}^d(91)$ = $C_{eb}^{'d}(91)\left(P^d(91) / \underset{e}{E}\,\underset{b}{E}\, C_{eb}^{'d}(91)\right)$

Step 4

Definition:

$p(e\,|\,b,d)$ = probability of being a member of ethnic group e given country of birth b and residence in district d

Method:

$p(e\,|\,b,d)$ = $P_{eb}^d(91) / \underset{e}{\sum} P_{eb}^d(91)$

Step 5

Definition:

$C_b^d(81)$ = 1981 Census count of persons born in country of birth b, resident in district d

Step 6

Definition:

$C_{eb}^d(81)$ = 1981 Census population estimate for persons of ethnicity e and country of birth b, resident in district d

Method:

$C_{eb}^d(81)$ $= p(e \mid b,d) \; C_b^d(81)$

Step 7

Definition:

$P_{eb}^d(81)$ = mid-1981 population estimate for persons of ethnicity e and country of birth b, resident in district d

Method:

$P_{eb}^d(81)$ $= C_{eb}^d(81) \left(P^d(81) / \sum_e \sum_b C_{eb}^d(81) \right)$

Step 8

Definitions:

$L_w^r(81)$ = Labour Force Survey counts of persons of ethnicity w (White, non-White) resident in region r, pooled from the 1979, 1981 and 1983 LFS

$P_w^r(81)$ = mid-1981 population estimate of persons of ethnicity w (White, non-White) resident in region r

Method:

$P_w^r(81)$ $= L_w^r \left(\sum_{d \epsilon r} P^d(81) / \sum_w L_w^r \right)$

Step 9

Definitions:

P' = mid-1981 adjusted population estimate

Method:

$P_{eb}^{'d}(81)$ $= P_{eb}^d(81) \left(P_w^r(81) / \sum_{d \epsilon r} \sum_{e \epsilon w} P_{eb}^d(81) \right)$

Step 10

$P_e^d(81)$ $= \sum_b P_{eb}^{'d}(81)$

$P_e^d(91)$ $= \sum_b P_{eb}^d(91)$

stationary over the intercensal decade. In practice, many people will have migrated. The LS enables the England and Wales 1991 Census population sampled to be classified by their 1981 location and so this difficulty could be overcome in part. Use of age-related weights in reconstructing the 1981 probabilities would be useful in order to allow for those who have died during the period 1981–91.

One modification to the Haskey procedure employed here is the reduction of the LFS constraint information, to just two numbers per control area; namely the estimates of Whites and non-Whites. The reason for doing this was to avoid the contamination of detailed reliable census counts (e.g. for country of birth groups) with far less reliable sample-based estimates. Country of birth by ethnic group matrices from the LFS, even when pooled, contain many zero counts, because of the small sample size. (This problem will be less serious with the post-1991 LFS with its larger sample size.)

The results of the estimation are set out in full in Appendix 2.2 for the 459 districts of Great Britain. These constitute a resource which readers can use for further study and/or critical evaluation. The district results are summarised in Appendix 2.1 for a 20-zone system. These 20 zones consist of the set of former metropolitan counties and region remainders which are frequently used to analyse population change and for which Labour Force Survey tabulations are available.

The nine minority ethnic populations are mapped in Figures 2.1 to 2.27. The maps have each been deliberately focused on England and Wales south of a line between Lancaster and Bridlington, and east of a line from Prestatyn to St Athan, as this area contains roughly 95 per cent of the minority ethnic population of Great Britain. Each group is portrayed on three maps. The first shows the absolute counts of members of the minority ethnic group for each district, represented by a circle the area of which is proportional to the count. The second shows the concentration of the group in the core districts, using the percentage that the group makes up of the district total population. The third map for each group presents the absolute counts of changes in the estimated size of the group in each district over the decade 1981–91. Most changes are positive, but in all groups there are a few districts where losses occur, and these are represented by open circles (shaded circles signifying gains).

2.3   The 1991 geography

In this section, we examine the geographical patterns of spread for the nine non-White minority ethnic groups, using two scales: metropolitan/non-metropolitan areas and local government district.

The metropolitan and non-metropolitan patterns

Appendix 2.1 sets out the statistics for the ethnic groups. There is a table for each ethnic group and for all minority ethnic groups combined. Each table contains the population estimates for 1981 and 1991, the absolute and percentage change between those two years, the row percentages for 1981 and 1991 (composition indicators), the column percentages for 1981 and 1991 (distribution indicators), and the location quotients for 1981 and 1991 (concentration indicators). The column labelled 'Row % 1991' contains the percentage that the group indicated in the table column makes up of the population of the area indicated in the table row. For example, 25.8 per cent of inner London's population at mid-1991 was estimated to be non-White, while 74.2 per cent was estimated to be White. There are two kinds of area: the first consists of metropolitan areas (either former metropolitan counties or parts of Greater London or statistical conurbations), the second of either whole regions lacking a metropolitan area (as here defined) or the remainders of a standard statistical region. The areas are ranked in descending order of non-White concentration/ascending order of White concentration.

The distribution statistics for each ethnic group are given in the columns labelled 'Column % 1981' and 'Column % 1991'. Each figure represents the percentage of the British population of a particular ethnic group found in the area indicated by the row in the table. For example, 36.1 per cent of the British population of the Black–Caribbean group is found in inner London in 1991, but only 0.06 per cent in central Clydeside. The final pair of columns contain the location quotients for each area. Location quotients (LQs) are the ratios of the ethnic group's row percentage for an area, divided by the row percentage for Britain as a whole. An LQ above 1 indicates that the group is more concentrated in an area than it is, on average, in Britain as a whole; an LQ below 1 indicates the group is less concentrated (than on average).

Whites and minority ethnic groups

The highest concentrations of minority ethnic populations are found in the large metropolitan areas of industrial and south east England. It is only in these areas that the percentage non-White rises above the British average of 5.6 per cent (this is 0.1 per cent higher than the 1991 Census figure given in OPCS and GRO(S) (1993) because of the allowances for differential under-enumeration). Nearly a quarter of inner London's population is non-White, compared with just over one in six in outer London and just under one in six in the West Midlands metropolitan area.

Note that the distributions of metropolitan and non-metropolitan areas overlap with respect to White/non-White concentration. The East Midlands, outer metropolitan area and the remainder of the North West region have higher non-White percentages than four of the metropolitan areas. As we shall see later these regional averages conceal much higher and lower percentages in particular districts.

Black groups

The concentration of individual minority ethnic groups is much lower than that of non-Whites as a whole, but the Black groups make up 13.5 per cent of the population of inner London. It is only in inner London, outer London and the West Midlands that Black–Caribbeans are over-represented; elsewhere they are under-represented with respect to their percentage of 0.93 for the population as a whole. Black–Africans are even more concentrated in inner and outer London, with these areas having the only percentages above the national average figure of 0.39. The Black–Other group, which includes many people of mixed origin, is more widespread and is over-represented in inner London, outer London, the West Midlands conurbation, Greater Manchester and East Anglia.

South Asian groups

The Indian group has its highest concentration in outer London, rather than inner London. The West Midlands concentration at 5.6 per cent is nearly double that of inner London at 3.0 per cent; a level which in turn is closely followed by 2.6 per cent for the East Midlands. Also above the national average of 1.56 per cent is the West Yorkshire metropolitan area. All other areas fall below the national average, though more than 1 per cent of the populations of the outer metropolitan area, Greater Manchester and the remainder of the North West are Indian.

The Pakistani population is the first whose distribution is not dominated by inner or outer London. The largest communities are found in the West Midlands and West Yorkshire metropolitan areas and above average (0.89 per cent) concentrations are found in the remainder of the North West, Greater Manchester, South Yorkshire and central Clydeside as well as inner and outer London.

The Bangladeshi population is highly concentrated in London, with 44 per cent of all Bangladeshis living in inner London alone (Tower Hamlets, Newham, Camden) and nearly 60 per cent in the London area (inner and outer London and the outer metropolitan area). Outside London there are above average (0.31 per cent) concentrations in the West Midlands and Greater Manchester.

Other groups

Although the Chinese, Other–Asian and Other–Other (i.e. other non-Asian) groups are all concentrated in London, their degree of concentration falls well short of that of the Bangladeshis. The Chinese constitute at least 0.1 per cent of the population of each area compared with an overall average of 0.29 per cent. This, of course, relates to their pattern of economic activity in the catering industry with a wide dispersion of establishments across the country. The Other–Asian pattern in a sense resembles that of Indians (with a larger number in outer London than inner London), but in other respects it differs in being more concentrated in the outer metropolitan area and less concentrated in the East Midlands.

The Other–Other group makes up just over half a per cent of the British population (0.54) but is, of course, a heterogeneous mixture of persons from a variety of ethnic and national backgrounds. They are well represented in all areas, though just over half are found in the three London areas (inner London, outer London and outer metropolitan area).

District patterns

The metropolitan/non-metropolitan classification conceals a great deal of vital local variation in minority ethnic group distribution between districts within areas. This variation is revealed when the maps of the 'ethnic core' districts are examined (Figures 2.1 to 2.27) along with Table 2.4, which picks out the districts with the largest district populations for each minority ethnic group (see Teague (1993) for equivalent lists ordered by degree of concentration).

Black groups

Figures 2.1 and 2.2 show the largest Black–Caribbean communities to be located in inner and outer London, Birmingham, Wolverhampton, Bristol, Nottingham, Manchester and Leeds, with smaller populations in a scattering of northern towns and towns to the north west of London. Within London itself, Black–Caribbeans are most concentrated in the boroughs of Lambeth, Hackney, Brent, Lewisham, Haringey and Southwark (three south of the Thames and three north, five in inner and one in outer London). Other inner and outer boroughs also house important concentrations. The single largest district population is, however, found in Birmingham.

The Black–African maps (Figures 2.4 and 2.5) resemble those of the Caribbeans most closely in London, but they are represented in fewer of the large towns of core England. Cardiff, Liverpool, Manchester, Leeds and Sheffield all have small communities of Black–Africans.

The Black–Other population (Figures 2.7 and 2.8) parallels that of the Black–Caribbeans throughout the country except that the relative importance of communities in cities and towns outside London is greater. This category contains many of the offspring born in the UK to one or more parents born in the Caribbean. Birmingham re-enters the top dozen districts, as does Liverpool. This group undoubtedly contains members of mixed origin. The one district which stands out on this map but not on those for the other Black groups is the city of Cambridge, where the Black–Other group is as concentrated as it is in parts of inner London.

South Asian groups

Figures 2.10 and 2.11 and the top dozen list in Table 2.4 reveal the concentration of Indians in the outer London boroughs (Ealing, Brent, Harrow, Hounslow, Redbridge and Barnet), and in Slough; in the Midlands in Leicester, Coventry, Birmingham, Wolverhampton and Sandwell; and in Bolton, Blackburn and Preston in the North West. The largest single district population is in Leicester, which has been the focus of Indian migrations from East Africa (see Owen and Johnson, Chapter 7 of this volume).

There is considerable contrast between the Indian distribution and the geographical spread of Pakistanis (Figures 2.13 and 2.14). Only Newham in London figures in the top dozen districts. The largest concentrations are in the textile towns of West

Yorkshire (Bradford and Kirklees), Greater Manchester (Manchester and Rochdale) and Lancashire (the Colne Valley towns), although the single largest district population is in Birmingham. Luton and Slough in the South East have larger Pakistani populations than all London boroughs bar Newham. Prominent in the top dozen list, for the first time, is a city outside the map area, namely Glasgow, with over 11,000 Pakistanis.

The Bangladeshi maps (Figures 2.16 and 2.17) show the concentration of this group in east London (particularly in Tower Hamlets), with lesser concentrations in neighbouring boroughs such as Newham, Camden, Hackney, Islington and Haringey. Outside London the largest Bangladeshi communities are to be found in Birmingham, Oldham, Luton, Bradford and Sandwell.

Other groups

The district maps of the Chinese population (Figures 2.19 and 2.20) confirm the finding of the metropolitan/non-metropolitan analysis; small numbers of Chinese are found in a majority of English districts with the largest communities (though only of a few thousand) in the major cities of Liverpool, Birmingham, Manchester and Glasgow. The Chinese are present in small numbers in all London boroughs.

The Other–Asian group is concentrated in London (Figures 2.22 and 2.23) but communities are found in all London boroughs, with greatest concentrations in north west London. The (outer) south London borough of Merton also figures in the top dozen list, indicating that this group may contain a wealthier middle class component (though more detailed investigation of the district tables giving information on the socio-economic status of each minority ethnic group would need to be undertaken to confirm this).

The Other–Other group displays a wide geographical spread on the percentage map (Figure 2.26) but the proportional circle map (Figure 2.25) features most of the larger cities and towns of industrial England as well as most of the London boroughs.

2.4   Growth and redistribution of minority ethnic group populations, 1981–91

In the analysis of recent changes in the geography of populations, it is usual to have available not only the statistics giving details of the population stocks themselves, but also details of the components that contribute to the change. These are the demographic components of fertility, mortality and migration, with the latter broken down into internal and international parts. It would be extremely valuable to have access to estimates broken down by age so that the cohort-replacement and ageing-in-place processes could be tracked for the various minority ethnic groups. Unfortunately, this information is not available and so the interpretation advanced here must be regarded as provisional, awaiting both the development of ethnic classifications of the principal population movements and the research needed to make estimates of those movements in the past.

What are the key features that should be looked for in the extensive information base reported in Appendices 2.1 and 2.2?

We need to examine:

1.   the overall level and pace of change in Great Britain for each group
2.   the degree of redistribution each group is experiencing
3.   the ways in which the relationships between ethnic group distributions, and in particular between each group and the White population, are evolving.

As these issues are addressed, we must keep in mind the likely errors introduced through the 1981 estimation procedures and the bias implicit in the spatial filters employed, namely the 459 local government districts of Great Britain and the 20 metropolitan/non-metropolitan areas used to summarise change.

Table 2.1   *Population change by ethnic minority group, 1981-91, Great Britain*

Group	Population 1981 (000s)	Population 1991 (000s)	Change 1981–91 (000s)	Per cent change 1981–91
White	52,600.0	53,062.3	452.3	0.9
Black–Caribbean	422.5	522.2	99.7	23.6
Black– African	141.4	219.2	77.8	55.0
Black–Other	143.8	188.2	44.5	30.9
Black groups	707.7	929.6	221.9	31.4
Indian	627.8	877	249.2	39.7
Pakistani	344.5	500.3	155.8	45.2
Bangladeshi	87.8	171.5	83.8	95.4
South Asian groups	1060.1	1548.8	488.8	46.1
Chinese	111.5	160.8	49.3	44.2
Other – Asian	110.4	202.3	91.9	83.2
Other – Other	214	302.2	88.2	41.2
Other groups	435.9	665.3	229.4	52.6
All ethnic minorities	2,203.7	3,143.7	940.1	42.7
Total	54,813.7	56,206.1	1,392.4	2.5

Source: Authors' estimates based on 1981 Small Area Statistics and 1991 Census Local Base Statistics, Crown Copyright, ESRC/JISC Purchase, and 1981 and 1991 OPCS mid-year population estimates, Crown Copyright.

The national picture

We start by looking at the population of Great Britain as a whole. Table 2.1 summarises the changes taking place over the decade between mid-1981 and mid-1991. In that period the population as a whole grew very modestly, by only 2.5 per cent over 10 years or nearly 1.4 million. Just over two thirds of this population increase was due to minority ethnic groups, with the White population contributing only 32 per cent, growing by less than 1 per cent over 1981–91.

Ethnic minorities in Table 2.1 are summed into three groups. The Other group, made up of the Chinese, Other–Asians and the Other–Other group, experienced the highest relative increase of 53 per cent (Table 2.1, last column), followed by the South Asian groups with a 46 per cent increase and the Black groups (31 per cent). However, this is too simple a classification – each grouping contains an ethnic minority with a high rate of increase. The highest rate is posted by the Bangladeshis who almost doubled their population in the decade, followed by the Other–Asians with an 83 per cent growth and Black–Africans (55 per cent growth). Much lower rates (though still substantially greater than that for the White population) were observed in the case of the Black–Caribbean (24 per cent) and Black–Other groups (31 per cent); with the Indian, Pakistani, Chinese and Other–Other groups experiencing growth in the 40–45 per cent range.

What factors account for this variation between the groups? Probably the most important influence is the high level of fertility experienced by most, though not all groups, coupled with the concentration of the population in the fertile age range. For example, if a minority ethnic population consisted of only married couples in their twenties, and if they had just two children over the course of a decade, this would double the group population. In the long run, this behaviour would just keep the population ticking over. Table 2.2 provides rough estimates of the total fertility rates (TFRs) for the White group, the Black groups, and the Other groups together with individual TFRs for Indians, Pakistanis and Bangladeshis.

Table 2.2   *Fertility indicators for ethnic groups, Great Britain, 1991*

Ethnic group	TFR Method 1	TFR Method 2
White	1.85	1.85
Black	1.58	1.73
Indian	2.09	2.10
Pakistani	3.80	3.86
Bangladeshi	5.22	5.33
Other	1.64	1.65

Notes: 1 TFR = total fertility rate = sum of age-specific fertility rates multiplied by the age interval = children per woman expected over a lifetime; 2 Method 1 converts births by mother's place of birth into ethnic group births using conditional probabilities from the 1991 Census. 3 Method 2 matches fertility rates for place of birth groups to the most closely linked ethnic group.
Sources: Authors' estimates using OPCS Birth Statistics and the 1991 Census, Crown Copyright.

The fertility of the Black groups is now lower, on average, than that of Whites and this explains their low growth compared with other groups. Their age structure is, however, still 'fertility-favourable'. The Black–African group, however, has much higher fertility than the Black–Caribbean and Black–Other groups, and a younger age structure. The high fertility of Bangladeshis and Pakistanis contributes to their above average growth rates.

The second set of factors at work concern the pace and direction of international migration. There is now net return migration to the Caribbean while the flow of family migrants from the Indian subcontinent continues at a steady level. Net immigration by members of the Other groups is probably the key factor in their growth, given the relatively low fertility levels reported in Table 2.2.

Spatial redistribution: the general perspective

The national changes subsume a variety of subnational experiences. In this section we examine these using a number of indicators of redistribution, to see to what extent the geographies of each group have changed. Table 2.3 provides this set of summary indicators. The indicators are computed from the summary statistics for the 20 metropolitan and non-metropolitan areas reported in Appendix 2.1. These give a succinct summary of the settlement structure in Britain. (The 20 areas were also those for which the Labour Force Surveys of 1979, 1981 and 1983 reported sample counts.)

The first panel of Table 2.3 shows how the ethnic composition of the Great Britain population is changing. The White percentage declined by 1.6 per cent between 1981 and 1991 while each minority group displayed at least a 0.1 per cent share increase.

The second panel reports the index of dissimilarity (ID) between the ethnic group's distribution over 20 metropolitan/non-metropolitan areas in 1981 and that in 1991. The ID ranges in theory from a minimum of zero when there are no differences in the relative distributions of the populations, to a maximum of 100 when the distributions are completely different.

It is clear that rather little in the way of redistribution has been occurring despite the high levels of growth. The greatest shifts are only 8 and 10 per cent (for the Other–Asian and Other–Other groups respectively), while the other groups show shifts below 7 per cent. However, all ethnic minority IDs are higher than those for Whites, indicating that their geographical redistributions are more dynamic, if not dramatically so.

The third panel of Table 2.3 compares the distribution of each minority ethnic group across the 20 metropolitan/non-metropolitan areas with that of the White population, while Whites are compared with all minority ethnic groups combined (using the ID). The IDs were computed for both 1981 and 1991, along with the change in IDs over the decade. For all groups their distance from Whites increased during the decade by between two and nine points on the ID scale. This is, in the main, the consequence of two processes. The first is the shift of the White population

Table 2.3 Indicators of spatial redistribution for ethnic groups, 1981-91, Great Britain

Indicator	Total	White	Black Caribbean	Black African	Black – Other	Indian	Pakistani	Bangla-deshi	Chinese	Other – Asian	Other – Other
GB population											
1981%	100	95.98	0.77	0.26	0.27	1.15	0.63	0.16	0.20	0.20	0.39
1991%	100	94.41	0.93	0.39	0.35	1.56	0.89	0.31	0.29	0.36	0.54
1981–91 change in %	0	-1.57	0.16	0.13	0.08	0.41	0.26	0.15	0.09	0.16	0.15
1981–91 change (000s)	1,392.4	452.3	99.7	77.8	44.5	249.2	155.8	83.8	49.3	91.9	88.2
1981–91 % change	2.5	0.9	23.6	55.0	30.9	39.7	45.2	95.4	44.2	83.2	41.2
Spatial redistribution											
1981 vs 1991 ID	1.5	2.1	4.5	5.8	3.6	6.1	4.1	5.4	6.5	8.2	10.4
Comparison with Whites											
1981 ID	1.7	41.6	55.1	61.1	38.5	45.3	40.6	47.4	23.6	40.8	59.3
1991 ID	2.5	45.0	58.3	67.6	40.5	48.9	43.3	51.8	27.8	48.0	68.0
1981–91 change in ID	0.8	3.4	3.2	6.5	2.0	3.6	2.7	4.4	4.2	7.2	8.7
Metropolitan concentration	9 areas	9 areas	9 areas	9 areas	9 areas	9 areas	9 areas	9 areas	9 areas	9 areas	9 areas
1981 % in metro areas	36.3	34.9	80.0	82.9	66.8	66.0	70.0	74.6	53.9	64.7	58.7
1991 % in metro areas	35.0	32.9	81.1	86.5	67.9	67.8	71.1	77.6	57.5	68.9	61.9
1981–91 change in %	-1.3	-2.0	1.1	3.6	1.1	1.8	1.1	3.0	3.6	4.2	3.2
Core concentration		15 areas	3 areas	2 areas	6 areas	5 areas	8 areas	4 areas	4 areas	2 areas	3 areas
1981 % in core areas	na	75.8	71.8	72.3	66.8	71.7	74.0	67.2	41.8	50.1	44.9
1991 % in core areas	na	77.3	72.8	77.9	67.9	74.3	75.6	70.8	45.3	58.0	48.3
1981–91 change in %	na	1.5	1.0	5.6	1.1	2.6	1.6	3.6	3.5	7.9	3.4
Southern concentration	7 areas	7 areas	7 areas	7 areas	7 areas	7 areas	7 areas	7 areas	7 areas	7 areas	7 areas
1981 % in core areas	49.5	48.9	73.3	84.4	68.9	62.8	34.7	64.7	62.8	75.9	67.4
1991 % in core areas	50.6	49.8	74.7	87.6	70.1	66.7	35.4	68.6	64.8	76.6	69.7
1981–91 change in %	1.1	0.9	1.4	3.2	1.2	3.9	0.7	3.9	2.0	0.7	1.7

Notes: na = not applicable; 1. ID = Index of Dissimilarity between one group and another
100 * 0.5 * sum (absolute value of the difference between % of one group in an area and the % of another). The IoD ranges between 0 (= no dissimilarity) and 100 (complete dissimilarity). (See Chapter 3, Box 3.1 for worked example).
2. Comparison with Whites:
The ID figures in the White column refer to a comparison of Whites with all Ethnic minority groups combined.
3. Metropolitan concentration: The 9 metropolitan areas are defined as Inner London, Outer London, West Midlands, West Yorkshire, Greater Manchester, South Yorkshire, Central Clydeside, Merseyside and Tyne and Wear.
4. Core concentration: Core areas are defined as those with Location Quotients (LQ) greater than one in 1991. Values above one show that the group is more concentrated in an area than in the country as a whole. See Appendix 2.1 for LQ numbers and areas for each group.
5. Southern concentration: Southern areas are defined as Inner London, Outer London, the Outer Metropolitan Area, Outer South East, East Anglia, South West and East Midlands.

away from metropolitan to non-metropolitan areas, a long-standing trend that encompasses both short distance migration within metropolitan commuting fields and also longer distance migration to smaller cities and towns (Stillwell et al., 1992). The second process consists of the large increases in minority ethnic group populations in areas of concentration, the metropolitan areas and selected cities elsewhere. It is possible that the method of estimation may still exaggerate the 1991 minority ethnic population of non-metropolitan areas, so producing a distancing from Whites over the decade that is artefact rather than reality. However, this probably has only a minor counter-effect, and can only be properly evaluated when better estimates are produced.

The extent to which minority ethnic populations are concentrated in large metropolitan areas is revealed in the fourth panel of Table 2.3. Although only a third of the White population resides in metropolitan areas between 54 and 83 per cent of ethnic minorities live there. While Whites experienced a 2 per cent decrease in the share residing in metropolitan areas, all minority ethnic groups experienced an increase.

There are minority ethnic group concentrations outside the metropolitan areas (e.g. Leicester for Indians and Luton for Pakistanis and Bangladeshis). The fifth panel of Table 2.3 aggregates the population estimates for those areas in which the minority ethnic group is more concentrated than it is in Britain as a whole (that is, where the Location Quotients (LQs) are greater than one). The table reports the number of such areas in 1991 for each group. These range from 15 for Whites to two for Black–Africans and Other–Asians. In all cases the percentage of the population located in the core areas increased over the decade 1981–91. For the Black–Caribbean and Black–Other groups the increase was around 1 per cent, but for Black–Africans and Other–Asians it was over 5 per cent.

The final aspect of spatial distribution over the decade addressed in Table 2.3 is that of concentration in southern Britain, defined as the metropolitan and non-metropolitan areas to the south east of the Severn–Humber line (see Table 2.3, note 5). Here trends between 1981 and 1991 were in agreement for both Whites and the minority ethnic groups: the southern share of all populations increased. However, the White increase at 0.9 per cent was below the national average of 1.1 per cent, while seven out of the nine minority groups experienced greater than national shifts.

To sum up, there is clear evidence from a comparison of the population estimates of ethnic groups in 1981 and 1991, of a widening of the differences between the spatial distribution of Whites on the one hand, and of minority ethnic groups on the other. This is principally a product of fast growth as a result of family expansion and new household formation among minority ethnic groups in their existing, established 1981 clusters, coupled with the migration of Whites out of metropolitan areas containing those clusters. However, this broad generalisation needs to be supplemented by a detailed examination of the spatial population history of each particular minority ethnic group.

Spatial redistribution for individual groups

Evidence for the changes in spatial distribution experienced by each group is assembled in the maps of change (Figures 2.3, 2.6, 2.9, 2.12, 2.15, 2.18, 2.21, 2.24 and 2.27), in Appendix 2.1, which provides a full battery of indicators over the 20 metropolitan/non-metropolitan areas, and in Table 2.4 which picks out the top 12 districts (by 1991 population size) for each group from Appendix 2.2 (where the full set of estimates are given). Appendix 2.1 includes eight indicators derived from the two population estimates:

1. The change in population between 1981 and 1991
2. The change as a per cent of the 1981 population
3. The row % in 1981, which is the percentage an ethnic group makes up of the area's total population
4. The row % in 1991
5. The column % in 1981, which is the percentage an ethnic group in an area makes up of the GB total population in that ethnic group in 1981
6. The column % 1991
7. The LQ (Location Quotient) 1981, which is the column % for the group divided by the column % for all groups in 1981
8. The LQ 1991.

We examine these statistics to see if there are signs of ethnic group redistribution within the broad categories discussed to date.

There is one persistent feature of the minority ethnic group tables listed in Appendix 2.1 which requires comment before the groups are discussed. One region, the remainder of the West Midlands (for 10 groups) records falls in minority ethnic group populations. These decreases seem anomalous and are probably artefacts of the clustered sampling method used in the 1979–81–83 Labour Force Surveys. Owen (1995b, Table 2) reports trends in the percentage of the population from minority ethnic groups based on the LFS. In the remainder of the West Midlands region (the counties of Hereford and Worcester, Staffordshire, Shropshire and Warwickshire) the pooled LFS for 1981 and 1983 gives a figure of 2.6 per cent whereas the pooled LFS for 1989 and 1991 suggests 1.5 per cent. In between, the series fluctuates widely between these extremes. What appears to have happened is that in 1979–81–83, the clustered sample (of enumeration districts) fell on pockets of high minority presence, while in 1991 the opposite was the case. Cluster sampling is poor at estimating trends in a clustered population if the sampled clusters change each year. Since 1991 the expanded LFS has been undertaken on a simple random basis within the regions (thereby avoiding the problems of shifting clusters). The results for the remainder of the West Midlands serve as a warning that the results as a whole must be treated with caution.

Black–Caribbeans

People of Black–Caribbean origin are found in virtually every English district and in most of the urban districts of Wales and Scotland. On the other hand the group is

Table 2.4   *The dozen largest district populations for each ethnic group*

District	1991	1981	Change	% 1991	% Change 81–91
Total					
Birmingham	1,006,500	1,004,130	2,370	100	0.2
Leeds	717,400	721,685	-4,285	100	-0.6
Glasgow City	688,500	769,394	-80,894	100	-10.5
Sheffield	529,300	544,437	-15,137	100	-2.8
Liverpool	480,700	514,911	-34,211	100	-6.6
Bradford	475,400	457,133	18,267	100	4.0
Edinburgh City	439,400	442,629	-3,229	100	-0.7
Manchester	438,500	453,423	-14,923	100	-3.3
Bristol	397,000	399,080	-2,080	100	-0.5
Kirklees	381,500	374,761	6,739	100	1.8
Wirral	336,000	341,236	-5,236	100	-1.5
Wakefield	316,200	318,727	-2,527	100	-0.8
White					
Birmingham	787,210	838,751	-51,541	78.21	-6.1
Leeds	675,019	690,047	-15,028	94.09	-2.2
Glasgow City	665,835	755,125	-89,290	96.71	-11.8
Sheffield	502,379	526,260	-23,881	94.91	-4.5
Liverpool	462,513	500,122	-37,609	96.22	-7.5
Edinburgh City	429,120	438,104	-8,984	97.66	-2.1
Bradford	399,860	401,490	-1,630	84.11	-0.4
Manchester	382,377	413,954	-31,577	87.20	-7.6
Bristol	376,418	381,764	-5,346	94.82	-1.4
Kirklees	340,246	342,952	-2,706	89.19	-0.8
Wirral	332,495	338,565	-6,070	98.96	-1.8
Wakefield	311,518	315,314	-3,796	98.52	-1.2
Black Caribbean					
Birmingham	47,277	39,585	7,692	4.70	19.4
Lambeth	32,702	27,564	5,138	12.74	18.6
Brent	25,618	19,932	5,686	10.30	28.5
Lewisham	24,519	19,205	5,314	10.18	27.7
Hackney	21,321	19,330	1,991	11.35	10.3
Haringey	19,958	17,275	2,683	9.42	15.5
Southwark	19,145	16,257	2,888	8.43	17.8
Wandsworth	16,259	14,623	1,636	6.13	11.2
Newham	16,015	13,528	2,487	7.24	18.4
Croydon	15,801	10,030	5,771	4.95	57.5
Waltham Forest	14,963	10,018	4,945	6.87	49.4
Ealing	12,599	8,919	3,680	4.47	41.3

Table 2.4   *continued*

District	1991	1981	Change	% 1991	% Change 81–91
Black African					
Lambeth	17,018	10,883	6,135	6.63	56.4
Southwark	16,783	8,289	8,494	7.39	102.5
Hackney	12,886	7,701	5,185	6.86	67.3
Newham	12,639	6,686	5,953	5.71	89.0
Haringey	11,864	7,802	4,062	5.60	52.1
Brent	10,305	5,888	4,417	4.15	75.0
Lewisham	9,087	5,233	3,854	3.77	73.6
Wandsworth	7,823	6,248	1,575	2.95	25.2
Barnet	6,317	3,525	2,792	2.11	79.2
Islington	6,308	4,356	1,952	3.64	44.8
Waltham Forest	6,269	3,588	2,681	2.88	74.7
Croydon	5,099	2,933	2,166	1.60	73.8
Black Other					
Birmingham	9,418	7,445	1,973	0.94	26.5
Hackney	7,696	6,140	1,556	4.10	25.3
Lambeth	7,073	5,531	1,542	2.76	27.9
Lewisham	6,125	4,796	1,329	2.54	27.7
Manchester	5,624	4,160	1,464	1.28	35.2
Brent	5,544	4,005	1,539	2.23	38.4
Southwark	5,161	4,044	1,117	2.27	27.6
Haringey	4,932	3,873	1,059	2.33	27.3
Wandsworth	4,535	3,574	961	1.71	26.9
Waltham Forest	3,702	2,538	1,164	1.70	45.9
Newham	3,560	2,832	728	1.61	25.7
Liverpool	3,555	2,965	590	0.74	19.9
Indian					
Leicester	64,669	44,132	20,537	22.71	46.5
Birmingham	54,410	42,865	11,545	5.41	26.9
Ealing	45,949	31,968	13,981	16.31	43.7
Brent	43,230	28,328	14,902	17.39	52.6
Harrow	33,246	17,515	15,731	16.31	89.8
Hounslow	30,291	18,597	11,694	14.49	62.9
Newham	29,105	22,259	6,846	13.15	30.8
Wolverhampton	28,887	23,184	5,703	11.62	24.6
Redbridge	24,078	13,130	10,948	10.41	83.4
Sandwell	23,539	19,286	4,253	7.98	22.1
Coventry	22,825	18,489	4,336	7.47	23.5
Barnet	22,499	13,400	9,099	7.50	67.9

Table 2.4   *continued*

District	1991	1981	Change	% 1991	% Change 81–91
Pakistani					
Birmingham	70,431	49,405	21,026	7.00	42.6
Bradford	48,059	34,116	13,943	10.11	40.9
Kirklees	18,185	13,267	4,918	4.77	37.1
Manchester	16,999	10,912	6,087	3.88	55.8
Waltham Forest	13,839	8,761	5,078	6.36	58.0
Newham	13,162	9,214	3,948	5.95	42.8
Glasgow City	11,605	7,015	4,590	1.69	65.4
Rochdale	11,402	7,505	3,897	5.57	51.9
Luton	10,987	7,238	3,749	6.29	51.8
Leeds	9,995	7,003	2,992	1.39	42.7
Sheffield	9,526	6,286	3,240	1.80	51.5
Slough	9,428	6,399	3,029	9.21	47.3
Bangladeshi					
Tower Hamlets	39,439	18,888	20,551	23.46	108.8
Birmingham	13,596	7,523	6,073	1.35	80.7
Newham	8,550	3,019	5,531	3.86	183.2
Camden	6,718	2,765	3,953	3.70	143.0
Oldham	5,286	2,559	2,727	2.41	106.6
Luton	4,819	2,576	2,243	2.76	87.1
Westminster,City	3,991	1,768	2,223	2.13	125.7
Bradford	3,877	2,259	1,618	0.82	71.6
Hackney	3,446	1,824	1,622	1.83	88.9
Haringey	3,238	1,355	1,883	1.53	139.0
Islington	2,857	1,277	1,580	1.65	123.7
Sandwell	2,289	1,552	737	0.78	47.5
Chinese					
Barnet	4,038	2,263	1,775	1.35	78.4
Liverpool	3,536	2,800	736	0.74	26.3
Birmingham	3,302	2,532	770	0.33	30.4
Lambeth	3,224	2,104	1,120	1.26	53.2
Manchester	3,205	2,419	786	0.73	32.5
Southwark	2,914	1,433	1,481	1.28	103.3
Westminster,City	2,910	2,270	640	1.55	28.2
Glasgow City	2,903	1,833	1,070	0.42	58.4
Camden	2,652	2,271	381	1.46	16.8
Brent	2,641	1,943	698	1.06	35.9
Ealing	2,538	1,544	994	0.90	64.4
Lewisham	2,500	1,361	1,139	1.04	83.7
Other Asian					
Brent	8,947	4,030	4,917	3.60	122.0
Barnet	8,946	4,216	4,730	2.98	112.2
Ealing	7,546	3,666	3,880	2.68	105.8
Newham	6,637	2,602	4,035	3.00	155.1
Birmingham	5,894	4,234	1,660	0.59	39.2
Westminster,City	5,347	3,141	2,206	2.85	70.2
Croydon	4,914	2,247	2,667	1.54	118.7
Haringey	4,852	2,254	2,598	2.29	115.3
Wandsworth	4,828	2,522	2,306	1.82	91.4
Merton	4,730	1,873	2,857	2.75	152.5
Harrow	4,674	2,020	2,654	2.29	131.4
Camden	4,040	2,526	1,514	2.22	59.9

Table 2.4 *continued*

District	1991	1981	Change	% 1991	% Change 81–91
Other–Other					
Birmingham	12,155	9,349	2,806	1.21	30.0
Westminster,City	8,239	5,284	2,955	4.39	55.9
Brent	7,842	4,757	3,085	3.15	64.9
Ealing	7,419	4,218	3,201	2.63	75.9
Croydon	6,227	3,935	2,292	1.95	58.2
Barnet	6,225	3,698	2,527	2.08	68.3
Manchester	6,033	4,258	1,775	1.38	41.7
Lambeth	6,031	4,331	1,700	2.35	39.3
Haringey	5,766	3,746	2,020	2.72	53.9
Kensington and					
Chelsea	5,364	3,619	1,745	3.69	48.2
Hackney	5,357	3,764	1,593	2.85	42.3
Camden	5,220	3,768	1,452	2.87	38.5

very concentrated in just a few areas: 51 per cent of the Great Britain population resided in the top dozen districts (listed in Table 2.4), in both 1981 and 1991. Eleven of these districts are in Greater London (both inner and outer), with the top district being Birmingham.

Although the general picture summarised in Table 2.3 is one of increased concentration over the decade 1981–91, at a finer spatial scale within metropolitan areas there is clear evidence of decentralisation. The percentage share of Black–Caribbean people located in inner London falls, while that in outer London rises (Appendix 2.1). In Table 2.4, the outer London boroughs show percentage increases at least double the national average for the group, while inner London boroughs exhibit gains at or below the national average. Clearly, a process of suburbanisation within Greater London is occurring.

In the rest of the country the growth of the Black–Caribbean population in the decade 1981–91 is above average (>24 per cent) in Greater Manchester, East Midlands, the remainder of the North West, South Yorkshire, Central Clydeside, and Tyne and Wear, and below average elsewhere.

Black–Africans

The Black–African group is the most spatially concentrated in metropolitan, core and southern areas of all the minority ethnic groups, and these concentrations all increased over the decade 1981–91 (Table 2.3). The dozen districts containing the largest clusters in 1991 were all London boroughs, eight in inner and four in outer London. The outer London boroughs all show higher than average growth, but so do the inner boroughs of Southwark, Newham and Lewisham in south and east London (Table 2.4). Some suburbanisation within Greater London is taking place though this process is not as advanced as that for the Black–Caribbean group. Gains outside London are all considerable but lower than in London, with the exception of the remainder of Scotland (though this region contains only 0.8 per cent of the group's national population – Appendix 2.1).

Black–Others

The Black–Other group consists in part of people of Caribbean descent who identify themselves now as Black and British, and in part of Black people with origins in areas outside both the UK and Africa. Some of the group are offspring of older Black–Caribbean parents. It is not surprising therefore that the ID between their respective 20 region distributions (Appendix 2.1) is low, at 19, in both 1981 and 1991. That is, only a fifth of either group would need to move to produce exactly matching spatial distributions. The group also experiences the second lowest ID in comparison with the White group (behind the dispersed Chinese group), and lower concentrations in metropolitan, core or southern areas than the other Black or South Asian groups (Table 2.3). The Black–Other group is concentrated in London and the West Midlands metropolitan county but to a lesser extent than either of the other Black groups (Appendix 2.1). Although it is only a third of the size of the Black–Caribbean group, it has a larger population in nine out of 20 regions. The Black–Other populations of the older port cities (Liverpool, Cardiff, Newcastle upon Tyne and Glasgow) have a long history: they derive from the settlement of African sailors serving on British ships from the 17th Century onwards. There has been intermarriage with the White population and many view themselves as of mixed heritage in ethnic and cultural terms. However, the Black–Other populations in the associated region have grown at slower rates than the national average (Appendix 2.1).

Indians

The Indian population is the largest ethnic minority recognised in the census classification, with 877,000 members in mid-1991. The term 'Indian' embraces people with a variety of origins within India (for example, Punjab and Gujarat) and East Africa (notably Kenya and Uganda), and a variety of religions (for example, Hinduism, Sikhism, Islam and Christianity), affiliations and mother tongues (principally Hindi, Punjabi and Urdu). Study of these groupings is, however, beyond the scope of this chapter (see Volume 2 of this series).

Indians differ in their geographical spread from the Black groups discussed above, first in having their largest populations in outer London rather than inner London, second in the size of their East Midlands population concentrated in the city of Leicester, and third in their clusters in the West Midlands districts of Wolverhampton, Sandwell and Coventry (Table 2.4, Figure 2.10).

The outer London boroughs feature prominently in the changing geography of the Indian population with Harrow and Redbridge, for example, showing an increase of over 80 per cent in the decade 1981–91 (Table 2.4), double the national average of 40 per cent. The Indian population of Outer London as a whole grew by 64 per cent. It is highly probable that outward migration is occurring to these more affluent areas within Greater London by a group that is also upwardly mobile in socio-economic terms. The Indian population has also grown in the outer metropolitan area by over 18,000, which is a sixth of total White gains in this region. Gains in the other parts of southern England are much smaller, both in absolute and relative terms.

Pakistanis

The unique feature of the spatial distribution of the Pakistani population is that it is not dominated by Greater London. Only 18 per cent of the Great Britain population was resident there in 1991 compared with 41 per cent of Indians and 53 per cent of Bangladeshis (Appendix 2.1). The Pakistani population also has the smallest gain in per cent share of the group resident in Greater London among the minority ethnic groups. In the top dozen districts, only two London boroughs figure (Table 2.4). There is, however, a clear pattern of outer London borough gains (Figure 2.15; Appendix 2.2), particularly in north east London (Waltham Forest and Redbridge) and north west London (Brent, Ealing and Hounslow).

The largest Pakistani populations and the greatest absolute changes are found in Bradford, Kirklees and Leeds in West Yorkshire, in Birmingham, and in a cluster of North West Districts – Manchester, Rochdale, Oldham in Greater Manchester, and Blackburn, Pendle and Hynburn in Lancashire. Relative change over the decade 1981–91 in other region populations lies fairly close to the national average of 45 per cent and the redistribution indicators show less change for this group than all except the Black–Other population.

Bangladeshis

The Bangladeshi population is the fastest growing ethnic group; highly concentrated in Greater London, particularly in east London (Figure 2.17), but with sizeable communities in the West Midlands (Birmingham and Sandwell) and the Pennine cities (Bradford and Oldham) (Table 2.4).

Above average gains (95 per cent) have been experienced in both inner and outer London, and in Tyne and Wear and the remainder of Scotland, though the populations are small in these latter two regions and sampling error may play a part in the 1981 estimates. The picture is generally one of population growth in place with a little displacement towards the outer London boroughs.

Chinese

The Chinese population is the most dispersed of all the ethnic minorities and closest to the White distribution. Nevertheless, eight of the top 12 districts for this group are London boroughs (Table 2.4). Above average relative gains were experienced in inner and outer London, the East Midlands, the remainder of the North West, South Yorkshire, Central Clydesdale and the remainder of Scotland. All of the indicators of spatial redistribution in Table 2.3 point to a modest degree of concentration over the decade.

Other–Asians

The Other–Asian group, with over half of its population in Greater London, shows the largest increase in London share of any group (Appendix 2.1), the largest gain in core and metropolitan concentration. This is consistent with continuing net immigration into Britain's largest cities from the Middle East, South East Asia (non-Chinese) and parts of South Asia outside India, Pakistan and Bangladesh.

However, like the South Asian groups, inner and outer London experience the greatest gains in this group (Figure 2.24, Appendix 2.1), with outer London boroughs gaining most. The outer metropolitan area and outer South East house the third (9 per cent in 1991) and fourth largest (5 per cent in 1991) regional populations of this group, although the relative increases were below average.

Other–Others (Other non-Asians)

Both Other–Asians and Other–Others exhibit a relatively high level of spatial redistribution between 1981 and 1991 (see the indicators in Table 2.3). However, it is difficult to intepret this as evidence of concentration because it may merely reflect the immigration of new groups while older, more established groups are dispersing a little. The two groups are heterogeneous collections of people with disparate identities. Insofar as they may conceivably have some 'community identity', this cannot be recognised using the broad classification on the 1991 Census.

2.5   Conclusions

This chapter has examined the geographical spread of the 10 ethnic groups recognised in the 1991 Census of Population. The ethnic geography of 1991 has been described in detail by Teague (1993) and Owen (1992a, 1994a, 1994b). However, such descriptions are just a snapshot in a continuously changing diorama. The 1991 geography can only attain true significance if seen in relation to earlier geographies. Accordingly, the estimation and interpretation of the directions of change in the ethnic geography of Great Britain have been the two principal objectives of this chapter.

Evaluation of 1981 estimates

The results presented here can only be regarded as provisional, and therefore a degree of caution is advisable. It is worthwhile spelling out at this point the problems inherent in our attempt to measure change in the geographical spread of ethnic groups:

(i)   The 1991 estimates can be regarded as fairly robust in that they are based principally on the direct counts of ethnic group members in the 1991 Census. The adjustments for under-enumeration both specific to ethnic group and specific to district were, however, important improvements.

(ii) The 1981 estimates must be regarded as a first attempt. The dependence of the estimates on the LFS sample numbers of Whites and minority ethnic group members turned out to be crucial. Despite the fact that counts from the 1979, 1981 and 1983 Labour Force Surveys were combined, it is likely that sample estimates of the per cent White and per cent ethnic minority in LFS region populations could depart considerably from their true value. Doubt was cast on the accuracy of estimates in the remainder of the West Midlands and the rest of Yorkshire and Humberside regions, which translated into improbable decreases in minority ethnic populations between 1981 and 1991. This doubt probably should be extended to about half of the 20 regions where ethnic minority numbers were relatively small. The LFS estimates were poor, for ethnic group composition, because of small sample size at regional scale and poor clustered sampling technique. Both problems have been addressed in post-1991 Labour Force Surveys.

(iii) The method adopted for the 1981 estimates is heavily dependent on the accuracy of the conditional probabilities of ethnic group membership given country of birth derived from the 1991 Census for each district, as estimates of the equivalent probabilities in 1981. There are two factors that make the 1991 probabilities biased estimates of the 1981 figures: age selectivity and geographical mismatching.

The 1991 Census population contains members, aged under 10, who were clearly not present in the 1981 Census population. Similarly, there will be members of the 1981 Census population not present in the 1991 Census population, principally as a result of death. How will these composition changes affect the conditional probabilities? The probability of being a minority ethnic group member given birth in this country is likely to have been much higher for the 0–9 age-group (the persons added in 1991 by virtue of birth during the preceding decade) than that for the 70-plus age-group (from which the subtracted persons would have principally been recruited). The geographical mismatching is the result of population movement into and out of the district populations. Our results have shown losses of Whites from the main metropolitan regions and gains in minority ethnic group populations. The probabilities of being White given birth in Britain would have been higher. The introduction of information from the LFS for 1979, 1981 and 1983 was an attempt to correct for this bias.

Despite these caveats about our estimates they can be confidently treated as superior to any alternative based on the country of birth statistics.

Geographical spread: a summary

It is useful to bring together the key features of Britain's ethnic geography:

(i) Representatives of all 10 ethnic groups into which the population can be classified in 1991 are found in most districts in Great Britain. Only in the most remote, rural districts is this not the case.

(ii) Minority ethnic populations, however, are highly concentrated; more so in England than Wales and Scotland, and in southern England rather than northern England.

(iii) Minority ethnic populations are concentrated in metropolitan areas, and within non-metropolitan areas in the largest urban districts. Only Whites are more concentrated in lower density districts in non-metropolitan areas.

(iv) Although all metropolitan areas have clusters of residents drawn from minority ethnic groups, some have more significant concentrations. Greater London, the West Midlands metropolitan area, West Yorkshire and Greater Manchester have ethnic minority location quotients greater than 1. In all other regions, Whites have location quotients above unity.

(v) There are a handful of districts lying outside metropolitan areas which figure, for one or more ethnic minorities, as important areas of residence. Nottingham, Luton and Bristol have important Black–Caribbean and Black–Other communities. Between a fifth and a quarter of Leicester's population is Indian and Slough, Blackburn, Derby and Luton have large Indian communities; Luton, Slough, Blackburn, Pendle and Hynburn are important residence districts for Pakistanis; Luton, Cardiff and Newcastle have Bangladeshi clusters; Edinburgh, Newcastle, Cardiff and Bristol have significant Chinese communities.

(vi) However, the maps of seven of the 10 ethnic groups are dominated by Greater London, which is home to 40 per cent or more of Britain's Black–Caribbean, Black–African, Black–Other, Indian, Bangladeshi, Other–Asian and Other–Other groups (Table 2.5). Every London borough has substantial numbers of all of these groups, though each have their own individual geography of concentration (see Chapter 6).

Table 2.5   *Degree of concentration of ethnic groups in Greater London, 1981-91*

Ethnic group	% of GB population		Change 1981-91
	1981	1991	
White	11.2	10.3	-0.9
Black–Caribbean	56.8	58.3	1.5
Black –African	72.3	77.9	5.6
Black–Other	44.0	45.3	1.3
Indian	37.1	41.2	4.1
Pakistani	17.3	18.3	1.0
Bangladeshi	47.6	52.7	5.1
Chinese	32.2	36.3	4.1
Other –Asian	50.1	58.0	7.9
Other –Other	37.8	41.8	4.0
Total	12.4	12.3	-0.1

Source: Computed from Appendix 2.1.

Geographical change: a summary

It is helpful to summarise what has been learnt about the geographical redistribution of ethnic groups:

(i)   There is a profound contrast between the almost static White population of Great Britain, which grew by less than 1 per cent between 1981 and 1991 and the minority ethnic populations which grew between 24 and 95 per cent.

(ii) Given this growth there was substantial potential for spatial redistribution. However, the degree of such redistribution (between 4 and 10 per cent) was relatively modest. The geographical spread of each minority ethnic group in 1991 was substantially the same as it had been in 1981.

(iii) The directions of these modest shifts were consistent across all ethnic minorities. All groups were marginally more separated from Whites in 1991 compared with 1981, across a set of 20 metropolitan and non-metropolitan areas. This involves a greater degree of metropolitan concentration for minorities in 1991 than in 1981, and an increased share of the group population in its core areas.

(iv) This increased concentration can be seen as a product of several processes. First, the White population is moving out of the areas of ethnic minority concentration. Second, ethnic minority families are growing with the addition of children. Third, new households are forming in each ethnic community and locating close to existing households. Fourth, new arrivals from abroad are joining existing communities, fitting into existing households or being sponsored by fellow ethnic group members. Fifth, minority ethnic group migrants within Great Britain may be relocating away from declining areas in the older industrial settings to southern urban areas promising greater opportunities for advancement. Each of these processes needs further investigation.

(v)   There is evidence of modest decentralisation within metropolitan areas of ethnic concentration. The spatial filters used in this chapter, namely metropolitan/non-metropolitan areas and local government districts, are not ideally suited to detecting this process. However, London boroughs provide a feasible, if coarse filter. The outer London boroughs experienced substantially higher growth for all minority ethnic groups and the outer metropolitan area had higher growth rates for four out of nine groups.

Directions for future research

It is clear that there are many ways in which the investigations reported in this chapter could be developed:

(i)   The 1981 estimates of ethnic group populations can be improved in two ways. First, data from the 2 per cent Sample of Anonymised Records (SARs, 1991 Census) can be employed to compute conditional probabilities for the population aged 10 and over for each district. Second, data from the Longitudinal Study for England and Wales incorporating 1981 and 1991 Census information can be used to improve the 1981 estimates of both the White/ethnic minority split and conditional probabilities of ethnic group given country of birth.

(ii) The estimation technique can be extended to smaller spatial scales such as wards. Here the difficult problem of spatial comparability will need to be tackled, choosing either the 1981 ward (Dorling, 1994) or a grid square unit (Bracken and Martin, 1995). Using this finer spatial filter the extent of suburbanisation within metropolitan areas could be examined.

(iii) The techniques developed for backwards estimation to 1981 can be used for forwards estimation with the much improved LFS data from 1991 onwards.

(iv) Decomposition of estimates by other characteristics such as age and sex would greatly help interpretation of changes. Development of age–sex disaggregated ethnic group populations using 1991 Census population, is fairly straightforward. Work by Rees (1993) has developed methods for making estimates of ethnic populations broken down by age–sex populations from 1981 Census information, but the techniques depend on special tabulations of district populations which may not be available for the whole country.

The 1991 Census has generated an enormous quantity of information on the geographical spread of Britain's ethnic minorities. This chapter has provided an overview for the country as a whole both for 1991 and for the previous decade. Britain's ethnic minority groups were revealed to be both expanding and redistributing in many interesting ways, which deserve further study.

References

Bracken, I. and Martin, D. (1995) Linkage of the 1981 and 1991 UK Censuses using surface modelling concepts. *Environment and Planning A*, 27, 3, 379–90.

Dorling, D. (1994) Visualising the geography of the population with the 1991 Census. *Population Trends*, 76, 29–39.

Haskey, J. (1991) Ethnic minority populations resident in private households – estimates by county and metropolitan district of England and Wales. *Population Trends*, 63, 22–35.

OPCS and GRO(S) (1992) 1991 Census. Local Base Statistics. Published in machine readable form and in the County and Scottish Region Reports. Purchased by ESRC/JISC for use in the academic community.

OPCS and GRO(S) (1993) 1991 Census. *Ethnic Group and Country of Birth. Great Britain.* Topic Monitor, CEN 91 TM EGCB. London: OPCS.

OPCS and GRO(S) (1994) 1991 Census. *Ethnic Group and Country of Birth. Great Britain.* Two volumes. CEN 91 EGCB. London: HMSO.

Owen, D. (1992a) *Ethnic minorities in Great Britain: settlement patterns.* Centre for Research in Ethnic Relations, University of Warwick, 1991 Census Statistical Paper No.1.

Owen, D. (1992b) *Census data and the analysis of spatial variations in the socio-economic circumstances of different ethnic groups.* Paper presented to the Census Analysis Group meeting, University of Leeds, 6–7 April 1992.

Owen, D. (1994a) Spatial variations in ethnic minority group populations in Great Britain. *Population Trends*, 78, 23–33.

Owen, D. (1994b) *Ethnic minority women and the labour market: analysis of the 1991 Census.* Manchester: Equal Opportunities Commission.

Owen, D. (1995b) *Integrating survey and Census data in estimating minority group populations.* Paper presented at the Institute of British Geographers Annual Conference, University of Northumbria, Newcastle upon Tyne, 5 January 1995.

Rees, P. (1993) *Ethnic group model: detailed specifications.* Documentation Paper 7, West Yorkshire Population Model and Information System, School of Geography and GMAP Ltd, University of Leeds

Stillwell, J., Rees, P. and Boden, P. (eds) (1992) *Migration patterns and processes, Volume 2: Population redistribution in the United Kingdom.* London: Belhaven.

Teague, A. (1993) Ethnic group: first results from the 1991 Census. *Population Trends*, 72, 12–17.

Figure 2.1 *Geographical spread in 1991: Black–Caribbean group*

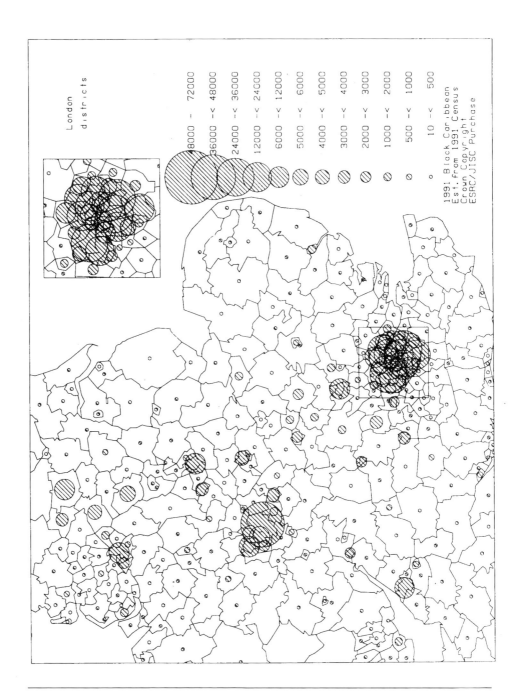

London
districts

8000 – 72000
36000 –< 48000
24000 –< 36000
12000 –< 24000
6000 –< 12000
5000 –< 6000
4000 –< 5000
3000 –< 4000
2000 –< 3000
1000 –< 2000
500 –< 1000
10 –< 500

1991 Black Caribbean
Est.from 1991 Census
Crown Copyright
ESRC/JISC Purchase

Figure 2.2   Geographical concentration in 1991: Black–Caribbean group

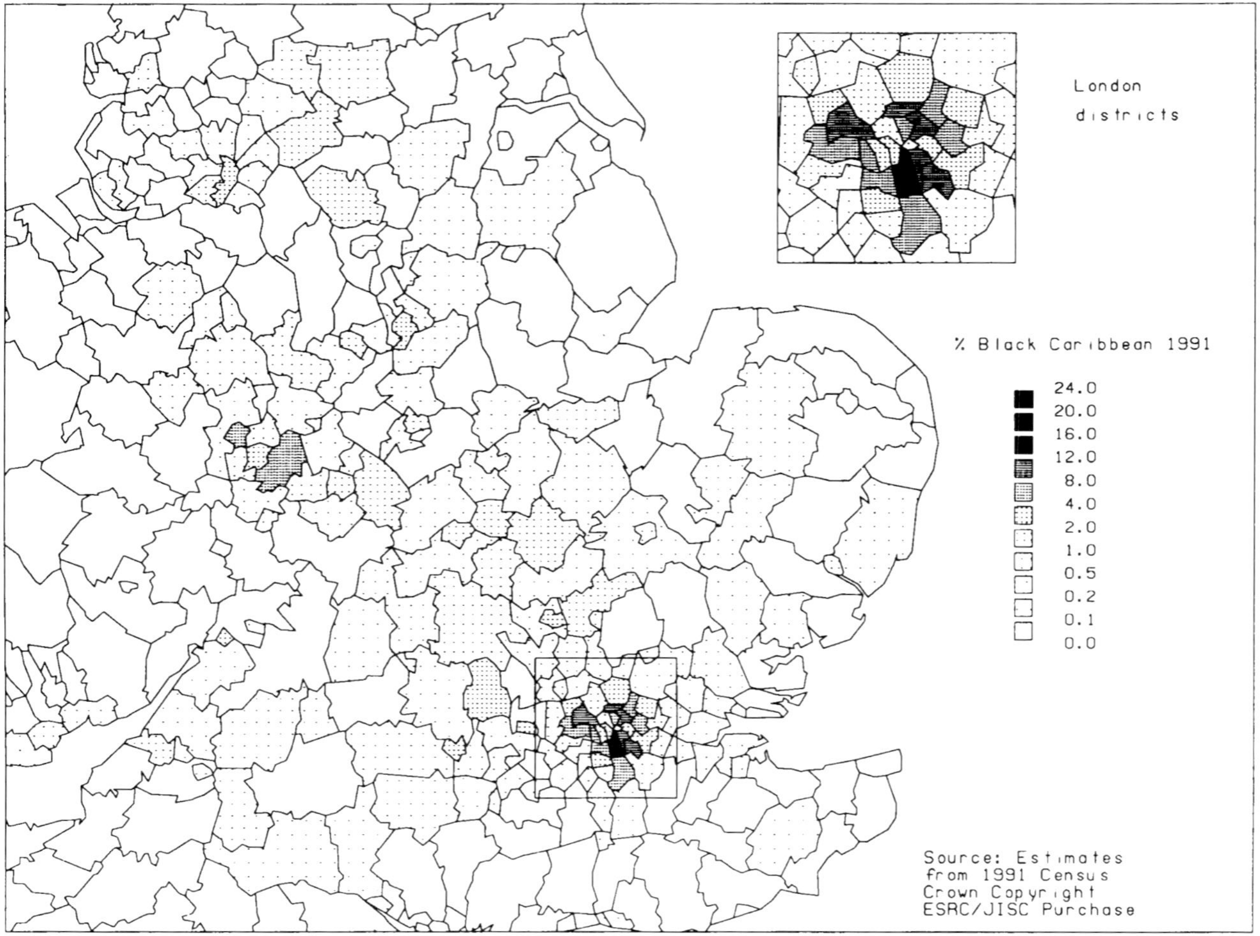

London
districts

% Black Caribbean 1991

24.0
20.0
16.0
12.0
8.0
4.0
2.0
1.0
0.5
0.2
0.1
0.0

Source: Estimates
from 1991 Census
Crown Copyright
ESRC/JISC Purchase

Figure 2.3 Population change 1981–91: Black–Caribbean group

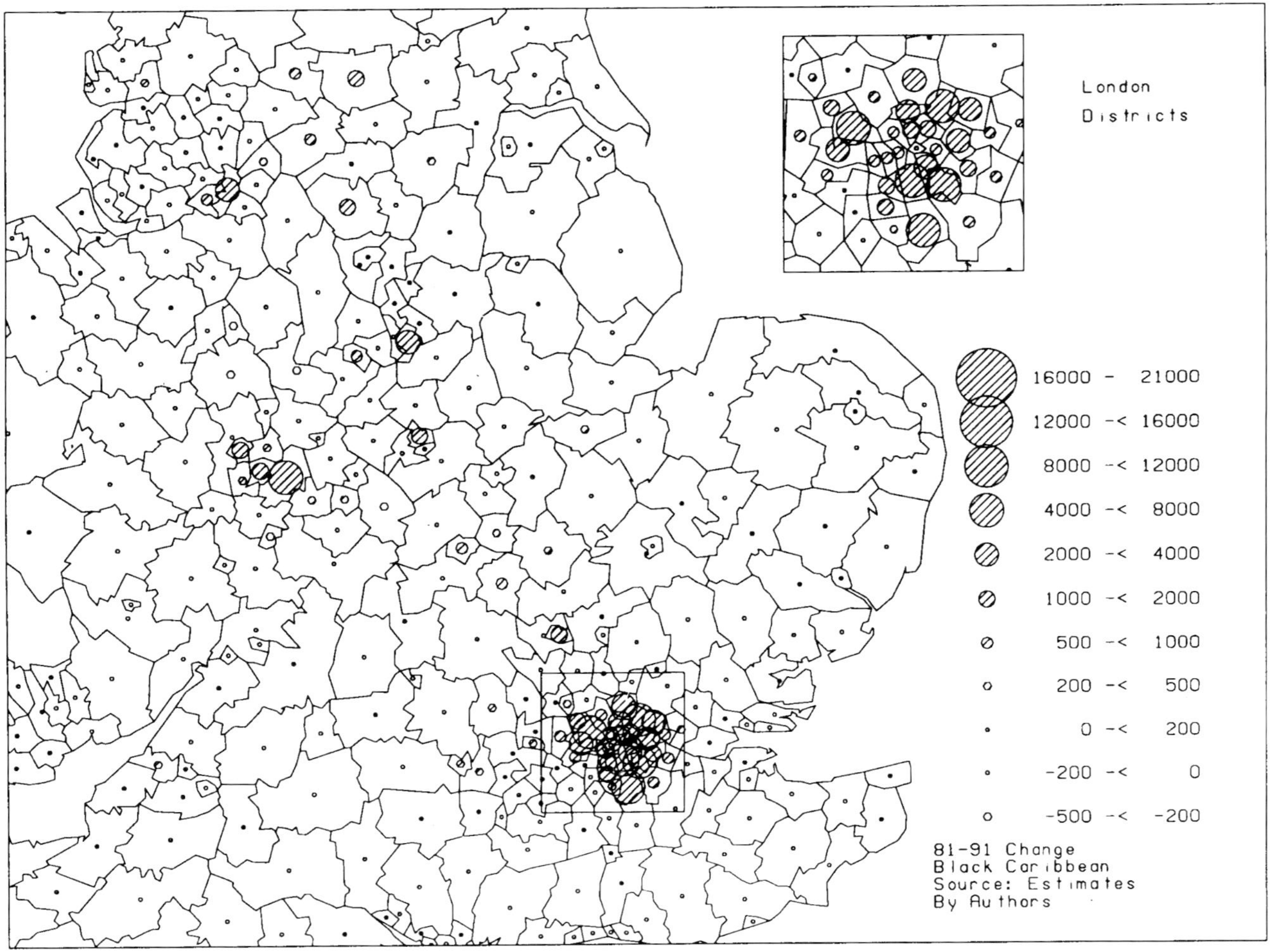

London
Districts

16000 – 21000
12000 – < 16000
8000 – < 12000
4000 – < 8000
2000 – < 4000
1000 – < 2000
500 – < 1000
200 – < 500
0 – < 200
–200 – < 0
–500 – < –200

81–91 Change
Black Caribbean
Source: Estimates
By Authors

Figure 2.4 *Geographical spread in 1991: Black–African group*

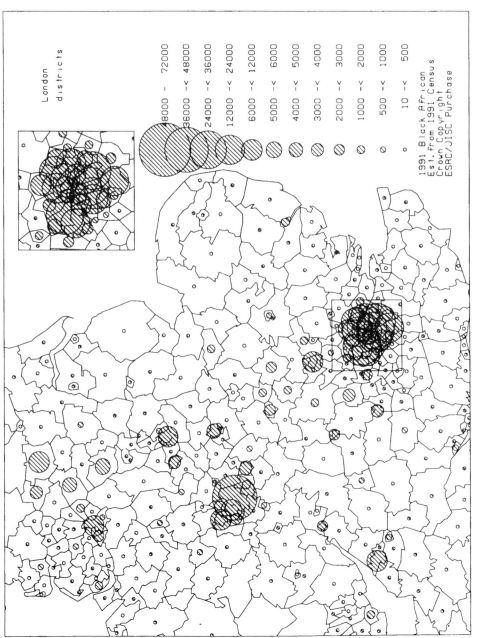

Figure 2.5   Geographical concentration in 1991: Black–African group

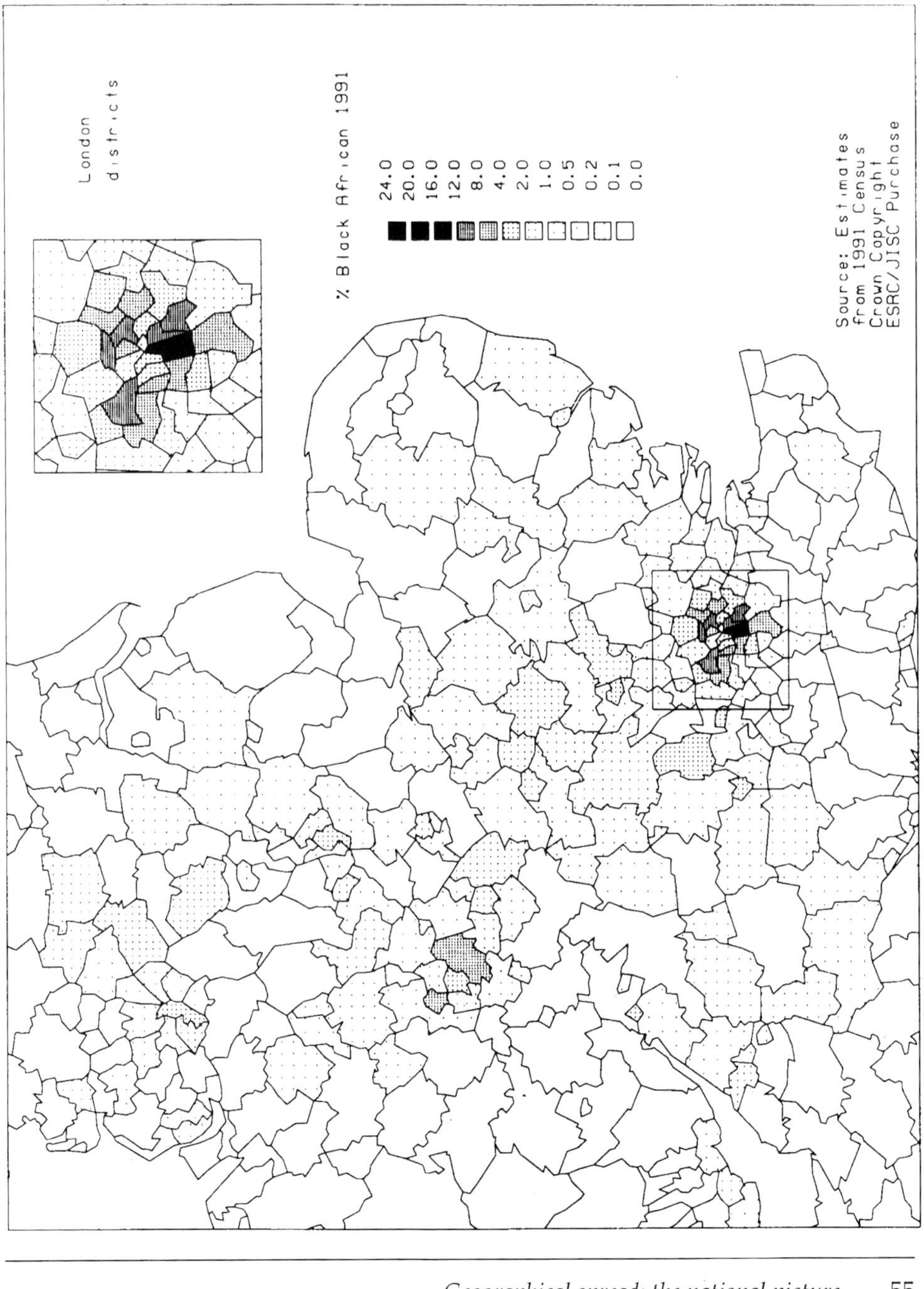

London
districts

% Black African 1991

24.0
20.0
16.0
12.0
8.0
4.0
2.0
1.0
0.5
0.2
0.1
0.0

Source: Estimates
from 1991 Census
Crown Copyright
ESRC/JISC Purchase

Figure 2.6 Population change 1981–91: Black–African group

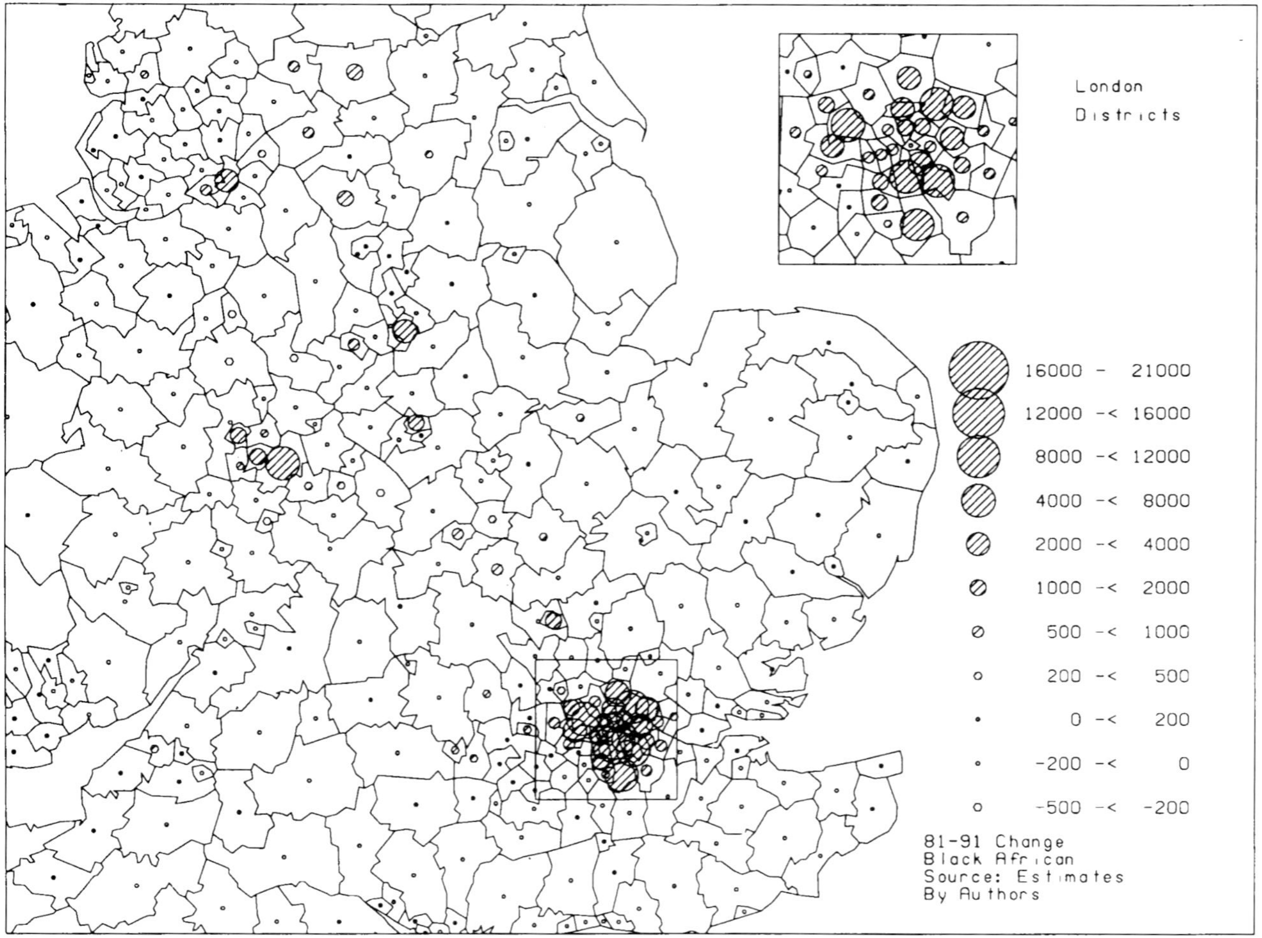

London
Districts

16000 – 21000
12000 – < 16000
8000 – < 12000
4000 – < 8000
2000 – < 4000
1000 – < 2000
500 – < 1000
200 – < 500
0 – < 200
–200 – < 0
–500 – < –200

81-91 Change
Black African
Source: Estimates
By Authors

Figure 2.7 Geographical spread in 1991: Black–Other group

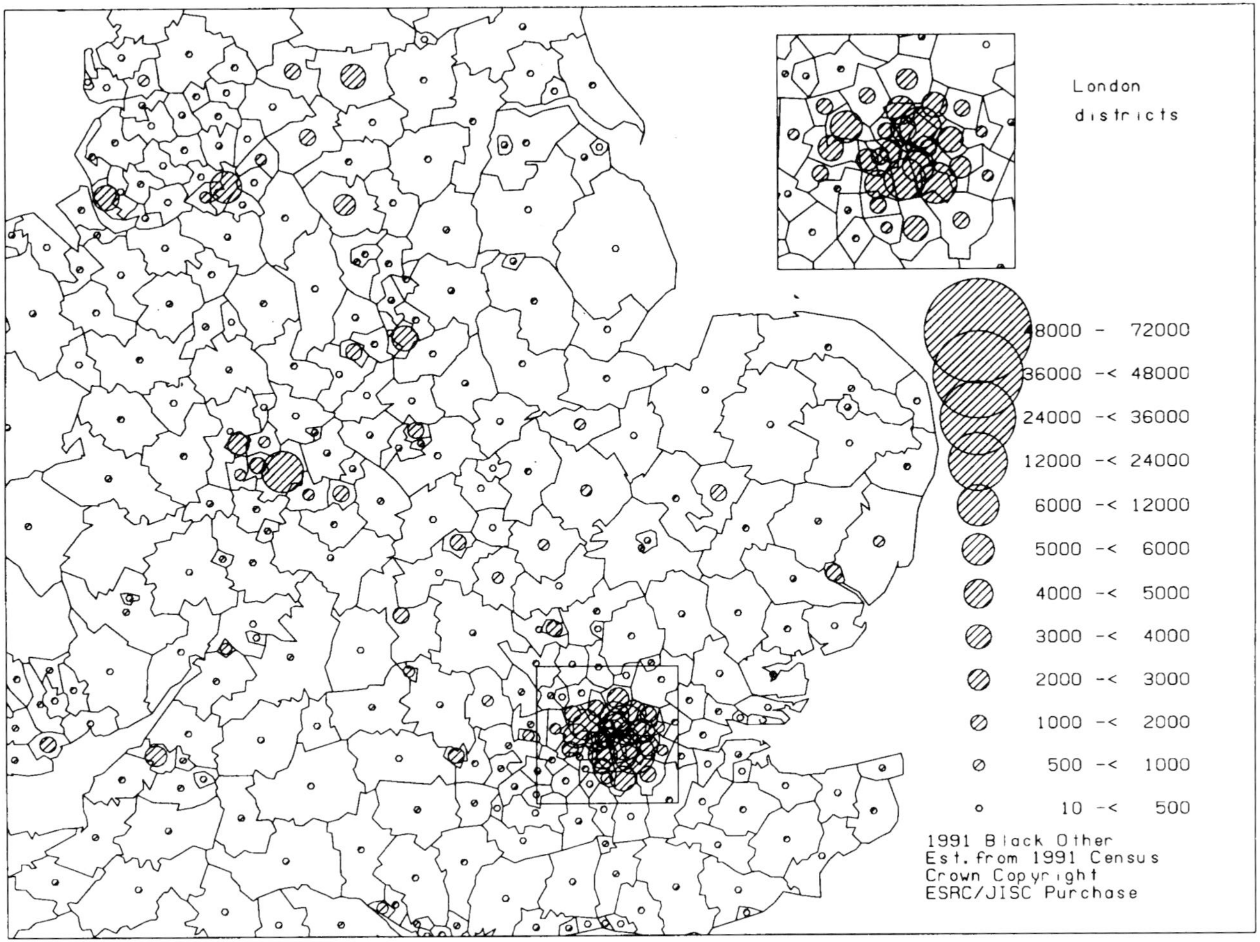

Figure 2.8 *Geographical concentration in 1991: Black–Other group*

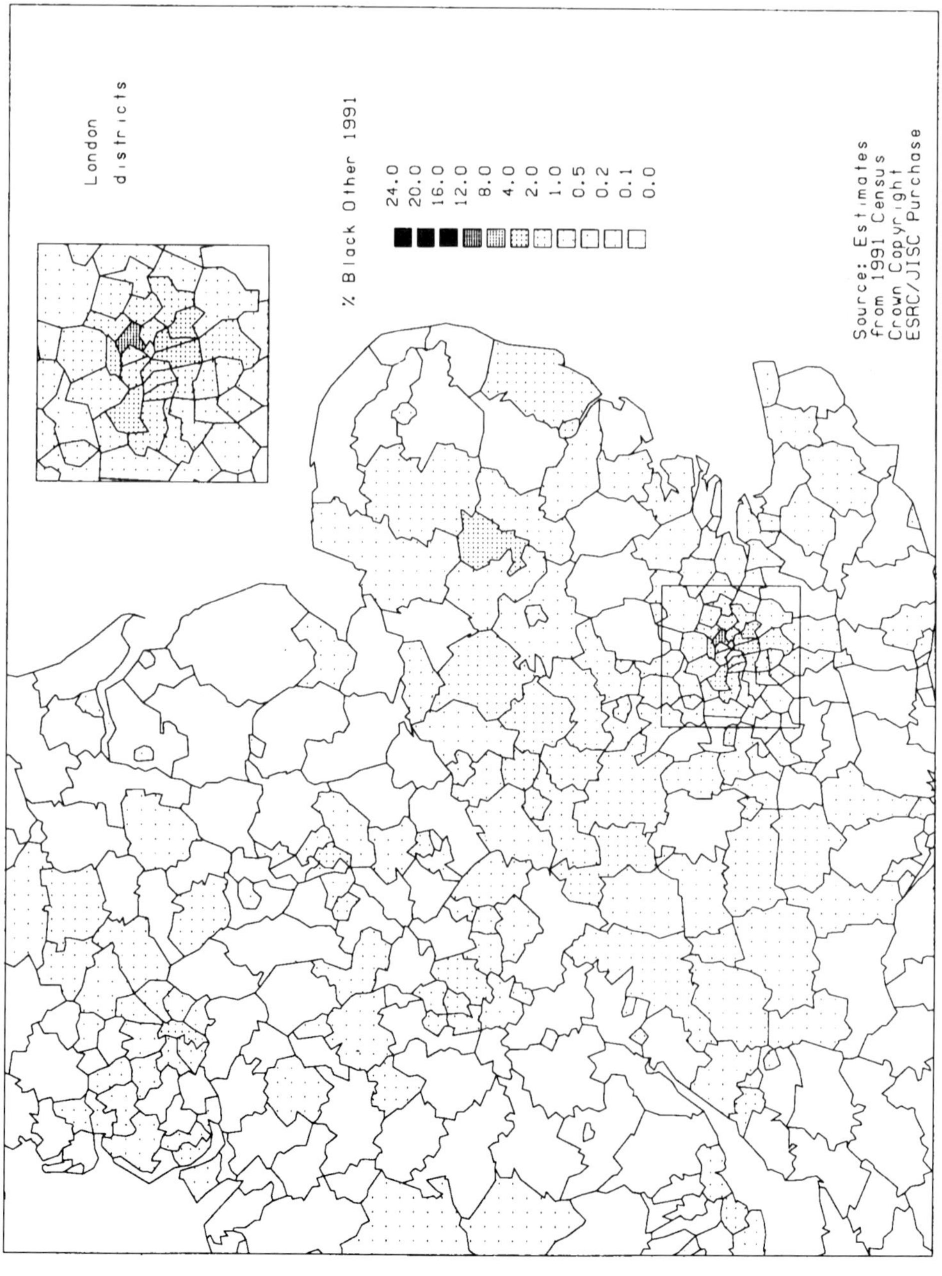

London
districts

% Black Other 1991

24.0
20.0
16.0
12.0
8.0
4.0
2.0
1.0
0.5
0.2
0.1
0.0

Source: Estimates
from 1991 Census
Crown Copyright
ESRC/JISC Purchase

Figure 2.9 *Population change 1981–91: Black–Other group*

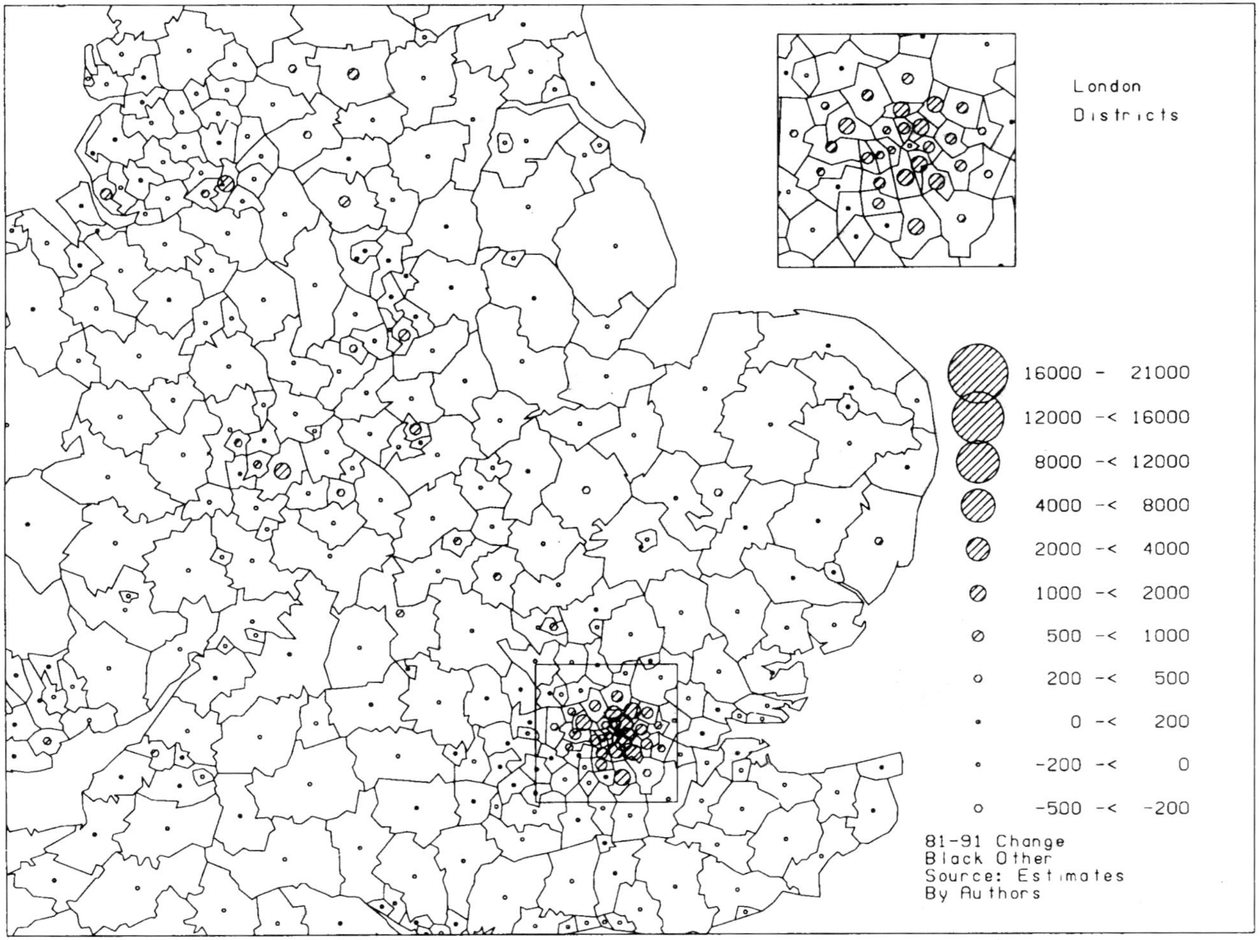

London
Districts

16000 — 21000
12000 — < 16000
8000 — < 12000
4000 — < 8000
2000 — < 4000
1000 — < 2000
500 — < 1000
200 — < 500
0 — < 200
−200 — < 0
−500 — < −200

81-91 Change
Black Other
Source: Estimates
By Authors

Figure 2.10 *Geographical spread in 1991: Indian group*

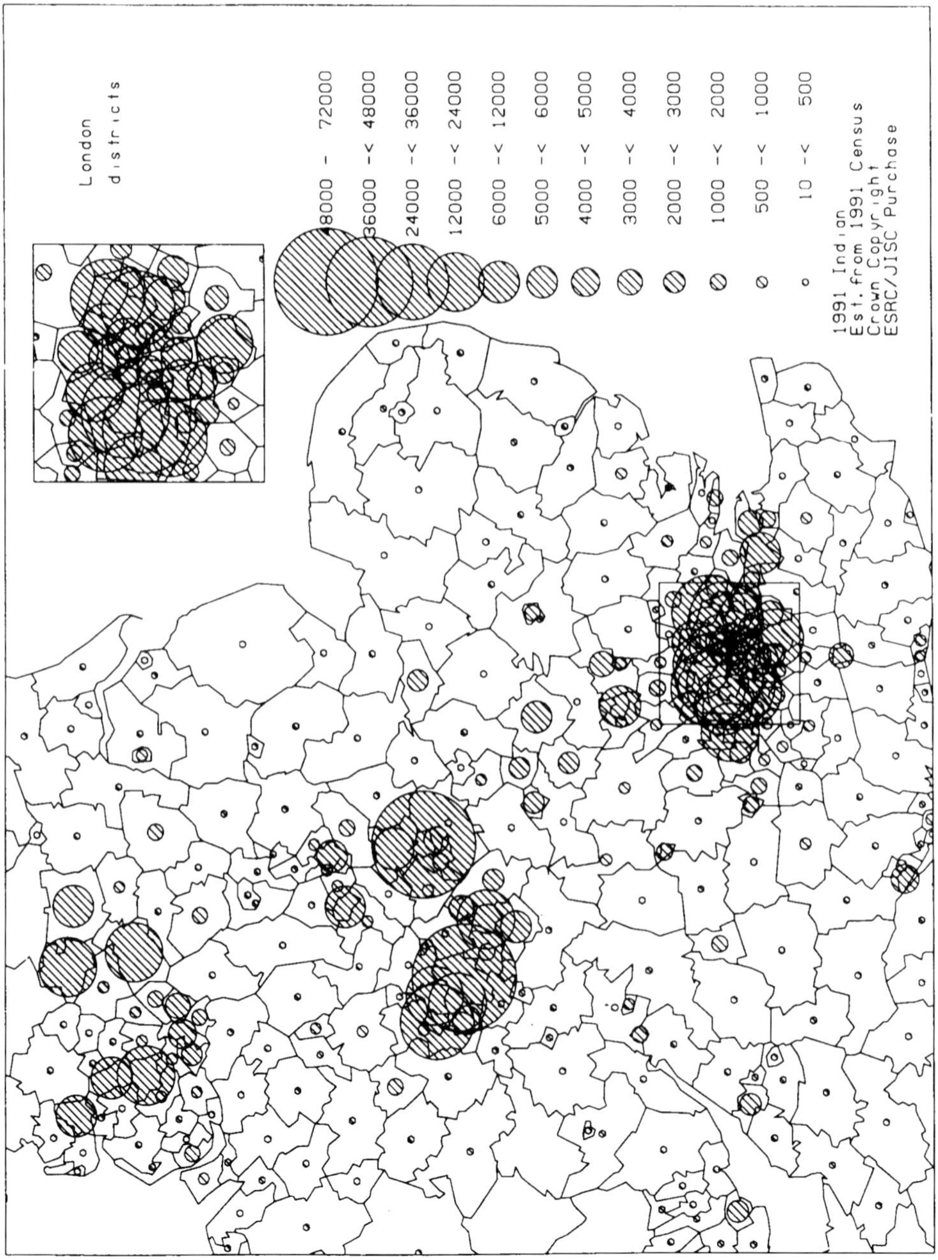

London
districts

8000 – 72000
36000 –< 48000
24000 –< 36000
12000 –< 24000
6000 –< 12000
5000 –< 6000
4000 –< 5000
3000 –< 4000
2000 –< 3000
1000 –< 2000
500 –< 1000
10 –< 500

1991 Indian
Est.from 1991 Census
Crown Copyright
ESRC/JISC Purchase

Figure 2.11 *Geographical concentration in 1991: Indian group*

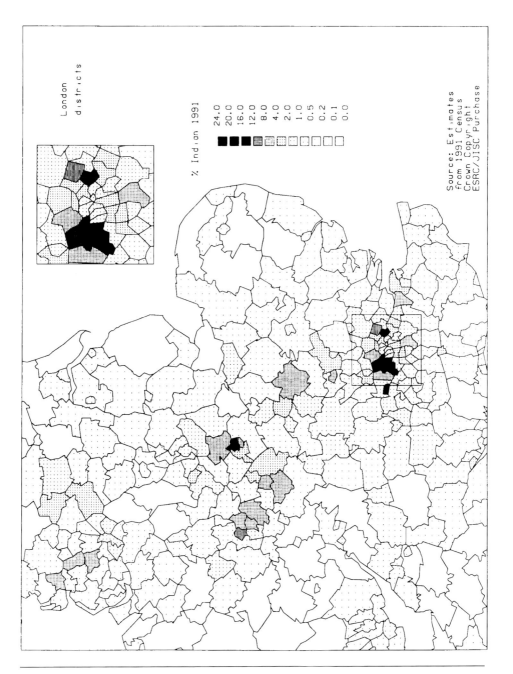

Figure 2.12 *Population change 1981–91: Indian group*

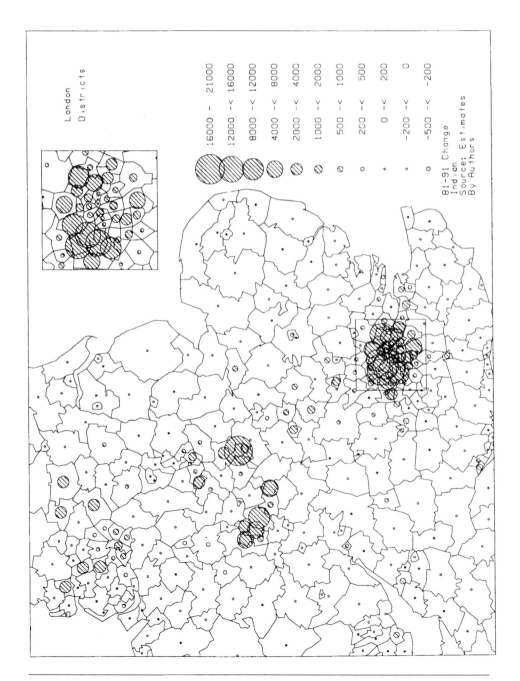

London
Districts

16000 – 21000
12000 – < 16000
8000 – < 12000
4000 – < 8000
2000 – < 4000
1000 – < 2000
500 – < 1000
200 – < 500
0 – < 200
–200 – < 0
–500 – < –200

81-91 Change
Indian
Source: Estimates
By Authors

Figure 2.13 *Geographical spread in 1991: Pakistani group*

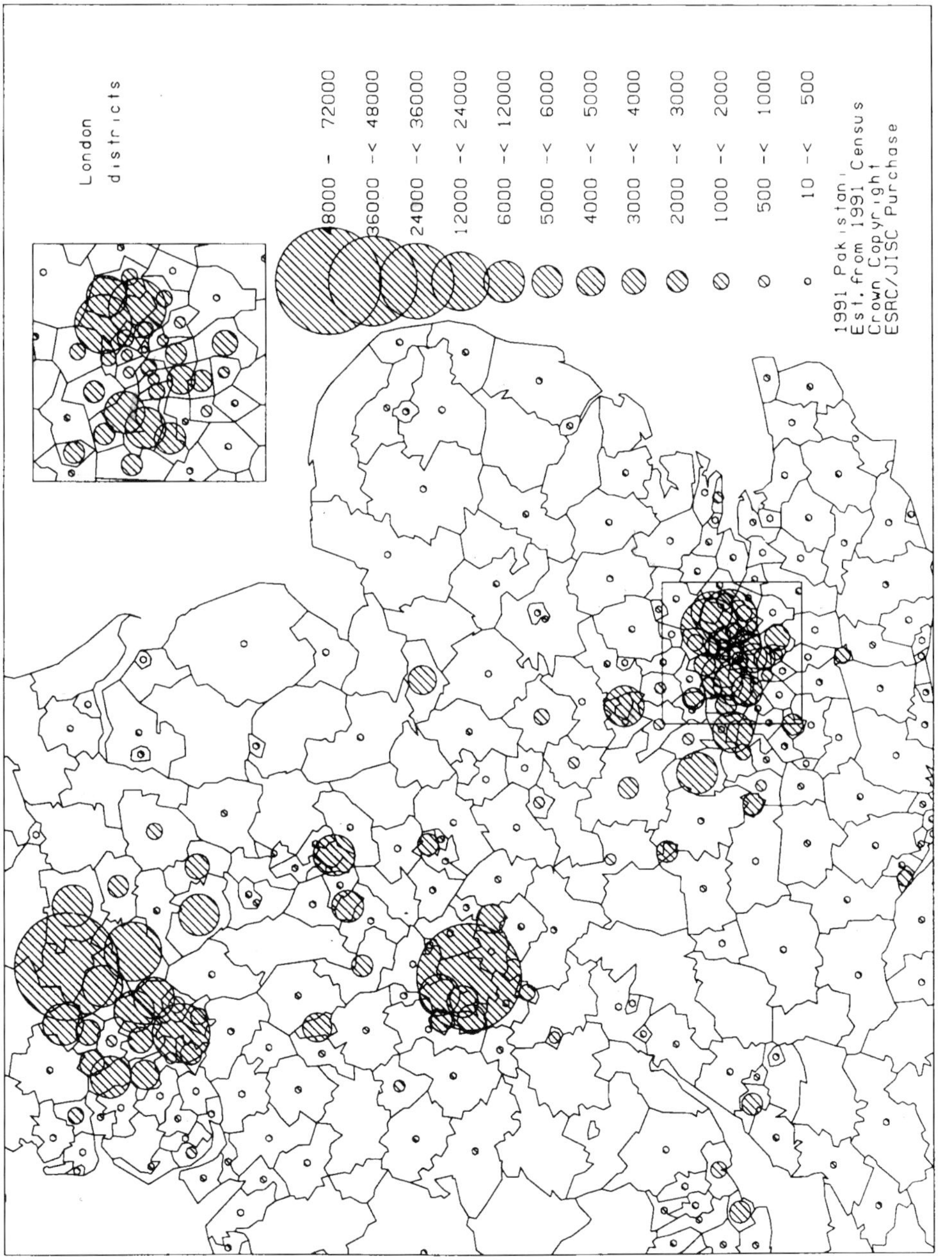

London
districts

18000 – 72000
36000 – < 48000
24000 – < 36000
12000 – < 24000
6000 – < 12000
5000 – < 6000
4000 – < 5000
3000 – < 4000
2000 – < 3000
1000 – < 2000
500 – < 1000
10 – < 500

1991 Pakistani
Est.from 1991 Census
Crown Copyright
ESRC/JISC Purchase

Figure 2.14 *Geographical concentration in 1991: Pakistani group*

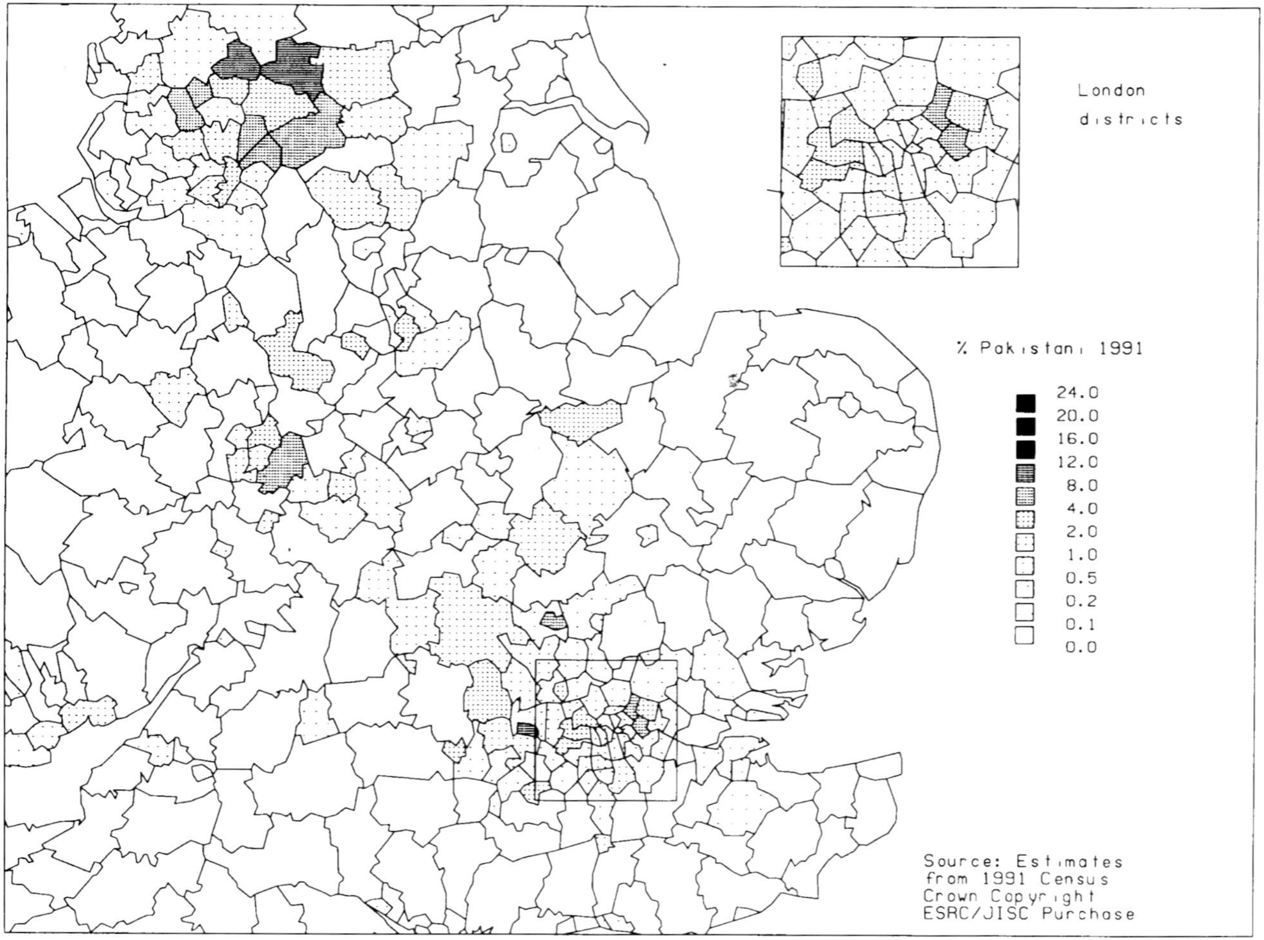

London
districts

% Pakistan, 1991

24.0
20.0
16.0
12.0
8.0
4.0
2.0
1.0
0.5
0.2
0.1
0.0

Source: Estimates
from 1991 Census
Crown Copyright
ESRC/JISC Purchase

Figure 2.15   Population change 1981–91: Pakistani group

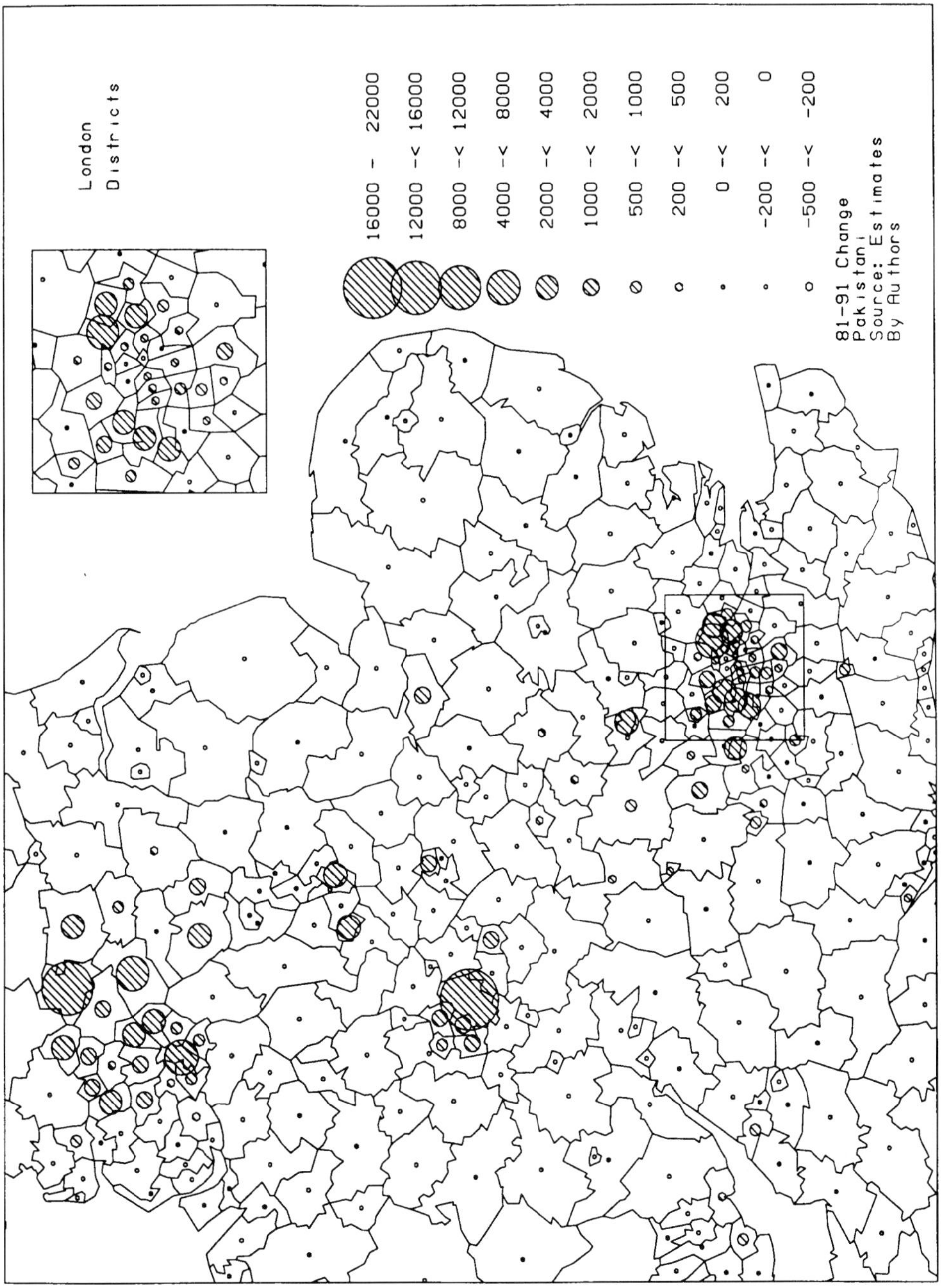

London
Districts

	81-91 Change
16000 – 22000	
12000 – < 16000	
8000 – < 12000	
4000 – < 8000	
2000 – < 4000	
1000 – < 2000	
500 – < 1000	
200 – < 500	
0 – < 200	
–200 – < 0	
–500 – < –200	

81-91 Change
Pakistani
Source: Estimates
By Authors

Figure 2.16 Geographical spread in 1991: Bangladeshi group

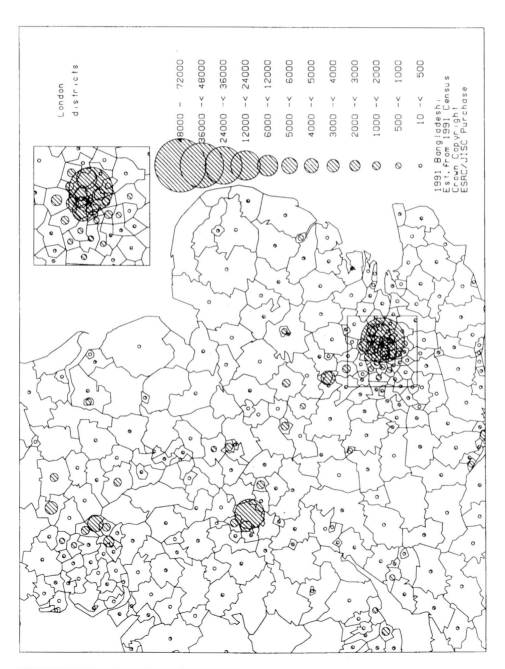

London districts

8000 – 72000
36000 –< 48000
24000 –< 36000
12000 –< 24000
6000 –< 12000
5000 –< 6000
4000 –< 5000
3000 –< 4000
2000 –< 3000
1000 –< 2000
500 –< 1000
10 –< 500

1991 Bangladeshi
Est. from 1991 Census
Crown Copyright
ESRC/JISC Purchase

Figure 2.17   Geographical concentration in 1991: Bangladeshi group

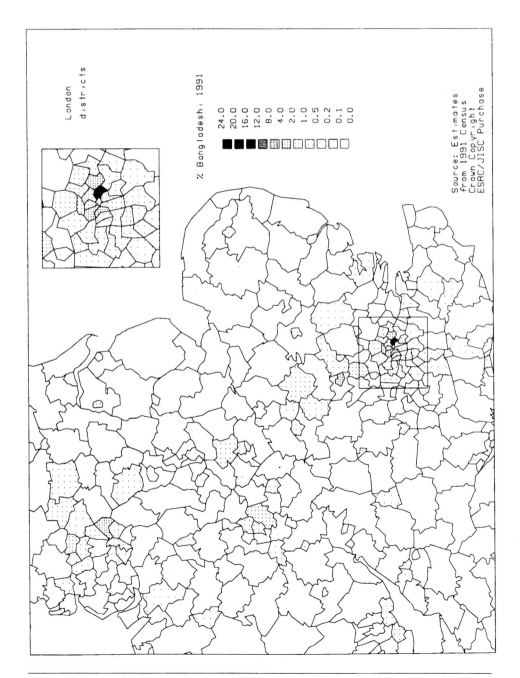

London
districts

% Bangladeshi 1991

24.0
20.0
16.0
12.0
8.0
4.0
2.0
1.0
0.5
0.2
0.1
0.0

Source: Estimates
from 1991 Census
Crown Copyright
ESRC/JISC Purchase

Figure 2.18 *Population change 1981–91: Bangladeshi group*

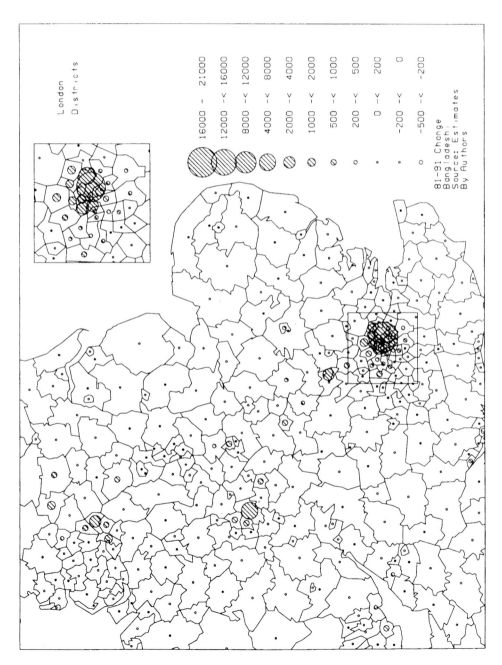

London
Districts

16000 – 21000
12000 – < 16000
8000 – < 12000
4000 – < 8000
2000 – < 4000
1000 – < 2000
500 – < 1000
200 – < 500
0 – < 200
–200 – < 0
–500 – < –200

81–91 Change
Bangladeshi
Source: Estimates
By Authors

Figure 2.19 *Geographical spread in 1991: Chinese group*

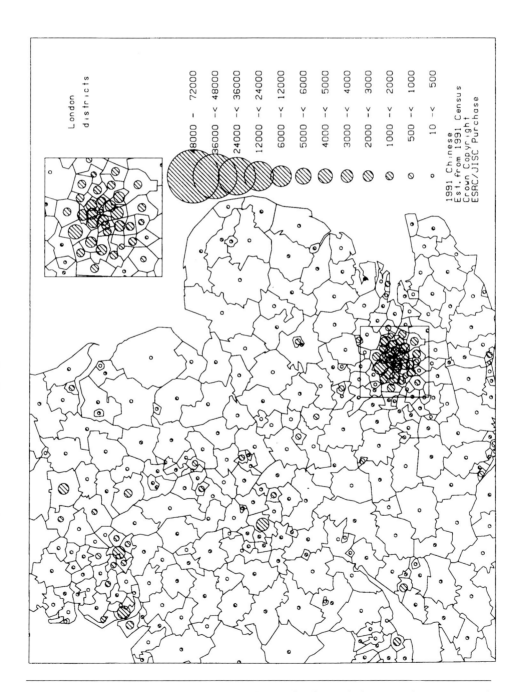

London
districts

8000 - 72000
36000 -< 48000
24000 -< 36000
12000 -< 24000
6000 -< 12000
5000 -< 6000
4000 -< 5000
3000 -< 4000
2000 -< 3000
1000 -< 2000
500   -< 1000
10   -<   500

1991 Chinese
Est. from 1991 Census
Crown Copyright
ESRC/JISC Purchase

Figure 2.20 *Geographical spread in 1991: Chinese group*

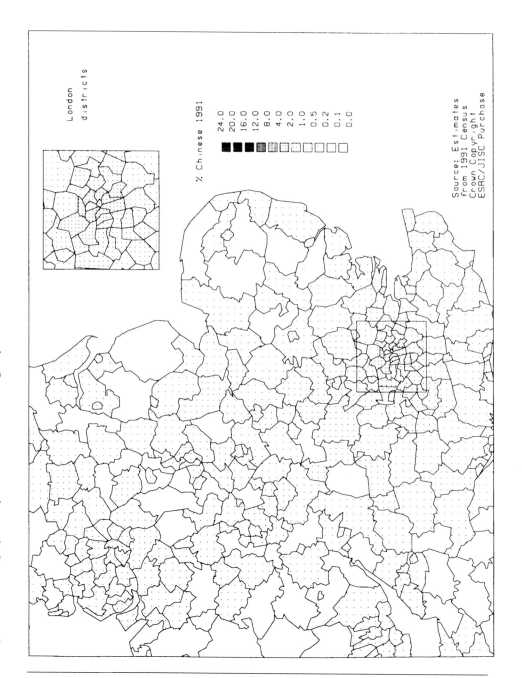

Figure 2.21 *Population change 1981–91: Chinese group*

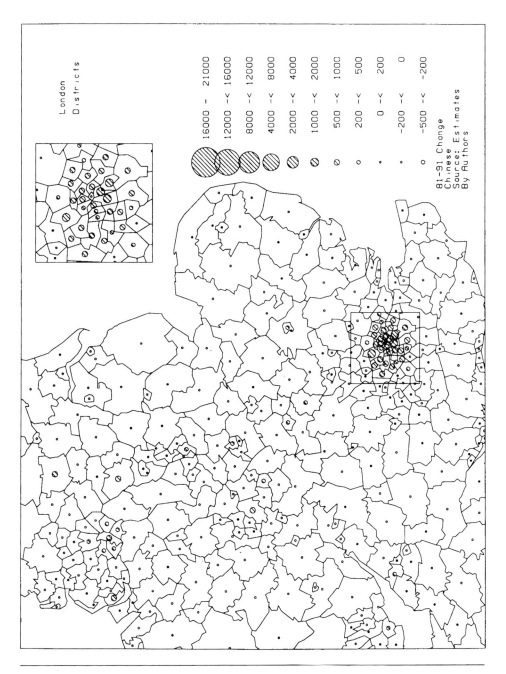

London
Districts

16000 – 21000
12000 – < 16000
8000 – < 12000
4000 – < 8000
2000 – < 4000
1000 – < 2000
500 – < 1000
200 – < 500
0 – < 200
–200 – < 0
–500 – < –200

81-91 Change
Chinese
Source: Estimates
By Authors

Figure 2.22 Geographical spread in 1991: Other–Asian group

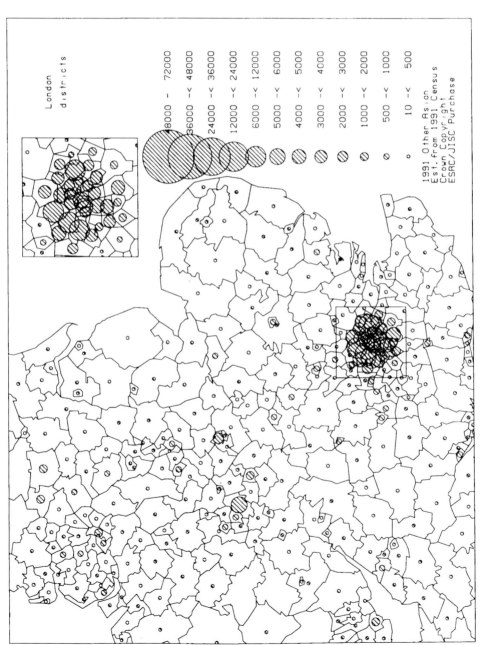

Figure 2.23 *Geographical concentration in 1991: Other–Asian group*

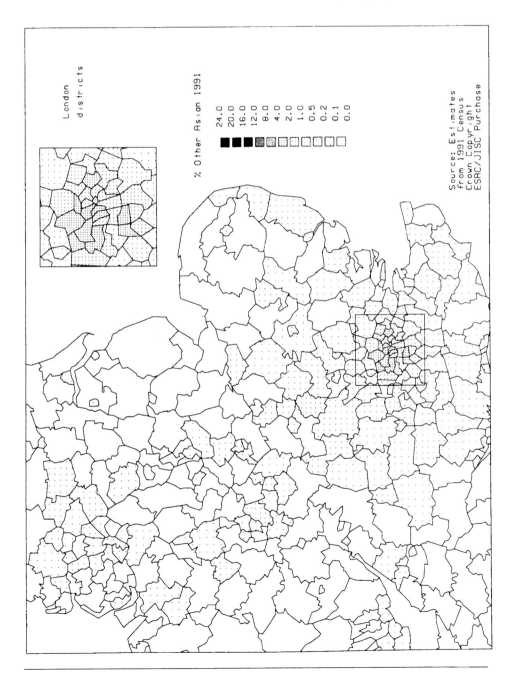

London
districts

% Other Asian 1991

24.0
20.0
16.0
12.0
8.0
4.0
2.0
1.0
0.5
0.2
0.1
0.0

Source: Estimates
from 1991 Census
Crown Copyright
ESRC/JISC Purchase

Figure 2.24 *Population change 1981–91: Other–Asian group*

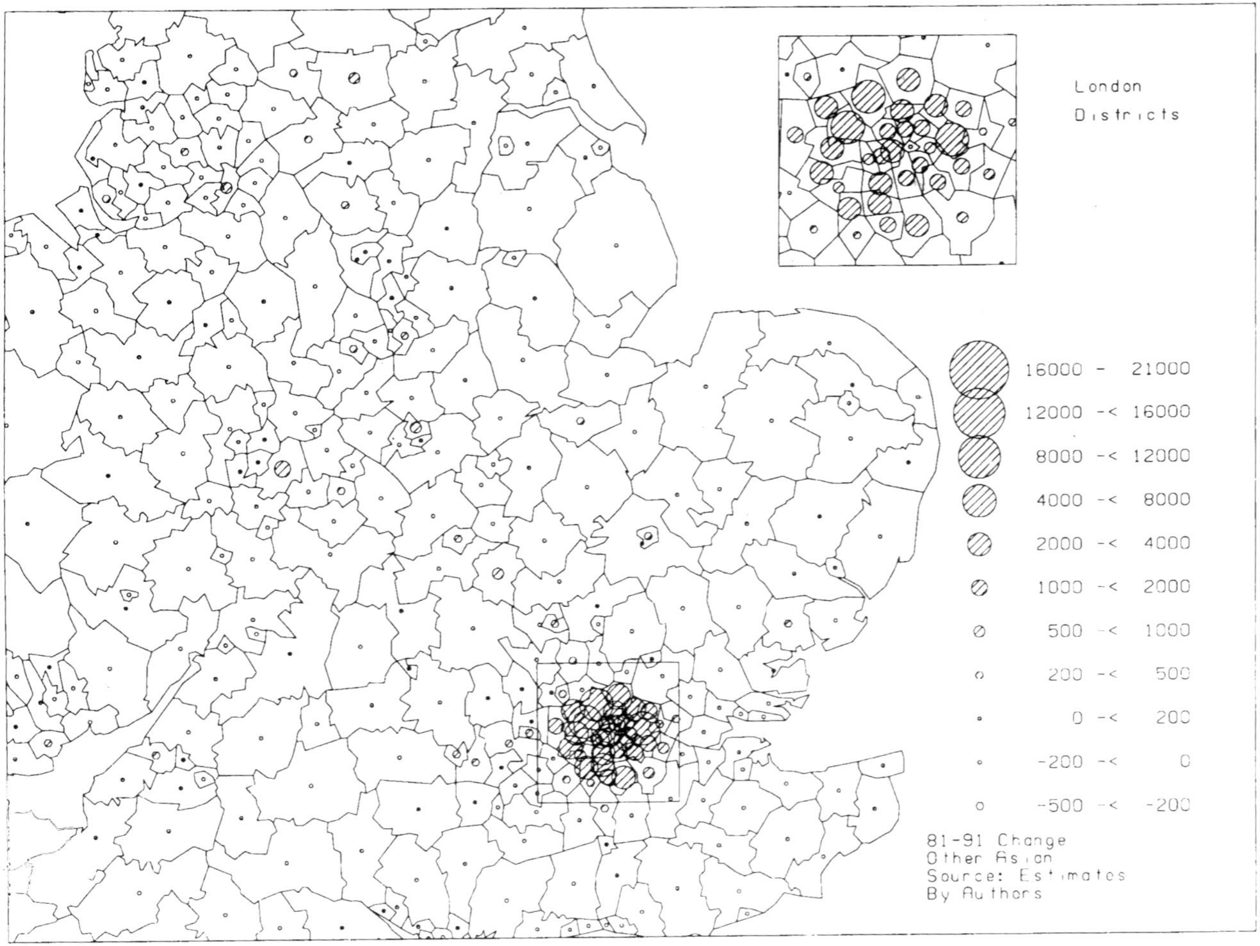

London
Districts

16000 – 21000
12000 – < 16000
8000 – < 12000
4000 – < 8000
2000 – < 4000
1000 – < 2000
500 – < 1000
200 – < 500
0 – < 200
-200 – < 0
-500 – < -200

81–91 Change
Other Asian
Source: Estimates
By Authors

Figure 2.25 *Geographical spread in 1991: Other–Other group*

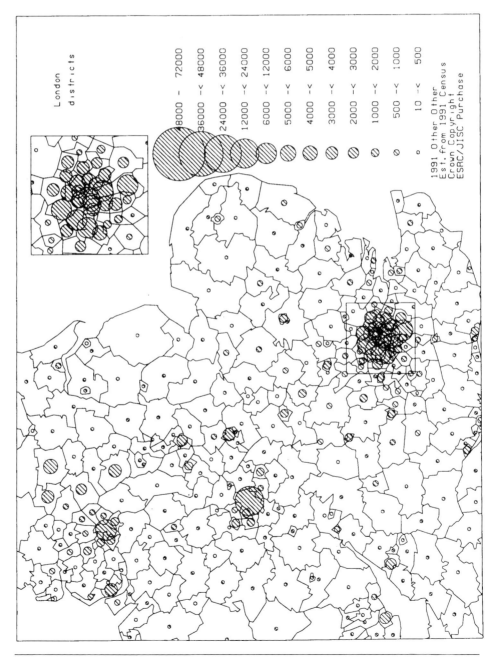

London
districts

48000 – 72000
36000 – < 48000
24000 – < 36000
12000 – < 24000
6000 – < 12000
5000 – < 6000
4000 – < 5000
3000 – < 4000
2000 – < 3000
1000 – < 2000
500 – < 1000
10 – < 500

1991 Other Other
Est. from 1991 Census
Crown Copyright
ESRC/JISC Purchase

Figure 2.26 Geographical concentration in 1991: Other–Other group

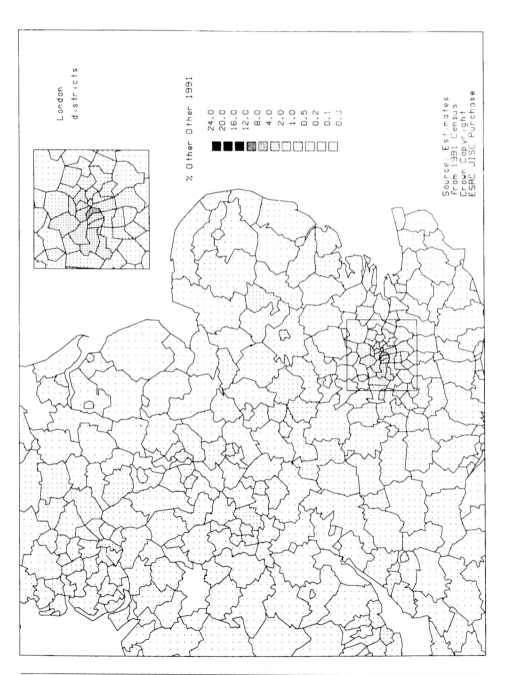

London
districts

% Other Other 1991

24.0
20.0
16.0
12.0
8.0
4.0
2.0
1.0
0.5
0.2
0.1
0.0

Source: Estimates
from 1991 Census
Crown Copyright
ESRC JISC Purchase

Figure 2.27 *Population change 1981–91: Other–Other group*

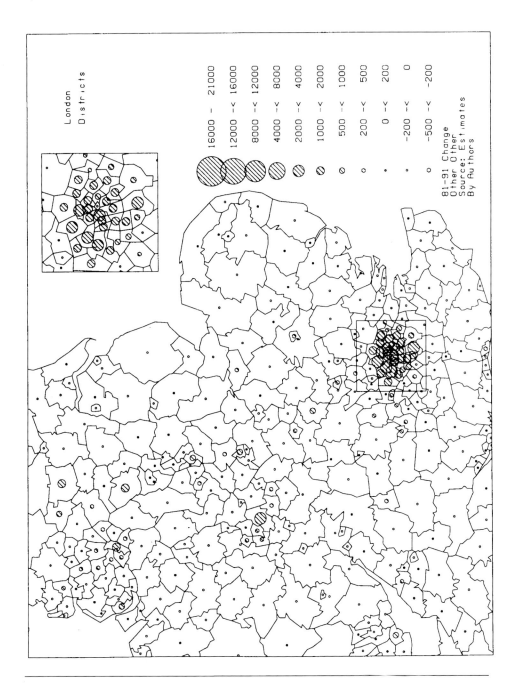

Appendix 2.1: *Estimates of ethnic group populations for GB regions with associated indicators*

Region	1981 Estimate	1991 Estimate	1981–91 Change	% Change 1981–91	Row %1981	Row %1991	Column %1981	Column %1991	LQ 1981	LQ 1991
White										
Inner London	2072832	1949430	-123402	-5.95	81.28	74.19	3.94	3.67	0.85	0.79
Outer London	3821141	3534783	-286358	-7.49	89.79	82.92	7.26	6.66	0.94	0.88
West Midlands	2371072	2237135	-133937	-5.65	88.70	85.08	4.51	4.22	0.92	0.90
West Yorkshire	1937375	1911618	-25757	-1.33	93.74	91.71	3.68	3.60	0.98	0.97
Gtr Manchester	2513545	2414417	-99128	-3.94	95.97	93.92	4.78	4.55	0.99	0.99
East Midlands	3720604	3836904	116300	3.13	96.56	95.08	7.07	7.23	1.01	1.01
Outer Met Area	5274859	5384160	109301	2.07	96.75	95.70	10.03	10.15	1.01	1.01
Remainder of NW	2270618	2302875	32257	1.42	97.96	96.93	4.32	4.34	1.02	1.03
South Yorkshire	1291660	1263799	-27861	-2.16	98.06	97.07	2.46	2.38	1.02	1.03
Outer South East	4665923	5005530	339607	7.28	98.14	97.75	8.87	9.43	1.02	1.04
East Anglia	1858272	2037328	179056	9.64	98.18	97.86	3.53	3.84	1.02	1.04
Central Clydeside	1711278	1595495	-115783	-6.77	98.85	97.99	3.25	3.01	1.03	1.04
Remainder of West Midlands	2448029	2584010	135981	5.55	97.39	98.03	4.65	4.87	1.01	1.04
Merseyside	1500267	1422453	-77814	-5.19	98.56	98.12	2.85	2.68	1.03	1.04
Tyne and Wear	1140786	1109420	-31366	-2.75	98.76	98.14	2.17	2.09	1.03	1.04
Wales	2780395	2848480	68085	2.45	98.83	98.51	5.28	5.37	1.03	1.04
South West	4329269	4653365	324096	7.49	98.82	98.63	8.23	8.77	1.03	1.04
Remainder of North	1947998	1942067	-5931	-0.30	99.27	99.02	3.70	3.66	1.03	1.05
Remainder of Scotland	3433961	3446523	12562	0.37	99.58	99.08	6.53	6.50	1.04	1.05
Remainder of Yorkshire & Humberside	1520093	1582496	62403	4.11	99.06	99.12	2.89	2.98	1.03	1.05
GB total	52609977	53062288	452311	0.86	95.98	94.41	100	100	1.00	1.00
Minority ethnic groups (all)										
Inner London	477266	678070	200804	42.07	18.72	25.81	21.66	21.57	4.66	4.62
Outer London	434360	727917	293557	67.58	10.21	17.08	19.71	23.15	2.54	3.05
West Midlands	302027	392265	90238	29.88	11.3	14.92	13.71	12.48	2.81	2.67
West Yorkshire	129326	172882	43556	33.68	6.26	8.29	5.87	5.50	1.56	1.48
Gtr Manchester	105553	156183	50630	47.97	4.03	6.08	4.79	4.97	1.00	1.09
East Midlands	132495	198396	65901	49.74	3.44	4.92	6.01	6.31	0.85	0.88
Outer Met Area	177241	241940	64699	36.50	3.25	4.30	8.04	7.70	0.81	0.77
Remainder of NW	47184	72925	25741	54.55	2.04	3.07	2.14	2.32	0.51	0.55
South Yorkshire	25541	38101	12560	49.18	1.94	2.93	1.16	1.21	0.48	0.52
Outer South East	88478	115070	26592	30.05	1.86	2.25	4.01	3.66	0.25	0.40
East Anglia	34529	44472	9943	28.80	1.82	2.14	1.57	1.41	0.46	0.38
Central Clydeside	19922	32705	12783	64.17	1.15	2.01	0.90	1.04	0.28	0.36
Remainder of West Midlands	65669	51890	-13779	-20.98	2.61	1.97	2.98	1.65	0.65	0.35
Merseyside	21932	27247	5315	24.23	1.44	1.88	1.00	0.87	0.36	0.34
Tyne and Wear	14314	20980	6666	46.57	1.24	1.86	0.65	0.67	0.31	0.33
Wales	32805	43020	10215	31.14	1.17	1.49	1.49	1.37	0.29	0.27
South West	51733	64535	12802	24.75	1.18	1.37	2.35	2.05	0.29	0.24
Remainder of North	14404	19133	4729	32.83	0.73	0.98	0.65	0.61	0.18	0.17
Remainder of Scotland	14538	32077	17539	120.64	0.42	0.92	0.66	1.02	0.10	0.16
Remainder of Yorkshire & Humberside	14408	14004	-404	-2.80	0.94	0.88	0.65	0.45	0.23	0.16
GB total	2203725	3143812	940087	42.66	4.02	5.59	100	100	1.00	1.00

Region	1981 Estimate	1991 Estimate	1981–91 Change	% Change 1981–91	Row %1981	Row %1991	Column %1981	Column %1991	LQ 1981	LQ 1991
Black Caribbean										
Inner London	161422	188333	26911	16.67	6.33	7.17	38.2	36.06	8.22	7.71
Outer London	78534	116359	37825	48.16	1.85	2.73	18.59	22.28	2.40	2.94
West Midlands	63597	75612	12015	18.89	2.38	2.88	15.05	14.48	3.09	3.09
West Yorkshire	13088	15552	2464	18.83	0.63	0.75	3.10	2.98	0.82	0.80
Gtr. Manchester	14119	18371	4252	30.12	0.54	0.71	3.34	3.52	0.70	0.77
East Midlands	19022	25684	6662	35.02	0.49	0.64	4.50	4.92	0.64	0.68
Outer Met Area	23403	28016	4613	19.71	0.43	0.50	5.54	5.36	0.56	0.54
Remainder of NW	1707	2436	729	42.71	0.07	0.10	0.40	0.47	0.10	0.11
South Yorkshire	4851	6365	1514	31.21	0.37	0.49	1.15	1.22	0.48	0.53
Outer South East	11268	13248	1980	17.57	0.24	0.26	2.67	2.54	0.31	0.28
East Anglia	4365	5001	636	14.57	0.23	0.24	1.03	0.96	0.30	0.26
Central Clydeside	220	329	109	49.55	0.01	0.02	0.05	0.06	0.02	0.02
Remainder of W. Mids	8406	5963	-2443	-29.06	0.33	0.23	1.99	1.14	0.43	0.24
Merseyside	1890	2208	318	16.83	0.12	0.15	0.45	0.42	0.16	0.16
Tyne and Wear	379	478	99	26.12	0.03	0.04	0.09	0.09	0.04	0.05
Wales	3099	3472	373	12.04	0.11	0.12	0.73	0.66	0.14	0.13
South West	11604	12894	1290	11.12	0.26	0.27	2.75	2.47	0.34	0.29
Remainder of North	525	647	122	23.24	0.03	0.03	0.12	0.12	0.03	0.04
Remainder of Scotland	284	590	306	107.75	0.00	0.02	0.07	0.11	0.01	0.02
Remainder of Yorkshire & Humberside	739	684	-55	-7.44	0.05	0.04	0.17	0.13	0.06	0.05
GB total	422522	522242	99720	23.60	0.77	0.93	100	100	1.00	1.00
Black African										
Inner London	70869	114330	43461	61.33	2.78	4.35	50.12	52.17	10.69	11.16
Outer London	31361	56463	25102	80.04	0.74	1.32	22.18	25.76	2.83	3.40
West Midlands	3602	4134	532	14.77	0.13	0.16	2.55	1.89	0.52	0.40
West Yorkshire	2236	2634	398	17.80	0.11	0.13	1.58	1.20	0.42	0.32
Gtr Manchester	4071	5638	1567	38.49	0.16	0.22	2.88	2.57	0.60	0.56
East Midlands	2454	3526	1072	43.68	0.06	0.09	1.74	1.61	0.24	0.22
Outer Met Area	6179	7414	1235	19.99	0.11	0.13	4.37	3.38	0.44	0.34
Remainder of NW	807	1159	352	43.62	0.03	0.05	0.57	0.53	0.13	0.13
South Yorkshire	968	1414	446	46.07	0.07	0.11	0.68	0.65	0.28	0.28
Outer South East	4590	5636	1046	22.79	0.10	0.11	3.25	2.57	0.37	0.28
East Anglia	1686	2099	413	24.5	0.09	0.10	1.19	0.96	0.34	0.26
Central Clydeside	809	1013	204	25.22	0.05	0.06	0.57	0.46	0.18	0.16
Remainder of W. Mids	1485	1126	-359	-24.18	0.06	0.04	1.05	0.51	0.23	0.11
Merseyside	2630	3093	463	17.6	0.17	0.21	1.86	1.41	0.66	0.55
Tyne and Wear	711	899	188	26.44	0.06	0.08	0.50	0.41	0.24	0.20
Wales	2236	2715	479	21.42	0.08	0.09	1.58	1.24	0.31	0.24
South West	2131	2571	440	20.65	0.05	0.05	1.51	1.17	0.19	0.14
Remainder of North	549	640	91	16.58	0.03	0.03	0.39	0.29	0.11	0.08
Remainder of Scotland	878	1695	817	93.05	0.03	0.05	0.62	0.77	0.10	0.12
Remainder of Yorkshire & Humberside	1133	970	-163	-14.39	0.07	0.06	0.80	0.44	0.28	0.16
GB total	141385	219169	77784	55.02	0.26	0.39	100	100	1.00	1.00

Region	1981 Estimate	1991 Estimate	1981–91 Change	% Change 1981–91	Row %1981	Row %1991	Column %1981	Column %1991	LQ 1981	LQ 1991
Black–Other										
Inner London	41220	52830	11610	28.17	1.99	2.71	28.67	28.07	7.37	7.74
Outer London	21988	32477	10489	47.7	0.58	0.92	15.29	17.25	2.13	2.63
West Midlands	13213	16638	3425	25.92	0.56	0.74	9.19	8.84	2.06	2.12
West Yorkshire	5446	6949	1503	27.6	0.28	0.36	3.79	3.69	1.04	1.04
Gtr. Manchester	7226	9939	2713	37.54	0.29	0.41	5.03	5.28	1.06	1.18
East Midlands	7744	11311	3567	46.06	0.20	0.32	5.39	6.01	0.75	0.91
Outer Met Area	8910	11512	2602	29.2	0.38	0.51	6.20	6.12	1.39	1.47
Remainder of NW	1725	2662	937	54.32	0.09	0.14	1.20	1.41	0.33	0.40
South Yorkshire	1953	2738	785	40.19	0.11	0.17	1.36	1.45	0.42	0.49
Outer South East	7535	9575	2040	27.07	0.14	0.18	5.24	5.09	0.53	0.51
East Anglia	6077	7405	1328	21.85	0.27	0.32	4.23	3.93	0.99	0.92
Central Clydeside	505	778	273	54.06	0.01	0.02	0.35	0.41	0.04	0.05
Remainder of W. Mids.	4071	3199	-872	-21.42	0.22	0.16	2.83	1.70	0.81	0.45
Merseyside	3824	4613	789	20.63	0.25	0.29	2.66	2.45	0.93	0.83
Tyne and Wear	679	876	197	29.01	0.00	0.00	0.47	0.47	0.00	0.00
Wales	3021	3645	624	20.66	0.11	0.13	2.10	1.94	0.4	0.37
South West	5626	6892	1266	22.5	0.13	0.15	3.91	3.66	0.48	0.42
Remainder of North	824	1075	251	30.46	0.04	0.06	0.57	0.57	0.16	0.16
Remainder of Scotland	938	1944	1006	107.25	0.03	0.06	0.65	1.03	0.10	0.16
Remainder of Yorkshire & Humberside	1243	1164	-79	-6.36	0.08	0.07	0.86	0.62	0.30	0.21
GB total	143768	188222	44454	30.92	0.27	0.35	100	100	1.00	1.00
Indian										
Inner London	60166	77999	17833	29.64	2.36	2.97	9.58	8.89	2.05	1.90
Outer London	172715	283286	110571	64.02	4.06	6.65	27.51	32.3	3.53	4.26
West Midlands	118101	148320	30219	25.59	4.42	5.64	18.81	16.91	3.84	3.62
West Yorkshire	29352	36762	7410	25.25	1.42	1.76	4.68	4.19	1.23	1.13
Gtr.Manchester	22053	30909	8856	40.16	0.84	1.20	3.51	3.52	0.73	0.77
East Midlands	69985	104986	35001	50.01	1.82	2.60	11.15	11.97	1.58	1.67
Outer Met Area	55016	73599	18583	33.78	1.01	1.31	8.76	8.39	0.88	0.84
Remainder of NW	16408	24228	7820	47.66	0.71	1.02	2.61	2.76	0.62	0.65
South Yorkshire	2444	3645	1201	49.14	0.19	0.28	0.39	0.42	0.16	0.18
Outer South East	21361	27038	5677	26.58	0.45	0.53	3.40	3.08	0.39	0.34
East Anglia	5372	6728	1356	25.24	0.28	0.32	0.86	0.77	0.25	0.21
Central Clydeside	3992	6280	2288	57.31	0.23	0.39	0.64	0.72	0.20	0.25
Remainder of W. Mids	23186	17849	-5337	-23.02	0.92	0.68	3.69	2.04	0.80	0.43
Merseyside	2248	2740	492	21.89	0.15	0.19	0.36	0.31	0.13	0.12
Tyne and Wear	3311	4477	1166	35.22	0.29	0.40	0.53	0.51	0.25	0.25
Wales	5251	6607	1356	25.82	0.19	0.23	0.84	0.75	0.16	0.15
South West	9349	11337	1988	21.26	0.21	0.24	1.49	1.29	0.19	0.15
Remainder of North	2823	3587	764	27.06	0.14	0.18	0.45	0.41	0.13	0.12
Remainder of Scotland	2038	4165	2127	104.37	0.06	0.12	0.32	0.47	0.05	0.08
Remainder of Yorkshire Humberside	2671	2455	-216	-8.09	0.17	0.15	0.43	0.28	0.15	0.10
GB total	627842	876997	249155	39.68	1.15	1.56	100	100	1.00	1.00

Region	1981 Estimate	1991 Estimate	1981–91 Change	% Change 1981–91	Row %1981	Row %1991	Column %1981	Column %1991	LQ 1981	LQ 1991
Pakistani										
Inner London	22730	30824	8094	35.61	0.89	1.17	6.60	6.16	1.41	1.32
Outer London	36710	60723	24013	65.41	0.86	1.42	10.66	12.14	1.37	1.60
West Midlands	65985	93426	27441	41.59	2.47	3.55	19.15	18.67	3.92	3.99
West Yorkshire	60803	84978	24175	39.76	2.94	4.08	17.65	16.99	4.67	4.58
Gtr. Manchester	33264	52107	18843	56.65	1.27	2.03	9.65	10.42	2.02	2.28
East Midlands	11760	18556	6796	57.79	0.31	0.46	3.41	3.71	0.48	0.52
Outer Met Area	32842	46683	13841	42.14	0.60	0.83	9.53	9.33	0.96	0.93
Remainder of NW	17658	27672	10014	56.71	0.76	1.16	5.13	5.53	1.21	1.31
South Yorkshire	9174	14017	4843	52.79	0.70	1.08	2.66	2.80	1.11	1.21
Outer South East	7746	10194	2448	31.60	0.16	0.20	2.25	2.04	0.26	0.22
East Anglia	4252	5999	1747	41.09	0.22	0.29	1.23	1.20	0.36	0.32
Central Clydeside	8684	14832	6148	70.80	0.50	0.91	2.52	2.96	0.80	1.02
Remainder of W. Mids	13085	10755	-2330	-17.81	0.52	0.41	3.80	2.15	0.83	0.46
Merseyside	716	912	196	27.37	0.05	0.06	0.21	0.18	0.07	0.07
Tyne and Wear	2914	4029	1115	38.26	0.25	0.36	0.85	0.81	0.40	0.40
Wales	4341	6021	1680	38.70	0.15	0.21	1.26	1.20	0.24	0.23
South West	3332	4139	807	24.22	0.08	0.09	0.97	0.83	0.12	0.10
Remainder of North	4438	5881	1443	32.51	0.23	0.30	1.29	1.18	0.36	0.34
Remainder of Scotland	3089	7483	4394	142.25	0.09	0.22	0.9	1.50	0.14	0.24
Remainder of Yorkshire & Humberside	1006	1064	58	5.77	0.07	0.07	0.29	0.21	0.10	0.07
GB total	344529	500295	155766	45.21	0.63	0.89	100	100	1.00	1.00
Bangladeshi										
Inner London	35014	75275	40261	114.99	1.37	2.86	39.90	43.89	8.58	9.24
Outer London	6778	15122	8344	123.10	0.16	0.35	7.72	8.82	1.00	1.14
West Midlands	11006	19131	8125	73.82	0.41	0.73	12.54	11.15	2.57	2.35
West Yorkshire	3845	6344	2499	64.99	0.19	0.30	4.38	3.70	1.16	0.98
Gtr. Manchester	6156	11958	5802	94.25	0.24	0.47	7.01	6.97	1.47	1.50
East Midlands	2274	4390	2116	93.05	0.06	0.11	2.59	2.56	0.37	0.35
Outer Met Area	6278	11282	5004	79.71	0.12	0.20	7.15	6.58	0.72	0.65
Rem of NW	1478	2813	1335	90.32	0.06	0.12	1.68	1.64	0.40	0.38
South Yorkshire	675	1249	574	85.04	0.05	0.10	0.77	0.73	0.32	0.31
Outer South East	4134	7401	3267	79.03	0.09	0.14	4.71	4.32	0.54	0.47
East Anglia	1004	1739	735	73.21	0.05	0.08	1.14	1.01	0.33	0.27
Central Clydeside	184	270	86	46.74	0.01	0.02	0.21	0.16	0.07	0.05
Remainder of W. Mids	1607	1380	-227	-14.13	0.06	0.05	1.83	0.80	0.40	0.17
Merseyside	489	764	275	56.24	0.03	0.05	0.56	0.45	0.20	0.17
Tyne and Wear	1313	2959	1646	125.36	0.11	0.26	1.50	1.73	0.71	0.84
Wales	2244	4046	1802	80.30	0.08	0.14	2.56	2.36	0.50	0.45
South West	1288	2431	1143	88.74	0.03	0.05	1.47	1.42	0.18	0.17
Remainder of North	443	798	355	80.14	0.02	0.04	0.5	0.47	0.14	0.13
Remainder of Scotland	363	912	549	151.24	0.01	0.03	0.41	0.53	0.07	0.08
Remainder of Yorkshire & Humberside	1189	1252	63	5.30	0.08	0.08	1.35	0.73	0.48	0.25
GB total	87762	171516	83754	95.43	0.16	0.31	100	100	1.00	1.00

Region	1981 Estimate	1991 Estimate	1981–91 Change	% Change 1981–91	Row %1981	Row %1991	Column %1981	Column %1991	LQ 1981	LQ 1991
Chinese										
Inner London	19382	29358	9976	51.47	0.76	1.12	17.38	18.26	3.80	3.85
Outer London	16556	29030	12474	75.34	0.39	0.68	14.85	18.05	1.95	2.35
West Midlands	4543	6119	1576	34.69	0.17	0.23	4.07	3.81	0.85	0.80
West Yorkshire	2912	3969	1057	36.30	0.14	0.19	2.61	2.47	0.70	0.66
Gtr. Manchester	5945	8580	2635	44.32	0.23	0.33	5.33	5.34	1.13	1.15
East Midlands	4883	7651	2768	56.69	0.13	0.19	4.38	4.76	0.63	0.65
Outer Met Area	11911	16032	4121	34.60	0.22	0.28	10.68	9.97	1.09	0.98
Remainder of NW	2136	3482	1346	63.01	0.09	0.15	1.92	2.17	0.46	0.51
South Yorkshire	1376	2241	865	62.86	0.10	0.17	1.23	1.39	0.52	0.59
Outer South East	9073	11392	2319	25.56	0.19	0.22	8.14	7.08	0.95	0.77
East Anglia	2912	3811	899	30.87	0.15	0.18	2.61	2.37	0.77	0.63
Central Clydeside	2731	4456	1725	63.16	0.16	0.27	2.45	2.77	0.79	0.94
Remainder of W. Mids	4151	3422	-729	-17.56	0.17	0.13	3.72	2.13	0.83	0.45
Merseyside	4719	5895	1176	24.92	0.31	0.41	4.23	3.67	1.55	1.40
Tyne and Wear	1995	2867	872	43.71	0.17	0.25	1.79	1.78	0.86	0.87
Wales	3970	4899	929	23.40	0.14	0.17	3.56	3.05	0.71	0.58
South West	5264	6875	1611	30.60	0.12	0.15	4.72	4.28	0.60	0.50
Remainder of North	1774	2216	442	24.92	0.09	0.11	1.59	1.38	0.45	0.39
Remainder of Scotland	2928	6289	3361	114.79	0.08	0.18	2.63	3.91	0.42	0.62
Remainder of Yorkshire & Humberside	2327	2222	-105	-4.51	0.15	0.14	2.09	1.38	0.76	0.48
GB total	111488	160806	49318	44.24	0.20	0.29	100	100	1.00	1.00
Other – Asian										
Inner London	24524	47703	23179	94.52	0.96	1.82	22.21	23.58	4.81	5.04
Outer London	30851	69594	38743	125.58	0.72	1.63	27.93	34.4	3.62	4.54
West Midlands	6654	9166	2512	37.75	0.25	0.35	6.02	4.53	1.24	0.97
West Yorkshire	3279	4771	1492	45.50	0.16	0.23	2.97	2.36	0.79	0.64
Gtr. Manchester	3252	5097	1845	56.73	0.12	0.20	2.94	2.52	0.62	0.55
East Midlands	4517	7497	2980	65.97	0.12	0.19	4.09	3.71	0.59	0.52
Outer Met Area	11404	19055	7651	67.09	0.21	0.34	10.33	9.42	1.05	0.94
Remainder of NW	1574	2762	1188	75.48	0.07	0.12	1.43	1.37	0.34	0.32
South Yorkshire	754	1407	653	86.60	0.06	0.11	0.68	0.70	0.29	0.30
Outer South East	6832	10169	3337	48.84	0.14	0.20	6.19	5.03	0.72	0.55
East Anglia	2706	3894	1188	43.9	0.14	0.19	2.45	1.92	0.71	0.52
Central Clydeside	931	1675	744	79.91	0.05	0.10	0.84	0.83	0.27	0.29
Remainder of W. Mids	2677	2636	-41	-1.53	0.11	0.10	2.42	1.30	0.53	0.28
Merseyside	889	1313	424	47.69	0.06	0.09	0.80	0.65	0.29	0.25
Tyne and Wear	1058	1716	658	62.19	0.09	0.15	0.96	0.85	0.46	0.42
Wales	2353	3660	1307	55.55	0.08	0.13	2.13	1.81	0.42	0.35
South West	2967	4488	1521	51.26	0.07	0.10	2.69	2.22	0.34	0.26
Remainder of North	922	1484	562	60.95	0.05	0.08	0.83	0.73	0.23	0.21
Remainder of Scotland	1219	2965	1746	143.23	0.04	0.09	1.10	1.47	0.18	0.24
Remainder of Yorkshire & Humberside	1078	1256	178	16.51	0.07	0.08	0.98	0.62	0.35	0.22
GB total	110441	202308	91867	83.18	0.20	0.36	100	100	1.00	1.00

Appendix 2.1: *continued*

Region	1981 Estimate	1991 Estimate	1981–91 Change	% Change 1981–91	Row %1981	Row %1991	Column %1981	Column %1991	LQ 1981	LQ 1991
Other–Other										
Inner London	41932	61416	19484	46.47	1.64	2.34	19.59	20.32	4.22	4.33
Outer London	38861	64858	25997	66.90	0.91	1.52	18.16	21.46	2.34	2.82
West Midlands	15327	19719	4392	28.66	0.57	0.75	7.16	6.53	1.47	1.39
West Yorkshire	8363	10923	2560	30.61	0.40	0.52	3.91	3.61	1.04	0.97
Gtr. Manchester	9467	13577	4110	43.41	0.36	0.53	4.42	4.49	0.93	0.98
East Midlands	9852	14790	4938	50.12	0.26	0.37	4.60	4.89	0.66	0.68
Outer Met Area	21304	28345	7041	33.05	0.39	0.50	9.96	9.38	1.00	0.93
Remainder of NW	3692	5718	2026	54.88	0.16	0.24	1.73	1.89	0.41	0.45
South Yorkshire	3345	5026	1681	50.25	0.25	0.39	1.56	1.66	0.65	0.71
Outer South East	15945	20407	4462	27.98	0.34	0.40	7.45	6.75	0.86	0.74
East Anglia	6160	7796	1636	26.56	0.33	0.37	2.88	2.58	0.83	0.69
Central Clydeside	1865	3063	1198	64.24	0.11	0.19	0.87	1.01	0.28	0.35
Remainder of W. Mids	7011	5553	-1458	-20.80	0.28	0.21	3.28	1.84	0.72	0.39
Merseyside	4531	5713	1182	26.09	0.30	0.39	2.12	1.89	0.76	0.73
Tyne and Wear	1956	2679	723	36.96	0.17	0.24	0.91	0.89	0.43	0.44
Wales	6295	7958	1663	26.42	0.22	0.28	2.94	2.63	0.57	0.51
South West	10176	12903	2727	26.80	0.23	0.27	4.76	4.27	0.60	0.51
Remainder of North	2104	2799	695	33.03	0.11	0.14	0.98	0.93	0.27	0.26
Remainder of Scotland	2797	6023	3226	115.34	0.08	0.17	1.31	1.99	0.21	0.32
Remainder of Yorkshire & Humberside	3018	2933	-85	-2.82	0.20	0.18	1.41	0.97	0.50	0.34
GB total	214001	302199	88198	41.21	0.39	0.54	100	100	1.00	1.00

Notes: The region definitions are as follows (see Appendix 2.2 for districts comprising each region except where indicated).
1.   Inner London: the London boroughs listed in Appendix 2.2
2.   Outer London: the London boroughs listed in Appendix 2.2
3.   West Midlands: the former West Midlands Metropolitan County
4.   West Yorkshire: the former West Yorkshire Metropolitan County
5.   Greater Manchester: the former Greater Manchester Metropolitan County
6.   East Midlands: Derbyshire, Leicestershire, Lincolnshire, Northamptonshire and Nottinghamshire
7.   Outer Metropolitan Area: the following districts:
     Bedfordshire (part): Luton, South Bedfordshire; Berkshire (part): Bracknell, Reading, Slough, Windsor and Maidenhead, Wokingham; Buckinghamshire (part): Chiltern, South Bucks, Wycombe; Essex (part): Basildon, Brentwood, Castle Point, Chelmsford, Epping Forest, Harlow, Rochford, Southend-on-Sea, Thurrock; Hampshire (part): Hart, Rushmoor; Hertfordshire: all districts; Kent (part): Dartford, Gillingham, Gravesham, Maidstone, Rochester upon Medway, Sevenoaks; Tunbridge and Malling, Tunbridge Wells; Surrey: all districts; West Sussex (part): Crawley, Horsham, Mid Sussex
8.   Remainder of the North West standard region: Cheshire and Lancashire
9.   South Yorkshire: the former South Yorkshire metropolitan county
10. Outer South East: all remaining parts of the South East region excluding London and the Outer Metropolitan Area
11. East Anglia: the counties of Cambridgeshire, Norfolk and Suffolk
12. Central Clydeside, the following districts: Clydesbank, Bearsden and Milngavie, Strathkelvin, Cumbernauld and Kilsyth, Falkirk, Clackmannan,Dunfermline, City of Edinburgh, Midlothian, West Lothian, Monklands, Motherwell, Hamilton,East Kilbride, City of Glasgow, Eastwood, Kilmarnock and Loudoun, Renfrew, Inverclyde,Dumbarton
13. Remainder of the West Midlands standard region: the counties of Hereford and Worcester, Shropshire, Staffordshire, Warwickshire
14. Merseyside: the former Merseyside metropolitan county
15. Tyne and Wear: the former Tyne and Wear metropolitan county
16. Wales: the home country
17. South West: the counties of Avon, Cornwall, Devon, Dorset, Gloucestershire, Somerset, Wiltshire
18. Remainder of the North standard region: Counties of Cleveland, Cumbria, Durham, Northumberland
19. Remainder of Scotland: Scotland less the districts of Central Clydeside
20. Remainder of Yorkshire and Humberside standard region: counties of Humberside and North Yorkshire

Appendix 2.2   Estimates of the population of ethnic groups in the 459 districts of Great Britain, 1981 and 1991

District	Year	White	Black–Caribbean	Black–African	Black–Other	Indian	Pakistani	Bangla–deshi	Chinese	Other–Asian	Other–Other	All groups
Inner London												
City of London	1981	5363	13	7	13	78	25	28	34	53	44	5659
	1991	3823	9	5	13	68	20	10	45	62	45	4100
Camden	1981	161478	2762	3196	1427	2442	608	2765	2271	2526	3768	183243
	1991	149490	3279	4664	1866	2974	796	6718	2652	4040	5220	181700
Hackney	1981	131797	19330	7701	6140	5405	1489	1824	1308	1385	3764	180145
	1991	124090	21321	12886	7696	6629	1845	3446	2016	2614	5357	187900
Hammersmith & Fulham	1981	132731	8427	2634	2126	2024	1006	466	757	1151	2565	153888
	1991	128641	9383	3918	2782	2483	1247	737	1153	2009	3848	156200
Haringey	1981	160099	17275	7802	3873	5811	1141	1355	1634	2254	3746	204990
	1991	149528	19958	11864	4932	7689	1565	3238	2407	4852	5766	211800
Islington	1981	145744	7501	4356	2540	1872	465	1277	1579	1202	2413	168949
	1991	140757	8824	6308	3340	2526	638	2857	2193	2434	3623	173500
Kensington & Chelsea	1981	127634	3148	2176	1257	1274	634	372	1108	2530	3619	143752
	1991	122936	3701	2891	1667	1711	867	613	1517	4033	5364	145300
Lambeth	1981	189718	27564	10883	5531	4328	1632	917	2104	1682	4331	248691
	1991	178168	32702	17018	7073	5500	2120	1646	3224	3119	6031	256600
Lewisham	1981	201060	19205	5233	4796	2047	563	353	1361	1391	2753	238764
	1991	187146	24519	9087	6125	2933	783	660	2500	3197	3850	240800
Newham	1981	141043	13528	6686	2832	22259	9214	3019	1109	2602	2108	204400
	1991	126708	16015	12639	3560	29105	13162	8550	1803	6637	3121	221300
Southwark	1981	181995	16257	8289	4044	1919	620	1208	1433	1163	2580	219508
	1991	170847	19145	16783	5161	2736	814	2284	2914	2670	3845	227200
Tower Hamlets	1981	108776	5270	2363	1378	1398	990	18888	1056	922	1702	142744
	1991	107481	6055	3969	1916	1730	1239	39439	1825	1861	2584	168100
Wandsworth	1981	221782	14623	6248	3574	6705	3502	774	1358	2522	3255	264341
	1991	211354	16259	7823	4535	8205	4488	1086	2199	4828	4523	265300
Westminster	1981	163612	6519	3295	1689	2604	841	1768	2270	3141	5284	191024
	1991	148461	7163	4475	2164	3710	1240	3991	2910	5347	8239	187700
Outer London												
Barking & Dagenham	1981	151037	1106	443	451	1859	1116	76	338	192	411	157029
	1991	136244	1840	929	661	2855	1715	187	599	511	658	146200
Barnet	1981	262111	2052	3525	983	13400	1362	512	2263	4216	3698	294123
	1991	243679	3041	6317	1529	22499	2397	1229	4038	8946	6225	299900
Bexley	1981	217886	896	580	419	3289	168	141	682	554	839	225454
	1991	206538	1497	958	651	5385	273	291	1237	1181	1389	219400
Brent	1981	152640	19932	5888	4005	28328	4714	434	1943	4030	4757	226670
	1991	136150	25618	10305	5544	43230	7565	758	2641	8947	7842	248600
Bromley	1981	302615	1715	628	692	1923	238	206	681	827	1498	311024
	1991	280804	2597	1012	1029	3202	391	449	1192	1678	2346	294700

Appendix 2.2: *Continued*

District	Year	White	Black–Caribbean	Black–African	Black–Other	Indian	Pakistani	Bangla-deshi	Chinese	Other–Asian	Other–Other	All groups
Croydon	1981	286146	10030	2933	2389	9080	2156	394	997	2247	3935	320307
	1991	262342	15801	5099	3543	15191	3518	817	1748	4914	6227	319200
Ealing	1981	204056	8919	2448	2076	31968	4926	416	1544	3666	4218	264236
	1991	189787	12599	4405	3040	45949	7720	797	2538	7546	7419	281800
Enfield	1981	243578	5854	2280	1644	5244	638	981	696	1364	2143	264423
	1991	225590	9730	4281	2477	9390	1083	2194	1179	3582	3693	263200
Greenwich	1981	202561	3506	1984	1476	4835	790	169	874	1037	1633	218865
	1991	186043	5335	4109	2182	7422	1304	397	1718	2429	2661	213600
Harrow	1981	164781	2857	941	926	17515	1395	290	1003	2020	2208	193937
	1991	149689	4537	1731	1396	33246	2406	552	1854	4674	3714	203800
Havering	1981	249017	844	269	337	1559	245	123	484	213	592	253683
	1991	225031	1321	393	492	2493	378	186	839	462	904	232500
Hillingdon	1981	222313	1264	475	532	8570	1123	401	624	1155	1513	237970
	1991	207460	2169	804	859	16079	2075	935	1205	2562	2652	236800
Hounslow	1981	167522	1586	1311	669	18597	3110	280	735	1957	2464	198233
	1991	157465	2309	2359	1046	30291	5410	626	1334	3999	4260	209100
Kingston upon Thames	1981	132290	329	305	204	1878	524	75	605	1369	979	138559
	1991	125528	518	491	327	3225	905	153	1137	3445	1771	137500
Merton	1981	152626	3165	1713	989	3572	1463	446	639	1873	1891	168376
	1991	143498	5065	3469	1502	5935	2313	908	1254	4730	3125	171800
Redbridge	1981	199984	3372	1410	1095	13130	3475	702	873	1271	1837	227148
	1991	181134	5691	2545	1627	24078	6552	1976	1574	2997	3025	231200
Richmond Upon Thames	1981	162836	371	213	214	1731	221	186	497	767	1153	168190
	1991	155277	555	349	328	2711	361	335	895	1563	1927	164300
Sutton	1981	171212	718	427	349	1537	285	189	417	767	925	176826
	1991	161201	1173	638	542	2807	518	388	771	1808	1555	171400
Waltham Forest	1981	175930	10018	3588	2538	4700	8761	757	661	1326	2167	210448
	1991	161323	14963	6269	3702	7298	13839	1944	1277	3620	3465	217700
Greater Manchester												
Bolton	1981	244673	524	335	350	9932	2745	111	341	386	729	260125
	1991	240815	704	387	497	13801	4386	216	453	610	1030	262900
Bury	1981	173773	297	118	230	487	2024	80	311	121	481	177922
	1991	172427	445	172	337	785	3365	118	514	223	713	179100
Manchester	1981	413954	9103	2684	4160	3489	10912	1112	2419	1331	4258	453423
	1991	382377	11473	3769	5624	4819	16999	2214	3205	1986	6033	438500
Oldham	1981	207910	832	104	445	1207	5910	2559	293	180	552	219992
	1991	200217	1085	149	621	1600	9204	5286	403	266	768	219600
Rochdale	1981	196512	281	111	308	556	7505	863	285	325	437	207184
	1991	188428	374	145	432	821	11402	1693	404	486	613	204800
Salford	1981	246412	248	192	354	674	493	173	461	163	717	249887
	1991	225890	326	260	486	949	710	289	663	279	1048	230900

Appendix 2.2: *Continued*

District	Year	White	Black–Caribbean	Black–African	Black–Other	Indian	Pakistan	Bangla-deshi	Chinese	Other–Asian	Other–Other	All groups
Stockport	1981	289232	337	163	283	918	988	154	589	236	748	293647
	1991	281376	503	233	405	1418	1629	234	970	414	1119	288300
Tameside	1981	213464	227	107	225	2577	1212	935	399	122	393	219662
	1991	210585	344	151	323	3437	1950	1653	610	188	559	219800
Trafford	1981	214061	2179	153	719	1861	1283	144	534	313	854	222099
	1991	203857	2983	222	994	2776	2156	208	849	509	1245	215800
Wigan	1981	313554	91	104	152	352	192	25	313	75	298	315157
	1991	308445	134	150	220	503	306	47	509	136	449	310900
Merseyside												
Knowsley	1981	172900	158	131	314	163	37	8	233	43	326	174312
	1991	155297	179	141	362	182	40	7	266	56	371	156900
Liverpool	1981	500122	1385	2239	2965	1140	522	270	2800	525	2943	514911
	1991	462513	1578	2636	3555	1359	669	429	3536	733	3691	480700
St. Helens	1981	189682	41	46	75	267	47	30	255	55	195	190692
	1991	179681	52	47	91	324	55	27	293	89	243	180900
Sefton	1981	298998	164	112	212	293	59	76	560	93	482	301048
	1991	292467	203	139	272	372	73	130	744	170	631	295200
Wirral	1981	338565	142	102	258	385	51	105	871	173	585	341236
	1991	332495	196	130	333	503	75	171	1056	265	777	336000
South Yorkshire												
Barnsley	1981	226528	52	41	96	261	46	9	141	39	160	227373
	1991	223074	73	58	139	433	93	21	204	72	233	224400
Doncaster	1981	288820	582	81	276	828	660	18	289	108	335	291997
	1991	288574	801	104	398	1223	1057	31	424	193	495	293300
Rotherham	1981	250052	83	59	118	306	2182	22	157	88	326	253394
	1991	249772	144	87	172	489	3341	33	224	153	486	254900
Sheffield	1981	526260	4134	787	1463	1049	6286	626	789	519	2524	544437
	1991	502379	5347	1165	2029	1500	9526	1164	1389	989	3812	529300
Tyne and Wear												
Gateshead	1981	212400	39	51	68	278	205	63	229	67	204	213604
	1991	201410	51	68	83	390	281	118	322	107	271	203100
Newcastle upon Tyne	1981	274972	173	418	216	1851	2367	612	821	663	778	282871
	1991	266824	211	528	281	2388	3196	1426	1220	1051	1074	278200
North Tyneside	1981	197413	49	63	150	360	90	149	339	77	191	198879
	1991	193358	59	78	193	498	135	299	507	119	253	195500
South Tyneside	1981	160368	51	104	152	310	95	200	136	74	514	162004
	1991	154738	66	137	194	473	158	424	188	127	696	157200
Sunderland	1981	295633	67	75	93	512	157	289	470	177	269	297742
	1991	293090	91	88	125	728	259	692	630	312	385	296400

District	Year	White	Black-Caribbean	Black-African	Black-Other	Indian	Pakistani	Bangla-deshi	Chinese	Other-Asian	Other-Other	All groups
West Midlands												
Birmingham	1981	838751	39585	2443	7445	42865	49405	7523	2532	4234	9349	100413
	1991	787210	47277	2807	9418	54410	70431	13596	3302	5894	12155	100650
Coventry	1981	292411	3021	347	942	18489	3034	757	538	758	1345	321642
	1991	266853	3457	423	1180	22825	4080	1271	806	1028	1676	305600
Dudley	1981	297935	2011	118	566	3250	3104	183	334	186	779	308467
	1991	295344	2489	141	747	4222	4396	236	468	290	1067	309400
Sandwell	1981	274239	6892	213	1336	19286	4071	1552	315	413	1346	309663
	1991	250941	8048	213	1623	23539	5662	2289	340	522	1623	294800
Solihull	1981	200359	1181	63	434	1107	292	40	216	111	524	204327
	1991	195285	1493	92	563	1912	484	52	380	214	725	201200
Walsall	1981	251718	2062	135	680	9920	4531	841	302	356	670	271214
	1991	237858	2484	139	852	12525	6299	1500	428	472	843	263400
Wolverhampton	1981	215659	8845	283	1810	23184	1548	110	306	596	1314	253656
	1991	201644	10364	319	2255	28887	2074	187	395	746	1630	248500
West Yorkshire												
Bradford	1981	401490	2927	575	1149	10375	34116	2259	541	1212	2489	457133
	1991	399860	3508	630	1494	12409	48059	3877	704	1678	3181	475400
Calderdale	1981	187572	234	72	228	405	4829	255	159	220	421	194395
	1991	184975	281	82	290	532	6487	335	186	300	531	194000
Kirklees	1981	342952	4026	348	1434	9809	13267	168	386	690	1681	374761
	1991	340246	4613	396	1833	12379	18185	234	501	958	2154	381500
Leeds	1981	690047	5751	1141	2478	8129	7003	1149	1529	1059	3396	721685
	1991	675019	6970	1392	3133	10623	9995	1885	2176	1642	4566	717400
Wakefield	1981	315314	150	100	157	634	1588	14	297	98	376	318727
	1991	311518	180	134	199	819	2252	13	402	193	491	316200
Avon												
Bath	1981	82296	569	50	229	171	23	37	224	111	360	84069
	1991	81973	589	63	263	207	29	80	287	162	447	84100
Bristol	1981	381764	5918	678	2003	2420	2422	334	867	540	2135	399080
	1991	376418	6409	786	2312	2969	2931	602	1165	812	2595	397000
Kingswood	1981	83975	153	21	78	106	20	16	106	39	140	84654
	1991	89500	226	32	99	166	29	31	158	75	184	90500
Northavon	1981	117055	171	37	96	239	23	9	136	77	221	118065
	1991	131192	244	54	133	330	38	27	211	155	316	132700
Wansdyke	1981	76946	30	29	32	54	4	0	59	18	123	77295
	1991	80351	38	38	40	64	5	0	77	31	156	80800
Woodspring	1981	161993	90	46	78	194	20	34	202	86	303	163047
	1991	178382	107	60	101	248	24	84	258	144	392	179800

Appendix 2.2: *Continued*

District	Year	White	Black–Caribbean	Black–African	Black–Other	Indian	Pakistani	Bangla-deshi	Chinese	Other–Asian	Other–Other	All groups
Bedfordshire												
Luton	1981	135058	5308	497	1158	5723	7238	2576	582	629	1232	160001
	1991	139554	6420	634	1512	7422	10987	4819	676	945	1631	174600
Mid Bedfordshire	1981	102734	167	96	302	338	42	12	203	177	369	104441
	1991	109662	193	108	359	477	49	33	234	229	454	111800
North Bedfordshire	1981	120146	2487	239	679	5084	1214	720	255	329	641	131794
	1991	122221	2714	284	818	5923	1505	1184	287	478	785	136200
South Bedfordshire	1981	105866	248	76	150	526	77	15	166	107	313	107542
	1991	107593	305	98	190	702	106	19	215	163	408	109800
Berkshire												
Bracknell Forest	1981	83388	219	99	131	350	80	22	164	165	368	84984
	1991	96318	275	155	191	534	121	54	274	325	554	98800
Newbury	1981	120362	207	68	222	302	44	49	149	99	337	121838
	1991	137053	328	108	343	412	69	64	218	188	518	139300
Reading	1981	125609	3441	492	901	1449	2251	120	376	410	910	135959
	1991	123330	3661	732	1095	1861	2984	230	497	640	1170	136200
Slough	1981	71908	2361	376	516	9900	6399	39	205	643	821	93168
	1991	73749	2788	429	674	12941	9428	101	266	925	1099	102400
Windsor & Maidenhead	1981	132149	186	129	167	1697	1248	93	322	430	581	137003
	1991	127664	225	171	209	2200	1652	125	441	722	790	134200
Wokingham	1981	114734	262	88	115	961	261	19	232	244	385	117303
	1991	137350	467	142	184	1761	516	26	410	506	638	142000
Buckinghamshire												
Aylesbury Vale	1981	129785	910	181	240	591	1384	28	217	220	529	134085
	1991	142169	1067	238	320	794	2018	31	289	371	702	148000
Chiltern	1981	87729	63	23	64	261	603	29	130	116	220	89238
	1991	87652	85	29	83	346	814	27	193	180	291	89700
Milton Keynes	1981	119876	1017	289	416	1560	398	388	325	402	765	125437
	1991	168679	1716	548	708	2946	842	717	688	940	1417	179200
South Buckinghamshire	1981	61358	70	21	66	590	92	37	118	103	221	62675
	1991	60374	99	30	85	979	159	57	162	155	300	62400
Wycombe	1981	145915	2756	157	529	826	4461	66	231	250	1117	156309
	1991	146362	3209	204	681	1037	6009	118	311	406	1462	159800
Cambridgeshire												
Cambridge	1981	96234	442	236	307	792	215	260	674	661	847	100667
	1991	101926	539	285	370	1025	290	526	936	984	1120	108000
East Cambridgeshire	1981	53693	30	17	56	87	12	9	34	27	113	54077
	1991	60649	33	26	87	120	14	10	50	50	161	61200
Fenland	1981	65022	26	12	50	92	6	9	83	17	87	65404
	1991	74923	43	20	70	148	6	18	98	46	128	75500

Appendix 2.2: *Continued*

District	Year	White	Black–Caribbean	Black–African	Black–Other	Indian	Pakistani	Bangladeshi	Chinese	Other–Asian	Other–Other	All groups
Huntingdonshire	1981	122346	244	164	727	301	255	27	165	180	461	124869
	1991	143135	287	226	987	385	310	75	215	264	616	146500
Peterborough	1981	124511	1013	155	455	2165	3411	39	232	536	591	133108
	1991	143318	1239	210	613	2732	4894	56	369	755	813	155000
South Cambridgeshire	1981	107205	91	61	117	228	58	8	148	94	303	108312
	1991	120902	125	84	158	313	85	17	221	175	421	122500
Cheshire												
Chester	1981	117534	38	37	57	109	40	67	116	72	177	118246
	1991	116760	68	64	90	162	59	148	202	155	291	118000
Congleton	1981	80299	22	17	22	94	12	3	86	26	65	80646
	1991	84685	40	27	35	144	18	9	165	62	115	85300
Crewe & Nantwich	1981	98471	196	32	118	123	10	31	98	30	121	99230
	1991	104177	261	55	189	173	10	95	160	70	209	105400
Ellesmere Port	1981	82836	26	20	32	57	20	8	65	38	74	83176
	1991	80986	38	26	48	82	31	8	101	63	109	81500
Halton	1981	123467	43	34	111	114	17	17	114	50	150	124131
	1991	123960	61	44	167	156	29	30	167	70	220	124900
Macclesfield	1981	149850	66	57	68	244	99	26	186	91	219	150907
	1991	149584	104	80	106	396	155	27	306	188	355	151300
Vale Royal	1981	111277	25	17	36	134	28	28	116	44	94	111784
	1991	113671	40	26	57	204	49	14	190	83	151	114500
Warrington	1981	169490	54	65	94	349	285	29	180	67	244	170855
	1991	182727	104	104	157	638	489	26	362	145	421	185200
Cleveland												
Hartlepool	1981	94506	15	25	21	96	98	36	78	33	61	94968
	1991	90864	19	32	27	151	107	71	97	54	79	91500
Langbaurgh-On-Tees	1981	150177	28	20	48	173	178	103	97	45	116	150986
	1991	145411	33	26	60	190	214	135	118	63	149	146400
Middlesbrough	1981	144189	143	208	193	788	2882	36	262	146	563	149411
	1991	139862	168	206	238	890	3860	56	250	178	692	146400
Stockton-on-Tees	1981	171427	38	56	79	455	962	6	206	130	273	173632
	1991	172533	41	68	102	554	1251	7	274	202	368	175400
Cornwall & Isles of Scilly												
Caradon	1981	67505	26	10	77	23	2	2	40	18	85	67787
	1991	77731	36	12	105	30	2	3	43	30	108	78100
Carrick	1981	75439	31	7	52	45	13	5	86	20	92	75791
	1991	83331	41	10	68	59	15	6	116	31	124	83800
Kerrier	1981	83280	40	50	52	32	3	2	68	29	141	83696
	1991	88209	50	56	70	36	4	9	61	36	169	88700
North Cornwall	1981	64626	15	17	53	24	6	2	31	24	88	64885
	1991	73943	21	22	71	28	7	8	45	36	118	74300

Appendix 2.2: Continued

District	Year	White	Black–Caribbean	Black–African	Black–Other	Indian	Pakistani	Bangla–deshi	Chinese	Other–Asian	Other–Other	All groups
Penwith	1981	53894	18	6	50	21	1	7	54	32	79	54162
	1991	59530	24	7	64	28	1	25	76	45	100	59900
Restormel	1981	78392	21	11	53	19	2	4	79	13	110	78704
	1991	86903	28	14	68	25	2	16	78	21	144	87300
Isles of Scilly	1981	2003	0	0	1	0	0	0	0	0	0	2004
	1991	1999	0	0	1	0	0	0	0	0	0	2000
Cumbria												
Allerdale	1981	95625	8	5	32	20	14	2	57	12	66	95841
	1991	96374	12	7	43	29	18	14	88	20	95	96700
Barrow-in-Furness	1981	73172	8	8	34	36	9	5	91	21	85	73470
	1991	73296	12	12	45	44	17	13	111	36	114	73700
Carlisle	1981	100657	20	18	53	78	12	28	103	26	94	101089
	1991	101288	25	23	71	100	18	82	128	42	124	101900
Copeland	1981	72799	20	8	35	22	11	4	40	21	38	72997
	1991	71722	25	11	44	33	19	7	50	40	51	72000
Eden	1981	43297	4	5	11	3	0	5	13	4	28	43371
	1991	45884	5	7	15	4	0	12	23	8	41	46000
South Lakeland	1981	94752	15	17	36	37	14	4	47	19	82	95023
	1991	98507	23	23	49	53	21	11	67	30	116	98900
Derbyshire												
Amber Valley	1981	109971	50	14	49	129	12	3	48	18	89	110384
	1991	112101	74	21	73	249	20	6	80	40	137	112800
Bolsover	1981	71692	21	7	25	80	5	3	35	6	45	71919
	1991	70941	31	10	35	131	8	4	61	13	66	71300
Chesterfield	1981	99636	214	40	88	115	95	12	135	36	100	100472
	1991	99057	271	65	125	204	136	28	202	63	150	100300
Derby	1981	198534	2524	193	902	6441	3708	79	397	428	854	214059
	1991	203223	3320	242	1314	8810	5828	152	572	687	1253	225400
Derbyshire Dales	1981	68532	11	10	12	26	4	2	40	9	52	68698
	1991	67840	14	15	19	34	7	9	63	19	80	68100
Erewash	1981	103999	223	17	120	400	40	0	81	28	140	105048
	1991	105972	306	24	173	611	60	0	114	40	199	107500
High Peak	1981	83065	34	18	37	46	15	2	70	22	117	83426
	1991	85523	58	27	56	68	22	1	115	49	180	86100
North East Derbyshire	1981	95663	31	15	27	92	7	0	55	26	92	96009
	1991	98247	43	24	41	156	12	0	88	46	142	98800
South Derbyshire	1981	68458	58	26	31	369	34	1	32	27	71	69107
	1991	71690	90	39	47	752	69	2	56	45	110	72900
Devon					East							
East Devon	1981	107313	29	20	38	24	9	3	82	25	114	107656
	1991	117655	38	27	50	29	12	3	104	33	149	118100

District	Year	White	Black–Caribbean	Black–African	Black–Other	Indian	Pakistani	Bangla-deshi	Chinese	Other–Asian	Other–Other	All groups
Exeter	1981	100463	39	56	62	187	29	75	133	100	379	101523
	1991	104032	52	69	80	226	39	88	182	150	481	105400
Mid Devon	1981	58557	16	11	39	19	2	0	31	13	90	58779
	1991	64800	22	14	51	25	3	0	44	20	122	65100
North Devon	1981	77953	24	12	28	75	2	20	72	21	91	78298
	1991	85047	31	16	36	95	2	36	90	31	114	85500
Plymouth	1981	251952	160	159	251	196	44	56	385	169	508	253880
	1991	252226	185	141	277	224	55	113	405	201	572	254400
South Hams	1981	66041	22	8	18	15	3	3	45	23	113	66290
	1991	78046	27	12	24	20	4	6	65	39	157	78400
Teignbridge	1981	94942	32	22	48	40	14	9	61	31	125	95325
	1991	109429	44	29	66	48	18	34	93	61	177	110000
Torbay	1981	112534	29	35	83	83	27	21	123	66	209	113211
	1991	121711	45	42	111	102	30	33	161	97	267	122600
Torridge	1981	48515	13	9	12	28	2	0	28	13	50	48671
	1991	52893	17	14	15	36	2	0	37	22	65	53100
West Devon	1981	42626	18	8	14	10	4	3	25	11	43	42762
	1991	46023	22	11	18	12	4	8	30	16	57	46200
Dorset												
Bournemouth	1981	141601	96	125	125	266	45	82	274	190	581	143385
	1991	156336	127	188	166	369	57	135	374	279	770	158800
Christchurch	1981	38159	13	7	17	33	12	11	26	21	46	38345
	1991	40938	17	9	23	46	14	23	40	32	58	41200
East Dorset	1981	68885	23	21	17	55	10	8	29	32	107	69187
	1991	78666	29	27	24	78	13	27	39	51	146	79100
North Dorset	1981	48889	18	10	16	12	1	16	35	12	60	49067
	1991	53557	18	14	20	15	1	43	41	17	73	53800
Poole	1981	119473	51	28	57	160	13	64	192	91	256	120386
	1991	133838	68	39	76	198	20	110	245	158	349	135100
Purbeck	1981	40393	13	3	19	12	1	5	33	15	60	40554
	1991	43302	14	5	27	13	1	6	35	22	75	43500
West Dorset	1981	79767	22	17	29	38	15	10	46	30	130	80103
	1991	86447	27	22	38	49	19	23	62	44	168	86900
Weymouth & Poole	1981	57708	20	17	43	30	4	11	79	35	111	58057
	1991	61747	24	21	56	37	4	31	94	46	140	62200
Durham												
Chester-le-Street	1981	52934	7	8	18	46	14	7	65	19	32	53150
	1991	52845	10	10	28	71	20	17	93	47	58	53200
Darlington	1981	97340	104	49	82	397	47	103	143	68	148	98480
	1991	98402	127	57	107	486	58	177	177	112	195	99900

Appendix 2.2: *Continued*

District	Year	White	Black–Caribbean	Black–African	Black–Other	Indian	Pakistani	Bangla-deshi	Chinese	Other–Asian	Other–Other	All groups
Derwentside	1981	88259	6	18	17	105	14	11	37	11	36	88514
	1991	86677	9	19	20	122	21	22	47	18	47	87000
Durham	1981	86733	12	31	20	105	28	15	118	113	141	87317
	1991	86164	16	41	33	157	40	43	141	172	194	87000
Easington	1981	101312	13	15	29	99	35	6	68	75	52	101703
	1991	98474	14	19	39	173	57	10	91	150	73	99100
Sedgefield	1981	93292	19	16	21	51	11	20	79	45	53	93607
	1991	91222	24	22	27	58	11	6	94	66	69	91600
Teesdale	1981	24771	11	5	5	6	1	0	10	12	12	24834
	1991	24408	15	6	7	8	1	4	12	20	18	24500
Wear Valley	1981	63971	28	10	20	45	5	3	46	19	29	64177
	1991	63096	34	15	25	66	11	8	59	47	38	63400
East Sussex												
Brighton	1981	145599	185	310	242	595	154	143	578	400	1043	149248
	1991	149571	232	398	297	735	197	268	609	555	1338	154200
Eastbourne	1981	76422	70	59	71	193	30	58	187	175	290	77554
	1991	83326	85	73	92	242	37	145	245	266	388	84900
Hastings	1981	74602	112	82	133	204	19	36	118	84	355	75746
	1991	81909	139	102	174	278	28	52	130	135	452	83400
Hove	1981	85502	85	151	146	445	79	141	273	204	674	87701
	1991	86748	111	180	178	585	107	242	366	311	872	89700
Lewes	1981	78399	47	61	68	141	10	46	86	77	196	79130
	1991	87582	62	78	90	185	16	83	119	122	264	88600
Rother	1981	76121	29	33	57	75	12	29	75	90	134	76656
	1991	82370	35	38	75	96	17	58	100	141	170	83100
Wealden	1981	118799	66	38	49	97	20	35	124	77	252	119556
	1991	130637	84	51	65	118	24	89	184	119	329	131700
Essex												
Basildon	1981	149910	375	151	231	640	145	43	265	163	476	152399
	1991	159252	465	180	308	867	188	94	388	308	648	162700
Braintree	1981	111309	157	84	84	248	38	48	159	190	318	112635
	1991	118295	203	67	110	312	51	82	149	181	351	119800
Brentwood	1981	71722	78	103	85	223	32	29	108	144	206	72730
	1991	69392	92	70	108	314	43	58	149	314	259	70800
Castle Point	1981	87218	59	33	67	193	38	53	117	49	178	88004
	1991	86041	72	39	83	260	53	88	153	86	225	87100
Chelmsford	1981	138015	256	151	152	500	119	77	292	214	405	140181
	1991	151063	335	181	210	690	161	126	413	357	564	154100
Colchester	1981	135730	205	222	220	447	71	78	412	307	608	138301
	1991	142671	245	215	271	542	76	131	464	524	761	145900

District	Year	White	Black–Caribbean	Black–African	Black–Other	Indian	Pakistani	Bangla-deshi	Chinese	Other–Asian	Other–Other	All groups
Epping Forest	1981	115289	168	98	114	746	104	32	201	147	352	117250
	1991	114015	231	118	144	1223	166	42	311	278	471	117000
Harlow	1981	77419	235	89	151	395	294	57	649	152	320	79761
	1991	72924	264	96	181	389	357	91	720	206	374	75600
Maldon	1981	48206	20	17	40	51	6	23	52	18	73	48505
	1991	52460	28	20	52	64	8	60	76	32	101	52900
Rochford	1981	73543	41	40	34	149	15	14	110	38	156	74141
	1991	75011	43	48	43	203	17	31	134	63	208	75800
Southend-on-Sea	1981	155097	177	118	164	761	388	146	492	231	541	158116
	1991	158353	237	149	217	1063	510	246	640	362	724	162500
Tendring	1981	114338	48	34	68	115	6	14	122	48	171	114964
	1991	126224	71	39	86	148	7	39	180	75	230	127100
Thurrock	1981	125328	228	149	129	965	80	47	390	168	324	127807
	1991	126496	331	172	168	1153	96	89	424	259	411	129600
Uttlesford	1981	62387	31	29	38	88	25	30	51	39	110	62827
	1991	65501	38	38	47	109	30	81	69	53	135	66100
Gloucestershire												
Cheltenham	1981	117533	112	54	126	892	21	88	187	152	255	119420
	1991	106064	118	50	141	895	22	127	213	195	276	108100
Cotswold	1981	70629	25	31	109	32	2	7	67	32	133	71067
	1991	74474	32	44	157	42	3	32	89	48	178	75100
Forest of Dean	1981	73077	28	23	27	35	4	0	48	17	50	73307
	1991	75612	34	30	33	41	5	1	58	24	62	75900
Gloucester	1981	101689	2113	137	573	1605	131	62	173	166	538	107188
	1991	98607	2132	131	654	1823	180	106	208	242	617	104700
Stroud	1981	89583	87	17	49	57	9	8	55	25	118	90007
	1991	103789	116	23	69	82	12	29	74	42	164	104400
Tewkesbury	1981	44977	26	13	27	67	9	3	46	15	62	45245
	1991	70592	50	23	50	120	16	20	82	33	114	71100
Hampshire												
Basingstoke & Deane	1981	130558	466	135	300	582	71	43	178	163	424	132920
	1991	142780	561	158	396	771	94	117	267	286	569	146000
East Hampshire	1981	91090	59	39	71	86	9	34	112	81	196	91778
	1991	103098	78	52	102	116	11	74	150	158	262	104100
Eastleigh	1981	91825	60	34	75	520	28	28	189	72	167	92997
	1991	105120	88	52	105	737	32	110	285	128	242	106900
Fareham	1981	88472	57	33	61	137	8	21	165	69	147	89168
	1991	98851	79	39	74	187	10	39	203	125	192	99800
Gosport	1981	77322	61	45	72	80	14	32	177	60	166	78030
	1991	75796	74	50	85	96	17	36	181	76	190	76600

Appendix 2.2: *Continued*

District	Year	White	Black–Caribbean	Black–African	Black–Other	Indian	Pakistani	Bangla-deshi	Chinese	Other–Asian	Other–Other	All groups
Hart	1981	63144	46	29	46	131	19	28	118	103	171	63836
	1991	79887	80	43	69	189	27	51	185	128	241	80900
Havant	1981	115024	57	96	102	142	24	51	170	70	184	115920
	1991	119184	70	109	145	185	29	76	185	90	226	120300
New Forest	1981	144995	55	49	75	137	8	44	136	93	237	145828
	1991	160721	78	59	95	175	11	80	171	115	294	161800
Portsmouth	1981	187599	164	254	293	643	57	614	701	282	758	191364
	1991	183934	184	258	395	751	65	1171	779	366	896	188800
Rushmoor	1981	91631	373	98	173	360	228	33	247	185	322	93649
	1991	84496	384	104	201	402	264	41	276	262	370	86800
Southampton	1981	200270	799	295	539	3602	863	334	611	538	1110	208961
	1991	197009	884	319	628	4147	1064	556	711	677	1305	207300
Test Valley	1981	93084	98	37	85	237	17	22	164	52	161	93954
	1991	102725	115	48	114	307	22	48	211	92	218	103900
Winchester	1981	92505	34	29	37	114	24	61	102	82	196	93184
	1991	97693	40	37	48	135	31	85	139	138	252	98600
Hereford & Worcester												
Bromsgrove	1981	86369	524	67	164	323	63	5	116	85	317	88032
	1991	90896	373	46	128	246	56	2	107	96	250	92200
Hereford	1981	47266	27	42	54	114	9	8	144	46	105	47816
	1991	50538	19	35	46	97	7	14	112	46	86	51000
Leominster	1981	37337	15	9	11	10	1	0	36	8	52	37480
	1991	39881	12	7	9	8	1	0	32	6	42	40000
Malvern Hills	1981	84162	49	63	46	98	8	2	138	64	150	84779
	1991	88095	37	50	37	84	6	5	107	58	120	88600
Redditch	1981	64726	851	78	272	311	1257	56	129	100	347	68127
	1991	76084	641	62	238	277	1106	73	112	99	309	79000
South Herefordshire	1981	46212	27	13	17	36	1	2	28	14	90	46441
	1991	51895	25	12	16	31	1	2	23	17	78	52100
Worcester	1981	76123	165	40	107	193	897	298	162	136	226	78347
	1991	82667	129	30	85	149	765	230	139	123	182	84500
Wychavon	1981	91936	89	34	49	84	6	26	102	39	151	92516
	1991	101807	62	28	42	72	4	33	91	34	128	102300
Wyre Forest	1981	90200	80	50	91	233	21	313	98	81	218	91383
	1991	94824	66	39	74	167	16	205	71	74	163	95700
Hertfordshire												
Broxbourne	1981	79183	212	55	87	230	34	36	112	96	224	80270
	1991	80755	315	75	115	339	44	49	135	170	302	82300
Dacorum	1981	128784	217	89	143	748	559	33	259	163	489	131483
	1991	130353	271	116	184	984	756	49	373	267	646	134000

Geographical spread: the national picture　　95

District	Year	White	Black–Caribbean	Black–African	Black–Other	Indian	Pakistani	Bangla-deshi	Chinese	Other–Asian	Other–Other	All groups
East Hertfordshire	1981	109125	74	42	65	249	45	55	167	120	265	110208
	1991	116178	111	58	86	372	73	107	239	211	366	117800
Hertsmere	1981	86293	194	110	127	769	63	48	358	226	524	88713
	1991	85262	237	140	161	1276	104	75	481	383	681	88800
North Hertfordshire	1981	103911	1047	73	253	2443	135	186	182	226	482	108939
	1991	106722	1194	86	326	3034	171	257	234	357	619	113000
St.Albans	1981	120848	721	243	243	705	359	695	348	408	656	125225
	1991	120240	832	231	315	1032	520	1284	479	902	864	126700
Stevenage	1981	72395	403	92	219	559	156	142	225	96	356	74643
	1991	73236	441	121	277	724	198	222	327	192	462	76200
Three Rivers	1981	79832	157	86	110	1051	143	38	191	203	448	82260
	1991	75533	216	110	140	1837	232	60	238	357	576	79300
Watford	1981	68178	802	202	280	1061	2040	78	222	325	624	73814
	1991	67972	1008	204	362	1416	2769	134	287	535	814	75500
Welwyn Hatfield	1981	92384	207	142	144	556	113	27	282	159	351	94364
	1991	92165	267	193	187	814	162	51	389	288	481	95000
Humberside												
Boothferry	1981	60400	17	21	36	76	3	0	40	18	57	60669
	1991	64405	19	21	36	83	5	0	45	24	62	64700
Cleethorpes	1981	68045	44	28	39	142	4	16	112	50	110	68590
	1991	69234	36	23	37	161	5	53	97	51	103	69800
East Yorkshire	1981	74888	21	19	27	22	5	14	76	10	71	75155
	1991	84993	23	21	30	23	6	34	76	15	78	85300
East Yorks, Borough of Beverley	1981	106083	31	57	61	282	47	13	119	72	224	106990
	1991	112284	30	62	60	267	53	9	119	90	225	113200
Glanford	1981	66450	20	13	22	118	17	7	115	35	82	66880
	1991	71732	21	12	21	127	19	19	124	43	84	72200
Great Grimsby	1981	91596	47	128	87	220	66	36	158	72	204	92615
	1991	90983	40	91	77	195	83	29	121	94	186	91900
Holderness	1981	46285	16	12	17	23	1	0	52	10	60	46475
	1991	51196	15	16	17	23	1	0	57	13	62	51400
Kingston Upon Hull	1981	270189	158	472	451	374	273	216	597	318	761	273808
	1991	263134	141	377	397	333	250	251	568	336	715	266500
Scunthorpe	1981	64213	52	137	101	689	205	713	137	65	157	66468
	1991	60423	40	109	81	580	233	636	103	62	132	62400
Isle of Wight												
Medina	1981	67648	44	19	40	64	8	41	56	31	99	68051
	1991	71517	38	26	49	91	8	37	65	44	124	72000
South Wight	1981	50099	16	5	38	13	5	0	30	19	99	50324
	1991	54108	19	7	45	17	5	0	44	26	129	54400

Appendix 2.2: *Continued*

District	Year	White	Black–Caribbean	Black–African	Black–Other	Indian	Pakistani	Bangla–deshi	Chinese	Other–Asian	Other–Other	All groups
Kent												
Ashford	1981	85978	143	82	95	209	39	30	104	131	193	87004
	1991	92160	175	109	121	246	49	45	144	207	244	93500
Canterbury	1981	120776	92	110	109	278	29	71	231	210	421	122327
	1991	128271	122	130	141	359	36	117	270	324	530	130300
Dartford	1981	81585	158	203	127	1267	41	52	191	258	343	84224
	1991	77820	166	128	152	1492	50	82	248	447	414	81000
Dover	1981	103034	37	44	76	150	13	29	94	62	178	103718
	1991	104531	43	43	90	190	13	66	111	96	217	105400
Gillingham	1981	93576	287	97	165	1379	364	36	157	151	413	96623
	1991	92620	392	107	211	1622	450	58	187	230	524	96400
Gravesham	1981	87717	225	71	126	4999	115	57	118	242	262	93932
	1991	85672	279	76	158	6373	160	93	139	328	323	93600
Maidstone	1981	129800	89	112	110	450	115	75	195	167	327	131440
	1991	135221	124	117	148	595	141	135	258	320	442	137500
Rochester upon Medway	1981	138637	274	139	232	2960	307	177	251	211	435	143623
	1991	140548	407	179	299	3594	390	340	330	344	569	147000
Sevenoaks	1981	107152	70	35	78	277	17	27	150	75	239	108119
	1991	108204	85	43	98	342	22	73	201	120	311	109500
Shepway	1981	85457	62	46	71	166	27	39	117	89	170	86243
	1991	92541	82	56	85	226	26	68	157	135	223	93600
Swale	1981	109510	44	55	85	248	15	36	96	40	190	110318
	1991	115809	44	68	105	322	19	76	133	79	244	116900
Thanet	1981	120874	73	74	118	210	34	15	229	104	269	122000
	1991	125461	92	95	146	276	35	24	288	156	328	126900
Tonbridge & Malden	1981	97574	33	62	57	192	39	34	107	78	205	98381
	1991	101392	42	81	75	241	48	61	147	143	271	102500
Tunbridge Wells	1981	98221	42	67	52	181	24	59	118	63	248	99075
	1991	100791	59	82	68	233	28	136	163	101	339	102000
Lancashire												
Blackburn	1981	121847	73	145	226	7485	5468	158	177	358	678	136614
	1991	116142	100	178	328	10824	8299	316	237	516	960	137900
Blackpool	1981	149523	56	31	88	110	45	35	167	46	158	150260
	1991	148591	81	44	134	164	91	106	263	88	239	149800
Burnley	1981	87755	30	53	71	225	1996	512	75	80	139	90936
	1991	86988	45	66	105	302	3260	991	105	137	202	92200
Chorley	1981	93391	93	16	78	147	110	4	54	26	116	94035
	1991	96110	130	24	122	220	147	11	97	55	185	97100
Fylde	1981	69255	21	13	23	74	26	5	38	21	81	69557
	1991	71753	34	23	36	132	50	27	61	50	135	72300

District	Year	White	Black–Caribbean	Black–African	Black–Other	Indian	Pakistani	Bangla–deshi	Chinese	Other–Asian	Other–Other	All groups
Hyndburn	1981	75807	21	23	41	118	2476	45	62	98	113	78804
	1991	74258	30	33	62	193	3900	105	95	159	165	79000
Lancaster	1981	124885	52	44	51	441	46	22	143	70	195	125949
	1991	128539	72	78	80	602	65	26	205	114	318	130100
Pendle	1981	78591	23	28	52	137	5199	6	52	64	152	84304
	1991	76845	32	38	76	182	8215	10	84	96	223	85800
Preston	1981	113931	720	94	350	5931	1177	81	119	246	433	123081
	1991	117901	960	125	546	8827	1852	189	205	424	671	131700
Ribble Valley	1981	55135	9	7	7	86	130	16	23	26	50	55488
	1991	51564	12	11	10	155	163	18	42	53	73	52100
Rossendale	1981	64055	26	13	26	63	393	370	51	28	102	65127
	1991	64490	42	21	41	96	654	560	85	54	158	66200
South Ribble	1981	95720	51	15	63	158	63	4	71	35	112	96293
	1991	101978	82	23	101	288	111	16	140	78	182	103000
West Lancashire	1981	107609	43	26	76	169	6	9	82	33	150	108203
	1991	108561	67	36	116	212	4	9	115	55	224	109400
Wyre	1981	99890	19	20	35	40	12	5	61	25	69	100176
	1991	102605	33	33	56	76	21	23	95	47	112	103100
Leicestershire												
Blaby	1981	76162	122	27	92	998	14	1	105	87	138	77746
	1991	80467	239	42	142	1896	24	2	196	171	221	83400
Charnwood	1981	134235	129	126	125	3716	53	414	291	249	453	139793
	1991	138383	189	172	187	6086	86	891	442	433	731	147600
Harborough	1981	61803	43	13	24	188	6	8	43	14	68	62209
	1991	67526	62	21	37	332	10	8	68	27	108	68200
Hinckley & Bosworth	1981	88483	45	21	41	252	33	13	84	25	105	89101
	1991	96039	70	34	64	526	61	26	166	48	168	97200
Leicester	1981	207109	3382	568	1350	44132	1827	591	495	1878	2266	263598
	1991	202332	4394	782	1889	64669	2827	1131	716	2726	3234	284700
Melton	1981	43712	24	4	23	168	4	1	13	8	44	44001
	1991	45069	36	6	36	241	6	5	22	13	65	45500
North West Leicestershire	1981	79734	34	21	37	171	2	8	54	18	75	80155
	1991	80734	52	35	54	274	3	8	90	34	115	81400
Oadby & Wigston	1981	50295	167	23	64	1731	106	19	85	127	196	52813
	1991	48403	241	34	91	3439	189	30	141	241	290	53100
Rutland	1981	33240	26	8	15	12	2	0	29	14	57	33403
	1991	32963	34	11	22	17	2	0	38	27	86	33200
Lincolnshire												
Boston	1981	52884	17	24	42	58	10	0	50	13	44	53142
	1991	53223	24	33	61	75	23	0	71	26	65	53600

Appendix 2.2: *Continued*

District	Year	White	Black–Caribbean	Black–African	Black–Other	Indian	Pakistani	Bangla-deshi	Chinese	Other–Asian	Other–Other	All groups
East Lindsey	1981	106478	48	15	65	40	15	9	54	30	95	106851
	1991	117378	71	23	103	71	22	21	86	59	166	118000
Lincoln	1981	76650	69	26	87	139	24	33	128	44	115	77315
	1991	83740	99	39	135	221	36	56	211	83	180	84800
North Kesteven	1981	80734	36	14	48	97	7	3	92	33	102	81165
	1991	79511	50	18	68	136	9	9	105	55	137	80100
South Holland	1981	62880	22	9	24	33	9	9	58	15	47	63098
	1991	67427	39	15	42	57	2	15	97	29	77	67800
South Kesteven	1981	99125	43	25	55	150	3	19	173	25	123	99748
	1991	109074	76	44	88	237	11	41	259	59	201	110100
West Lindsey	1981	78413	56	12	52	65	21	5	42	24	92	78764
	1991	76221	73	16	71	90	3	4	53	42	126	76700
Norfolk												
Breckland	1981	96082	85	41	190	61	40	9	76	46	200	96831
	1991	107295	110	58	271	71	56	21	81	72	265	108300
Broadland	1981	97616	24	36	47	152	11	4	128	49	182	98249
	1991	106360	28	45	60	182	13	8	172	78	253	107200
Great Yarmouth	1981	80986	25	36	59	92	35	6	72	69	143	81522
	1991	88133	33	55	72	122	45	6	117	128	189	88900
King's Lynn & West Norfolk	1981	122538	51	38	146	141	22	23	151	65	205	123381
	1991	130681	61	42	175	158	43	22	170	103	246	131700
North Norfolk	1981	83127	19	27	53	34	3	1	49	31	110	83453
	1991	91583	21	35	66	41	4	7	60	46	135	92000
Norwich	1981	124607	73	95	217	252	53	75	241	118	461	126192
	1991	125238	90	114	251	311	74	131	264	168	561	127200
South Norfolk	1981	95003	25	21	44	56	9	8	47	46	117	95375
	1991	103564	37	27	56	71	13	28	65	77	160	104100
Northamptonshire												
Corby	1981	52737	60	18	43	165	3	7	44	15	79	53171
	1991	52954	86	27	64	243	7	14	61	25	118	53600
Daventry	1981	58272	52	12	42	102	35	0	54	32	62	58665
	1991	62400	74	17	65	161	36	0	91	57	98	63000
East Northamptonshire	1981	62720	51	12	61	112	15	30	36	24	61	63123
	1991	67926	83	22	94	213	22	25	67	51	96	68600
Kettering	1981	70602	112	41	67	636	13	14	244	86	143	71958
	1991	75018	165	66	104	953	22	29	267	153	223	77000
Northampton	1981	151817	1897	244	654	1544	327	622	409	303	608	158425
	1991	173457	2806	397	1065	2704	536	1254	720	625	1035	184600
South Northamptonshire	1981	64575	44	52	137	87	3	9	39	34	119	65101
	1991	70201	73	93	242	137	4	15	64	65	206	71100

Appendix 2.2: *Continued*

District	Year	White	Black–Caribbean	Black–African	Black–Other	Indian	Pakistani	Bangla-deshi	Chinese	Other–Asian	Other–Other	All groups
Wellingborough	1981	60531	949	65	281	1785	85	65	59	97	215	64130
	1991	63623	1267	86	418	2378	124	130	98	153	323	68600
Northumberland												
Alnwick	1981	28903	3	1	5	10	3	0	6	3	13	28948
	1991	30241	4	1	7	13	3	0	6	7	17	30300
Berwick-upon-Tweed	1981	26203	2	3	5	3	0	2	8	2	17	26244
	1991	26730	2	7	6	6	0	7	11	3	27	26800
Blyth Valley	1981	77569	8	12	10	55	40	12	73	35	63	77876
	1991	79831	11	16	16	78	53	53	101	53	87	80300
Castle Morpeth	1981	49647	3	6	17	99	19	17	49	36	33	49925
	1991	49756	4	6	22	171	29	26	71	66	49	50200
Tynedale	1981	54063	4	5	11	22	2	1	23	14	35	54181
	1991	57212	6	6	16	32	2	5	38	29	53	57400
Wansbeck	1981	62400	6	0	22	72	39	17	55	13	34	62658
	1991	61268	8	0	28	98	50	12	69	21	45	61600
North Yorkshire												
Craven	1981	47602	17	11	25	25	196	12	33	8	64	47994
	1991	50296	22	11	24	30	204	7	34	11	61	50700
Hambleton	1981	74746	15	19	27	47	23	6	80	17	81	75060
	1991	79172	14	20	27	48	28	4	75	26	86	79500
Harrogate	1981	139304	91	68	145	178	54	58	248	104	349	140597
	1991	144073	86	64	161	158	66	61	243	134	354	145400
Richmondshire	1981	43178	45	5	32	51	3	0	56	40	81	43490
	1991	45789	35	3	30	47	2	1	57	52	83	46100
Ryedale	1981	85087	34	17	31	91	12	9	104	53	127	85567
	1991	90938	31	16	30	77	12	14	103	58	120	91400
Scarborough	1981	101664	41	29	46	91	33	15	111	69	164	102263
	1991	108591	46	28	44	83	41	16	107	79	164	109200
Selby	1981	79380	18	51	18	46	7	0	84	48	109	79762
	1991	91998	20	49	18	46	7	6	89	57	109	92400
York	1981	100983	72	46	78	196	57	74	205	89	317	102118
	1991	103255	65	47	74	174	49	112	204	111	309	104400
Nottinghamshire												
Ashfield	1981	107537	78	22	58	124	20	5	91	15	71	108022
	1991	108968	104	32	83	197	35	10	134	30	106	109700
Bassetlaw	1981	103566	133	26	54	115	14	16	80	19	110	104133
	1991	104481	150	36	75	177	23	25	124	50	161	105300
Broxtowe	1981	103969	167	60	99	524	127	5	169	66	213	105398
	1991	106266	266	100	146	954	258	18	312	138	342	108800
Gedling	1981	110682	593	57	178	467	157	2	175	48	242	112600
	1991	108450	776	74	249	706	236	5	264	94	346	111200

Appendix 2.2: *Continued*

District	Year	White	Black–Caribbean	Black–African	Black–Other	Indian	Pakistani	Bangla-deshi	Chinese	Other–Asian	Other–Other	All groups
Mansfield	1981	100234	161	24	94	263	24	52	82	46	96	101077
	1991	100378	217	32	133	407	34	59	126	78	137	101600
Newark & Sherwood	1981	97749	111	21	66	112	5	4	88	25	89	98269
	1991	102899	169	35	98	178	8	9	124	47	132	103700
Nottingham	1981	251841	7037	494	2365	3673	4761	194	522	443	1944	273275
	1991	250155	9244	669	3336	5170	7491	327	919	752	2836	280900
Rushclife	1981	92285	148	30	110	628	132	14	102	60	220	93728
	1991	96644	248	48	166	1026	232	21	168	104	344	99000
Oxfordshire												
Cherwell	1981	105510	257	195	822	472	422	20	222	235	627	108782
	1991	120476	360	248	1050	633	755	55	296	318	807	125000
Oxford	1981	131958	2312	572	824	1703	2265	465	832	756	1428	143116
	1991	118337	2114	639	872	1834	2515	626	929	885	1549	130300
South Oxfordshire	1981	102356	115	24	80	172	22	31	108	91	276	103275
	1991	119410	140	37	110	237	24	47	147	163	385	120700
Vale of White Horse	1981	102502	79	43	102	222	70	16	225	104	277	103638
	1991	111333	105	63	139	281	90	43	315	162	369	112900
West Oxfordshire	1981	81109	83	39	101	90	2	12	70	94	238	81839
	1991	91102	108	48	108	128	5	33	84	106	278	92000
Shropshire												
Bridgnorth	1981	49850	37	7	29	98	12	31	96	34	68	50263
	1991	50390	34	6	23	72	11	19	64	29	51	50700
North Shropshire	1981	50641	42	7	37	54	5	6	58	17	58	50924
	1991	53365	31	5	30	48	7	2	47	17	47	53600
Oswestry	1981	31236	9	20	20	30	0	37	20	10	55	31437
	1991	34309	7	18	17	28	0	46	16	8	50	34500
Shrewsbury & Altcham	1981	86570	56	40	51	167	21	42	204	58	215	87423
	1991	91595	45	30	40	125	16	50	154	71	175	92300
South Shropshire	1981	33818	10	16	25	35	9	7	38	6	54	34019
	1991	38408	9	15	23	35	12	6	36	7	48	38600
The Wrekin	1981	120428	772	75	408	2193	1047	73	271	365	504	126135
	1991	136910	594	65	344	1837	897	67	272	471	441	141900
Somerset												
Mendip	1981	89565	29	27	64	37	3	10	51	25	110	89919
	1991	97329	39	34	80	46	3	18	69	38	144	97800
Sedgemoor	1981	89651	23	13	53	45	18	9	54	26	124	90017
	1991	98809	32	18	68	59	25	19	72	39	159	99300
South Somerset	1981	132707	51	45	72	52	13	18	94	39	180	133270
	1991	142656	66	52	94	63	19	26	131	62	230	143400

Appendix 2.2: *Continued*

District	Year	White	Black-Caribbean	Black-African	Black-Other	Indian	Pakistani	Bangla-deshi	Chinese	Other-Asian	Other-Other	All groups
Taunton Deane	1981	87956	26	23	48	70	12	23	125	39	164	88486
	1991	95110	33	28	62	78	16	42	165	58	208	95800
West Somerset	1981	29434	7	3	8	9	0	5	22	13	39	29541
	1991	31951	9	3	10	12	0	9	34	22	51	32100
Staffordshire												
Cannock Chase	1981	83955	95	28	77	306	48	47	136	38	123	84852
	1991	89234	75	23	60	291	29	41	110	39	98	90000
East Staffordshire	1981	91673	763	47	279	380	3464	33	165	67	311	97182
	1991	94231	509	37	212	292	2607	49	147	79	238	98400
Lichfield	1981	87575	120	20	89	351	48	87	115	68	209	88681
	1991	92256	98	15	70	310	36	69	110	64	173	93200
Newcastle-under-Lyme	1981	118736	158	77	134	392	75	28	181	92	272	120144
	1991	120588	121	64	102	310	68	35	176	108	227	121800
South Staffordshire	1981	95761	242	35	80	564	23	7	109	103	157	97079
	1991	105135	183	28	65	546	11	9	97	96	130	106300
Stafford	1981	114361	604	120	255	865	92	47	274	125	513	117255
	1991	117825	386	76	192	593	60	43	170	117	338	119800
Staffordshire Moorlands	1981	94786	57	18	53	126	27	7	55	24	120	95273
	1991	95721	42	14	39	82	21	14	49	26	92	96100
Stoke-on-Trent	1981	243216	1026	201	641	1196	5007	343	441	294	818	253183
	1991	245046	671	145	480	898	4316	309	349	256	630	253100
Tamworth	1981	63922	269	61	130	327	27	16	109	51	137	65049
	1991	70144	187	45	104	259	17	6	88	42	108	71000
Suffolk												
Babergh	1981	73611	59	17	91	72	5	13	57	36	148	74110
	1991	79883	71	18	107	85	6	27	69	55	179	80500
Forest Heath	1981	49540	150	351	1388	57	4	15	79	222	643	52449
	1991	56237	160	402	1598	67	6	14	103	259	754	59600
Ipswich	1981	114410	1739	99	1148	448	66	440	295	149	640	119435
	1991	113367	1798	99	1209	485	82	616	311	170	663	118800
Mid Suffolk	1981	70448	36	23	52	50	6	3	52	28	120	70818
	1991	78747	47	25	59	61	7	13	67	30	143	79200
St.Edmundsbury	1981	86318	91	46	171	128	18	17	96	78	230	87192
	1991	91689	107	49	187	143	20	44	110	93	259	92700
Suffolk Coastal	1981	95371	97	176	692	110	9	29	134	164	412	97194
	1991	112082	123	238	926	142	12	76	215	234	552	114600
Waveney	1981	99604	45	35	67	54	14	9	99	90	147	100163
	1991	107616	49	41	83	66	19	24	118	107	178	108300
Surrey												
Elmbridge	1981	110062	101	114	95	690	107	116	367	542	547	112740
	1991	110438	138	172	129	1010	149	182	571	925	785	114500

Appendix 2.2: *Continued*

District	Year	White	Black–Caribbean	Black–African	Black–Other	Indian	Pakistani	Bangla–deshi	Chinese	Other–Asian	Other–Other	All groups
Epsom & Ewell	1981	66470	192	294	121	535	109	83	289	703	390	69186
	1991	64175	159	239	147	879	161	123	365	1154	498	67900
Guildford	1981	123905	95	65	73	397	83	35	263	209	380	125503
	1991	124276	113	90	93	527	109	59	370	341	523	126500
Mole Valley	1981	77280	22	35	41	153	17	49	109	75	171	77952
	1991	78599	30	42	55	209	24	89	181	134	238	79600
Reigate & Banstead	1981	115036	131	117	106	505	371	73	259	297	468	117362
	1991	115503	154	135	140	712	431	152	359	499	613	118700
Runnymede	1981	71404	53	48	69	340	48	49	160	154	262	72586
	1991	72918	64	53	96	501	72	107	220	301	368	74700
Spelthorne	1981	90764	107	63	78	983	167	65	195	215	355	92993
	1991	88101	138	71	102	1397	221	66	272	351	481	91200
Surrey Heath	1981	73628	69	63	73	355	166	39	188	166	303	75048
	1991	77954	92	85	102	518	218	69	241	294	429	80000
Tandridge	1981	75344	63	51	76	256	8	53	132	135	251	78370
	1991	75944	80	53	96	359	14	58	175	207	315	77300
Waverley	1981	111733	51	54	59	192	40	46	182	130	258	112745
	1991	114746	59	72	77	239	48	104	236	187	332	116100
Woking	1981	78722	85	121	95	349	1561	87	206	287	368	81880
	1991	82289	119	155	133	478	2420	173	329	480	524	87100
Warwickshire												
North Warwickshire	1981	59187	92	18	48	193	28	1	46	21	100	59733
	1991	60824	76	15	37	184	22	2	38	24	79	61300
Nuneaton & Bedworth	1981	108815	288	76	190	4290	251	16	192	196	332	114647
	1991	113530	217	60	147	3475	203	7	141	161	259	118200
Rugby	1981	82317	1292	87	378	3128	437	20	213	155	499	88526
	1991	81138	852	63	273	2205	302	12	164	129	361	85500
Stratford-on-Avon	1981	99356	81	38	79	155	31	11	176	87	231	100244
	1991	105182	63	30	62	125	28	10	138	75	187	105900
Warwick	1981	107495	566	98	257	6934	170	38	299	293	579	116728
	1991	111492	399	63	204	5003	130	20	262	264	463	118300
West Sussex												
Adur	1981	58178	25	37	35	122	5	20	79	37	161	58700
	1991	58208	30	41	42	153	5	57	104	58	202	58900
Arun	1981	118036	50	82	51	136	20	51	139	68	213	118845
	1991	130152	63	105	69	178	22	124	195	109	283	131300
Chichester	1981	98331	37	65	45	61	20	18	166	119	228	99090
	1991	101527	54	73	57	71	26	48	180	120	244	102400
Crawley	1981	85621	173	120	150	2408	1249	47	166	319	512	90767
	1991	81560	220	150	184	3349	1755	75	242	513	652	88700

Geographical spread: the national picture   103

Appendix 2.2: *Continued*

District	Year	White	Black–Caribbean	Black–African	Black–Other	Indian	Pakistani	Bangla-deshi	Chinese	Other–Asian	Other–Other	All groups
Horsham	1981	96548	44	39	44	159	40	26	110	75	203	97289
	1991	109203	66	57	65	199	45	65	176	131	294	110300
Mid Sussex	1981	109117	55	58	69	272	35	80	137	139	326	110287
	1991	120894	70	69	95	366	40	161	202	253	451	122600
Worthing	1981	91506	46	59	58	191	75	78	184	144	267	92609
	1991	96598	57	82	74	223	94	184	241	210	338	98100
Wiltshire												
Kennet	1981	65296	62	11	80	51	9	0	64	54	126	65754
	1991	69124	62	13	105	64	14	0	80	78	160	69700
North Wiltshire	1981	103939	201	27	119	200	6	26	143	65	214	104940
	1991	112511	229	36	152	244	7	50	190	101	280	113800
Salisbury	1981	101965	97	25	57	97	20	38	134	66	184	102683
	1991	105694	107	32	71	120	23	73	155	94	231	106600
Thamesdown	1981	147209	589	106	311	1368	296	120	272	284	670	151225
	1991	167449	777	142	422	1715	405	211	438	447	895	172900
West Wiltshire	1981	99120	408	46	133	101	3	22	78	44	259	100215
	1991	107439	438	58	171	121	4	58	101	68	341	108800
Clwyd												
Alyn & Deeside	1981	71917	24	15	29	56	7	14	105	33	71	72271
	1991	73858	28	19	36	66	11	45	97	49	90	74300
Colwyn	1981	48852	19	9	20	35	15	11	74	36	70	49141
	1991	55995	24	13	27	41	20	18	98	65	99	56400
Delyn	1981	66360	22	9	18	30	13	0	44	21	63	66581
	1991	68116	25	8	22	38	20	4	52	34	81	68400
Glyndwr	1981	40034	9	2	15	13	1	10	19	9	40	40151
	1991	42137	12	2	19	17	1	13	29	19	52	42300
Rhuddlan	1981	52116	20	13	30	70	42	26	44	13	69	52442
	1991	54890	25	16	35	84	68	28	50	22	81	55300
Wrexham Maelor	1981	112619	26	37	50	125	57	46	117	122	95	113294
	1991	115923	32	42	60	145	80	69	121	204	124	116800
Dyfed												
Carmarthen	1981	51858	14	8	19	38	10	5	25	16	68	52059
	1991	55772	24	11	29	50	23	14	35	41	102	56100
Ceredigion	1981	60708	23	38	19	51	25	23	109	79	152	61228
	1991	65847	23	49	28	67	48	58	149	116	215	66600
Dinefwr	1981	37326	7	8	9	16	2	0	22	11	45	37446
	1991	38812	11	10	13	28	3	3	37	23	60	39000
Llanelli	1981	75605	15	4	27	66	33	7	62	11	57	75888
	1991	74998	21	5	32	89	59	22	79	25	71	75400

Appendix 2.2: *Continued*

District	Year	White	Black–Caribbean	Black–African	Black–Other	Indian	Pakistani	Bangla–deshi	Chinese	Other–Asian	Other–Other	All groups
Preseli Pembrokeshire	1981	68926	14	9	55	57	11	15	53	38	90	69268
	1991	70240	15	11	67	69	19	35	61	68	116	70700
South Pembrokeshire	1981	38015	13	2	14	20	6	7	28	16	24	38146
	1991	42109	17	2	19	30	5	24	42	22	31	42300
Gwent												
Blaenau Gwent	1981	79092	10	9	29	89	24	3	70	17	49	79391
	1991	76499	13	14	33	127	39	4	84	26	61	76900
Islwyn	1981	67382	24	13	26	83	37	5	113	18	59	67760
	1991	66443	28	17	29	109	60	14	115	21	65	66900
Monmouth	1981	73164	22	15	51	103	10	3	67	30	100	73566
	1991	75983	27	18	63	130	10	21	86	43	120	76500
Newport	1981	126341	447	129	250	317	1293	323	212	178	587	130078
	1991	132070	465	161	297	403	1645	577	262	277	743	136900
Torfaen	1981	90226	43	22	47	94	24	35	118	40	125	90774
	1991	90757	53	26	54	110	33	42	130	48	146	91400
Gwynedd												
Aberconwy	1981	51061	17	12	20	37	9	13	71	9	96	51346
	1991	53410	24	15	26	46	12	22	100	18	126	53800
Arfon	1981	54030	5	53	38	67	60	44	111	51	150	54608
	1991	55000	6	82	49	81	115	59	126	71	211	55800
Dwyfor	1981	25876	4	5	7	8	0	1	11	2	22	25935
	1991	27123	7	5	11	8	0	4	13	5	24	27200
Meirionnydd	1981	31316	3	5	6	13	2	0	31	8	52	31436
	1991	32826	4	8	8	21	3	0	49	14	66	33000
Ynys Mon-Isle of Anglesey	1981	67791	21	15	25	35	16	3	78	24	67	68074
	1991	69043	26	17	29	39	30	9	91	34	82	69400
Mid Glamorgan												
Cynon Valley	1981	67531	15	7	17	76	62	13	67	20	57	67866
	1991	65342	17	8	20	95	106	28	85	32	68	65800
Merthyr Tydfil	1981	59887	13	7	14	137	38	11	67	17	58	60249
	1991	59451	16	7	17	158	57	15	85	27	66	59900
Ogwr	1981	129546	48	33	68	179	50	37	149	152	136	130397
	1991	132327	58	38	89	225	74	66	179	277	168	133500
Rhondda	1981	81831	16	13	37	91	36	19	89	11	44	82187
	1991	78937	20	14	43	125	61	24	115	13	49	79400
Rhymney Valley	1981	104840	39	28	67	130	34	27	125	29	167	105485
	1991	103867	43	32	74	159	40	26	139	35	185	104600
Taff-Ely	1981	93935	34	34	46	164	38	9	169	78	148	94656
	1991	97555	43	39	55	226	73	20	250	153	187	98600

District	Year	White	Black-Caribbean	Black-African	Black-Other	Indian	Pakistani	Bangla-deshi	Chinese	Other-Asian	Other-Other	All groups
Powys												
Brecknock	1981	40863	17	1	30	13	0	3	28	27	61	41043
	1991	41282	20	1	36	18	0	4	34	34	70	41500
Montgomeryshire	1981	48254	15	3	40	24	10	13	23	13	59	48453
	1991	52912	20	5	58	31	15	18	35	22	84	53200
Radnor	1981	21259	6	1	17	5	0	1	12	6	20	21326
	1991	23799	9	1	24	8	0	2	15	10	31	23900
South Glamorgan												
Cardiff	1981	265016	1776	1475	1470	2313	2086	1026	916	777	2270	279124
	1991	275279	1952	1801	1747	2889	2879	1762	1163	1205	2924	293600
Vale of Glamorgan	1981	107875	113	50	192	187	103	24	147	91	324	109106
	1991	113410	141	63	237	244	156	33	180	133	401	115000
West Glamorgan												
Lliw Valley	1981	59398	11	9	32	53	18	10	49	12	70	59663
	1991	63326	17	13	42	79	32	8	73	19	92	63700
Neath	1981	67240	10	4	24	78	18	37	85	17	55	67567
	1991	65660	12	4	28	97	19	72	112	26	69	66100
Port Talbot	1981	54479	117	6	53	41	20	36	39	4	46	54840
	1991	50888	117	6	56	41	27	68	45	4	49	51300
Swansea	1981	187826	67	133	110	337	131	384	421	317	629	190355
	1991	186594	77	132	133	414	178	815	483	425	749	190000
Borders												
Berwickshire	1981	18351	1	0	1	0	1	0	3	1	5	18365
	1991	19065	3	0	3	0	4	0	9	2	13	19100
Ettrick & Lauderdale	1981	33329	0	6	9	7	2	0	13	7	12	33385
	1991	34279	0	12	19	14	4	0	32	15	26	34400
Roxburgh	1981	35360	1	1	9	10	3	0	11	1	8	35405
	1991	35305	3	3	18	22	7	0	22	3	17	35400
Tweeddale	1981	14223	0	1	4	0	3	0	2	4	5	14242
	1991	15248	0	2	8	0	15	0	4	11	10	15300
Central												
Clackmannan	1981	47992	0	1	7	11	69	2	27	16	23	48147
	1991	48146	1	2	14	21	163	5	58	39	51	48500
Falkirk	1981	144489	8	20	27	68	180	2	71	17	68	144950
	1991	142355	14	33	52	105	429	2	146	35	129	143300
Stirling	1981	79914	4	6	19	47	49	3	48	30	56	80176
	1991	80840	9	12	42	95	119	13	84	66	121	81400
Dumfries & Galloway												
Annandale & Eskdale	1981	35660	1	1	3	11	5	0	13	3	8	35705
	1991	37080	3	2	7	25	21	0	35	9	19	37200

District	Year	White	Black–Caribbean	Black–African	Black–Other	Indian	Pakistani	Bangla-deshi	Chinese	Other–Asian	Other–Other	All groups
Nithsdale	1981	56578	1	4	6	20	29	1	40	6	24	56709
	1991	56894	2	12	14	40	61	11	99	16	52	57200
Stewarty	1981	22854	1	0	2	0	0	0	9	1	7	22875
	1991	23553	3	0	5	1	0	0	20	3	15	23600
Wigtown	1981	30279	1	0	4	4	1	0	7	2	5	30304
	1991	29951	2	1	7	9	3	0	13	4	9	30000
Fife												
Dunfermline	1981	126074	5	15	27	46	100	7	101	18	60	126454
	1991	127654	10	34	57	97	265	26	189	43	124	128500
Kirkcaldy	1981	148721	9	20	30	88	182	11	115	28	72	149275
	1991	147129	20	41	61	174	518	24	222	65	147	148400
North East Fife	1981	65291	1	22	15	23	8	3	37	28	56	65484
	1991	69551	2	49	34	47	24	4	82	77	130	70000
Grampian												
Aberdeen City	1981	210343	24	185	54	137	56	70	319	191	288	211667
	1991	211130	59	324	129	311	160	178	709	503	696	214200
Banff & Buchan	1981	82713	5	3	9	8	4	3	44	11	31	82832
	1991	85513	11	7	22	20	12	14	99	29	72	85800
Gordon	1981	63594	3	4	10	23	4	3	24	22	46	63732
	1991	76847	8	9	27	53	11	9	63	62	110	77200
Kincardine & Deeside	1981	42181	3	16	19	12	1	0	14	21	63	42330
	1991	53446	7	34	42	27	3	0	38	50	153	53800
Moray	1981	83284	10	7	14	11	26	8	60	7	42	83468
	1991	83728	17	16	27	22	58	20	112	18	83	84100
Highland												
Badenoch & Strathspey	1981	9808	2	1	2	0	0	0	5	2	4	9825
	1991	10960	5	2	6	0	0	0	13	4	10	11000
Caithness	1981	27533	3	7	19	6	13	0	9	11	23	27625
	1991	26501	3	16	48	12	26	2	13	30	50	26700
Inverness	1981	56858	4	7	15	19	12	4	55	22	55	57049
	1991	62127	8	15	35	48	31	17	131	55	132	62600
Lochaber	1981	19526	3	0	6	3	2	0	3	0	10	19554
	1991	19237	6	0	11	5	5	5	7	1	22	19300
Nairn	1981	9901	0	2	0	0	2	5	7	1	4	9922
	1991	10549	0	4	0	0	4	18	12	4	8	10600
Ross & Cromarty	1981	46808	7	7	10	7	13	0	16	8	27	46903
	1991	49003	13	14	21	12	28	7	30	15	57	49200
Skye & Lochalsh	1981	10615	2	0	1	1	0	0	2	1	8	10630
	1991	11760	5	0	2	2	0	0	6	2	22	11800
Sutherland	1981	13327	1	1	3	1	3	0	1	2	3	13341
	1991	13166	1	2	8	2	5	1	1	4	9	13200

Appendix 2.2: *Continued*

District	Year	White	Black–Caribbean	Black–African	Black–Other	Indian	Pakistani	Bangla-deshi	Chinese	Other–Asian	Other–Other	All groups
Lothian												
East Lothian	1981	80614	5	9	12	24	18	0	29	16	49	80777
	1991	85025	9	23	27	53	54	0	68	34	106	85400
Edinburgh City	1981	438104	88	276	205	598	1152	126	873	370	837	442629
	1991	429120	184	553	418	1232	2820	351	1995	919	1809	439400
Midlothian	1981	83135	7	15	21	34	57	1	23	4	47	83344
	1991	79683	15	21	40	58	141	2	44	7	88	80100
West Lothian	1981	138458	12	32	36	46	201	1	92	81	112	139072
	1991	145211	27	68	76	88	471	1	190	213	255	146600
Strathclyde												
Argyll & Bute	1981	64489	6	33	114	31	2	3	35	35	84	64831
	1991	64526	11	64	217	59	5	12	73	67	165	65200
Bearsden & Milngavie	1981	38263	6	16	20	348	131	8	73	29	61	38955
	1991	39774	11	20	35	693	241	16	149	56	103	41100
Clydebank	1981	52830	5	6	8	26	35	0	31	7	27	52975
	1991	46214	8	7	10	30	44	0	41	9	35	46400
Cumbernauld & Kilsyth	1981	61805	8	37	12	63	108	0	49	83	93	62257
	1991	62807	11	43	20	100	218	0	93	154	154	63600
Cumnock & Doon Valley	1981	44849	2	4	2	18	19	0	14	1	10	44919
	1991	42823	4	8	4	41	58	0	34	4	24	43000
Cunninghame	1981	136962	7	12	20	106	32	4	71	16	40	137271
	1991	138612	15	23	40	264	70	9	152	39	76	139300
Dumbarton	1981	78590	6	5	16	34	62	10	70	19	50	78861
	1991	78143	12	10	33	65	131	15	148	39	105	78700
East Kilbride	1981	83068	3	10	8	76	44	3	81	36	53	83382
	1991	83779	4	13	13	122	91	5	120	63	90	84300
Eastwood	1981	52700	5	8	16	234	364	2	89	42	99	53557
	1991	58727	11	18	31	500	945	2	197	84	184	60700
Glasgow City	1981	755125	152	616	338	2465	7015	128	1833	562	1159	769394
	1991	665835	224	750	509	3561	11605	197	2903	997	1917	688500
Hamilton	1981	109208	3	25	15	75	123	1	133	22	66	109672
	1991	106114	5	37	23	116	235	1	224	40	104	106900
Inverclyde	1981	100918	4	6	38	70	13	1	67	14	42	101172
	1991	91237	7	9	70	128	31	1	111	32	74	91700
Kilmarnock & Loudon	1981	82269	7	2	11	27	34	1	70	10	27	82459
	1991	81084	15	5	23	61	89	1	143	23	56	81500
Kyle & Carrick	1981	112921	5	21	11	55	23	1	101	17	45	113200
	1991	113023	10	41	21	107	59	1	209	38	89	113600
Clydesdale	1981	57088	5	5	4	43	46	11	33	5	26	57265
	1991	57815	9	11	7	82	124	24	68	9	50	58200

Appendix 2.2: *Continued*

District	Year	White	Black–Caribbean	Black–African	Black–Other	Indian	Pakistani	Bangla–deshi	Chinese	Other–Asian	Other–Other	All groups
Monklands	1981	111245	14	10	15	44	211	4	45	12	32	111632
	1991	103485	20	16	22	62	332	4	86	23	50	104100
Motherwell	1981	150911	8	13	21	70	375	13	118	31	55	151616
	1991	143744	11	16	34	90	649	12	202	62	79	144900
Renfrew	1981	209632	12	41	40	204	154	5	156	61	144	210450
	1991	199917	19	59	61	327	265	6	219	104	223	201200
Strathkelvin	1981	86491	4	27	12	387	124	20	123	46	76	87310
	1991	85099	5	34	20	679	207	27	222	83	124	86500
Tayside												
Angus	1981	92840	7	11	32	25	17	3	73	12	45	93067
	1991	94525	14	23	68	47	48	4	150	28	94	95000
Dundee City	1981	181861	11	78	62	334	570	74	191	124	211	183515
	1991	168988	18	132	120	661	1232	126	406	286	432	172400
Perth & Kinross	1981	128357	6	23	20	19	38	0	113	13	111	128700
	1991	124400	13	44	43	37	95	0	219	28	221	125100
Island Areas												
Orkney	1981	19130	0	3	2	1	2	0	2	1	14	19155
	1991	19533	1	5	6	4	8	0	8	1	33	19600
Shetland	1981	26248	4	3	4	8	9	4	10	17	23	26330
	1991	22377	7	3	6	10	15	7	14	25	35	22500
Western Isles	1981	31522	2	3	3	2	26	1	5	3	11	31578
	1991	29381	4	6	6	4	56	2	8	8	24	29500

Chapter 3
Level and nature of spatial concentration and segregation of minority ethnic populations in Great Britain, 1991

Ceri Peach and David Rossiter

3.1 Background

The analysis of segregation of minority ethnic groups has a long history in the United States, but a much more fragmentary record in the United Kingdom. Studies in the United States by Duncan and Duncan (1957), Duncan and Lieberson (1959), Lieberson (1963), Taeuber and Taeuber (1965), Morrill (1965), Kantrowitz (1969), Lieberson and Waters (1988) and Massey and Denton (1993) have achieved classic status. These studies demonstrated a uniquely high level of segregation of African Americans, irrespective of class, size and percentage of population, and regional location of the cities studied. They also showed that there was a hierarchy of segregation of ethnic groups when measured against the distribution of the native White population.

Methodology has converged on the use of the index of dissimilarity (ID), which measures the proportion of a group which would have to shift its area of residence in order to have the same distribution as the group with which it is being compared (see Box 3.1). In the United States the 'old' north west European groups had low rates of segregation (20 to 40), the 'new' southern and eastern Europeans had moderate rates (40 to 50), newer groups such as the Latino and recent Asian migrants tended to have high rates (50 to 70), but African Americans had extraordinarily high rates in the 70s, 80s and 90s. Massey and Denton (1993) coined the term 'hypersegregation' to describe this phenomenally high incidence.

The richness of the American literature was in part due to the major importance of immigration and ethnic minority groups in American life, in part to the wealth of census information about ethnic (or, at least, birthplace) groups, and in part to the publication of such data for relatively small census areas such as tracts and since 1960, blocks.

In Britain, although there is a long history of immigration, that which has occurred since 1945 marks, in terms both of volume and character, a clear departure from earlier migratory flows. Although it is wrong to see immigration as an exclusively post-war phenomenon, certainly those groups which are chronicled under the 1991 Census ethnic group question were not resident in Britain on the current scale until this period. Interest in numbers and characteristics, particularly in relation to the working of the current Race Relations Act (1976), have been offset by the fear of asking census questions which are in effect 'racially' categorised, as well as the

Box 3.1 *Index of dissimilarity (ID)*

The index of dissimilarity (ID) is derived from the formula:

$$ID = 1/2 \sum_{i=1}^{k} |x_i - y_i|$$

where k = the total number of subareas in the city

x_i = the percentage of the city total of the x population in area i

y_i = the percentage of the city total of the y population in area i

Translated into ordinary language it means that the index is half the sum of the differences between the percentage of the x population group and y population group living in each of the k areas of the city. All differences are taken as positive. To give an example, if we had a city with four tracts (A, B, C and D) and population was evenly distributed over the four tracts 10 per cent, 20 per cent, 30 per cent and 40 per cent, the calculation of the ID would be 30 calculated as follows:

Tract	Per cent of x population	Per cent of y population	Difference between between x and y
A	25	10	15
B	25	20	5
C	25	30	5
D	25	40	15
Total	100	100	60
Half sum of difference			30

resistance to potential questions by some sections of the population (Sillitoe, 1978; 1987). Thus, until 1991, census questions were always posed in the more neutral form of birthplace rather than in the more informative mode of ethnicity. The result is that Britain differs from the United States both in the nature and length of its immigration history, and also lacks the long run of statistics which informs American analysis.

Birthplace is not only a poor surrogate for ethnicity, but may be profoundly misleading. For example, nearly two thirds of those living in Britain and born in East Africa are of Indian, rather than African, descent. About 15 per cent of those born in India and living in Great Britain are White rather than ethnic Indians; indeed, in earlier censuses the proportion may have been even higher (Peach and Winchester, 1974). Most significant of all, large sections of the minority ethnic population living in Britain are British-born. For example, over half of Britain's Black–Caribbean population is British-born and the same is true of the Pakistani population.

Attempts to circumvent the lack of an ethnic group question were made in 1971 by asking for parental birthplace. It was assumed that persons whose parents were both born in the British West Indies, for example, would be ethnically West Indian. However, the published volumes of the census generally used much cruder areal definitions for parental birthplace, and although the data were better than birthplace data based on individuals, they were nevertheless unsatisfactory. They were, however, better than the 1981 data. Estimates of the 1981 ethnic population rely largely on the birthplace of the head of household. Attempts to pioneer an ethnic group question for the 1981 Census (Sillitoe, 1978; 1987) were thwarted at a late stage. Quite apart from opposition to the question from powerful forces within the government, there was evidence of a marked suspicion of officialdom, in particular among poor urban Blacks. (The census year of 1981, it may be remembered, was the year of major urban riots in Britain (Peach, 1986).)

Despite all of these qualifications, there was a significant early blooming of spatial analysis of ethnic groupings in Emrys Jones's classic work *A Social Geography of Belfast* (1960). The 1951 Census enumeration district records were made available for analysis, the first time such data had been released in the United Kingdom. The Census of Northern Ireland also included a question on religion (not asked in the rest of the United Kingdom). Jones was therefore able to measure the degree of separation of Protestants and Catholics for the smallest units of data aggregation available. The point is important because larger units such as wards or boroughs hide significant levels of segregation. Sadly, economists rather than geographers were entrusted with the records from the 1961 Census and, through an error, lost all of the enumeration district material by aggregating it upwards into wards.

It was not until the 1971 Census that enumeration district material began to become more freely available in Britain, but then only in difficult-to-access computer tapes, which had to be purchased and specially commissioned. The 1981 Census saw a more broadly accessible release of census enumeration district material (but of course, with only birthplace, and not ethnic, data). Thus, 1991 marks a new era for the analysis of ethnicity in Britain, putting us more on a par with the USA; though, of course, we lack longitudinal comparative material. The ESRC has made available the whole of the 1991 Census of Great Britain through the Manchester University Computing Centre.

Significant work on the segregation of ethnic minority groups in Great Britain appeared in the 1970s and 1980s. Of these, work by Jones (1970), Lee (1977) and Robinson (1986) are the most notable. Robinson's work is particularly important as it analysed the degree of segregation within the South Asian communities in Blackburn, and produced levels of disaggregation not available from the census.

3.2 Conceptual issues

Before embarking on detailed analysis, it is important to discuss some conceptual problems about the meaning of segregation (Peach, 1981). Underlying the concept of segregation is a belief that unevenness of residential distributions within an urban area reflect social differences: the greater the degree of spatial difference, the greater the social difference. Unevenness can be measured in a variety of ways, however, and can produce paradoxical results. The same distribution can be conceived of as showing either no segregation or total segregation depending upon the concept of segregation employed. For example, if we were to take the case of Bute Town in

Cardiff, an early area of minority ethnic settlement (Little 1947; Halliday, 1992), we could agree perhaps that all the Black population lived in this dockland area of the city in the 1940s. According to Little (1947) this meant that the Black population of Cardiff was segregated, and confined to a small territory with few links to the outside world. However, even if all of the minority ethnic population was in Bute Town, not all of the population of Bute Town was Black. Indeed, the minority ethnic population was a minority within the area as well.

Thus, conceptualising segregation in a different way, we could argue that Bute Town was integrated because it had a mixed population, while the bulk of the White population, outside the docks, was segregated because it contained no Black population. In other words, the same agreed distribution could be interpreted in diametrically opposing ways. The Black population is segregated because it is confined to Bute Town; the Black population is unsegregated because it lives alongside White people; the White population is unsegregated because it is found in every area of the city; the White population is segregated because the large majority is found in White-only areas; Bute Town is segregated because Black people are restricted to that area; Bute Town is the only integrated area in the city.

As stated above, the most commonly used measure of ethnic segregation is the index of dissimilarity, which assesses the degree of unevenness between the residential distribution of two populations in terms of a symmetrical relationship. The index tells the observer what percentage of either group would have to change its area of residence in order to replicate exactly the distribution of the group with which it is being compared. In this system, zero represents identical distributions and no segregation; 100 represents total segregation with no areal overlap between the groups. If the Bute Town example were as described above and we were to measure it on the ID, it would produce a high value, probably of the order of 90.

Other indices which have enjoyed some popularity include Lieberson's P* (Lieberson, 1981). The key point of this index is that it recognises the asymmetry of the exposure of two groups in a given situation. For example, in the Cardiff case, the Black population of Bute Town would everywhere have had the possibility of meeting White people. White people in Cardiff, on the other hand, would have had very limited possibilities of meeting Black people because only a small percentage of the Whites lived in Bute Town. (The dramatic contrasts in contacts between different ethnic groups are explored in a later section of this chapter.)

Some studies of segregation have been almost exclusively concerned with areas of concentration, such as 'Chinatowns', and have paid little attention to dispersed members of the group. This kind of discussion is caught up with the hunt for ghettos, a labelling process which is too often infected by the looseness of everyday discourse, and by a variety of pejorative connotations linking urban decay with the alleged moral/cultural identity of the residents of such areas. To avoid such confusions, and to raise the level of conceptual clarity, it is useful at this juncture to outline the difference between a 'ghetto' and an 'ethnic village'.

Eyles in the *Dictionary of Human Geography* defines the term 'ghetto' as 'a residential district which is almost exclusively the preserve of one ethnic or cultural group'

(Johnston et al, 1983). This definition is unsatisfactory since it fails to capture one half of the critical characteristics that define the 'Black ghetto' in the American context. It is more instructive to see the ghetto as dual. First, a single ethnic or 'racial' group forms the whole population of the residential district. Second, all of that group is found in such areas. The point is well made in relation to Chicago by Philpott, where he distinguishes between 'ethnic villages' (enclaves) and the true ghetto. Although it was common to refer to Irish, German or Polish 'ghettos', Philpott (1978) demonstrates that only a minority of most European ethnics lived in such areas and that they rarely formed a majority of the population in the areas that were identified with them as a group. For example, the Irish areas of Chicago in the 1930s contained only 3 per cent of the Irish population and only one third of the population of 'Irish' areas of the city was Irish. The same was broadly true of other European ethnicities, with only the Poles forming a slight majority of the 'Polish' areas and having more than half of the Polish population living in such areas (see Table 3.1). For African Americans, on the other hand, Black areas were over 80 per cent Black and over 90 per cent of Blacks lived in such areas.

Table 3.1 *'Ghettoisation' of ethnic groups, Chicago, 1930*

Group	Group's city population	Group's 'ghetto' population	Total 'ghetto' population	Percentage of group 'ghettoised'	Group's percentage 'ghetto' population
Irish	169,568	4,993	14,595	2.9	33.8
German	377,975	53,821	169,649	14.2	31.7
Swedish	140,013	21,581	88,749	15.3	24.3
Russian	169,736	63,416	149,208	37.4	42.5
Czech	122,089	53,301	169,550	43.7	31.4
Italian	181,161	90,407	195,736	49.7	46.2
Polish	401,306	248,024	457,146	61.0	54.3
Negro	233,903	216,846	266,051	92.7	81.5

Source: Philpott (1978) Table 7.

3.3   Findings from the 1991 Census

Macro-scale geography

At the macro-scale, it is clear that the minority ethnic population of Great Britain is concentrated in England rather than Scotland or Wales (Owen, 1992). While 86 per cent of the total population of Great Britain lives in England, so 99 per cent of the Black–Caribbean, 98 per cent of the Indian, 97 per cent of the Black–Other, 97 per cent of the Bangladeshi, 94 per cent of the Pakistani and 90 per cent of the Chinese (see Table 3.2).

Table 3.2 *Relative concentration of ethnic groups in Great Britain by country of residence*

	Total	White	Black–Caribbean	Black–African	Black–Other	Indian	Pakistani	Bangla-deshi	Chinese
Gt Britain	54,888,844	51,873,794	499,964	212,362	178,401	840,255	476,555	162,835	156,938
England	47,055,204	44,144,339	495,682	206,918	172,282	823,821	449,646	157,881	141,661
Wales	2,835,073	2,793,522	3,348	2,671	3,473	6,384	5,717	3,820	4,801
Scotland	4,998,567	4,935,923	934	2,773	2,646	10,050	21,192	1,134	10,476
Percentage in England	85.73	85.10	99.14	97.44	96.47	98.04	94.33	96.96	90.27

Source: 1991 Census, Ethnic Group and Country of Birth, Great Britain, Volume 2, London: OPCS, 1993, Table 6.

It is also clear that minorities are concentrated in large urban areas to a greater extent than the White population, although the degree varies from group to group (see Table 3.3). For example, a quarter of the total population of Great Britain lives in Greater London, Greater Manchester and the metropolitan counties of the West Midlands and West Yorkshire combined. However, 83 per cent of the Black–Africans, 79 per cent of the Black–Caribbeans, 75 per cent of the Bangladeshis and nearly two thirds of the Black–Others, Indians and Pakistanis do so as well. Only the Chinese, at still nearly double the rate of the total population, are less concentrated.

Unlike the USA, there are no towns or cities in which minority ethnic groups constitute a majority, and at district level this is also true. The London Borough of Brent is the local authority with the highest percentage of minority population at 44.8 per cent, followed by Newham (42.3) and Tower Hamlets (35.6).

The highest percentage that Black–Caribbeans form of a single ward in Great Britain, is 30.1 per cent in Roundwood (in Brent, London). The Black–African population reaches a surprising 26.6 per cent in Liddle ward in Southwark; surprising since this figure is only a little lower than the Caribbean maximum figure, while the Black–Caribbean population is more than twice as numerous as the Black–African population. For the Indian population, the highest ward percentage is also in London: 67.2 per cent in Northcote in Ealing (although there are several figures

Table 3.3 *Relative concentration of ethnic groups in large metropolitan areas, Great Britain, 1991*

	Total	White	Black–Caribbean	Black–African	Black–Other	Indian	Pakistani	Bangla-deshi	Chinese
Gt Britain	54,888,844	51,873,794	499,964	212,362	178,401	840,255	476,555	162,835	156,938
Gtr London	6,679,699	5,333,580	290,968	163,635	80,613	347,091	87,816	85,738	56,579
W. Midlands Metropolitan	2,551,671	2,178,149	72,183	4,116	15,716	141,359	88,268	18,074	6,107
Gtr Manchester	2,499,441	2,351,239	17,095	5,240	9,202	29,741	49,370	11,445	8,323
West Yorkshire met county	2,013,693	1,849,562	14,795	2,554	6,552	34,837	80,540	5,978	3,852
Percentage ethnic groups in named areas	25.04	22.58	79.01	82.66	62.83	65.82	64.21	74.45	47.70

Source: 1991 Census *Ethnic Group and Country of Birth, Great Britain.* Volume 2. London: OPCS, 1993, Table 6.

almost as high in Leicester). The most highly concentrated Bangladeshi ward is 60.7 per cent in Spitalfields in Tower Hamlets. This figure is even more surprising than that of the Black–Africans, since the Bangladeshi population are even less numerous. The highest concentration of Pakistanis is in University ward in Bradford, where they form 52.8 per cent of the total population. The Black–Other population seems to be heavily represented in several areas with US military bases. Numerically, they are a relatively unimportant part of the Black–Other population, but they stand out because of their concentrated distribution in bases. There is a maximum concentration of less than 10 per cent (Iceni ward, near Mildenhall in East Anglia). Other areas that stand out are more expected, such as Moss Side in Manchester, Granby ward in Liverpool and Brent in London. The Chinese achieve a maximum of only 5.6 per cent (Abercromby ward in Liverpool), while the mysterious Other–Other category (in which the Arabs seem to figure prominently) have a maximum concentration of 11.6 per cent in Bryanston ward in Westminster, and a strong localisation in the richer parts of London: Knightsbridge, Mayfair and South Kensington. The highest proportion of a ward's population formed by the Irish-born is 17.7 per cent, in Cricklewood ward in Brent.

Taking these figures together, a number of conclusions can be drawn:

1. The proportions that individual minority ethnic groups form, of the population of even quite small areas like wards, is nowhere as high as that formed almost uniformly by the African American population in the United States.
2. The number of wards with high concentrations is small and the proportion of a given ethnicity living at such high densities is generally low.
3. There are significant differences between the ethnic groups in the extent to which they form the population of the wards in which they have the highest concentrations. However, if all minorities are taken together, very high levels can be achieved, but there are few such areas. Northcote ward in Ealing has a non-White population of 90 per cent. Two other wards in the country have percentages above 80 (see Table 3.4).

Table 3.4 *Wards with highest level of minority ethnic group presence, Great Britain, 1991*

District	Ward	Total population	Non-White population	**Non-White percentage**
Ealing	Northcote	11,177	10,083	**90.21**
Leicester	Spinney Hill	10,035	8,281	**82.52**
Ealing	Glebe	12,858	10,424	**81.07**
Blackburn	Brookhouse	8,121	6,339	**78.06**
Leicester	Crown Hills	9,585	7,261	**75.75**
Newham	Kensington	7,902	5,910	**74.79**
Ealing	Mount Pleasant	12,550	9,307	**74.16**

Source: Special tabulations prepared from ESRC 1991 Census archive at Manchester University.

On the other hand, a high proportion of minority ethnic groups live in areas where they constitute a small proportion of the total population, or of the White population. Figure 3.1 presents a Lorenz curve showing the cumulative proportion of minority ethnic groups against the total population. The wards are ranked in percentage terms for each group, and are marked along the horizontal axis. The proportion of the total population living in the same wards is marked on the vertical axis. If the minority population had an identical distribution to that of the total population, it would form a perfect diagonal line. The White population nearly produces this effect. The further from the diagonal the line for a particular group is, the more uneven is its distribution in comparison with that of the total population. It shows, for example, that 80 per cent of the Bangladeshis are living in wards that contain only 10 per cent of the total population, and that half of the Irish-born are living in wards that contain a fifth of the total population.

Figure 3.1 *Ward-level Lorenz curves, Great Britain, 1991*

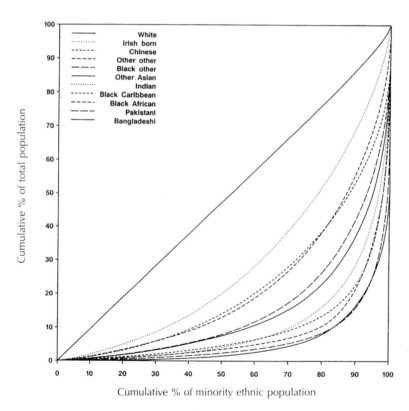

As the size of area decreases, the level of ethnic minority presence in the most concentrated areas increases. At ward level, 61 per cent of Spitalfields ward in Tower Hamlets is Bangladeshi. At enumeration district level, 90 per cent of the most densely Bangladeshi-dominated enumeration district in Spitalfields was Bangladeshi. This level of concentration, however, is very unusual. The highest level of Black–Caribbean concentration in any London enumeration district was 62 per cent (in Brent). It is very clear therefore that nowhere in Britain do we witness the levels of concentration common in North American cities: sustained 100 per cent levels for block and tract data being observed in the case of African Americans.

Micro-scale analysis

Indices of dissimilarity and indices of segregation (IS) (see Boxes 3.1 and 3.2) were calculated for the 10 ethnic groups given in the census (together with those for persons born in Ireland) at both the ward and enumeration district level for all major cities and centres of settlement in Britain. Tables were also generated for birthplace groups in order to provide direct comparison with results for earlier censuses. Results for comparable birthplace and ethnic groups are rather similar. Tables for Greater London (Tables 3.5 and 3.6) and Birmingham (Tables 3.7 and 3.8) are presented as examples (see also Chapters 6 and 7).

As expected, using the finer mesh of enumeration districts, the levels of segregation are higher than for wards. There are some surprises, however. The Chinese in both cities have low levels of segregation from most groups at the ward level, but leap to very high levels at the enumeration district level. This suggests that the Chinese are well distributed across the city, but in a series of segregated clusters that reveal themselves at the finer scale (a phenomenon argued, by Rees and Phillips in Chapter 2, to be related to their particular, and distinctive, economic niche). Chinese numbers are small, which might also be a contributory factor, but the African population which is also small, has high levels at the ward and at the enumeration district level.

Box 3.2 *Index of segregation (IS)*

The index of segregation (IS) is a variant of ID.
It compares the degree of difference between the x population and the total population minus itself. It will be seen from the tables that the ID and the IS are very similar for all groups except for the White population, which constitutes the large majority in British cities. The IS can be calculated by dividing ID for the target group by 1 minus the target population divided by the total population. The formula is given below:

$$IS = \frac{ID}{1 - \dfrac{\sum\limits_{i=1}^{k} y_i}{\sum\limits_{i=1}^{k} t_i}}$$

where k = the total number of subareas in the city
   x_i = the percentage of the city total of the x population in area i
   y_i = the percentage of the city total of the y population in area i
   t_i = the percentage of the city total population in area i

---

Table 3.5 Indices of dissimilarity and segregation for Great London, by ethnic groups, 1991

Ethnic group	White	Black–Caribbean	Black–African	Black–Other	Indian	Pakistani	Bangla-deshi	Chinese	Other–Asian	Other–Other	Irish–born	ID	IS	Number
White	0	49	46	41	51	54	65	30	34	29	26	8	35	5,050,537
Black–Caribbean	54	0	21	15	56	51	62	42	43	35	38	43	45	289,712
Black–African	56	35	0	19	56	51	57	34	39	33	36	40	41	161,660
Black–Other	52	32	39	0	55	51	60	35	39	29	31	35	36	80,368
Indian	56	62	64	65	0	33	67	49	38	45	45	46	49	345,901
Pakistani	66	62	64	65	48	0	65	51	41	46	47	48	49	87,452
Bangladeshi	77	74	71	74	78	77	0	59	60	59	61	62	63	85,298
Chinese	52	60	57	60	64	70	77	0	27	23	24	26	26	55,499
Other–Asian	47	54	54	55	50	58	76	53	0	22	27	28	29	111,701
Other–Other	39	46	47	46	54	61	74	52	43	0	17	22	23	120,118
Irish–born	31	45	49	45	52	60	74	51	44	34	0	21	22	253,211
ID	9	47	49	46	51	60	74	49	42	34	26			—
IS	40	49	50	47	54	61	75	50	43	34	27			6,641,457

ED numeration district level below the diagonal, ward level above.
Source: Calculations from the ESRC 1991 Census holdings at the University of Manchester Computing Service.

Table 3.6 Indices of dissimilarity and segregation for Greater London, by birthplace groups, 1991

Birthplace	Ireland	Old Common-wealth	East Africa	Other Africa	Caribbean	Bangla-desh	India	Pakistan	South East Asia	Europe	China	IOD	IS	Number
Ireland	0	30	38	36	36	60	39	44	23	25	31	21	22	253,011
Old Commonwealth	47	0	53	46	50	66	54	56	26	20	32	36	36	52,586
East Africa	48	65	0	52	49	67	21	36	38	48	49	40	40	107,755
Other Africa	49	65	63	0	25	59	54	51	41	42	41	40	40	74,142
Caribbean	43	63	57	41	0	61	51	48	44	44	46	41	42	150,010
Bangladesh	74	82	79	74	74	0	65	63	60	61	61	61	62	56,321
India	48	65	33	64	58	78	0	29	39	50	50	41	42	151,194
Pakistan	59	71	53	67	61	77	46	0	44	54	53	46	46	44,331
South East Asia	46	51	56	61	60	77	56	63	0	23	26	23	23	41,214
Europe	35	40	56	55	53	76	56	66	45	0	28	30	32	241,319
China	76	76	79	78	79	86	81	82	70	74	0	33	33	6,888
IOD	26	48	47	50	45	74	46	59	43	35	77			—
IS	27	48	48	51	46	74	47	59	44	36	77			1,178,771

ED numeration district level below the diagonal, ward level above.
Source: Calculations from the ESRC 1991 Census holdings at the University of Manchester Computing Service.

Table 3.7 Indices of dissimilarity and segregation for Birmingham by ethnic group 1991

Ethnic group	White	Black–Caribbean	Black–African	Black–Other	Indian	Pakistani	Bangla-deshi	Chinese	Other–Asian	Other–Other	Irish–born	ID	IS	Number
White	**0**	54	49	43	60	74	80	37	57	44	22	14	53	641,018
Black–Caribbean	58	**0**	20	14	30	49	45	32	22	29	39	40	42	42,341
Black–African	72	56	**0**	18	34	46	47	23	20	21	35	36	36	2,473
Black–Other	55	33	59	**0**	37	49	50	28	26	22	27	29	29	8,227
Indian	68	49	66	60	**0**	53	57	39	28	41	46	48	50	49,798
Pakistani	82	63	71	68	61	**0**	33	55	36	39	59	62	66	57,803
Bangladeshi	88	66	74	71	70	50	**0**	59	40	46	67	67	68	12,181
Chinese	70	67	70	70	70	78	81	**0**	31	28	29	28	28	2,918
Other–Asian	71	57	65	63	54	56	65	68	**0**	25	42	43	43	5,183
Other–Other	52	43	60	46	58	57	67	67	56	**0**	28	30	30	10,517
Irish–born	27	46	65	46	59	70	79	68	64	44	**0**	13	13	35,000
ID	15	46	65	46	56	69	78	67	61	42	22	22		—
IS	57	48	65	46	60	74	79	67	62	42	22		22	867,459

ED numeration district level below the diagonal, ward level above.
Source: Calculations from the ESRC 1991 Census holdings at the University of Manchester Computing Service.

Table 3.8 Indices of dissimilarity and segregation for Birmingham, 1991, by birthplace group

Birthplace	Ireland	Old Common-wealth	East Africa	Other Africa	Caribbean	Bangla-desh	India	Pakistan	South East Asia	Europe	China	ID	IS	Number
Ireland	**0**	30	37	34	37	67	45	61	29	23	39	12	13	38,088
Old Commonwealth	66	**0**	48	30	53	80	55	73	27	12	34	23	23	1,324
East Africa	54	75	**0**	39	35	56	32	42	37	45	44	41	41	6,722
Other Africa	75	79	74	**0**	34	61	40	54	18	30	31	32	32	976
Caribbean	46	78	55	70	**0**	45	28	49	36	46	47	39	40	19,227
Bangladesh	80	92	71	83	67	**0**	58	35	61	76	68	68	68	7,653
India	59	78	46	74	47	71	**0**	55	40	51	53	47	48	21,482
Pakistan	71	89	59	80	62	51	63	**0**	56	69	62	62	65	31,234
South East Asia	64	73	66	72	68	80	66	76	**0**	25	25	26	26	2,186
Europe	42	59	61	74	59	87	62	79	63	**0**	35	16	16	7,099
China	88	84	85	83	85	89	84	90	73	84	**0**	38	38	511
ID	21	64	54	75	45	78	56	70	61	35	88	38		—
IS	22	64	54	76	46	79	57	72	61	35	88		38	136,502

ED numeration district level below the diagonal, ward level above.
Source: Calculations from the ESRC 1991 Census holdings at the University of Manchester Computing Service.

Table 3.9 *Indices of segregation of the Bangladeshi population at ward and enumeration district (ED) level in selected cities, 1991, together with comparisons of segregation levels (IOD) against the Indian and Pakistani populations*

City	Bangladeshis versus Indians ward level	Pakistanis ward level	IS ward level	Indian ED level	Pakistanis ED level	IS ED level
Leeds	60	33	79	84	67	93
Sheffield	64	47	71	90	77	93
Bradford	54	49	70	86	73	89
Leicester	64	43	74	83	74	89
Coventry	41	36	65	71	61	86
Blackburn	48	34	48	78	71	86
Manchester	50	46	63	73	66	83
Birmingham	57	33	68	70	50	79
London	67	65	63	78	77	75

Source: Special tabulations prepared from ESRC 1991 Census archive at Manchester University.

Table 3.10 *Indices of segregation of the Pakistani population at enumeration district (ED) level in selected cities, 1991*

City	Pakistani index of segregation at ED level	Pakistani total population
Oxford	60	2,025
Greater London	61	87,452
Leicester	62	2,669
Greater Manchester	77	49,270
Leeds	78	9,274
Bradford	79	45,265
Birmingham	79	65,974
Liverpool	86	615

Source: Special tabulations prepared from ESRC 1991 Census archive at Manchester University.

Table 3.11 *Indices of segregation of the Chinese population at enumeration district (ED) level in selected cities, 1991*

City	Chinese index of segregation at ED level	Chinese total population
Oxford	47	824
Greater London	50	55,499
Liverpool	60	3,305
Birmingham	68	3,159
Leicester	70	705
Greater Manchester	70	8,164
Leeds	73	2,006
Bradford	81	664

Source: Special tabulations prepared from ESRC 1991 Census archive at Manchester University.

The startling feature revealed by the figures is the high level of segregation of the Bangladeshis. Indices of segregation for Bangladeshis in nine cities are presented in Table 3.9. At enumeration district level, the IS for the Bangladeshis in Sheffield is 93, and in Leeds likewise. In Bradford and Leicester, the IS is 89 and in Manchester 83. These high levels mean that their distribution is in marked contrast to almost every other group. It is not simply that Bangladeshis are highly segregated from the White population (although they do show very high rates – 86 at enumeration district level in Manchester, 88 in Birmingham), they also show high rates against other minority ethnic groups. Their lowest level is with the Pakistanis (a group with which they once shared nationality). At ward level they show low levels of segregation from Pakistanis, often in the 30s. At enumeration district level, however, the values are generally in the 60s and 70s. The lowest level is in Birmingham, but the index of 50 (again with the Pakistanis) is still moderately high.

In all other cities examined, the Bangladeshi IS has high values. In some of these cities, the numbers are very small, in which case a high value may constitute a form of statistical 'mirage', rather than representing a 'real' phenomenon worthy of sociological investigation. For example, if there are fewer Bangladeshis than enumeration districts (as is the case in Blackburn), indices are bound to be high. However, the fact that levels are high without exception, including cities in which there are substantial numbers, indicates an important phenomenon. From Table 3.9 it can be seen that although Bangladeshis have very high levels of segregation, these rates are consistently lower with their co-religionists, the Pakistanis, than with Indians. However, the fact that this is a matter of degree, and that isolation exists in relation to all other groups, including co-religionists, suggests that positive factors favouring group solidarity are important. After all, Bangladeshis in Britain are culturally and linguistically distinct from the majority of the Pakistani population. Bangladeshis are as spatially segregated from Pakistanis in London as they are from the White population (see Table 3.5). In other words, Bangladeshi segregation may not be high simply because this group has been, and/or is being, marginalised by the White majority. Part of the explanation may lie in a desire to maintain a degree of isolation from all other groups.

The second most segregated group is the Pakistani population (see Table 3.10). In Birmingham they have an ID of 78 at enumeration district level, and an IS of 79. In Greater Manchester, their ID is 76 and their IS, 77. Similarly high rates apply in relation to their segregation from almost all other ethnic groups. Their lowest ID with any group in Manchester is 69 (with the Indians). In Birmingham, their lowest ID is 51 (with the Bangladeshis).

The Black–African and Chinese populations also show a high degree of segregation at the enumeration district level, although below the Bangladeshi and Pakistani levels (see Table 3.11).

Caribbean segregation levels show some variability between the South East and Midlands on the one hand, and northern towns on the other (see Table 3.12). Greater London and Birmingham, which together contain over two thirds of the Black–Caribbean population, have ISs of 49 and 48 respectively, at enumeration district level. This suggests a major decline in levels of concentration, if one compares these

Table 3.12 *Indices of segregation of the Black–Caribbean population at enumeration district (ED) level in selected cities, 1991*

City	Caribbean index of segregation at ED level	Caribbean total population
Leicester	43	4,070
Oxford	46	1,732
Birmingham	48	42,431
Greater London	49	289,712
Bradford	56	3,223
Greater Manchester	56	10,390
Liverpool	68	1,479
Leeds	72	5,102

Source: Special tabulations prepared from ESRC 1991 Census archive at Manchester University.

with figures quoted in earlier studies. Taking the birthplace group, for which direct comparisons can be made, the IS at enumeration district level was 48 for Greater London and a rather more substantial 64 for Birmingham. Comparison of data for Greater London at a variety of scales, from 1961 to 1991, reveals a consistent, progressive decline in the levels of segregation (see Table 3.13). Given that the initial levels of segregation were not high (by, say, US standards), and that the trend is downwards, it may be that there are significant differences in 'social', as well as spatial, distance between minority ethnic groups in Britain as compared with the USA, specifically in the area of 'ethnic tolerance'.

There is also cartographic evidence suggesting a progressive dispersal of the Black–Caribbean population in London (see also relevant data in the previous chapter, and the discussion of Black–Caribbean 'internal migration' by Champion in Chapter 4). Figure 3.2 is a map of London showing wards which had experienced an increase (or decrease) in their Caribbean-born populations between 1981 and 1991. The decreases are greatest in the central areas (which coincide with the areas of densest settlement). The growth areas are on the outer edges of the areas of concentration.

The Sample of Anonymised Records (SARs) also seem to reflect this point in terms of social interaction. Over a quarter of households (26.8 per cent) containing Black–Caribbean heads or partners contained a Black–Caribbean male and White female.

Table 3.13 *Comparison of IDs for Greater London Caribbean-born population, 1961–91*

Year	Borough level ID	Ward level ID	Enumeration district ID	Source
1961	Not available	56		Lee (1973)
1971	38	49	65	Woods (1976)
1981	37	46	53	Peach*
1991	34	41	50	Peach**

* derived from 1981 Census data held at ESRC archive, Manchester University
** derived from 1991 Census data held at ESRC archive, Manchester University

Figure 3.2 *Change in Caribbean-born population, Greater London, 1981–1991: absolute change by ward*

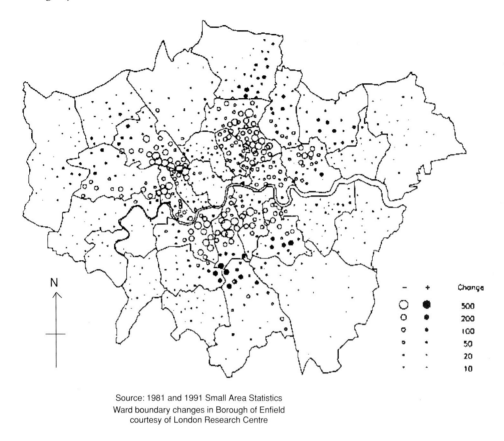

	−	+	Change
	○	●	500
	○	●	200
	○	•	100
	○	•	50
	•	•	20
	·	·	10

Source: 1981 and 1991 Small Area Statistics
Ward boundary changes in Borough of Enfield
courtesy of London Research Centre

A further 4.8 per cent contained a White male and Black–Caribbean female. This again contrasts sharply with the US experience. Extremely high levels of segregation in the case of American Blacks are accompanied by an extremely low incidence of 'mixed' households (of both the above types).

Lieberson's P* index

An alternative way of viewing segregation of minority ethnic groups is through Lieberson's P^* index (Lieberson, 1981). The index of dissimilarity which, as we have seen, measures the proportion of a given population which would have to shift its area of residence, in order to replicate the distribution of the groups with which it is compared, is symmetrical. This means that the proportion which would have to move is identical for both groups. Lieberson's P^* index is asymmetrical (as we saw in the Bute Town example earlier in the chapter). It measures the degree of exposure of one group to another (see Box 3.3). If a minority ethnic group is very small, its degree of exposure to the majority group is greater than the majority group's exposure to it. P^* estimates are therefore very sensitive to the relative size of the groups concerned. Tables of P^* statistics may be interpreted as the probability of the row label group in the table living in an area containing the column heading population.

Box 3.3

P* Index

The P* index was developed by Lieberson (1981) to describe asymmetric relationships between groups in cities. (IS and ID are symmetric. They measure the proportion of either of the compared groups which would have to shift their area of residence to replicate the distribution of the other. In other words, the values are identical for both groups.) P* measures the hypothetical probability that the next person a member of group X will randomly meet will be another member of group X, or Y or whatever group is under investigation. In Lieberson's formulation he uses subscripts preceding and following P* to indicate, respectively, the group from whom and to whom the interaction is directed. Thus for a randomly selected member of group X in a city, the probability that someone else selected from the same subarea will be a member of group Y is denoted by $_xP^*_y$. Only in the unusual case that X and Y are the same size in a city will $_xP^*_y$ be identical with $_yP^*_x$. The degree of isolation of members of group X is represented by $_xP^*_x$. For a member of group X randomly selected in the city, $_xP^*_x$ gives the probability that someone else chosen from the same subarea will also be a member of group X. In other words, it gives the average proportion X is of the population in each subarea weighted by the number of Xs living in each of these subareas.

In its most general form the formula is

$$_xP^*_y = \sum_{i=1}^{k} \{(x_i/X)\,(y_i/t_i)\}$$

where X is the total number of group X in the city
          x_i is the total number of group X in a given subarea
          y_i is the total number of group Y in a given subarea
          t_i is the total population in a given subarea.

P* values for Birmingham and Greater London are presented in Tables 3.14 and 3.15. The tables illustrate some interesting features. For example, the enumeration district level tables for Birmingham show that there is a higher probability of Pakistanis living close to other Pakistanis (38.3 per cent chance) than to Whites (34.3 per cent). Whites have a very low probability of living in enumeration districts containing Pakistanis (3 per cent chance), while Pakistanis have a much higher probability of living in enumeration districts containing Whites (34.3 per cent). Bangladeshis in Birmingham, however, have a greater probability of meeting Pakistanis in areas where they live (28.6 per cent) than meeting Bangladeshis (13 per cent). The high degree of Bangladeshi clustering in London, however, means that they have a 24 per cent chance of meeting other Bangladeshis in enumeration districts where they live, although they have twice as great a chance of meeting Whites. Whites in London have only a 1 per cent chance of living in enumeration districts which contain Bangladeshis.

Table 3.14 P* Indices of segregation for Birmingham, 1991

Ethnic group	White	Black–Caribbean	Black–African	Black–Other	Indian	Pakistani	Bangla-deshi	Chinese	Other–Asian	Other–Other	Number
At Ward level											
White	85.2	3.5	0.2	0.8	3.6	4.3	0.7	0.3	0.4	1	751,391
Black–Caribbean	58.5	9.7	0.5	1.6	11.5	11.7	3.2	0.5	1.1	1.8	44,542
Black–African	63.2	8.3	0.5	1.4	9.7	10.9	2.7	0.5	1	1.8	2,649
Black–Other	65.3	7.9	0.4	1.4	8.8	10.7	2.5	0.4	0.9	1.6	8,801
Indian	53.7	10	0.5	1.5	17.3	10.9	2.5	0.5	1.2	1.7	50,948
Pakistani	48.4	7.9	0.4	1.4	8.4	25.2	4.3	0.4	1.2	2.3	65,974
Bangladeshi	43.7	11.3	0.6	1.8	10	22	6.4	0.5	1.4	2.4	12,724
Chinese	70.9	6.6	0.4	1.2	7.9	8.1	1.9	0.5	0.9	1.5	3,159
Other–Asian	56.8	8.6	0.5	1.4	11.3	14.7	3.2	0.5	1.2	1.9	5,600
Other–Other	64.9	6.8	0.4	1.2	7.5	13.2	2.7	0.4	0.9	1.9	11,464
At enumeration district											
White	87.2	3.4	0.2	0.8	3.2	3	0.5	0.3	0.4	0.9	751,391
Black–Caribbean	57.5	12.8	0.6	2	10.6	10.3	2.8	0.5	1.1	2	44,542
Black–African	62.0	9.3	1.6	1.6	8.6	10.1	2.5	0.8	1.4	2.1	2,649
Black–Other	65.6	10	0.5	2.4	7.6	8.7	2.2	0.5	0.8	1.9	8,801
Indian	47.8	9.2	0.4	1.3	23.4	11.8	2.7	0.5	1.3	1.6	50,948
Pakistani	34.3	7	0.4	1.2	9.1	38.3	5.5	0.4	1.5	2.4	65,974
Bangladeshi	31.6	9.7	0.5	1.5	10.7	28.6	13.0	0.4	1.6	2.3	12,724
Chinese	68.2	6.9	0.7	1.3	7.9	7.6	1.7	2.3	1.5	2	3,159
Other–Asian	50.7	8.4	0.7	1.2	12.1	17.4	3.7	0.8	2.9	2.1	5,600
Other–Other	62.2	7.8	0.5	1.4	7.2	13.6	2.6	0.5	1	3.2	11,464

Source: 1991 Census. Crown Copyright.

Table 3.15 *P* Indices of segregation for Greater London, 1991*

Ethnic group	White	Black–Caribbean	Black–African	Black–Other	Indian	Pakistani	Bangla-deshi	Chinese	Other–Asian	Other–Other	Number
At Ward level											
White	82.7	3.8	2.1	1.1	4.2	1.1	1.0	0.8	1.5	1.7	5,303,748
Black–Caribbean	69.4	9.6	4.7	2.3	5.7	1.8	1.4	1.0	1.9	2.3	289,712
Black–African	70.0	8.4	5.3	2.2	5.2	1.7	1.7	1.2	2.0	2.3	161,660
Black–Other	71.9	8.3	4.4	2.2	5.0	1.6	1.5	1.0	1.8	2.3	80,368
Indian	64.4	4.7	2.5	1.2	17.4	3.3	1.1	0.8	2.6	2.1	345,901
Pakistani	64.3	6.0	3.1	1.5	13.0	4.8	1.9	0.8	2.6	2.1	87,452
Bangladeshi	63.4	4.7	3.2	1.4	4.5	1.9	16.2	1.0	1.7	2.0	85,298
Chinese	76.7	5.2	3.4	1.5	5.0	1.3	1.5	1.3	2.1	2.2	55,499
Other–Asian	73.4	5.0	2.9	1.3	8.1	2.0	1.3	1.0	2.7	2.2	111,701
Other–Other	75.5	5.5	3.1	1.5	5.9	1.5	1.4	1.0	2.1	2.5	120,118
At enumeration district level											
White	83.5	3.6	2.0	1.1	4.0	1.0	0.9	0.8	1.5	1.7	5,303,748
Black–Caribbean	66.5	11.6	5.1	2.6	5.6	1.8	1.5	1.0	1.9	2.4	289,712
Black–African	66.2	9.2	7.5	2.4	5.3	1.7	1.9	1.3	2.1	2.4	161,660
Black–Other	69.4	9.3	4.9	3.2	4.9	1.6	1.5	1.0	1.9	2.3	80,368
Indian	60.7	4.7	2.5	1.1	20.5	3.6	1.2	0.8	2.7	2.1	345,901
Pakistani	59.9	6.1	3.2	1.5	14.2	7.2	2.2	0.9	2.8	2.1	87,452
Bangladeshi	54.4	5.0	3.6	1.4	4.8	2.2	23.7	1.1	1.8	2.0	85,298
Chinese	74.2	5.1	3.7	1.4	5.2	1.3	1.7	2.7	2.4	2.2	55,499
Other–Asian	70.9	5.0	3.0	1.3	8.5	2.2	1.4	1.2	4.3	2.4	111,701
Other–Other	73.7	5.7	3.3	1.5	6.0	1.5	1.4	1.0	2.2	3.6	120,118

Source: 1991 Census. Crown Copyright.

3.4 Positive and negative, dominant and recessive factors in segregation

Segregation comes about as the result of a complex interplay of forces. Chain migration processes have a strong influence on locating minorities in clusters. Hostility from the society within which the settlement takes place can reduce the ability of the group to disperse, and defence may be an important element in clustering. There are both positive and negative reasons for most ethnic clustering patterns and, given their simultaneous presence in many situations, it is difficult to disentangle the dominant from recessive factors in any given situation. Nevertheless, it is important to recognise that not all segregation results from negative factors such as racism.

Substantial parts of the 1960s, 1970s and early 1980s literature centred on the 'choice versus constraints' debate. Rex and Moore (1967) demonstrated high levels of discrimination against immigrants, particularly against Pakistanis, in their fieldwork area of Sparkbrook in Birmingham; and showed a high concentration of Pakistanis in their lowest 'housing class', the rooming house. Dahya (1974), on the other hand, argued that Pakistani concentration in multi-occupied accommodation was a preferred, as distinct from an enforced, strategy. He argued that chain migration by village and family, the desire to maximise savings, shared language and religion, culinary needs and so forth, all argued in favour of sharing accommodation. Thus, although the existence of discrimination could not be denied, it was not material to the patterns of concentration that arose. Later work by Sarre et al. (1989) attempted to use structuration theory to resolve the choice–constraint duality. They argued that the discriminatory constraints of White society were internalised within a minority ethnic group's behaviour. Minority ethnic groups would sometimes appear to choose particular localities, when in fact they were accepting only what they knew they would be allowed to have. This new theoretical approach generated some new insights, but arguably led, in the end, to little more than a variant of the constraint school of thought.

It is clear that segregation is not simply of Black from White, or majority from minority, but takes place between the minority ethnic groups as well. Tables 3.5 to 3.8 clearly demonstrate high levels of segregation between the various minority ethnic populations; Bangladeshis from Pakistanis, Black–Caribbeans from Black–Africans, and so forth. The 1991 Census does not, by definition, allow us to measure the levels of segregation within groups that are treated as homogeneous, such as the Indian or Pakistani population. However, Robinson's work (1986) in Blackburn demonstrates the significant levels of segregation between Hindus, Sikhs and Muslims from the same South Asian ultimate origins. A sample census by Leicester City and County Councils in 1983 (Leicester, 1988) showed similar results. Peach's work on segregation between different Caribbean island groups in London makes the same point (Ley et al., 1984).

3.5 Class explanations of ethnic segregation

In attempting to partial out the relative contribution of different factors to the net pattern, socio-economic position is an important variable for assessment. We may follow Taeuber and Taeuber (1965) and Lieberson (1963) in using indirect standardisation to estimate the importance of economic factors in residential segregation. This exercise is performed by taking the class distribution of a city's population as given. Next, the percentage that a given ethnic group forms of each economic class in the city as a whole is calculated. These percentages are then applied to the given numbers of each economic group in each area of the city. This produces the number of that ethnic group which would be expected to be in any given area on the basis of its proportion of each economic group in the city as a whole. For example, if Black–Caribbeans formed 5 per cent of skilled manual workers in a city, they would be expected to form 5 per cent of the manual worker population, wherever that population was found, and so forth. Given that not all groups have the same socio-economic profile and given that socio-economic groups are segregated from one another, some degree of ethnic segregation would be expected for 'class' rather than 'ethnic' reasons.

The results of this simulation are shown for London (Table 3.16). The table demonstrates that all ethnic groups would manifest a much lower degree of segregation if economic factors alone controlled their distribution. The table can be interpreted by expressing the ID value below the diagonal as a percentage of the corresponding value above the diagram. For example, the expected level of segregation of the Black–Caribbean population from the White population from the socio-economic pattern at ward level was 4, while the observed level was 50. Thus, only 8 per cent of the observed level of segregation is explained by socio-economic factors. (It is worth noting that the figures for the IDs differ from those given in other tables for two reasons. First, they are based on persons aged 16 and over and in work. Hence they omit the unemployed and economically inactive. Second, they are based on the 10 per cent sample data, and hence are liable to sampling error.)

The results of the comparison for other groups show a similarly low degree of economic class explanation. Class explains 9 per cent of the high levels of Bangladeshi segregation from Whites; it explains nearly 11 per cent of the (much lower degree of) Irish segregation from the White population. It explains less than 2 per cent of either the Indian or Pakistani segregation from the White population. The London figures are not very different in kind from various American findings. In Chicago in 1960, for example, only 12 per cent of racial segregation could be attributed to income differentials (Taeuber and Taeuber, 1965).

3.6 Conclusion

The minority ethnic population in Great Britain is very unevenly spread, showing particular concentrations in Greater London and the other major metropolitan counties. The Chinese, whose high representation in the restaurant and take-away trade, has led them to shadow the distribution of the population which they serve,

Table 3.16 *Comparison of observed segregation (above diagonal) and expected segregation on the basis of social class (below diagonal) for ethnic groups in Greater London, 1991*

Ethnic group	White	Black–Caribbean	Black–African	Indian	Pakistani	Bangla-deshi	Chinese	Other–Asian	Other–Other	Irish–	ID	IS	Number
White	**0**	50	50	52	56	64	38	40	34	28	7	34	233,247
Black–Caribbean	4	**0**	33	55	53	65	53	47	42	41	44	46	11,704
Black–African	3	2	**0**	61	61	65	51	48	42	43	46	46	4,060
Indian	1	4	2	**0**	43	70	52	43	50	44	47	50	13,635
Pakistani	1	3	2	1	**0**	70	58	48	52	49	51	52	2,050
Bangladeshi	6	2	3	5	5	**0**	66	63	62	62	62	62	1,088
Chinese	2	6	5	3	3	8	**0**	40	38	37	36	37	2,188
Other–Asian	0	4	3	1	1	6	2	**0**	34	34	35	36	4,457
IOD	0	4	2	1	1	5	3	1	2	3			—
IOS	2	4	2	1	1	5	3	1	2	3			290,875

The table is based upon Table 93 of the Local Base Statistics which gives social class and ethnic group for residents aged 16 and over, employees and self-employed.

be more broadly spread. The Bangladeshi line on the Lorenz curve starts off as the most distinct curve of any minority ethnic group, but its later distribution crosses over the curves of other groups (see Figure 3.1).

Within the major urban areas, the distribution of minority ethnic groups is also uneven, with a marked tendency towards inner urban concentrations. Indians in London, with a western outer suburb pattern of settlement are a major exception to this rule. This may be due in part to the high socio-economic position of the Indian population. It is also related to a settlement pattern that reflects the importance of Heathrow airport, as opposed to railway termini as in the case of the Black–Caribbean population (which began its major immigration earlier than the Indians). The Chinese tend to have a low level of segregation from the White population at ward level but a much higher degree at enumeration district level, suggesting highly localised clusters within a broad scatter.

If we were to reproduce Philpott's table of Chicago ghettoisation (see Table 3.1) for London, the extent of the difference between the US and British situations would become even more apparent. If, for example, we define ghettoisation in as similar a way to Philpott as possible, by selecting those wards where the minority formed 30 per cent or more of the population, then the London position in 1991 would be as shown in Table 3.17. Black–Caribbean segregation levels appear at about the same level as Irish segregation in Chicago in 1930. Only 3 per cent of the Black–Caribbean population lived in Caribbean areas and they formed only a third of the population there. A quarter of the Indian population is living in wards where they form nearly half of the population. One third of Bangladeshis are ghettoised on this basis and they form half of the population of Bangladeshi areas. However, this distribution is more like those of the Polish or Italian populations in Philpott's table than that of the African Americans. If one combines the London minority ethnic populations, however, a picture more akin to the Bangladeshi/Polish pattern emerges. Half of the combined minority ethnic groups live in wards where they form nearly half of the population.

Table 3.17 *'Ghettoisation' of ethnic groups at enumeration district level, Greater London, 1991: 30% cutoff*

Ethnic	Group's city population	Group's 'Ghetto' population	Total 'Ghetto' population	Percentage of group 'ghettoised'	Group's percentage of 'ghetto' population
Black–Caribbean	290,968	7,755	22,545	2.6	34.4
Black–African	163,635	3,176	8,899	2.0	35.6
Black–Other	80,613	nil	nil	nil	nil
Indian	347,091	88,887	202,135	25.6	44.0
Pakistani	87,816	1,182	3,359	1.4	35.2
Bangladeshi	85,738	28,280	55,000	33.0	51.0
Chinese	56,579	38	111	0.0	34.2
Other–Asian	112,807	176	572	0.2	30.8
Other–Other	120,872	209	530	0.2	39.4
Irish-born	256,470	1,023	2,574	0.4	39.8
Non-White	1,346,119	721,873	1,589,476	53.6	45.4

Source: 1991 Census: Crown Copyright.

Levels of segregation of the Black groups are generally much lower than those of the South Asian groups. The highest density or proportion of the local population formed by the Black–Caribbean, Black–African and Black–Other groups either singly or jointly is less than half the population of any ward in Britain. South Asian groups, on the other hand, achieve a majority position in a number of wards, both as individual ethnic groups and *a fortiori* as combined groups. Black–Caribbean indices of dissimilarity at ward level are generally in the 40s and 50s in British cities and only occasionally rise into the 60s and 70s. Indian segregation levels are generally lower than those for Black–Caribbeans, while Pakistani levels are generally higher. Bangladeshi levels of segregation, in contrast, are almost uniformly high.

Despite fears of following the African American model of inner city segregation, the 1991 Census suggests rather more optimistic conclusions. Ghettos on the American model do not exist and in the case of the Black–Caribbean population, despite an unfavourable economic position and substantial evidence of continuing discrimination, the segregation trend in London is downwards, albeit very slightly.

References

Dahya, B. (1974) The nature of Pakistani ethnicity in industrial cities in Britain. In: Cohen, A. (ed.), *Urban Ethnicity*. London: Tavistock.

Duncan, O. D. and Duncan, B. (1957) *The Negro Population of Chicago*. Chicago: The University of Chicago Press.

Duncan, O.D. and Lieberson, S. (1959) Ethnic segregation and assimilation. *American Journal of Sociology*, 64, 364–74. Reprinted in Peach, C. (ed.), Urban Social Segregation. London: Longman, 1975.

Halliday, F. (1992) *Arabs in Exile*. London: I.B. Taurus and Co.

Johnston, R. J., Gregory, D., Haggett, P., Smith, D. and Stoddart, D.R. (1983) *The Dictionary of Human Geography*. Oxford: Blackwell.

Jones, E. (1960) *A Social Geography of Belfast*. Oxford: Oxford University Press.

Jones, P. N. (1970) Some aspects of the changing distribution of coloured immigrants in Birmingham, 1961-66. *Transactions of the Institute of British Geographers*, 50, 199–219.

Kantrowitz, N. (1969) Ethnic and racial segregation in the New York Metropolis. *American Journal of Sociology*, 74, 685–95. Reprinted in Peach, C. (ed.), Urban Social Segregation. London: Longman, 1975.

Lee, T. R. (1977) *Race and Residence: The Concentration and Dispersal of Immigrants in London*. Oxford: Clarendon Press.

Leicester (1988) *Survey of Leicester 1983:* Ward Tables. Leicester City Council and Leicestershire County Council, Leicester.

Ley, D., Clarke, C. and Peach, C. (eds) (1984) *Geography and Ethnic Pluralism*. London: Allen and Unwin.

Lieberson, S. (1963) *Ethnic Patterns in American Cities*. New York: The Free Press of Glencoe.

Lieberson, S. (1981) An asymmetrical approach to segregation. In: Peach, C., Robinson, V. and Smith, S. J. (eds), *Ethnic Segregation in Cities*. London: Croom Helm.

Lieberson, S. and Waters, M. (1988) *From Many Strands: Ethnic and Racial Groups in Contemporary America*. New York: Russell Sage Foundation.

Little, K. S. (1947) *Negroes in Britain*. London: Routledge and Kegan Paul.

Massey, D.S. and Denton, N.A. (1993) *Apartheid American Style*. Cambridge, MA: Harvard University Press.

Morrill, R. L. (1965) The Negro ghetto: problems and alternatives. *Geographical Review,* 55(3), 339–61.

Owen, D.W. (1992) *Ethnic minorities in Great Britain: settlement patterns*. National Ethnic Minority Data Archive 1991 Census Statistical Paper No.1. University of Warwick, Centre for Research in Ethnic Relations.

Peach, C. (1981) Conflicting interpretations of segregation. In: Jackson, P. and Smith, S. (eds), *Social Interaction and Ethnic Segregation*. London: Academic Press for Institute of British Geographers, Special Publication, No 12, 19–33.

Peach, C. (1986) A geographical perspective on the 1981 urban riots in England. *Ethnic and Racial Studies*, 9(3), 396–411.

Peach, G.C.K. and Winchester, S.W.C. (1974) Birthplace, ethnicity and the enumeration of West Indians, Indians and Pakistanis. *New Community*, 3, 386–94.

Philpott, T.L. (1978) *The Slum and the Ghetto: Neighborhood Deterioration and Middle Class Reform*, Chicago, 1880–1930. New York: Oxford University Press.

Rex, J. and Moore, R. (1967) *Race, Community and Conflict*. London: Oxford University Press.

Robinson, V. (1986) *Transients, Settlers and Refugees: Asians in Britain*. Oxford: Clarendon Press.

Sarre, P., Phillips, D. and Skellington, R (1989) *Ethnic Minority Housing: Explanations and Policies*. Aldershot: Avebury.

Sillitoe, K. (1978) Ethnic origins: the search for a question. *Population Trends*, 13, 25–30.

Sillitoe, K. (1987) Questions on race/ethnicity and related topics for the Census. *Population Trends*, 49, 5–11.

Taeuber, K. E. and Taeuber, A. (1965) The Negro as an immigrant group. *American Journal of Sociology*, 69(4), 374–82. Reprinted in Peach, C. (ed.), (1975) *Urban Social Segregation*. London: Longman.

Taeuber, K.E. and Taeuber, A. (1964) *Negroes in Cities: Residential Segregation and Neighborhood Change*. Chicago: Aldine Publishing Co.

Woods, R. I. (1976) Aspects of the scale problem in the calculation of segregation indices: London and Birmingham, 1961 and 1971. *Tijdschrift voor Economische en Sociale Geografie*, 67(3), 169–74.

Acknowledgements

The work was carried out with assistance from the OPCS and from the ESRC Research Grant R45126412793. Grateful acknowledgement is made of the use of the ESRC census data at the Manchester Computing Centre of the University of Manchester and of the Samples of Anonymised Records (SARs) made available through the ESRC at the Census Microdata Unit at the University of Manchester. Grateful acknowledgement is made to the Hon. Editor, *Transactions the Institute of British Geographers*, for permission to draw extensively on Peach, C. Does Britain have Ghettos? *Transactions, Institute of British Geographers*, 1996, New series vol. 21, 1, 216–235.

Chapter 4
Internal migration and ethnicity in Britain

Tony Champion

4.1 Introduction

Migration can be regarded as a key indicator of people's quality of life and of their ability to improve their lot, but great care needs to be taken in interpreting the patterns observed from analyses of change-of-address data. When dealing with population subgroups like the ethnic minorities, it is conventional to examine their rates and patterns of residential mobility and compare them with those of the majority group, taking the 'assimilationist' approach that significant differences (specifically, lower levels of mobility on the part of minorities) will be the result of negative factors impinging on life-style and life chances. Lower than 'average' levels of movement, for instance, may perhaps be interpreted as the result of factors which are 'trapping' people in certain environments and preventing access to wider opportunities, while high migration propensities may reflect the failure to find a suitable labour market, housing or social niche. Alternatively, however, low levels of mobility can indicate satisfaction with current circumstances, while high levels of movement can occur during periods of economic dynamism and rapid social advancement.

In the past, it has been enormously difficult even to monitor the internal migration of Britain's minority ethnic groups and assess its demographic impact, let alone address questions concerning what this means for the individuals and groups involved. In the first place, researchers of any aspect of internal migration in Britain have traditionally faced problems of inadequate data (though this situation has improved somewhat since the mid-1970s). It has also been very difficult to distinguish the ethnic components in the internal migration records which do exist. This latter problem has now been addressed by the inclusion of the ethnic group question on the 1991 Census form, and the use of the answers to this question in some of the census output on change of address, most notably one table in the Special Migration Statistics.

This chapter presents the results of an initial examination of the 1991 Census data, on migration in Britain by ethnic grouping. It begins by outlining the strengths and weaknesses of these data in comparison with what was available previously from the census and other sources. It then looks at migration propensities by ethnic group, distinguishing internal from international migration and investigating levels of shorter and longer distance movement within Britain. This analysis is carried out at the national level, and the geographical variations across Britain are the subject of the following section. The chapter goes on to examine the patterns of net population redistribution by ethnic grouping arising from migration, identifying the main gaining and losing areas and assessing whether these shifts denote trends towards greater spatial concentration or the reverse. The final substantive section explores some of the patterns of gross population movement underlying the net shifts, and provides an impression of the dynamics of migration and the extent to which this varies between groups.

For those readers who are interested principally in the results of this analysis and intend to go straight to the substantive sections or the summary of findings at the end of the chapter, a word of caution. It should be remembered that the migration data from the 1991 Census are not in reality data on migration, but data on whether or not people were normally resident at the same address on census night as they had been exactly one year before, i.e. irrespective of any changes in address during the intervening 12 months. In addition, around one person in 20 who should have been entered on a census form was not, either being imputed for the purposes of census output or omitted entirely. Importantly in the current context, these people are believed to have been disproportionately concentrated in the most migratory age-groups in the population. It should also be recognised that some of those who were included on census forms were not entered as being at a different address 12 months earlier when in fact they should have been, and also that a number of people who were declared as migrants did not provide enough information to allow their previous address to be identified with certainty. Finally, care must be taken in generalising from this information, given that the year leading up to the census in April 1991 saw one of Britain's worst ever recessions and was therefore markedly different in economic terms from the previous few years. These potential weaknesses are outlined in more detail in the next section, and are assessed in relation to the undoubted strengths of the 1991 Census data.

4.2   Data on internal migration by ethnic group

The fundamental importance of the 1991 Census for the study of the internal migration of Britain's minority ethnic populations is that it allows researchers to do something that has been virtually impossible up till now. In the words of Britain's foremost researcher in this field, 'Data on the internal migration of Britain's ethnic minorities are extremely limited' (Robinson, 1992). Indeed, in recent years it has been hard enough to gauge the overall size of Britain's minority ethnic (i.e. non-White) population, let alone provide details of its geographical distribution, how this has been changing, and what role internal migration has played compared with international migration, births and deaths (see, for example, Haskey, 1990; 1991; Shaw, 1988).

Traditional data sources

In recent years two main sources of data have been used for research on the geographical distribution and mobility of Britain's minority ethnic populations. One is the Labour Force Survey (LFS) which has the great value of providing information specifically on respondents' ethnic group. It was used by Owen and Green (1992) to examine differences between ethnic groups in migration propensities in 1986–87, showing that while 10.5 per cent of Whites had moved house during the 12-month period, all the larger minority ethnic groups, with the exception of Indians, had seen higher levels of movement, though the ranking of groups by mobility rate differed when inter-regional moves were treated separately from migration within regions.

Because of limitations of sample size, however, the LFS has not been considered a reliable indicator of population characteristics below the scale of standard regions and metropolitan counties. The study of migration in the case of minorities is particularly badly affected, given their small proportion of the total population and the relatively small proportion of most groups moving house in a particular year. In 1986–88, for example, the annual average number of LFS respondents identifying themselves as something other than White in response to the ethnic group question was 6,994, with certain groups comprising very small numbers indeed — only 188 Arabs, 289 Bangladeshis, 298 Africans and 343 Chinese (Haskey, 1990). The total number of non-White migrants in the sample will therefore have been under 1,000 and for certain groups it will have been under 50, raising problems of large sampling error for the spatial analysis of migration flows. These problems are exacerbated by the geographical clustering used in the sample design at this time (see Chapter 2 for a more detailed discussion of this issue).

The other main source is the birthplace information provided by the population census. This has hitherto furnished virtually all we know about the geography of the minority ethnic population, based on the various assumptions that the latter was reasonably adequately represented by people born in the New Commonwealth and Pakistan (NCWP), or by certain elaborations such as 'people with both parents born in the NCWP' (1971 Census) and 'people whose head of household was NCWP-born' (1981 Census); see Chapter 2 for further discussion of this issue.

Irrespective of the validity of this approach for a single census year or for tracing change in the ethnic population between censuses, however, this information can tell us nothing about migration *per se* unless it is cross-tabulated against the answers to the change of address question. Unfortunately, such analyses were not provided in any of the standard output from either the 1971 or 1981 Censuses. The only exception is Table 5 in the 1981 Census Topic Report on Country of Birth, but this gives data on one-year migrants by place of birth only for persons who were migrating into the UK from elsewhere and not for people already living in Britain.

Two ways have nevertheless been found for using the previous population censuses to trace the migration within Britain of people who had entered the country previously. One is through the generation of additional tabulations by the census authorities: a number were commissioned from the 1981 Census, involving the cross-tabulation of one-year migrants with birthplace for various combinations of origin and destination areas (see OPCS Census 1981 User Guide 130/6). The other is via the use of the OPCS Longitudinal Study (LS), with its linkage of individuals identified in both 1971 and 1981 Censuses. Robinson (1992) has used this source to study the scale and pattern of between-region movement between 1971 and 1981 of West Indian, Indian and Pakistani immigrants in comparison with those of people born in the UK and, furthermore, has taken advantage of other information on their two census records to investigate the degree of social mobility associated with such geographical movements. The LS can also be used to produce customised analyses of the one-year change of address data (and five-year in 1971) from the two censuses, though this approach provides no information about people's circumstances before the move.

The value of the 1991 Census

Against this background of extremely limited information, the 1991 Census represents a major step forward. The inclusion of the ethnic group question in the 1991 Census, together with the enhanced importance attached to issues surrounding the geographical mobility of the minority ethnic population, has ensured that each relevant standard dataset derived from the census contains cross-tabulations of the responses to the ethnic group and change-of-address questions, or makes this possible on a customised basis. The next few paragraphs outline the nature of the information available in each of these datasets.

The County Reports, Local Base Statistics and Small Area Statistics can be considered as a single group, as their table structure is broadly similar. In all these datasets, one table (Table 17) provides counts of the numbers of residents that are one-year migrants by ethnic group, giving the standard 10 categories of ethnic group in the County Report tables for counties and districts and in the Local Base Statistics for census wards, and using the four broad categories of ethnic group in the Small Area Statistics for enumeration districts. Table 17 also provides counts of the total population aged 1 year and over for the relevant ethnic group categories, so that a meaningful calculation of migration rate can be made. The result indicates the proportion of the usual residents of an area on census night that had been living at a different address 12 months before. It is not possible from this table to differentiate between those who had moved house within the same area (i.e. county, district, ward or enumeration district) and those who had entered the area from elsewhere in the country or indeed from outside Britain. The table which breaks down migrants by type of move in this way (Table 15) is not cross-tabulated by ethnic group. Similarly, there are other tables providing information on migrants, but not their ethnicity. Finally, these datasets provide no information about people leaving an area.

Among the 1991 Census topic reports, those on 'Country of Birth and Ethnic Group' and 'National Migration' contain tables where one-year migration data are given by ethnic group. The former, however, is of no use in the present context because its one potentially relevant table (Table 9) refers only to people whose address was outside the UK one year before the census, not to people moving within Britain. By contrast, Table 11 of *National Migration (Part 1)* covers all types of move, and breaks down one-year migrants by the 10 ethnic groups, sex, broad age-group (1–4, 5–15, 16–19, 20–29, 30–44, 45 to pensionable age, pensionable age and over) and type of move (all migrant residents, moving within the 'area', moving within regions, moving within districts, moving to and from the rest of Great Britain, moving to and from Northern Ireland, moving from outside the UK and moving from origins not stated). The principal drawback of this table is its limited geography, since the 'areas' in question are Great Britain and its constituent countries of England, Wales and Scotland – contrary to the impression given in the list of full table titles (National Migration (Part 1)). A fuller breakdown of 'areas' is given in Table 10 of the 'Regional Migration (Part 1)' datasets, comprising regions, metropolitan counties, other main urban centres and regional remainders, but these are being produced in machine-readable form rather than as published volumes and are not available at the time of writing.

The 1991 Census dataset which is of most interest to migration researchers is the Special Migration Statistics (SMS). One table (Table 5 in SMS, set 2) provides counts for the four-fold ethnic grouping. The great value of this dataset is that it contains full (i.e. 100 per cent) and unmodified (i.e. not subject to blurring) counts of one-year migrants by their district of residence on census night and by their district of residence one year previously (or country of residence if they were then living outside Great Britain). This means that it is possible to construct a district-to-district matrix of migrant flows separately for Whites, Blacks, South Asians and Others. The principal drawback is that, for confidentiality reasons, no flow of less than 10 migrants is given an ethnic group breakdown. Given the relatively sparse nature of the migration matrix (arising from the fact that migration is essentially a short distance process), this is a very common feature of the table and severely restricts the extent of origin- and destination-based analyses at the level of districts or groupings of districts. The only qualification to this generalisation is that the SMS data include two higher-order sets of flow matrices on a county-to-district and district-to-county basis, which allow the construction of a county-to-county migration matrix with a relatively low degree of data suppression. This feature, together with the fact that the SMS include total counts of numbers moving into and out of each district by ethnic group, raises hopes that in due course a fairly accurate district level flow matrix can be generated for each of the four ethnic categories.

Finally, there are two ways of using 1991 Census data on migration and ethnicity without being constrained by pre-ordained table structures. One is the Sample of Anonymised Records (SAR), or more strictly the two SARs – the 2 per cent sample of individual persons and 1 per cent sample of households. As outlined by Dale and Marsh (1993), the 1991 Census is the first to be used to generate datasets of individual records directly available to the user. In the case of the 2 per cent SAR this permits the characteristics of any individual migrant to be examined, including ethnic group and change of address. The latter, however, is limited in its geographical detail, comprising the SAR district of residence on census night and the region of residence one year previously (where region refers to the 10 standard regions, except for the South East which is split into inner London, outer London and the remainder).

The geographical detail in the household SAR is even more limited, with usual address on census night being given in no more detail than the regional level. In terms of the spatial analysis of migrant flows, this is unfortunate because of the predominance of short distance migration. Preliminary exploration of the individual person SAR, for instance, shows that, out of 7,919 non-Whites in the sample who are migrants, 565 did not state the location of their previous address, 1,720 had been living outside Britain 12 months before, 4,328 had been living at a different address somewhere in the same region and only 1,306 had moved in from one of the other 12 regions (only 661, if the South East is treated a a single region). So, while the sample size is considerably larger than that yielded by the LFS, caution nevertheless needs to be exercised in drawing conclusions, particularly where the migration behaviour of the separate minority ethnic groups is being studied.

The other way of using the census data is through the Longitudinal Study (LS), whose value for studying migration between 1971 and 1981 has already been stressed. In more detail, this is an approximately 1 per cent sample of people in England and Wales, comprising all residents whose birthday falls on one of four undisclosed dates (see Dale, 1993). This has, in the past, sometimes been used in a similar way to the SARs, in that customised analyses can be produced drawing on data from a single census. With the SAR providing 1991 Census data on this basis, the LS is unlikely to be used much for migration analysis in this manner, because although it provides district level data on usual residence 12 months before the census and on census night, the analyses which can be released to users have to satisfy certain confidentiality constraints. Where the LS will prove extremely valuable (once the 1991 Census records are entered into the dataset) is in the ability to compare the addresses of members of the LS sample in 1991 with those of 1981 and/or 1971, where records can be linked to one or both of the previous censuses. This not only has the advantage of enabling the examination of changes in people's characteristics and circumstances between censuses alongside any change in residential location, but also makes it possible to identify the ethnicity of such LS members (since this is a characteristic that by definition will not have changed over time). This provides the opportunity to rework the original 1971–81 analyses of migration (which had to use a birthplace-derived indicator of ethnicity), and permits the updating (to 1991) of such analyses. Moreover, the intercensal time periods over which these analyses can be made yields a far larger sample size of migrants than the one-year change of address data provided by the 1991 Census on its own.

Given that the purpose of this chapter is to describe the main features of the internal migration of the minority ethnic population and compare them with those of Whites, the main sources to be used comprise the Special Migration Statistics, together with the unmodified data on migrants available at district level and above, available in the County Reports and in machine-readable form from the ESRC/JISC Census purchase mounted at the Manchester Computing Centre. For basic descriptive analysis the SARs do not provide nearly as much information as these other sources, while as mentioned above, the LS was not ready for use with the 1991 data at the time of writing. The tables in the topic reports mentioned will be drawn upon where relevant, for though their geographical detail is much less than in the two main sources, they provide additional information, notably in adopting the 10-fold categorisation of ethnic group and providing some cross-tabulations with sex and (broad) age-group.

A cautionary note on the use of the 1991 Census migration data

Before proceeding with the substantive part of the paper, it is important to draw attention to a number of weaknesses of the census data, over and above the limitations outlined above relating to the structure of the tabulations available and issues of sample size.

Some of these are traditional problems arising from the nature of the question on the census form. As the question asks specifically about usual address one year ago, the information provided by the census cannot tell us about all the residential movements taking place over the intervening 12-month period. For instance, if a person moved house more than once, only a single move is recorded. If a person left their previous address and returned to it during that year, no migration is recorded. If someone moves and then dies before census night, no migration is recorded and, by definition, no one under one year of age at the census can be a migrant because they had no previous address. Furthermore, those who left Great Britain during the pre-census year are omitted entirely from the census and its migration statistics (though this is not of direct concern for this study of internal migration).

The other main problem relates to the fact that a proportion of those who should have been recorded as migrants according to the census definition, has been omitted. This problem of omission can arise for three reasons. In the first place, as noted above, not everyone who was resident in Britain on census night was returned on a census form. Even after special imputation procedures were adopted, the census count of residents is believed to omit just over 1.2 million, around 2.2 per cent short of the true figure. This is likely to affect migration rates as well as the actual counts of migrants, since the missing million are drawn disproportionately from those aged 16–29 years old, the most mobile period of the life course (Marsh, 1993). Second, some of those who were included on census forms were not entered as living at a different address 12 months before when they should have been. According to the Census Validation Survey, the question on usual address one year ago was answered incorrectly for 1.8 per cent of all persons, giving a net undercount of migrants of around 10 per cent. Third, analyses of geographical patterns of migration cannot be undertaken in cases where the location of the previous address is not stated or is inadequately described. In the 1991 Census, the number of 'origin not stated' cases totalled 325,630, 6.1 per cent of the 5.35 million migrants included in the census output.

As a final cautionary word, it is important to point out that the census change-of-address data cover a single year which may well not be typical of migration behaviour over the past few years. Data from the National Health Service Central Register show that overall levels of migration in the year to April 1991 were running at their lowest for a decade. Moreover, some very marked swings had taken place over the previous few years, particularly in patterns of net migration (Stillwell et al., 1992). Until the results of the 10-year change-of-address analysis are available from the LS, it will not be clear how confidently the patterns shown by the 1991 Census's migration data can be generalised over a longer period.

4.3   Migration by ethnic group: the national picture

In this first section of findings, we examine the numbers of migrants and compare ethnic groups on the basis of several ratios relating to the proportion of migrants among the base populations. This work draws on the statistics available in the Local Base Statistics, the County Reports and the Topic Reports. It is thus able to make use of the 10-fold ethnic group classification, though the four-fold summary groupings are also included for cross-referencing with the subsequent account based on the Special Migration Statistics. It should be noted that this part of the analysis must be couched in terms of the characteristics of 'migrant residents' and their share of the total number of residents in an area, because it is based entirely on data for people at their place of usual residence on census night, i.e. their home after their change of address.

Table 4.1 shows the number of Britain's usual residents who on census night were resident at an address different from that one year previously. Approximately 5.35 million people recorded by the census admitted to being migrants in this sense, representing almost 1 in 10 of the number of residents aged one year or over. It should be stressed (in keeping with comments in the previous section) that this is the raw count and is not adjusted in any way either to allow for errors in answering the change of usual address question or to compensate for the missing million factor.

In terms of ethnic group, the vast majority of migrants were, not surprisingly, White – 4.96 million or 92.8 per cent of all migrants (Table 4.1). This proportion is, however, somewhat lower than their 94.5 per cent share of the base population, and this is reflected in the somewhat lower than average proportion of Whites who were migrants, 9.70 per cent as opposed to the overall figure of 9.88 per cent. The minority ethnic populations had a propensity to migrate one third higher on average than the White population.

Among the nine minority ethnic groups, the largest absolute number of migrants is

Table 4.1   Migrant residents by ethnic group, Great Britain, 1991

Ethnic group	Migrant residents 1991 (number)	All residents aged 1+ 1991 (000s)	Migrants as proportion of all resident (percentage)
All	5,350,466	54,147.5	9.9
White	4,964,828	51,198.7	9.7
All ethnic minorities	385,638	2,948.8	13.1
Black total	124,202	870.5	14.3
Caribbean	45,229	492.5	9.2
African	53,102	207.0	25.7
Other	25,871	171.0	15.1
South Asian	138,500	1,448.8	9.6
Indian	73,279	826.3	8.9
Pakistani	45,848	464.4	9.9
Bangladeshi	19,373	158.0	12.3
Chinese and Other	122,936	629.4	19.5
Chinese	29,257	154.8	18.9
Other–Asian	43,965	194.5	22.6
Other–Other	49,714	280.1	17.7

Source: 1991 Census Local Base Statistics, Table 17, (ESRC/JISC purchase). Crown copyright.

found in the Indian population; at 73,279, these comprise 1.37 per cent of migrant residents in Britain. This, however, is entirely the product of their importance in the population at large, because their propensity to be migrants is, at 8.87 per cent, the lowest of all the ethnic groups, including Whites. The only other group below the propensity for Whites are the Black–Caribbeans. The level for Pakistanis is almost exactly the same as for the whole population, and after this in ascending order of mobility rate come the Bangladeshis, Black–Others, Other–Others, Chinese, Other–Asians and Black–Africans. For the last group, fully one quarter were recorded as having changed their address in the 12 months before census night – over two and a half times the overall average. In terms of the three-way summary grouping of the minority ethnic groups, the Chinese and Other category proves twice as mobile, and Blacks one and a half times as mobile, as Whites, while South Asians are shown to be slightly less mobile than the White population (Table 4.1).

Now, this chapter's primary concern is with internal migration, and it can be expected that the proportions of migrants among the minority ethnic populations are more likely to be swelled by people moving into Britain over the pre-census year than they will be for the White population. The next question therefore is: how much of the difference between Whites and the minority ethnic groups remains after the effect of recent immigration is removed? Table 4.2 attempts to answer this question, though it is complicated by the number of people whose previous address is not known, which is not only significant (particularly in comparison to the numbers moving into Britain from elsewhere in the world), but also differs considerably between ethnic groups. The true internal migration rate will lie somewhere between the results derived by assuming that all the 'origin not stated' people had moved into Britain during the pre-census year and those derived by assuming that they had all been living somewhere else in Britain a year before.

Table 4.2 presents the results achieved by taking both these extreme assumptions. The second data column shows the proportion of residents at census night who gave an address outside Great Britain as their residence one year before. For the White population, this was 0.5 per cent (or 1 in every 200), but for the minority ethnic populations the overall proportion was over five times as large, at 2.7 per cent. In terms of the three-way summary categories, it was highest for the Chinese and Others at 6.0 per cent, followed by Blacks at 2.5 per cent and South Asians at 1.5 per cent. For the nine separate minority ethnic groups, the proportion was particularly high for Other–Asians (9.4 per cent) and Black–Africans (7.5 per cent), both well over 10 times the level for Whites. At the other extreme, the figure for Black–Caribbeans was only slightly above the level for Whites, and those for Indians, Pakistanis, Black–Others and Bangladeshis are all below the overall level for the minority ethnic populations.

If these known recent immigrants are excluded from the calculation in order to produce a maximum possible estimate of the internal residential mobility rate, there is seen to be remarkably little difference between the White and the minority ethnic populations. The 10.35 per cent rate for the latter is just one eighth higher than the 9.20 per cent rate for the White population, as shown in the third data column of Table 4.2. Furthermore, the degree of variation between the minority ethnic groups is also much smaller. The mobility rate for Black–Africans remains the highest on

Table 4.2 *Migrant residents classified by place of origin as a proportion of residents, by ethnic group, Great Britain, 1990–91*

Ethnic group	Migrants as a percentage of residents aged 1+				
	All origins	From outside Great Britain	Remainder	Origin not stated	From within Great Britain
All	9.9	0.6	9.3	0.6	8.7
White	9.7	0.5	9.2	0.6	8.6
All ethnic minorities	13.1	2.7	10.4	1.4	8.9
Black total	14.3	2.5	11.8	2.1	9.6
Caribbean	9.2	0.6	8.6	1.4	7.1
African	25.7	7.5	18.1	4.0	14.1
Other	15.1	1.8	13.3	1.9	11.5
South Asian	9.6	1.5	8.1	0.8	7.3
Indian	8.9	1.2	7.7	0.6	7.0
Pakistani	9.9	1.7	8.2	1.0	7.2
Bangladeshi	12.3	2.1	10.1	1.5	8.6
Chinese and other	19.5	6.0	13.5	1.8	11.8
Chinese	18.9	5.3	13.7	1.5	12.1
Other –Asian	22.6	9.4	13.3	1.9	11.3
Other –Other	17.7	4.1	13.7	1.8	11.9

Note: Rows may not sum as indicated because of rounding. Final column refers to those specifying somewhere in Great Britain as their address a year before the Census, i.e. excluding migrants from outside Britain and 'origin not stated'.
Source: Calculated from 1991 Census National Migration 100%, Great Britain, Table 11 and Local Base Statistics, Table 17. Crown copyright.

Table 4.3 *Within-Britain migrants as a percentage of residents by ethnic group and age, Great Britain, 1991*

Ethnic group	Age group (years)					
	1–15	16–19	20–29	30–44	45+	All ages 1+
All	8.6	9.6	20.6	8.7	3.7	8.7
White	8.7	9.1	20.9	8.7	3.7	8.6
All ethnic minorities	7.7	8.0	15.9	8.9	4.1	8.9
Black total	9.3	9.9	15.9	9.8	2.9	9.6
Caribbean	7.2	8.4	13.2	7.1	2.3	7.1
African	11.2	12.5	21.1	14.0	6.1	14.1
Other	10.4	10.6	16.2	10.9	4.2	11.5
South Asian	6.2	6.5	13.0	7.1	4.4	7.3
Indian	5.8	6.1	13.6	6.7	3.8	7.0
Pakistani	6.3	5.9	11.9	7.5	4.7	7.2
Bangladeshi	7.4	9.4	12.9	9.1	7.6	8.6
Chinese and Other	9.4	9.8	21.3	11.5	5.2	11.8
Chinese	7.9	9.6	23.5	11.1	5.4	12.1
Other–Asian	9.1	10.5	19.4	11.1	5.8	11.3
Other–Other	10.1	9.5	21.2	12.3	4.6	11.9

Source: Calculated from 1991 Census National Migration 100%, Great Britain, Table 11.

this basis, at 18.1 per cent, but otherwise the range is down to six percentage points, from 7.7 per cent for Indians to 13.7 per cent for both the Chinese and Other–Others.

If the 'origin not stated' category of migrant is excluded from the analysis in order to deal only with those who can confidently be assigned a previous address within Great Britain, then the differences become even smaller. As shown in the fifth data column of Table 4.2, the proportion of the minority ethnic population that is known to have been an internal migrant in the year before census night is, at 8.9 per cent, only 0.3 per cent higher than the 8.6 per cent level for the White population. The Black–African rate is now down to 14.1 per cent, and the range for the other eight minority groups is now as little as five percentage points (ranging from 7.1 for Black–Caribbeans to 12.1 for the Chinese). Even so, if compared directly with one another, it can equally be seen that the Indian population contains only half as many 1990–91 internal migrants per capita as the Black–African population, and that the proportion of Black–Caribbean and Pakistani populations moving house within Britain over that 12-month period was also significantly below the proportion for the White population.

At the same time, it is important to check how far these differences are the result of age-structure effects, because it is well known that migration levels vary through the life course and also that the minority ethnic populations are much younger on average than the White population. Table 4.3 shows the proportion of migrants in each of five broad age-groups. At this scale it can be seen that 20–29-year-olds contain particularly high proportions of within-Britain migrants, whereas the 45+ age-group contains relatively few. For all minority ethnic groups taken together, the proportion of migrants is below the level for Whites in the three younger age-groups (particularly the 20–29-year-olds) and just slightly above the level for Whites for the age-groups 30–44 and 45+. These last two age-groups comprise only 42 per cent of the minority population as a whole, compared to 61 per cent of Whites, so it is clearly the youthful structure of the former that pushes their overall proportion of migrants as high as 8.9 per cent. If their age-specific proportion of migrants was to be applied to the age distribution of Whites, the within-Britain migration rate for the minority ethnic population would be significantly lower than that for Whites.

This conclusion holds for some of the nine minority ethnic groups but by no means all of them. As already noted, the overall proportion of migrants for Black–Caribbeans, Indians and Pakistanis is lower than for Whites, and Table 4.3 demonstrates that this is the case for all age-groups except for Indians and Pakistanis in the 45+ category. The overall differences between these groups and Whites would therefore be even greater were age structure to be standardised. At the other extreme, however, the high overall proportions of migrants found for Black–Africans, Black–Others, Chinese, Other–Asians and Other–Others would remain above the level for Whites even after age standardisation, judging by their generally higher percentages across the five age-groups (Table 4.3).

Within-Britain migration by type and distance of move

In Tables 4.1 and 4.2 we have looked at the proportion of the 1991 Census resident population that can be considered migrants, and differentiated between those moving into Britain from elsewhere in the world and those moving house within Britain (as far as is possible given the 'origin not stated' phenomenon). It should be noted that none of the ratios presented in Tables 4.1 to 4.3 should be interpreted as a mobility rate in the strict sense of the term, because these ratios have not been calculated on the basis of the population at risk but only as a proportion of the population identified after the change of address has taken place. Also, no indication has been given of the extent of mobility in terms of the distance of move, except perhaps implicitly in terms of the breakdown between internal migrants and migrants from outside Great Britain. This section seeks to rectify both of these inadequacies.

Table 4.4 presents the numbers of 1991 residents in Britain found by the census to have migrated within Britain during the pre-census year, and differentiates between those moving between the 10 standard regions and those moving within regions. (These counts necessarily exclude migrants classed as origin not stated.) The percentage figures in Table 4.4 denote true migration rates because the base population shown in the first column has been adjusted so as to represent the number of people at risk of being a declared internal migrant one year before the census, i.e. the 1991 population minus the numbers of both migrants entering Britain during the year and the numbers of 'origin not stated' migrants. Comparison of the third data column in Table 4.4 with the last data column in Tables 4.2 and 4.3 reveals that, as a result of these adjustments to the population base, the migration rates are higher than the proportions of residents admitting to being internal migrants — 8.77 and 8.66 respectively for the total population, but with larger differentials for the minority ethnic populations owing to the greater incidence of recent immigrants and 'origin not stated' for these.

Turning to the separate rates for between-region and within-region migration shown in Table 4.4, the overall differences between the White and non-White populations are found to be relatively small, but significant. Overall, the minority ethnic populations have a lower propensity than Whites for inter-regional migration (by around 15 per cent), but the reverse is the case for intra-regional moves (with minority populations being the higher by around 15 per cent). The contrast with the White population is particularly clear for the Black group, with its well below average overall rate of movement between regions and above average rate within regions. This results from the combination of very high intra-regional mobility for Black–Caribbeans, Black–Africans and Black–Others and very low inter-regional mobility for Black–Caribbeans. This pattern is also followed by the Bangladeshis, but Indians and Pakistanis are less mobile than the White population both between and within regions. By contrast, all three groups under the Chinese and Other group heading are characterised by higher rates than the White group for both types of migration (Table 4.4).

Table 4.4 *Between region and within region migration rates by ethnic group, Great Britain, 1990–91*

Ethnic group	Population at risk (000s)	Migration within Britain		Migration between regions		Migration within regions	
		000s	%	000s	%	000s	%
All	53,485	4,688.2	8.8	629.7	1.2	4,058.4	7.0
White	50,659	4,425.1	8.7	601.2	1.2	3,823.9	7.0
All ethnic minorities	2,826	263.0	9.3	28.5	1.0	234.6	8.0
Black total	830	83.9	10.1	6.1	0.7	77.8	9.0
Caribbean	482	35.0	7.3	2.4	0.5	32.6	6.0
African	183	29.2	16.0	1.9	1.0	27.3	14.0
Other	165	19.6	11.9	1.7	1.0	17.9	10.0
South Asian	1,415	105.1	7.4	12.8	0.9	92.4	6.0
Indian	811	58.0	7.2	8.2	1.0	49.8	6.0
Pakistani	45	33.4	7.4	3.4	0.8	30.0	6.0
Bangladeshi	152	13.7	9.0	1.1	0.7	12.6	8.0
Chinese and Other	581	74.0	12.8	9.7	1.7	64.4	11.0
Chinese	144	18.8	13.0	3.0	2.0	15.8	10.0
Other–Asian	173	22.0	12.8	2.4	1.4	19.6	11.0
Other–Other	264	33.3	12.6	4.3	1.6	29.0	11.0

Note: Population at risk refers to the number of residents estimated to be at risk of migrating between and within regions of Britain in the year proceeding the 1991 Census. It is calculated as the total number of residents aged one year or over at the 1991 Census, minus those whose address a year earlier was outside Great Britain or not stated.
Source: Calculated from 1991 Census National Migration 100%, Great Britain, Table 11.

Looking down the migration rate columns of Table 4.4, it is clear that, certainly for the pre-census year (1990/91), the Chinese were the most mobile between regions, with nearly 1 in 50 of those at risk being involved. This is four times the rate of inter-regional movement experienced by Black–Caribbeans. After the Black–Caribbeans, Pakistanis and Bangladeshis are the least mobile, while Other–Asians and Other–Others are the next most mobile after the Chinese. As regards migration within regions, it is the Black–Africans who proved most prone; at 14.9 per cent they were nearly two and a half times more mobile than Indians. Pakistanis and Black–Caribbeans have the next lowest mobility, while Black–Other and all three Chinese and Other groups lie close to the 11 per cent mark.

Table 4.5 presents the distribution of within-Britain migrants by type of move, for each ethnic heading, not only showing the proportion of moves that crossed regional boundaries but also breaking down within-region moves into three categories according to level of geographical boundary crossed. At first glance, the most impressive feature of Table 4.5 is the predominance of short distance moves, a well known feature of migration behaviour. Not only are between-region moves relatively uncommon, but among the within-region moves it is those that do not cross a local authority district boundary that are by far the most numerous. This pattern is found for all the groups shown.

Nevertheless, Table 4.5 reveals some significant differences between groups in the importance of the various types of migration – differences that are not regular over

Table 4.5 *Distribution of within-Britain migration by type of move and ethnic group, 1990–91*

Ethnic group	Within district	Between district within county	Between county within region	Between region
All	61.2	13.8	11.6	13.4
White	61.3	13.7	11.4	13.6
All ethnic minorities	58.7	15.9	14.5	10.8
Black total	59.2	17.2	16.4	7.2
Caribbean	63.5	14.7	15.0	6.8
African	49.9	22.8	20.7	6.6
Other	65.2	13.4	12.5	8.9
South Asian	62.2	14.2	11.4	12.1
Indian	56.3	16.3	13.3	14.2
Pakistan	73.5	8.5	7.6	10.3
Bangladeshi	59.8	19.4	12.8	8.0
Chinese and Other	53.3	16.8	16.9	13.1
Chinese	49.5	17.2	17.6	15.8
Other–Asian	52.9	17.8	18.2	11.1
Other–Other	55.7	15.9	15.6	12.8

Note: Data refer to composition of type of move for each group identified, with each row summing to 100 per cent (apart from effects of rounding). The term 'district' includes the London Boroughs, the term 'county' includes the Scottish regions, and the term 'regions' refers to the 10 standard regions of Great Britain.
Source: Calculated from 1991 Census National Migration, 100%, Great Britain, Table 11.

distance in every case. Thus, for the minority ethnic populations overall, the proportion of moves taking place between regions is lower than for the White population, but so also is their proportion of within-district moves according to these data, with the two intermediate types being over-represented. This pattern is particularly characteristic of Black–Africans, with much lower levels of within-district and between-region migration than average; it is also found to a lesser extent in the case of Other–Asians and Other–Others. Among the rest of the groups, the Chinese are similar to Black–Africans in their low proportion of within-district moves, but have much the higher proportion of inter-regional moves. Indians, with all but within-district moves being above average, contrast sharply with Pakistanis, with their great emphasis on within-district moves.

Looking down the columns in Table 4.5, it is clear that, among those who changed address within Britain, shorter distance moves (i.e. within districts) were particularly important for Pakistanis, followed by Black–Others and Black–Caribbeans. For all other minority ethnic groups, within-district moves were less common than for the White population, and were especially rare for the Chinese and Black–Africans. At the other extreme, the Chinese recorded the highest proportion of between-region moves, followed by the Indians, but for all the other minority groups inter-regional migration was less important than for the White population. The two intermediate categories are relatively most important for Black–Africans, Other–Asians, Chinese and Other–Others, and are of well below average importance for Pakistanis.

Table 4.6 *Within district moves as a proportion of within-Britain migration by ethnic group and age, 1990–91*

Ethnic group	Age group (years)					
	1–15	16–19	20–29	30–44	45+	All ages 1+
All	68.1	62.0	57.5	58.7	64.4	61.2
White	68.2	62.1	57.8	58.8	64.4	61.3
All ethnic minorities	67.4	60.1	52.2	56.0	64.7	58.7
Black total	68.3	61.0	53.4	55.0	68.1	59.2
Caribbean	73.3	62.6	58.3	59.5	73.4	63.5
African	56.5	52.7	45.0	50.1	57.3	49.9
Other	72.8	66.8	57.6	57.8	63.0	65.2
South Asian	69.9	62.1	54.3	60.7	66.8	62.2
Indian	63.8	58.5	48.7	56.2	62.7	56.3
Pakistani	79.6	73.9	66.2	71.1	76.9	73.5
Bangladeshi	63.8	52.0	54.9	58.5	63.7	59.8
Chinese and Other	61.9	55.2	48.3	51.1	56.7	53.3
Chinese	56.3	49.2	46.0	48.7	59.5	49.5
Other–Asian	59.8	56.0	48.8	52.2	55.1	52.9
Other–Other	64.0	58.1	49.6	51.7	56.1	55.7

Source: Calculated from 1991 Census National Migration 100%, Great Britain, Table 11.

Bangladeshis score relatively strongly on between district but within county moves, while Black–Caribbeans are notably above average for between county but within region moves (Table 4.5).

Because the importance of the various types of move differs with age (as shown in Table 4.3), it is important to check that the patterns seen in Table 4.5 are not the result largely of differences in age composition between ethnic groups. A partial check is provided in Table 4.6, which focuses on the importance of within-district moves for the same broad age-groups as in Table 4.3. For the population as a whole, it can be seen that there is a much higher than average proportion of such short-distance migration among the youngest and oldest age-groups, with relatively low proportions for the 20–29 and 30–44-year-olds. The proportion of within-district moves among the minority ethnic group migrants is close to the average for the 1–15 and 45+ age-groups, but significantly lower than average for the intermediate age-groups, notably the 20–29-year-olds. Clearly the lower significance of within-district moves shown by the minority populations as a whole is not simply due to their younger age structure, but instead reflects a clear difference in migration behaviour.

Furthermore, inspection of the ethnic group breakdown in Table 4.6 reveals the existence of contrasts in migration behaviour within the minority ethnic population. The low overall importance of these shorter-distance moves for the Chinese and Other group (53.3 per cent) is reflected in the details for all five age-groups – all significantly below the overall figure for the minority ethnic population and very much lower than for the White population. The proportions for South Asians are significantly higher than for the minority population overall (in all five age-groups), while the slightly above average proportion for Blacks is mirrored in all age-groups except 30–44-year-olds. The proportions shown for the nine separate minority ethnic groups are not quite so regular across the age-groups, but in general there are substantial differences in movement distances between ethnic groups that do not result from their varied age structure.

Finally, the 1991 Census allows an examination of within-Britain migration on the basis of the more precise measure of 'distance of move', though this is possible for ethnic groups only through customised tabulations from the SARs as it is not a standard output in any census dataset or report. The results of analysing the 2 per cent sample of individuals are shown in Table 4.7. Almost 55 per cent of the minority ethnic group migrants who moved within Britain, and stated their previous address, had moved less than 5 km, one sixth more than for the White population, while under 7 per cent had moved at least 200 km, barely half the percentage of the White population. Only the Chinese came close to the figure for the White population, with 13.1 per cent living at least 200 km from their previous address, and they were also the only group to record a smaller proportion of 0–4 km migrants than Whites. All three Black groups share the distinction of being least involved in 200+ km moves, and on aggregate contain the highest proportion of shorter distance moves – 77.5 per cent moving less than 10 km, compared with 69.4 per cent for South Asians, 63.9 per cent for Chinese and Other groups, and 59.8 per cent for Whites.

Table 4.7   *Within Britain migrants' distance of move by ethnic group, 1990–91*

Ethnic group	Distance of move (km)					
	0–4	5–9	10–49	50–199	200+	Number
All	47.1	13.2	14.4	12.4	12.9	95,177
White	46.7	13.1	14.4	12.5	13.3	89,815
All ethnic minorities	54.6	15.9	12.6	10.0	6.9	5,362
Black total	56.9	20.6	12.9	6.0	3.7	1,780
Caribbean	58.4	21.0	11.0	6.2	3.4	762
African	51.6	23.9	15.4	5.4	3.7	591
Other	61.6	15.2	12.9	6.3	4.0	427
South Asian	57.3	12.1	11.0	11.8	7.7	2,055
Indian	52.1	14.0	13.3	13.5	7.1·	1,175
Pakistani	66.3	7.7	6.7	9.3	10.0	627
Bangladeshi	59.3	14.6	10.7	10.3	5.1	253
Chinese and Other	48.3	15.5	14.3	12.3	9.6	1,527
Chinese	40.2	14.5	14.5	17.6	13.1	358
Other–Asian	49.7	17.9	15.5	9.7	7.1	491
Other–Other	51.6	14.3	13.3	11.3	9.4	678

Note: Rows may not sum to exactly 100 per cent because of rounding. The final column indicates sample size. In addition to the 95,177 within-Britain migrants analysed here, the dataset contains 7,498 migrants from outside Great Britain and 8,110 migrants with 'origins not stated'.
Source: Calculated from 1991 Census two per cent individual Sample of Anonymised Records. (ESRC/ JISC purchase). Crown copyright.

The national picture: a summary of key findings

This national-scale analysis of the migration behaviour of Britain's population, by ethnic group, has revealed some clear similarities and contrasts. Taking all nine minority ethnic groups as a single population, they were found to contain a higher proportion of migrants than the White population, but this difference evaporated when allowance was made for both those who had been living outside Great Britain a year before census night and those classified as 'origin not stated'. In fact, when attention is focused on the within-Britain moves of the under 30-year-olds, the age-group in which the major part of the minority ethnic population is concentrated, it is found that minority ethnic populations change address within Britain rather less than Whites. Moreover, those who did migrate within Britain tended to move over shorter distances than Whites. Though the proportion moving within the same district is lower than for Whites, the proportion moving less than 5 km is significantly higher, while the proportions moving between regions and moving at least 200 km are both much lower than for Whites.

The analysis has also identified some major differences between the individual minority ethnic groups in both migration rate and distance of move, though these two measures are not closely related. In terms of the three broad groupings, 'Chinese and Other' displays both the highest migration rate and the highest proportion of long-distance movement; Blacks exhibit the next highest migration but the lowest proportion of long-distance moves. Other significant differences have been found between the nine separate groups; most notably, the higher migration rates for Black–Africans, Chinese, Other–Asians and Other–Others, the high proportion of long distance moves by the Chinese and the very low proportion of long-distance moves by all three Black groups.

4.4 Migration by ethnic group: the geographical dimension

All the analyses so far have examined the residential mobility of each of the various ethnic groupings as a single national population. The question to be addressed now is the extent to which the scale and nature of migration varies between different parts of the country and whether any such geographical variations follow patterns across the ethnic groups.

There are several alternative ways of examining geographical variations in within-Britain migration, given that for any particular area people can change address within that area, move away from it to another part of the country or move into it from elsewhere in Britain. The options for study are as follows:

(i)   Numbers changing address within the area
(ii) Numbers moving from an address in the area to one outside the area
(iii) Numbers moving from an address outside the area to one inside the area
(iv) Numbers leaving an address in the area for any destination in Britain, i.e. (i) plus (ii)
(v)   Numbers entering an address in the area from any origin in Britain, i.e. (i) plus (iii).

Option (i) can be referred to as 'local turnover', involving movement between addresses within a particular area and not altering the area's population size or composition. Options (iv) and (v) constitute alternative measures of overall turnover (with respect to within-Britain moves) and have the advantage that they are not affected by the rather arbitrary nature of area boundaries and differences in the size of areas (i.e. the things that determine which moves are 'local' and which are not). Options (ii) and (iii), by identifying moves into and out of an area, have the advantage of providing a measure of the 'non-local turnover', movement which can be influenced by the relative attractiveness of places. These two measures are, of course, needed to calculate the migration balance for each area so as to gauge the net effect of migration on population distribution. Net migration is dealt with in the next section; here the emphasis is on variations between areas in the propensity to migrate.

The following constitutes a brief account of the main results derived from calculating these measures. Counties and Scottish regions are used as the areas, with the Orkneys, Shetlands and Western Isles being treated as a single area (called 'Islands') to give a total of 64. The raw data are taken from the Special Migration Statistics, Set 2, Table 5 and relate to all migrants with known origin and destination within Great Britain. As explained earlier, only four ethnic groupings can be recognised from this source: White, Black, South Asian, and Chinese and Other. The results in this section are not affected by data suppression because of the nature of the data needed from the SMS matrices: the marginals, which are not subject to suppression, and the diagonals, which in the 'County-District' version of the table are all large enough to escape suppression. It must be noted, however, that there is a small numbers problem, even at the county level, and with minorities collapsed into only three categories. As a result, areas with very few migrants or very small population bases can appear to have very low or very high migration rates respectively. Partly to overcome this problem, as well as for ease of comparison with Whites, an overall rate for minority ethnic groups combined has also been calculated in each case.

Migration within and out of areas

We begin with the movements for which migration propensities can be calculated in relation to the population at risk, i.e. the local residents of each area (albeit measured at the end of the observation period rather than at the beginning). Table 4.8 gives details of the areas with the five highest and lowest rates of within-area migration for Whites, for all three minority ethnic groups together, and then for the latter separately. This is option (i) above, the local turnover rate, though note that, given the large size of areas like North Yorkshire and Highlands, the distances moved within them can be quite substantial. Among the White population, it can be seen that Tayside and Grampian experienced the most movement during this one year, with at least 8.5 per cent changing address within these areas; Scotland dominates the top of the list, perhaps reflecting the relative buoyancy of its housing market during this period. At the other extreme, the level of movement among Whites was lowest in Warwickshire – at 5.0 per cent, under three fifths of the Tayside level. For the minority ethnic population as a whole, the range between highest

Table 4.8 *Local turnover rates by ethnic group: five highest and lowest county-level areas, 1990–91*

Highest rates/areas		Lowest rates/areas	
Whites			
8.6	Tayside	5.0	Warwickshire
8.5	Grampian	5.1	Powys
8.0	Lothian	5.1	Cheshire
7.8	Strathclyde	5.3	Mid Glamorgan
7.6	Devon	5.3	Clwyd
All ethnic minorities			
10.1	West Glamorgan	2.9	Powys
10.1	Strathclyde	4.0	Warwickshire
10.0	Tayside	4.1	Isle of Wight
9.9	Tyne and Wear	5.0	Northumberland
9.8	East Sussex	5.2	Hereford and Worcester
Blacks			
11.6	Lothian	2.8	Powys
11.5	East Sussex	2.9	Isle of Wight
11.4	Devon	4.8	Hereford and Worcester
11.1	West Glamorgan	4.9	Central
11.0	Gwynedd	5.9	Highland
South Asians			
11.1	Gwynedd	0.6	Dumfries and Galloway
10.4	Cornwall	1.1	Powys
9.4	Highland	2.3	Isle of Wight
9.2	Borders	3.0	Warwickshire
8.9	Tayside	3.4	Gwent
Chinese and Others			
13.7	West Glamorgan	3.3	Powys
13.2	Strathclyde	4.9	Northumberland
12.5	Tyne and Wear	5.0	Mid Glamorgan
11.9	Tayside	5.0	Cheshire
11.4	South Glamorgan	5.0	Warwickshire

Note: Data refer to the percentage of the relevent 1991 population that changed address within the named area.
Source: Calculated from 1991 Census Special Migration Statistics and Local Base Statistics (ESRC/JISC purchase). Crown copyright.

and lowest is nearly three times that for Whites. At the top end, 1 in 10 changed address within the same area, while at the other extreme the level for Powys was only 1 in 35, and for three other areas it was fewer than 1 in 20. Similarly wide variations in within-county movement are found for the three separate minority ethnic groupings, with particularly high local mobility (around one in six) recorded by the Chinese and Other group in Strathclyde, West Glamorgan, and Tyne and Wear – none of these three areas being subject to the small numbers problem.

The level of out-migration – option (ii) in the list above – can also be treated as a migration propensity, because the population at risk of moving away is that of the local area. As shown in Table 4.9, for the White population, Greater London lies at one extreme, with 3.7 per cent of its population moving out of the county to

Table 4.9 *Out-migration rates by ethnic group: five highest and lowest county-level areas, 1990–91*

Highest rates/areas		Lowest rates/areas	
Whites			
3.7	Greater London	1.1	Strathclyde
3.5	Berkshire	1.3	Mid Glamorgan
3.5	Oxfordshire	1.3	Gwent
3.5	Surrey	1.3	Cleveland
3.3	Buckinghamshire	1.3	Merseyside
All ethnic minorities			
7.5	Cumbria	1.0	West Midlands
7.4	Isle of Wight	1.4	West Yorkshire
7.2	Gwynedd	1.4	Greater Manchester
6.8	Dumfries and Galloway	1.5	Leicestershire`
6.6	Norfolk	1.6	Lancashire
Blacks			
12.1	Dumfries and Galloway	0.8	West Midlands
9.4	Northumberland	1.2	Greater Manchester
9.3	Islands	1.3	Nottinghamshire
9.1	Cumbria	1.4	West Yorkshire
9.1	Norfolk	1.6	South Glamorgan
South Asians			
18.0	Isle of Wight	0.0	Islands
12.9	Powys	0.9	West Midlands
9.4	Cumbria	1.1	Bedfordshire
9.2	Cornwall	1.2	West Yorkshire
8.6	Gwynedd	1.2	Greater Manchester
Chinese and Others			
7.4	Dumfries and Galloway	2.2	West Midlands
6.8	Gwynedd	2.6	West Yorkshire
6.3	Central	2.6	Greater Manchester
6.1	Mid Glamorgan	2.7	Merseyside
6.0	Cumbria	2.8	Powys

Note: Data refer to the percentage of the relevent 1991 population that moved out of the named area to an address elsewhere in Britain.
Source: Calculated from 1991 Census Special Migration Statistics and Local Base Statistics (ESRC/JISC purchase). Crown copyright.

somewhere else in Britain during the year before the census. Berkshire, Surrey and Oxfordshire share rates of around 3.5 per cent, reflecting the high propensity of people in the south east of England to engage in these longer distance moves. By contrast, larger conurbations and coalfields outside southern England dominate the list of areas with the lowest rates of out-migration, with only 1.1 per cent of Strathclyde's White population moving out of the region and 1.3 per cent for four others. Similarly low rates are found for the minority ethnic populations in the same types of areas, including West Midlands county, West Yorkshire and Greater Manchester. The highest rates of departure at this county level are found for Blacks and South Asians, and generally for areas where these groups are very weakly represented in the whole population, suggesting a lack of retention where there is not already a certain critical mass.

Table 4.10 shows the combined effect of within-county moves and departures from these areas, as an overall measure of the migration propensity of the local populations and one which is not distorted by the position of the area boundaries – option (iv) above. For the White population, the propensity to change address during the year before the census ranged from 10.7 per cent of residents in Oxfordshire to 6.5 per cent in Mid Glamorgan. For the minority ethnic population as a whole, the least mobile areas have similarly low rates (e.g. 6.7 per cent for Warwickshire), but at the upper end the rates are significantly higher than for Whites. This is particularly the case for Blacks and South Asians in more peripheral and sparsely populated parts of Britain.

Table 4.10 *Propensity to leave an address by ethnic group: five highest and lowest county-level areas, 1990–91*

Highest rates/areas		Lowest rates/areas	
Whites			
10.7	Oxfordshire	6.5	Mid Glamorgan
10.5	Tayside	6.8	Merseyside
10.3	Grampian	6.9	Gwent
10.1	Berkshire	6.9	Clwyd
10.0	Lothian	6.9	West Glamorgan
All ethnic minorities			
16.7	Gwynedd	6.7	Warwickshire
15.6	Cumbria	6.9	Leicestershire
15.2	Norfolk	7.0	West Midlands
15.0	Cornwall	7.1	Bedfordshire
14.9	Grampian	7.5	West Yorkshire
Blacks			
22.4	Dumfries and Galloway	6.8	Isle of Wight
18.2	Fife	7.2	West Midlands
18.2	Norfolk	7.9	Highland
17.8	Devon	8.5	Hereford and Worcester
17.7	Gwynedd	8.6	Nottinghamshire
South Asians			
20.4	Isle of Wight	4.7	Dumfries and Galloway
19.7	Gwynedd	5.3	Warwickshire
19.6	Cornwall	5.5	Gwent
15.2	Grampian	5.8	Bedfordshire
14.6	Cumbria	6.0	Leicestershire
Chinese and Others			
18.2	West Glamorgan	6.2	Powys
16.8	Tayside	8.6	Northumberland
16.5	Tyne and Wear	8.7	Warwickshire
16.2	Central	9.6	Hertfordshire
16.2	Strathclyde	9.7	Cheshire

Note: Data refer to the percentage of the relevent 1991 population that changed address within the named area or moved out to an address elsewhere in Britain.
Source: Calculated from 1991 Census Special Migration Statistics and Local Base Statistics (ESRC/JISC purchase). Crown copyright.

Table 4.11 *In-migration rates by ethnic group: five highest and lowest county-level areas, 1990–91*

Highest rates/areas		Lowest rates/areas	
Whites			
3.7	Buckinghamshire	0.9	Strathclyde
3.6	Oxfordshire	1.0	Merseyside
3.6	Surrey	1.1	Cleveland
3.5	Wiltshire	1.1	Greater Manchester
3.4	Berkshire	1.2	West |Midlands
All ethnic minorities			
9.9	Isle of Wight	0.9	West Midlands
8.5	Northumberland	0.9	West Yorkshire
8.1	Dumfries and Galloway	1.3	Lancashire
8.0	Gwynedd	1.4	Leicestershire
7.6	Borders	1.5	Greater Manchester
Blacks			
15.1	Powys	0.7	West Yorkshire
13.9	Borders	0.8	West Midlands
12.4	Gwynedd	0.9	Lancashire
11.7	Cornwall	1.1	Leicestershire
11.2	Dyfed	1.3	Greater Manchester
South Asians			
25.7	Dumfries and Galloway	0.7	West Midlands
15.8	Isle of Wight	1.1	West Yorkshire
13.2	Islands	1.4	Greater Manchester
10.2	Powys	1.4	Nottinghamshire
9.4	Northumberland	1.4	Borders
Chinese and Others			
8.4	Northumberland	1.9	Strathclyde
8.3	Islands	2.1	West Midlands
7.8	Borders	2.3	Merseyside
7.6	Highlands	2.4	West Yorkshire
7.0	Isle of Wight	2.5	Greater Manchester

Note: Data refer to the percentage of the relevent 1991 population that moved into the named area from elsewhere in Britain.
Source: Calculated from 1991 Census Special Migration Statistics and Local Base Statistics (ESRC/JISC purchase). Crown copyright.

In-migration and migrant residents

Table 4.11 shows the reverse of the process portrayed in Table 4.9, namely people who moved into the named areas from elsewhere in Britain during the year before the census, i.e. option (iii) in the earlier list. These in-migration rates, however, have more limited meaning than those in Table 4.9, because they merely denote the significance of in-migration for the relevant population and cannot be used to represent the mobility propensies of individual groups of people. They could equally be called newcomer rates, in that they refer to the proportion of residents who are new to the area compared to the year before.

Viewed in this light, it can be seen that in 1990–91 in-migration boosted the White population most in Buckinghamshire, Oxfordshire and Surrey, all with newcomers making up at least 3.6 per cent of those populations, while Strathclyde and Merseyside were attracting fewest newcomers to their White populations. For the minority ethnic population as a whole, the newcomer rate was considerably higher than the maximum level for the White population in many counties, most notably in some more rural northern and western areas where newcomers comprised at least 1 in 12 of the minority population. In the areas of more established minority settlement, however, in-migrants from the rest of Great Britain during 1990–91 made up only around 1 per cent of the minority ethnic population – a figure comparable to that for Whites in the least attractive areas.

With respect to option (v) in the earlier list, it is possible to measure the proportion of the relevant population that was new to its address – people who can be termed migrant residents in that they were living in the area at the time of the census and had moved house during the previous 12 months, in this context from somewhere else in Britain (including an address in the same area). The results are shown in Table 4.12. As regards the White population, Grampian is found to contain the largest proportion of these migrant residents in a list which is dominated by Scottish regions and English university counties, while Mid Glamorgan and Merseyside are shown to have the smallest proportions. The proportions of migrant residents in the minority ethnic population as a whole are similar to Whites at the bottom of the ranking – around 7 per cent for Leicestershire, Warwickshire, West Midlands and West Yorkshire – but much higher than for Whites at the top end, with those at a new address making up around 1 in 6 of the minority population in Gwynedd, Borders and Islands. Admittedly, there is an element of the small numbers problem here, especially with Borders and Islands, but Gwynedd's rate is based on 174 migrants among 1,873 residents and both Dorset and Norfolk contained over 5,000 minority residents in 1991.

Patterns of net migration and population redistribution

So far, attention has been focused primarily on the propensity for residential mobility and secondarily on the importance of migrants in the population. These aspects have been examined first at national scale and then at the level of counties and Scottish regions. This work has been based entirely on measures of gross migration, including all recorded one-year changes of address taking place in Britain for which the census could confidently locate the previous address. This section tackles the question of the net effect of these changes of address on the distribution of the various ethnic groups. For Great Britain as a whole, the net effect is nil because the study covers only those who were alive and living in Britain at both the beginning and end of the year. As the net migration balance for any area must be calculated by subtracting out-migration from in-migration, this analysis can be undertaken only by reference to the SMS, limiting the treatment to the four broad ethnic groupings as used in the previous section.

The purpose of this analysis is primarily descriptive. Most attention is given to the three minority ethnic groups because the patterns for Whites are very close to those

Figure 4.1 *Net migration of minority ethnic groups between counties and Scottish regions,* 1990–91: (a) all ethnic minorities; (b) Blacks; (c) South Asians; (d) Chinese and Others*

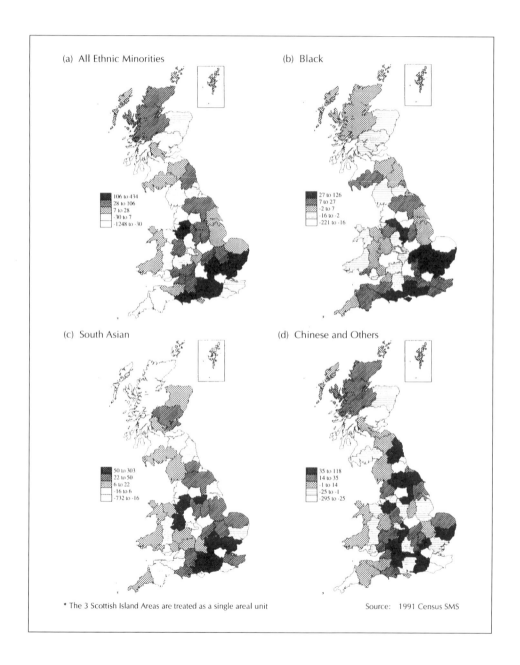

of the total population, which are already well documented elsewhere (see, in particular, Stillwell et al, 1992). The availability for the first time of census migration data by ethnic group, however, makes it possible to address two more specific questions. One relates to whether migration is leading to any dispersal of the minority ethnic populations away from the well established concentrations in certain parts of the country, or is reinforcing the existing geographical disparities. The second is the degree of correspondence between the minority ethnic population shifts resulting from within-Britain migration and the redistribution of the White population; notably whether ethnic minority redistribution is taking place along clearly defined channels that are markedly different from those followed by Whites or parallels those of the Whites in a way that might be interpreted as constituting an integrated migration system.

Figure 4.1 shows the absolute levels of net migration for counties and Scottish regions both for the minority ethnic population as a whole and for the three separate groupings. Taking the former, it can be seen that the largest net gains took place in a line of counties stretching from Dorset to Suffolk. The leading county was Berkshire (+434), followed by Bedfordshire (+253), Surrey (+238), Buckinghamshire (+231) and West Sussex (+205). Cheshire and Greater Manchester form a secondary core of large gains. The main losers were principally areas with major urban centres, with the largest numbers of net out-migrants being in Greater London (-1,248), West Yorkshire (-666), West Midlands county (-378), Lancashire (-195) and Strathclyde (-174). Thus, there would seem to be a deconcentration from most of the major conurbations, with Greater Manchester and South Yorkshire as significant exceptions.

When the picture is broken down into the three separate ethnic groupings (Figures 1 (b) to (d)), it is easier to generalise about the losers than the gainers. Certain areas feature regularly among the heavier losers, with Strathclyde, West Yorkshire, Leicestershire and London falling in the bottom quintile for all three ethnic groupings, and several others like Lancashire, Mid Glamorgan and West Midlands appearing there twice. As regards the gainers, only Hertfordshire and West Sussex feature consistently in the top quintile, and even if the top two quintiles are considered, the list expands only as far as eight more: Dorset, Berkshire, Surrey, Buckinghamshire, Bedfordshire, Northamptonshire, Cheshire and North Yorkshire. Both Blacks and South Asians had their largest concentrations of gaining areas in the Greater South East (South East and immediately adjacent counties) and a common outlier in Greater Manchester, but they also exhibit considerable differences. Meanwhile, the pattern of net gains for the Chinese and Others is much more fragmented geographically.

Since the patterns produced by using absolute numbers is influenced by the distribution of the relevant populations, a more meaningful perspective is usually provided by these data being expressed as rates of the base population. On this basis, Highland region emerges with the greatest percentage migration gains of minority ethnic population, equivalent to 3.3 per cent of the 1991 numbers, followed by Borders (2.7), Islands (2.6) and Isle of Wight (2.5). The largest percentage losses are found for Mid Glamorgan (-1.3), Cornwall (-0.9), South Glamorgan (-0.7) and Cleveland (-0.6). The full pattern is shown in Figure 4.2 (a). Clearly these results

Table 4.12 *Within-Britain migrant resident rate by ethnic group: five highest and lowest county-level areas, 1990–91*

Highest rates/areas		Lowest rates/areas	
Whites			
11.1	Grampian	6.5	Mid Glamorgan
10.8	Tayside	6.5	Merseyside
10.8	Oxfordshire	6.9	West Glamorgan
10.5	Highland	7.0	Gwent
10.5	Cambridgeshire	7.1	West Midlands
All ethnic minorities			
17.5	Gwynedd	6.7	Leicestershire
16.9	Borders	6.8	Warwickshire
15.9	Islands	6.9	West Midlands
15.5	Dorset	7.1	West Yorkshire
15.3	Norfolk	7.6	Bedfordshire
Blacks			
36.2	Dumfries and Galloway	7.1	Hereford and Worcester
20.8	Islands	7.1	West Midlands
18.7	Isle of Wight	8.6	West Yorkshire
18.2	Devon	8.7	Nottinghamshire
18.2	Dorset	9.0	London
South Asians			
23.5	Gwynedd	5.0	Warwickshire
23.1	Borders	5.9	Leicestershire
22.1	Cornwall	5.9	Gwent
17.1	Dorset	6.0	West Yorkshire
16.8	Grampian	6.3	West Midlands
Chinese and Others			
18.0	Islands	5.9	Powys
17.5	Borders	9.7	Lincolnshire
16.6	Central	9.7	Derbyshire
16.6	West Glamorgan	10.0	Hertfordshire
15.9	Oxfordshire	10.2	Bedfordshire

Note: Data refer to the percentage of the relevent 1991 population that changed address within the named area or moved into it from elsewhere in Britain.
Source: Calculated from 1991 Census Special Migration Statistics and Local Base Statistics (ESRC/JISC purchase). Crown copyright.

need to be treated with care because the most extreme values tend to be associated with areas with rather small minority populations. (The three individual minority groupings, of course, suffer even more from this problem and are not shown separately here.)

An alternative perspective which tackles the small numbers problem is to express the net changes as a proportion of the total population of each area, i.e. in terms of the contribution of the ethnic minority net migration to overall population change. The results for all minority ethnic groups combined are presented in Figure 4.2 (b), with extreme areas listed in Table 4.13. The impacts as measured this way are small, needing to be expressed in terms of persons per 10,000. The largest positive effect is

Table 4.13 Impact of net within-Britain migration on overall population size of counties and Scottish regions: the greatest gainers and losers, 1990–91

All ethnic minorities		Blacks		South Asians		Chinese & Others	
Greatest gainers							
5.9	Berkshire	2.7	Isle of Wight	4.1	Berkshire	1.6	Berkshire
4.8	Bedfordshire	2.0	Suffolk	3.3	Bedfordshire	1.5	Wiltshire
3.7	Buckingham	1.1	Bedfordshire	3.0	Buckingham	1.3	Warwickshire
3.2	Suffolk	0.7	Cambridgeshire	1.8	Surrey	1.3	Suffolk
2.9	West Sussex	0.6	Northumberland	1.5	West Sussex	1.3	Highlands
Greatest losers							
−3.3	West Yorkshire	−0.8	Oxfordshire	−2.9	West Yorkshire	−2.1	South Glamorgan
−3.3	South Glamorgan	−0.5	Fife	−1.6	Cleveland	−1.0	West Glamorgan
−2.0	Leicester	−0.5	Hereford and Worcester	−1.4	Lancashire	−0.7	Durham
−1.9	Greater London	−0.5	West Midlands	−1.0	Leicestershire	−0.6	Dumfries and Galloway

Note: Data refer to net migration of the named group as a proportion of the area's total 1991 population, expressed as persons per 10,000.
Source: Calculated from 1991 Census Special Migration Statistics and Local Base Statistics (ESRC/JISC purchase). Crown copyright.

Table 4.14 *Extent of inter-county redistribution produced by net within-Britain migration by ethnic group, 1990–91*

Ethnic group	Redistribution produced by net migration	Total population in group (000s)	Percentage of population in group
All ethnic groups	89,468	54,889	0.16
Whites	87,344	51,874	0.17
All ethnic minorities	3,459	3,015	0.11
Blacks	824	891	0.09
South Asians	2,158	1,480	0.15
Chinese and Others	1,124	645	0.17

Note: 'Redistribution produced by net migration' refers to the total net in-migration of counties and Scottish regions gaining from elsewhere in Britain.
Source: Calculated from 1991 Census Special Migration Statistics and Local Base Statistics (ESRC/JISC purchase). Crown copyright.

Figure 4.2 *Significance of net migration of ethnic minorities, 1990–91: (a) as a proportion of minority ethnic population (%); (b) as a proportion of total population (per 10,000)*

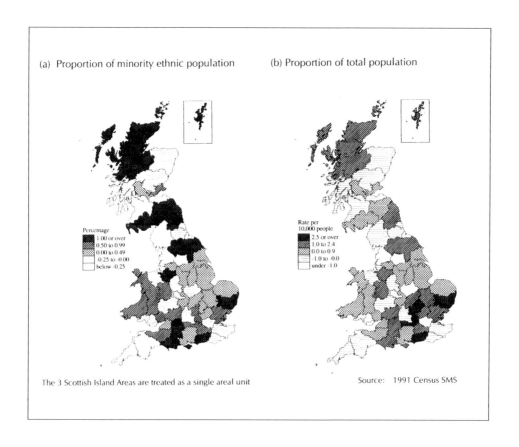

(a) Proportion of minority ethnic population

(b) Proportion of total population

Percentage
- 1.00 or over
- 0.50 to 0.99
- 0.00 to 0.49
- -0.25 to -0.00
- below -0.25

Rate per 10,000 people
- 2.5 or over
- 1.0 to 2.4
- 0.0 to 0.9
- -1.0 to -0.0
- under -1.0

The 3 Scottish Island Areas are treated as a single areal unit

Source: 1991 Census SMS

a 5.9 per 10,000 increase in Berkshire's total population and the largest negative effect a 3.3 per 10,000 decrease for West Yorkshire. But the general pattern can be fairly readily interpreted. The strongest population growth produced by the migration of ethnic minority members is found in south east England to the south, west and north of London. Even so, some of the more peripheral and rural parts of Britain have also been affected significantly by their gains, notably Highlands, Islands, Northumberland and North Yorkshire. Moreover, dividing by the total population does not remove from the frame the major losers in absolute terms, with the total populations of West Yorkshire, South Glamorgan, Leicestershire, Greater London, West Midlands and Lancashire (in that order) being the hardest hit by the net out-migration of ethnic minority residents.

Table 4.13 also shows the results of the same form of analysis for the three separate minority ethnic groupings. In terms of contribution to population growth, Berkshire is the county most affected by the migration of both South Asians and Chinese and Others, but has been very little affected by the redistribution of Blacks. The latter have had a much more substantial impact on the populations of the Isle of Wight and Suffolk than any other part of Britain during 1990–91. The negative impact of South Asian migration was clearly most marked for West Yorkshire, losing the equivalent of 2.9 per 10,000 of the county's total population, and for Chinese and Others, South and West Glamorgan were affected most. The biggest negative impact of Black migration was for Oxfordshire, but at the relatively low level of 0.8 per 10,000.

From the above analyses, there appear to be significant differences between ethnic groups in the level of population redistribution between counties. One way of measuring this in a single statistic is to divide total net migration by the total number in the relevant population. The results are shown in Table 4.14. Overall net migration over this pre-census year produced a 0.16 per cent redistribution of population between counties and Scottish regions. The level of redistribution of the (total) minority ethnic population produced by within-Britain migration was considerably smaller than for the White population, involving only a 0.11 per cent shift compared to a 0.17 per cent shift for the latter. Among the separate groups, the redistribution of Chinese and Others was proceeding as rapidly as for the White population, but the level was somewhat lower for South Asians and particularly low for Blacks. For the latter category, the total net migratory flow from losing counties to gaining ones was only 824 people, equivalent to less than 0.1 per cent of Britain's Black population.

As regards the question of whether these net migration changes are producing an increase or a decrease in the proportion of the population that is made up of ethnic minority members in particular areas, this can be tackled by comparing the percentage change produced for the minority population with that for the White population. The two variables are graphed for the 64 areas in Figure 4.3 (a) and the results mapped in Figure 4.3 (b). In two situations the outcome is clear-cut. For areas in sector 3, the White population is growing through net in-migration from the rest of Britain, while the minority population is falling through net out-migration, giving rise to an increased proportion of Whites in the population. Cornwall, Devon, East Sussex, Clwyd, Cumbria and Grampian are in this category.

The reverse pattern of sector 6, with White net out-migration and the net in-migration of ethnic minority members, is found in rather fewer cases: Bedfordshire, Berkshire, Nottinghamshire, South Yorkshire and Greater Manchester. In the top right quadrant, a distinction is drawn between which of the two populations is growing the faster as a result of this migration. Six counties, confined to central and eastern England, saw their proportion of Whites increase, but 28 counties – the largest single group distinguished here, and representing all parts of the country outside the major conurbations – recorded the faster growth of their minority ethnic populations.

Finally, in the bottom left quadrant where both populations were experiencing net out-migration to the rest of Britain, only two counties – Greater London and West

Figure 4.3 *Net migration rates for Whites and ethnic minorities by county and Scottish region, 1990–91: (a) relationship between the two; (b) classification of areas based on relationship*

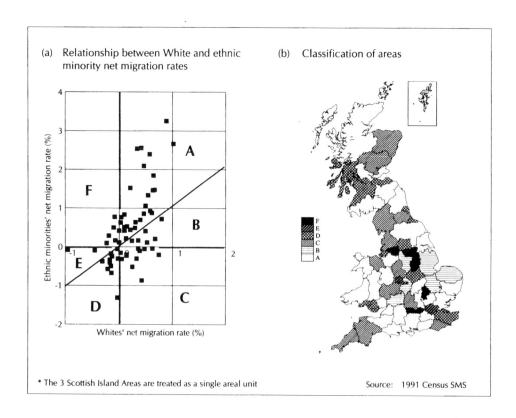

(a) Relationship between White and ethnic minority net migration rates

(b) Classification of areas

* The 3 Scottish Island Areas are treated as a single areal unit

Source: 1991 Census SMS

Midlands – saw greater losses by their White populations (sector 5). The other 11 (sector 4) recorded a faster contraction through migration of their minority ethnic population. These include two counties with well-established minority communities – Leicestershire and West Yorkshire – as well as a number of counties facing severe problems of economic restructuring, such as the Glamorgans, Merseyside, Tyne and Wear and Strathclyde.

Pending a more elaborate analysis of the implications of these changes for the degree of concentration and dispersal of the minority ethnic population, this information can be used to suggest how patterns developed in this one year. Of the five counties with ethnic minority members making up at least 8 per cent of their 1991 populations, three saw their minority proportion increase as a result of this one year of within-Britain migration (Greater London, West Midlands and Bedfordshire), while Leicestershire and West Yorkshire saw it decrease. Of the seven counties with between 4 and 8 per cent, five are found from Figure 4.3 (b) to have seen this migration lead to an increase in their minority proportions (Greater Manchester, Nottinghamshire, Hertfordshire, Berkshire and Buckinghamshire), with the proportion falling in Lancashire and South Glamorgan. The position among the counties which contain the largest concentrations of Britain's minorities therefore varies, but the dominant pattern is one of net shift towards these areas relative to the redistribution of the White population, i.e. towards even greater concentration.

4.5   The geographical patterning of gross flows by ethnic group

Attention thus far has focused on areas defined by individual counties and Scottish regions, noting the scale of migration within each area and between each area and the rest of Britain (treated as a single unit). This final substantive section of the chapter examines the migration flows which link areas together, identifying the areas which have the largest exchanges between them. The emphasis here is on gross movement (i.e. all moves between place A and place B including moves from B to A as well as from A to B), but for each pair of places it is also possible to calculate the scale and direction of the net flow.

This is definitely not a straightforward task. In the first place, there are a large number of potential pairings to examine – 4,032 gross flows for the 64 counties and Scottish regions (i.e. excluding the 64 within-area flows) and 2,016 net flows, for each type of migrant (i.e. per ethnic group in this case). Second, a great number of these flows cannot be fully disaggregated by ethnic group of migrant because of data suppression in the SMS, even in the county-district matrices used for the present analysis. Work is currently underway at the University of Leeds to estimate the composition of the suppressed flows, but in the meantime attention is concentrated on the largest flows, with the number of migrants for whom ethnic group is not available being given as an aid to gauging the confidence that can be placed in the conclusions drawn.

First we look at each of the three minority ethnic groupings in the SMS to identify their largest inter-county flows. Then, in recognition of its pivotal role in Britain's migration system, Greater London's links with other parts of Britain are examined. Finally, a brief look is taken at the impact of migration at the district level.

The largest inter-county flows for the three minority ethnic groupings

Table 4.15 shows the main flows for Blacks, including the counterflows in each case and the net redistribution resulting. The top 10 all comprised flows between Greater London and other counties, so a separate list is given of the 10 largest inter-county flows elsewhere in Britain.

Table 4.15 *Largest flows of Blacks between counties and Scottish regions, 1990–91*

Direction of main flow		Flow	Counter-flow	Net flow	Suppressed	
Origin	Destination				Flow	Counter-flow
Ten largest flows						
Greater London	Essex	237	120	117	—	—
West Midlands	Greater London	234	199	35	5	—
Greater London	Kent	198	154	44	—	—
Greater London	Hertfordshire	196	132	64	—	8
Greater London	Surrey	156	132	24	—	—
Greater London	Bedfordshire	135	111	24	—	1
Greater London	Buckinghamshire	121	83	38	—	2
Greater London	Berkshire	118	91	27	—	2
Greater London	Greater Manchester	116	115	1	—	2
West Yorkshire	Greater London	107	98	9	3	—
Ten largest flows excluding London						
Norfolk	Suffolk	81	28	53	—	—
West Midlands	Staffordshire	55	40	15	—	—
Hereford	West Midlands	43	25	18	—	—
Greater Manchester	West Midlands	40	28	12	—	—
Hertfordshire	Bedfordshire	40	10	30	—	—
Lancashire	Greater Manchester	37	26	11	—	—
West Yorkshire	Greater Manchester	34	20	14	—	—
Nottinghamshire	Derbyshire	33	19	14	—	—
Greater Manchester	Cheshire	31	19	12	—	—
West Midlands	Warwickshire	31	20	11	—	—

Source: Derived from 1991 Census Special Migration Statistics (ESRC/JISC purchase). Crown copyright.

The largest single flow of Blacks during this one-year period was from London to Essex, while the second largest was to London from West Midlands county. Next largest were flows from London to Kent, Hertfordshire, Surrey, Bedfordshire, Buckinghamshire and Berkshire. The pattern is clearly dominated by flows from London to other, mainly adjacent, counties in south-east England, and from London to other metropolitan counties. In all cases there is a sizeable counterflow, as is predicted by migration theory, resulting in relatively small net flows in most cases. The net redistribution of 117 Blacks from London to Essex is the most impressive figure. Among this top 10, all net flows are away from London, except those for West Midlands and West Yorkshire. Note that in none of these cases is the level of data suppression at all high, hence the conclusions drawn here are unaffected; the one possible exception being the direction of net flow between London and Manchester.

Flows of Blacks not involving London as either origin or destination are much smaller. The largest – that of 81 people migrating from Norfolk to Suffolk – has a very low counterflow compared with other cases and may result from a special feature such as redeployment of US military personnel during the year. Most of the flows involve a metropolitan county or other more heavily populated area, indicating a deconcentration tendency, as for the net flows from West Midlands county to Staffordshire and Warwickshire and from Greater Manchester to Cheshire, but there are also examples of redistribution towards the more urbanised county: from

Hereford and Worcester to West Midlands and from Lancashire to Greater Manchester.

As regards South Asian flows between areas (Table 4.16), London again emerges as pivotal. Here we note the net deconcentration of people from London to other counties in south-east England, and net gains by London from some more distant counties. Excluding exchanges with London, the main source counties are West Yorkshire and West Midlands, while Greater Manchester is the only county to appear as the net gainer more than once in this list. There are also some three-way linkages, in the sense that in net terms Lancashire gained South Asians from West Yorkshire but was itself a net loser to Greater Manchester. Similarly, West Midlands county gained from West Yorkshire, but was a net loser to several other counties.

The picture for the Chinese and Others (Table 4.17) largely mirrors the previous two, particularly in relation to the flows involving London. In this respect, the only exceptions are the net flows into London from two south-east England counties (Kent and East Sussex) and the clear net gain by London from Greater Manchester. Outside London, most of the main flows are in a deconcentration pattern; for instance, West Midlands to Staffordshire and Warwickshire, Greater Manchester to Cheshire, and the apparent 'cascading' from Surrey (a net gainer from London) to Berkshire and Hampshire, with Hampshire in turn losing to Wiltshire. As with South Asians, Greater Manchester is the recipient of three of these largest main flows, but the net gains involved are very small in two cases.

Table 4.16 *Largest flows of South Asians between counties and Scottish regions, 1990–91*

Direction of main flow		Flow	Counter-flow	Net flow	Suppressed	
Origin	Destination				Flow	Counter-flow
Ten largest flows						
West Midlands	Greater London	494	420	74	5	—
Greater London	Surrey	369	223	146	—	—
Greater London	Berkshire	354	188	166	—	2
Greater London	Hertfordshire	331	211	120	—	8
Leicestershire	Greater London	313	221	92	10	—
Greater London	Essex	276	152	124	—	—
Greater London	Greater Manchester	244	235	9	—	2
West Yorkshire	Greater London	236	188	48	3	—
Greater London	Kent	228	190	38	—	—
Greater London	Buckinghamshire	219	90	129	—	2
Ten largest flows excluding Greater London						
West Yorkshire	Greater Manchester	177	87	90	—	—
West Yorkshire	West Midlands	153	87	66	—	—
West Midlands	Leicestershire	147	127	20	—	—
Lancashire	Greater Manchester	144	88	56	—	—
West Midlands	Greater Manchester	120	103	17	—	—
West Midlands	Warwickshire	117	80	37	—	—
West Midlands	South Yorkshire	113	73	40	—	—
West Midlands	Berkshire	100	87	13	—	—
West Yorkshire	Lancashire	87	48	39	—	—
West Midlands	Staffordshire	85	77	8	—	—

Source: Derived from 1991 Census Special Migration Statistics (ESRC/JISC purchase). Crown copyright.

Table 4.17 *Largest flows of Chinese and Others between counties and Scottish regions, 1990–91*

Direction of main flow		Flow	Counter-flow	Net flow	Suppressed	
Origin	Destination				Flow	Counter-flow
Ten largest flows						
Greater London	Surrey	437	335	102	—	—
Greater London	Hertfordshire	317	174	143	—	8
Greater London	Essex	239	214	25	—	—
Kent	Greater London	230	209	21	—	—
Greater London	Berkshire	198	162	36	—	2
Greater Manchester	Greater London	151	106	44	2	—
Greater London	Hampshire	149	114	35	—	3
East Sussex	Greater London	134	121	13	6	—
Greater London	Buckinghamshire	122	110	12	—	2
West Yorkshire	Greater London	120	86	34	3	—
Ten largest flows excluding Greater London						
Hampshire	Wiltshire	85	25	60	—	—
Surrey	Hampshire	66	41	25	—	—
West Midlands	Staffordshire	66	41	25	—	—
Greater Manchester	Cheshire	64	44	20	—	—
West Midlands	Warwickshire	57	28	29	—	—
Lancashire	Greater Manchester	54	51	3	—	—
Surrey	Berkshire	53	38	15	—	—
Merseyside	Greater Manchester	52	28	24	—	—
West Yorkshire	Greater Manchester	46	45	1	—	—
Derbyshire	Nottinghamshire	39	30	9	—	—

Source: Derived from 1991 Census Special Migration Statistics (ESRC/JISC purchase). Crown copyright.

Selected flows to, from and within London

Given that there is a fair degree of similarity between the three minority groupings for the patterns of largest absolute inter-county flow just described, the opportunity is taken here of viewing them side by side for a selection of cases. This is done in Table 4.18 by presenting an ethnic breakdown of flows between Greater London and five other counties, giving details for the White population alongside those of the minority ethnic groups. Four of the counties selected are ones which have appeared regularly in Tables 4.15 to 4.17, and Cornwall is added in order to provide an example of a rural county which, despite being relatively lightly populated and at a considerable distance from London, nevertheless has sizeable migration links with London.

Essex and Surrey are taken as representatives of the situation of counties in southeast England which were gaining minority ethnic migrants from London in net terms. Table 4.18 confirms that both these counties were net gainers of all three minority groups, leading to a lowering of London's minority population by these amounts in 1990–91. This process, however, needs to be seen alongside the level of net out-migration of Whites from London to these two counties. In all, the ethnic minorities make up only 3.8 per cent of the net migration from London to Essex and 4.9 per cent of that from London to Surrey. When related to the ethnic composition of the populations of these counties (in 1991 minorities comprised 20.2 per cent in London, 1.9 per cent in Essex and 2.8 per cent in Surrey), it can be

Table 4.18 *Ethnic composition of selected flows to and from Greater London, 1990–91*

Origin/ destination	Unsuppressed flows					Suppressed flows
	Whites	Blacks	South Asians	Chinese and Others	Total	
Essex						
To GL	6,945	120	152	214	7,431	0
From GL	13,595	237	276	239	14,347	0
Net to GL	−6,650	−117	−124	−25	−6,916	0
Surrey						
To GL	8,887	132	223	335	9,577	0
From GL	14,212	156	369	437	15,174	0
Net to GL	−5,325	−24	−146	−102	−5,597	0
West Midlands						
To GL	2,104	234	494	177	3,009	5
From GL	1,868	199	420	132	2,619	0
Net to GL	+236	+35	+74	+45	+390	+5
West Yorkshire						
To GL	1,752	107	236	120	2,215	3
From GL	1,970	98	188	86	2,342	0
Net to GL	−218	+9	+48	+34	−127	+3
Cornwall						
To GL	780	8	4	13	805	6
From GL	1,256	5	9	7	1,277	5
Net to GL	−476	+3	−5	+6	−472	+1

Note: GL = Greater London. Negative figure for 'net to GL' denotes a net flow from Greater London to the named county.
Source: Derived from 1991 Census Special Migration Statistics (ESRC/JISC purchase). Crown copyright.

gauged that the effect of these migrations is to increase the proportion of the ethnic minorities in the populations of all three counties.

In terms of net flows, West Midlands county provides the opposite picture, with net gains of all four ethnic groups accruing to London. In this case, ethnic minority migration makes up 39.5 per cent of London's net gains and therefore serves to increase the relative size of the ethnic minority component of London's population while reducing it in the West Midlands (where the 1991 proportion was 14.6 per cent). The effect is the same for West Yorkshire, though more obvious in this case given that it was gaining Whites from London in net terms while losing ethnic minority members to it.

The case of Cornwall demonstrates how little, minority ethnic groups are involved in such long distance migration in and out of rural Britain, either in net or gross terms. Cornwall is a strong net migration gainer from London, and in net terms this is entirely accounted for by Whites. In fact, there is a net shift of minority population from Cornwall to London, though this does not apply to South Asians and the number is very small in aggregate (Table 4.18).

Also in relation to the deconcentration theme, the SMS Set 2 county-district matrices provide data on flows between inner London and outer London, because for census

Table 4.19 *Ethnic composition of migration flows between inner and outer London, 1990–91*

Origin/ destination	Unsuppressed flows					Suppressed flows
	Whites	Blacks	South Asians	Chinese and Others	Total	
To IL	24,360	3,734	1,721	2,058	31,873	0
From IL	37,108	5,748	3,176	3,283	49,315	0
Net to IL	−12,748	−2,014	−1,455	−1,225	−17,442	0

Note: IL = inner London.
Source: Derived from 1991 Census Special Migration Statistics (ESRC/JISC purchase). Crown copyright.

purposes these are treated as two separate counties. Table 4.19 presents data for this on the same basis as in Table 4.18. It is clear that net out-migration from inner to outer London was occurring at this time not only for Whites but for all three minority ethnic groups as well. In aggregate, minorities comprised 26.1 per cent of this net population shift. This level is very similar to their proportion of inner

Table 4.20 *Districts with greatest absolute net gains and losses resulting from migration within Great Britain by ethnic group, 1990–91*

Greatest net gains		Greatest net losses	
Whites			
Wealden	1,547	Birmingham	−5,631
Perth and Kinross	1,478	Manchester	−4,178
Suffolk Coastal	1,468	Glasgow	−3,925
Northavon	1,461	Lambeth	−3,751
Huntingdon	1,452	Liverpool	−3,366
All ethnic minorities			
Harrow	1,118	Hackney	−1,113
Redbridge	875	Brent	−952
Enfield	675	Lambeth	−909
Hillingdon	501	Haringey	−853
Barnet	365	Newham	−624
Blacks			
Enfield	475	Hackney	−678
Lewisham	381	Lambeth	−362
Croydon	288	Haringey	−365
Redbridge	195	Southwark	−355
Harrow	194	Brent	−305
South Asians			
Harrow	679	Brent	−506
Redbridge	552	Ealing	−488
Hillingdon	334	Newham	−441
Solihull	175	Birmingham	−394
Hounslow	166	Leicester	−351
Chinese and Others			
Harrow	245	Lambeth	−242
Redbridge	128	Kensington and Chelsea	−228
Barnet	126	Haringey	−171
Kingston upon Thames	114	Hackney	−168
Enfield	102	Glasgow	−159

Source: Calculated from 1991 Census Special Migration Statistics (ESRC/JISC purchase). Crown copyright.

London's total population (25.6 per cent), thus producing no significant change in the latter, but is considerably higher than the ethnic minority share of outer London's population (16.9 per cent) which will thus have been boosted by this shift.

Impacts of migration on district populations by ethnic group

This chapter has focused almost exclusively at the level of county and Scottish region in order to describe the broad patterns of migration and to side-step the problem of data suppression which is much greater in the district-to-district datasets. But the marginal data in the latter are not subject to suppression and can be used to calculate the net impact of within-Britain migration for each of the four ethnic groups. Table 4.20 identifies the five local authority districts which have gained most migrants in each ethnic group from exchanges with the rest of Great Britain, and the five that have lost most.

For Whites, the biggest losers in absolute terms during this one-year period were the large provincial city authorities of Birmingham, Manchester and Glasgow. The London Borough of Lambeth and Liverpool come next, both losing well over 3,000 Whites. The gainers of Whites were more widely spread, as shown by the smaller absolute gains of around 1,500 for the leading districts, though four of the top five share the distinction of being less heavily populated areas in the southern half of Britain: Wealden (East Sussex), Suffolk Coastal, Northavon (Avon) and Huntingdon (Cambridgeshire).

For the three minority ethnic groups in aggregate and separately, however, the list of biggest net losers and gainers is very different from this (Table 4.20). The list of losers is dominated by London boroughs in each case, the only exceptions among the five being Birmingham and Leicester for South Asians, and Glasgow for Chinese and Others. They are predominantly inner London Boroughs, but Brent and Ealing feature as the two most important districts for South Asian net out-migration, and Brent is also fifth most important for Blacks.

In even greater contrast to the pattern for Whites, London boroughs also dominate the lists of largest net gainers for the minority ethnic groups, in this case all outer London (Table 4.20). The only exception is Solihull (West Midlands), with its significant net gain of South Asians. Clearly, in terms of absolute numbers of minority migrants, movements within London dominate the district level redistribution caused by within-Britain migration just as much as Greater London emerges as by far the most important element of between-county migration. At this more local level, deconcentration from inner to outer area emerges as strongly for minorities as for Whites, but involves shifts over much more restricted distances than for Whites.

4.6 Concluding comments

The 1991 Census, with its inclusion of a question on ethnic group and the availability of an ethnic group table in the Special Migration Statistics, marks a major step forward in terms of the potential for analysing ethnic differentials in migration in Britain. This chapter has reported the results of an initial exploration of these data on people living at a different address on census night from that a year before. This final section summarises some of the main findings.

First, while the minority ethnic population as a whole contained a proportion of migrants one third greater than that for Whites, it has been found that this difference evaporates when allowance has been made for people arriving from outside Great Britain. Also, age for age, minorities move house less frequently on average than Whites. Ethnic minority movers also tend to have moved over shorter distances than Whites. There are, however, substantial variations between groups, with the proportion of Chinese and Black–African movers being twice as high as the equivalent rates for Indians, Black–Caribbeans and Pakistanis. The Chinese tended to move greater distances than Whites, whereas a much higher than average proportion of Blacks and Bangladeshis moved only short distances.

Migration rates also vary more between different parts of the country for the ethnic minorities than for Whites, both for the minority population as a whole and for the three separate groups identifiable in the Special Migration Statistics. Local turnover in West Glamorgan and Strathclyde, for instance, was nearly three times that in Powys and Warwickshire. Rates of departure were found to be particularly high from more remote rural areas like Cumbria, Gwynedd and Norfolk, where the relatively small minority ethnic communities appeared much less stable than established minority ethnic concentrations in areas such as West Midlands, West Yorkshire and Leicestershire. At the same time, arrival rates were also much higher in the more remote rural areas, so that in net terms some of these (notably Highland, Borders and Islands) saw the strongest migration-induced growth in minority ethnic population in Britain. These results, however, need to be viewed with caution because of the small numbers problem.

In absolute terms, the biggest net impacts of ethnic minority migration in 1990–91 were felt in south-east England and in the more urbanised areas elsewhere. The largest net gains occurred in a belt of counties stretching from Dorset to Suffolk, while the largest losses were registered by Greater London, West Yorkshire, West Midlands, Lancashire and Strathclyde. While this pattern broadly accords with the trends exhibited by Whites, more detailed analysis suggests that the overall effect of within-Britain migration is an increase in the proportion of minority ethnic residents in areas where it is already high. In general, as revealed by a brief examination in trends in inner and outer London, tendencies toward minority deconcentration appear to be effective over shorter distances than for Whites.

There remains much more to be learnt from the 1991 Census about ethnic minority migration patterns. The present account has concentrated on the level of the county and Scottish region and, even here, has only scratched the surface of this huge dataset, in particular giving relatively little attention to migration streams between areas. Much more can be done both on this and also by using the district-level migration matrices. In relation to the latter, however, the data suppression problem needs to be overcome and – even more at this level than for counties – care will need to be taken over the small numbers problem and the fact that these data relate only to a single year. Finally, on the positive side, in terms of future research it is clear that further important insights can be derived, first from the 10- and 20-year changes of address which can be detected from the OPCS Longitudinal Study, and second, from the customised analyses which the Samples of Anonymised Records permit.

References

Dale, A. (1993) The OPCS Longitudinal Study. In Dale, A. and Marsh, C. (eds), *The 1991 Census User's Guide*. London: HMSO, pp. 312–29.

Dale, A. and Marsh, C. (eds) (1993) *The 1991 Census User's Guide*. London: HMSO.

Haskey, J. (1990) The ethnic minority populations of Great Britain. *Population Trends*, 60, 35–38.

Haskey, J. (1991) Ethnic minority populations resident in private households – estimate by county and district. *Population Trends*, 63, 22–36.

Marsh, C. (1993) The validation of census data, II. General issues. In: Dale, A. and Marsh, C. (eds), *The 1991 Census User's Guide*. London: HMSO, pp. 155–67.

OPCS (1986) 1981 Census – published, unpublished and related tables, topic: migration, OPCS Census 1981 User Guide 130/6 (revised August 1986).

Owen, D. and Green, A. (1992) Migration patterns and trends. In: Champion, A. G. and Fielding, A. J. (eds), *Migration Processes and Patterns Volume 2: Research Progress and Prospects*. London: Belhaven, pp. 17–40.

Robinson, V. (1992) Move on up: the mobility of Britain's Afro-Caribbean and Asian populations. In: Stillwell, J., Rees, P. and Boden, P. (eds), *Migration Processes and Patterns Volume 2: Population Redistribution in the United Kingdom*. London: Belhaven, pp. 271–91.

Shaw, C. (1988) Components of growth in the ethnic minority population. *Population Trends*, 52, 26–30.

Stillwell, J., Rees, P. and Boden, P. (eds) (1992) *Migration Processes and Patterns Volume 2: Population Redistribution in the United Kingdom*. London: Belhaven.

Chapter 5
Inter-generational differences in ethnic settlement patterns in Britain

Vaughan Robinson

5.1 Introduction

It has been argued elsewhere that the study of the geography of ethnic relations in the UK has passed through a number of phases since its inception in the late 1950s (Robinson, 1987), and that each of these phases has tended to have its roots in a different geographical paradigm. Over the same period, geographers have also reduced the scale of their analysis and sharpened its resolution. We have thus seen geographers abandoning broad regional analysis (e.g. Peach, 1968) in favour of the use of small-scale data, often relating to urban neighbourhoods (e.g. Cater and Jones, 1979). And we have also seen geographers changing the resolution of their analyses away from meaningless, and clearly 'racialised', amalgams such as the coloured population (e.g. Griffiths, 1960; Jones, 1970), the New Commonwealth and Pakistani (NCWP) population or the Asian population (Hussain, 1975) towards progressively more precisely defined population fractions based upon characteristics such as country of origin (Jones, 1978), religion (Robinson, 1979), precise regional origins (Peach, 1984), or combinations of region of origin and language (Robinson, 1986).

However, as geographers have sought to define groups more precisely for analysis, so they have tended to rely increasingly upon diacritical markers which are (a) associated with the primordial school of ethnicity, (b) depend upon labels derived from the societies of origin, and (c) ascribed and static. While such primordial and affective characteristics can certainly act as bases for social action and can also underpin spatial agglomeration in the early stages of settlement (see Boal, 1976), it could be argued that other diacritical markers are more determinant of how groups will fare in the longer term. Central to these will be the extent to which those of minority ethnic origin are seen as outsiders or immigrants, the social class profile assigned to, or acquired by, the group on arrival, and the subsequent direction and rate of social mobility. It is these factors, rather than which Asian mother tongue is spoken, or which West Indian island a person comes from, that will determine access to resources (Glazer and Moynihan, 1975) or the possibilities open to a minority.

Perhaps then, given the fact that it is several decades since the peaks of West Indian and South Asian migration to the UK, geographers should begin to employ different criteria to define the groups which they use as their units of analysis, and criteria which are more instrumental in nature and more forward looking. To date, few concerted efforts have been made to understand the impact of social class upon ethnic settlement patterns in the UK; the work of Ceri Peach being a notable exception (see, for example, Peach, Winchester and Woods (1975); Peach and Byron

(1993); and Chapter 3 in this volume). And only Robinson (1986) – using the example of East African Asian refugees and South Asian labour migrants – has considered how differing circumstances and reasons for migration might impact upon subsequent long-term settlement strategies and patterns within the UK.

This chapter thus seeks to achieve three things. First, it extends the continuing trend to finer resolution analysis. Second, in defining population groups for analysis it attempts to use acquired, not proscribed, characteristics. And third, the defining characteristics which have been selected are ones which have instrumental salience, in the sense of being central to a meaningful explanation of observed patterns. More particularly, the account considers a number of related questions; namely, whether there are significant differences in the settlement patterns of immigrant members of the minority ethnic population and their British-born and raised counterparts, whether such differences are a simple period effect – resulting from different age and social class profiles – which will disappear with time, or whether differences are a consequence of the contrasting trajectories of social mobility of the immigrant and British-born groups.

Figure 5.1 *Cumulative proportions of the overseas-born minority ethnic populations of Great Britain by year of entry*

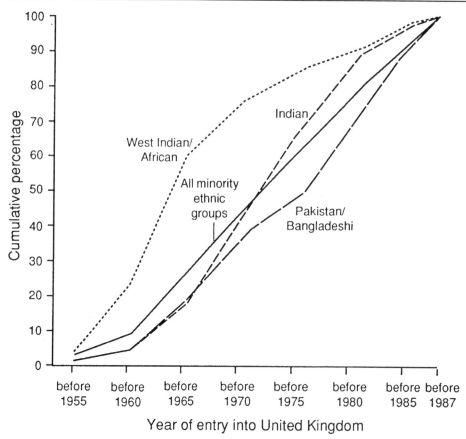

Source: Labour Force Survey

5.2 Waves of migration

Any analysis of ethnic minority settlement patterns within the UK needs to take account of the fact that those groups which collectively form Britain's minority population did not all arrive in Britain at the same time. As Figure 5.1 demonstrates, the peaks of West Indian, Indian and Pakistani migration to the UK were separated by as much as 15 years, with West Indian immigration having effectively peaked before the threat of immigration control in 1961. Bangladeshi migration, being of more recent origin than that of the other South Asian groups, has resulted, not surprisingly, in a population which contains relatively few British-born adults. As a result, Bangladeshis are excluded from the analysis which follows. The three groups selected (Black–Caribbean, Indian and Pakistani) have contrasting age structures, entered the family reunion or creation phases at different times, and therefore have different proportions that are British-born. Table 5.1 documents this, and shows the lagged effect of later arrival, albeit modified by contrasting fertility rates once in Britain. Clearly then, the Black–Caribbean group is further along its journey than either the Indian or Pakistani populations (see Robinson, 1993 for further details).

5.3 Inter-generational differences in settlement patterns

Table 5.2 contains data on the distribution of ethnic minority household heads across England, Scotland and Wales, and also draws the distinction between immigrants and those who were British-born. While it is clear that England dominates the

Table 5.1 *The demographic imprint of successive waves of ethnic minority migration to the UK*

	Total period fertility rate		Number of births (000)			% Aged <16 years	% Change in population
	1981	1987	1971	1976	1987/90	1985–87	1981–87/9
West Indian	2.0	1.9	12.5	7.1	3.8	25	−9
Indian	3.1	2.7	13.3	12.0	8.6	31	7
Pakistani				8.1	12.9	43	52
Bangladeshi				1.4	4.8	50	116

Note: Births; Pakistani and Bangladeshi figures are for 1987, others are for 1990.
Source: % Change figures from `In brief', *Population Trends*, 63 (1991).

Table 5.2 *The distribution of immigrant and British-born members of the minority ethnic population by country, 1991 (%)*

	Black–Caribbean		Indian		Pakistani	
	Immigrant	British-born	Immigrant	British-born	Immigrant	British-born
England	99.3	98.7	97.6	96.7	94.5	92.3
Scotland	0.1	0.3	1.5	2.1	4.2	6.1
Wales	0.5	1.0	0.9	1.1	1.3	1.6

Note: Household heads only.
Source: Calculated from 1991 Census Small Area Statistics (SAS).

distribution of Black–Caribbeans, Indians and Pakistanis, regardless of place of birth, it is also noticeable that the British-born are relatively more numerous outside England than their immigrant counterparts. In some cases (e.g. Pakistanis in Scotland), the discrepancy is of the order of 50 per cent.

Table 5.3 reduces the scale of analysis to the regions of England. Indices of dissimilarity (ID) suggest that, at this scale, there is very little difference between the distributions of those born in Britain and those not. The largest index (still only 6.7) is for the ethnic Indian population, and results from the relative under-representation of British-born in the South East, and their over-representation in all other regions except the East Midlands. British-born Black–Caribbeans are also under-represented in the South East and over-represented in the West Midlands (ID 2.9). Within the Pakistani ethnic group, the British-born are less numerous in the areas of traditional settlement (South East, Yorkshire and Humberside, and the North West) and are more numerous in some areas of limited settlement (the North and the East Midlands), giving an overall ID of 2.5.

Table 5.3 The distribution of immigrant and British-born members of the minority ethnic population by English region, 1991 (%)

	Black–Caribbean		Indian		Pakistani	
	Immigrant	British-born	Immigrant	British-born	Immigrant	British-born
North	0.16	0.33	1.29	1.80	2.02	3.33
Yorkshire and Humberside	4.61	4.79	5.78	6.59	20.62	19.96
East Midlands	5.16	5.08	11.17	9.04	3.98	5.00
East Anglia	0.97	1.03	0.78	1.21	1.39	1.11
South East	66.68	64.02	50.45	45.93	32.68	31.34
South West	2.61	2.43	1.44	2.22	0.98	1.05
West Midlands	15.21	17.25	21.74	24.93	21.36	21.43
North West	4.57	5.06	7.34	8.28	16.96	16.76

Note: Household heads only.
Source: Calculated from 1991 Census Small Area Statistics (SAS).

Table 5.4 The distribution of immigrant and British-born members of the minority ethnic population by English conurbation, 1991 (%)

	Black–Caribbean		Indian		Pakistani	
	Immigrant	British-born	Immigrant	British-born	Immigrant	British-born
Inner London	36.2	36.3	8.9	11.1	6.5	8.4
Outer London	22.4	19.9	28.5	21.7	12.5	11.1
Greater Manchester	3.6	3.9	3.7	4.4	10.1	10.1
Merseyside	0.4	0.6	0.4	0.9	0.2	0.5
South Yorkshire	1.2	1.5	0.5	0.9	2.8	3.5
Tyneside	0.1	0.2	0.7	1.0	0.8	1.2
West Midlands	13.9	15.9	18.8	21.9	18.0	18.1
West Yorkshire	3.2	3.1	4.7	4.9	16.4	14.6
Of national population	81.0	81.4	66.2	66.8	67.3	67.5

Note: Household heads only.
Source: Calculated from 1991 Census Small Area Statistics (SAS).

Figure 5.2 *Black-Caribbeans: ratio of British-born to immigrant, relative to the national average*

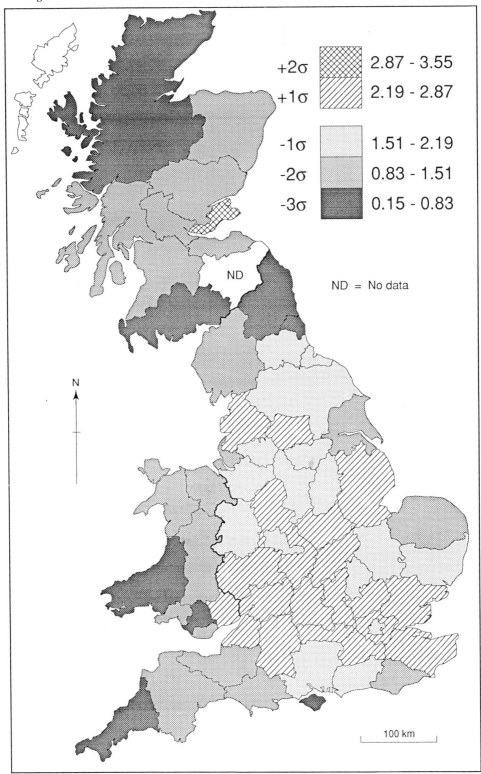

Table 5.4 narrows the focus further to the English conurbations. It reveals that a slightly greater proportion of the British-born of each group can be found in the conurbations than their immigrant counterparts. It also shows how the British-born tend to be significantly under-represented in outer London, significantly over-represented in inner London and the West Midlands, and over-represented in all of the conurbations beyond London.

Figures 5.2, 5.3 and 5.4 reduce the scale to county level and indicate for each county whether the ratio of British-born to immigrant members of an ethnic group deviates from the national average for that group. Areas denoted as being above the mean thus represent counties where the British-born are relatively under-represented. Those below the mean represent counties with more British-born than might have been expected.

Figure 5.2 relates to the Black–Caribbean population. It shows a bipolar distribution, with British-born over-representation in major English conurbations and in remoter rural areas not usually associated with ethnic minority settlement. It is noticeable, for example, how with increasing distance west, south west, south or north east from London the degree of British-born over-representation becomes greater. It should also be noted, however, that absolute levels of under-representation for Black–Caribbeans are relatively small, with the most extreme level of under-representation being within two standard deviations of the average ratio for the country.

It is much less easy to generalise about Figure 5.3, relating to ethnic Indians. There are, however, some similarities with Figure 5.2. The conurbations are areas of British-born over-representation, as are the South Coast, the South West, much of the North and Scotland, west and mid-Wales and East Anglia. The counties immediately surrounding London are areas of under-representation, as are a swathe of rural counties in England running from Gloucestershire, through Warwickshire and Northamptonshire into Lincolnshire. However, there are also some contrasts between Figures 5.2 and 5.3. British-born ethnic Indians are over-represented in a band of counties on the outer edge of London's influence (Oxfordshire, Buckinghamshire and Bedfordshire), and in counties around other major conurbations (Wiltshire, Herefordshire and Staffordshire).

Some similar themes emerge from Figure 5.4, which relates to Pakistanis. Again, the British-born are over-represented in the conurbations, the South West, most of Wales, the South Coast, East Anglia and much of the North. However in the non-conurban counties of England the Pakistani pattern differs considerably from the Indian pattern. British-born Pakistanis are under-represented in the outer Home Counties and in the counties to the west of the West Midlands, and they are slightly over-represented in the more rural counties running from south east Wales to Humberside.

Table 5.5 refines the description further, by reducing the scale to local authority districts and looking only at household heads. It is designed to show the extent to which immigrant and British-born members of an ethnic group tend to live in areas of ethnic concentration or areas of sparse ethnic settlement and it reveals a clear

Figure 5.3 *Indians: ratio of British-born to immigrant, relative to the national average*

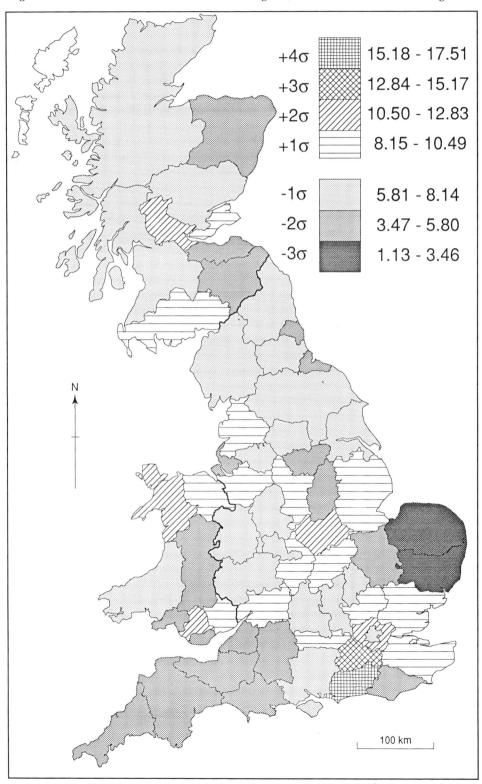

+4σ   15.18 - 17.51
+3σ   12.84 - 15.17
+2σ   10.50 - 12.83
+1σ   8.15 - 10.49

-1σ   5.81 - 8.14
-2σ   3.47 - 5.80
-3σ   1.13 - 3.46

N

100 km

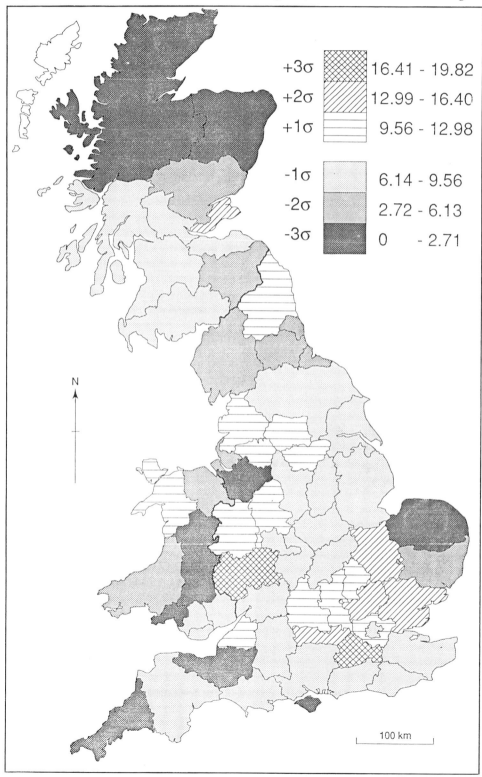

Table 5.5 *The distribution of ethnic minority household heads between areas of varying ethnic concentration*

% Of household heads in a district from that ethnic group	Indian		Pakistani		Black–Caribbean	
	Immigrant	British-born	Immigrant	British-born	Immigrant	British-born
0.0–0.099	2.3	1.9	3.6	5.3	1.6	2.6
0.1–0.49	10.7	9.4	13.8	16.7	5.5	5.6
0.5–0.99	13.0	40.8	15.4	16.2	5.3	5.7
1.0–1.49	7.7	5.6	14.5	14.1	7.6	7.3
1.5–1.99	6.5	4.7	7.8	8.0	5.8	5.1
2.0–2.49	5.3	3.1	6.6	6.2	4.6	4.3
2.5–2.99	11.8	9.6	7.0	6.0	6.0	5.7
3.0–3.49	1.0	0.7	16.8	16.7	1.3	1.2
3.5–3.99	5.2	3.8	0	0	5.9	6.0
4.0–4.49	8.0	5.0	1.8	1.5	0	0
4.5–4.99	0	0	12.7	9.3	7.3	7.1
5.0–5.99	3.9	1.7	0	0	15.2	20.6
6.0–6.99	12.7	8.0	0	0	2.8	2.9
7.0–7.99	5.6	2.6	0	0	2.9	3.1
8.0–8.99	6.3	2.8	0	0	3.6	4.1
9.0–9.99	0	0	0	0	3.9	3.6
10.0+	0	0	0	0	20.6	19.3

Note: Figures may not sum to 100% because of rounding.
Source: Calculated from1991 Census Small Area Statistics (SAS).

picture. For all of the groups, a higher proportion of the *British-born* heads of household live in areas of relatively sparse ethnic settlement. This is particularly true for Indians, with 26 per cent of all heads of household who are of Indian ethnicity and born in India living in areas where Indians form less than 1 per cent of all household heads, while the same is true for 52 per cent of all British-born Indians. This confirms the role of British-born Indians as social and spatial pioneers. For Pakistanis and Black–Caribbeans the respective percentages are 33 per cent versus 38 per cent, and 12 per cent versus 14 per cent.

To summarise then, description of the spatial distribution of the British-born and immigrant components, of each of the three principal minority ethnic populations, has revealed that, while the pattern of settlement of the two components is not radically different, there are persistent and consistent discrepancies. These discrepancies suggest that British-born Black–Caribbeans, Indians and Pakistanis are less numerous within the south east of England and in outer London but are more numerous both in the major conurbations and in areas not usually associated with ethnic minority settlement, especially peripheral rural counties. Not surprisingly then, the British-born tend to record a bipolar pattern of distribution with substantial numbers in areas of dense ethnic settlement, but above average numbers in areas with little ethnic settlement. The former are likely to be children born to immigrant parents, while the latter are more likely to be households headed by a British-born 'ethnic'.

5.4 Changes over time in inter-generational differences in settlement patterns

Given that the last section has demonstrated that differences do exist between the spatial distribution of immigrant and British-born members of each minority ethnic population, it is important to discover whether these differences have increased over the last decade. If this can be shown to be the case, it might suggest that the two elements within each population are on divergent social trajectories.

Inter-county migration, 1981–91

The first way of answering this question is to consider the extent to which those of minority ethnic origin have remained within the same locations between 1981 and 1991. The OPCS Longitudinal Study (LS) provides an appropriate dataset for such an analysis (see also discussion of this data source in Chapter 4). The LS, as noted in Chapter 4, is based upon a 1 per cent subsample drawn from the census in 1971 (and selected by birthday), to which are regularly added new respondents who have entered the population through immigration or birth, and from which those who have died are deleted. OPCS has then attempted to trace the 1971, 1981 and 1991 Census records for each respondent and to link them for the purposes of analysis. While the LS is thus not truly longitudinal, it does provide linked data for the same individual over time. Estimates based on LS data were made of the percentage of a county's minority ethnic population in 1981 who were also resident in that same county in 1991.

It should be noted, however, that because the data are not truly longitudinal we are not able to distinguish between those LS respondents who have been immobile during the decade 1981–91 and those who have moved out of the county and then returned later in the decade. With this proviso in mind, the data do indicate interesting patterns.

Black–Caribbeans

The LS Black–Caribbeans are found to be the least mobile of all minority ethnic groups, with the immigrant component being even less mobile than the British-born counterpart; inter-county migration rates are 49 and 87 per thousand, respectively, over the decade. Greater London was the most likely to retain its Black–Caribbean population over time, and Merseyside the least. In addition, disaggregation of the data shows the main difference between the British-born and immigrant Black–Caribbean populations to be their willingness, or at least propensity, to remain within the English conurbations. These are capable of retaining their immigrant populations but are much less able to keep their British-born Black–Caribbeans. The same is also true of many of the non-conurban counties which already had sizeable populations of Caribbean origin (e.g. Avon, Gloucester, Northamptonshire, Nottinghamshire, Leicestershire and Buckinghamshire). These two points taken together suggest a leakage of British-born from traditional areas of Black–Caribbean settlement.

Indians

For the Indian population, almost the opposite is true. The group is highly mobile, with decennial inter-county mobility rates of 133 and 128 per thousand for the British-born and immigrant components respectively. The conurbations have proved less effective at retaining their Indian populations than their Black–Caribbean populations, although Greater London still holds its pre-eminent position as the most attractive of the major metropolitan areas. Disaggregation shows the British-born Indians to be rooted in existing areas of concentration; namely Greater London, Greater Manchester, Lancashire, Leicestershire, Derbyshire, Bedfordshire and the West Midlands. In contrast many of the areas of existing concentration have experienced a leakage of immigrant Indians, particularly the conurbations (other than London and the West Midlands), Lancashire, Warwickshire, Kent and Northamptonshire. Areas proving capable of retaining their immigrant Indians include such counties as Oxfordshire, Hampshire, Cambridgeshire, West Sussex and Wiltshire. This suggests that the British-born are remaining near areas of concentration, perhaps because they are minors or perhaps because they wish to make use of protected markets, employment niches, and community- and family-based social networks. Immigrants on the other hand are more likely to move from areas of concentration, perhaps for career reasons, or to more fully match their status with their address.

Pakistanis

The Pakistani members of the LS are also more mobile than the Black–Caribbeans, with decennial inter-county mobility rates of 91 and 90 per thousand for the British-born and immigrant components respectively. It is interesting to note that the Pakistanis no longer appear to be the most mobile of the principal minority ethnic groups (c.f. the 1971–81 period analysed in Robinson, 1993). The second point of note is that there is much less variability in the extent to which counties can retain their Pakistani populations. The conurbations are highly likely to keep their existing Pakistani populations; something which cannot be said for the other major area of Pakistani concentration, Lancashire. Within the Pakistani group, there are some differences between British-born and immigrant. For both, the conurbations are the key. The immigrants are most likely to remain in the West Midlands and Greater Manchester, while the British-born find Greater London more attractive. However, both groups are strongly attracted to the major English conurbations. Outside the conurbations there are few areas which are consistently attractive, although Nottinghamshire and Staffordshire prove themselves capable of retaining the British-born, and Berkshire, Cambridgeshire and Nottinghamshire can retain immigrant Pakistanis.

Migration flows, 1981–91

The second way of answering the question of whether differences in the geographical distribution of British-born and immigrant members of the minority ethnic population are increasing or decreasing over time is to compare the migration flows

Figure 5.5 *Immigrant Indian flows*

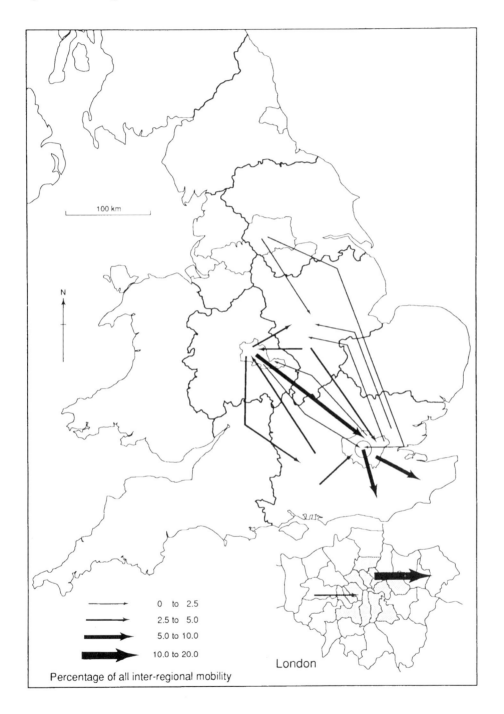

100 km

N

0 to 2.5
2.5 to 5.0
5.0 to 10.0
10.0 to 20.0

Percentage of all inter-regional mobility

London

Figure 5.6 *British-born Indian flows*

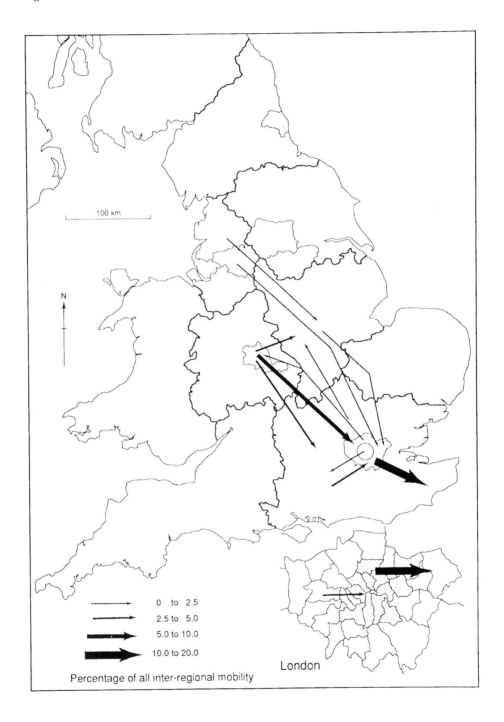

Figure 5.7 *Immigrant Black–Caribbean flows*

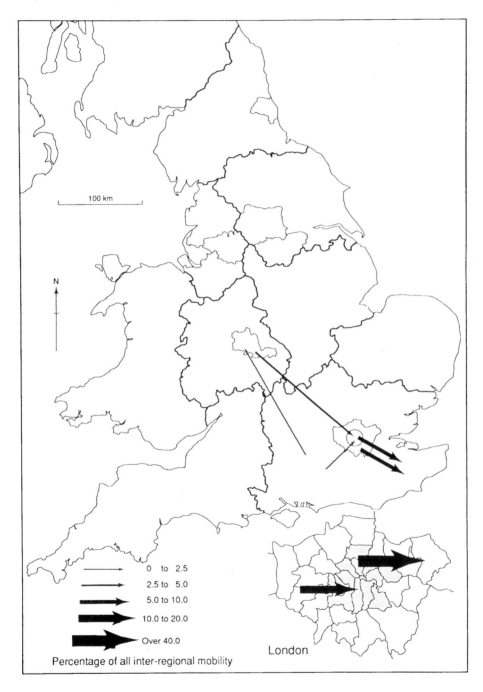

100 km

N

0   to   2.5
2.5 to   5.0
5.0 to 10.0
10.0 to 20.0
Over 40.0
Percentage of all inter-regional mobility

London

Figure 5.8 *British Black–Caribbean flows*

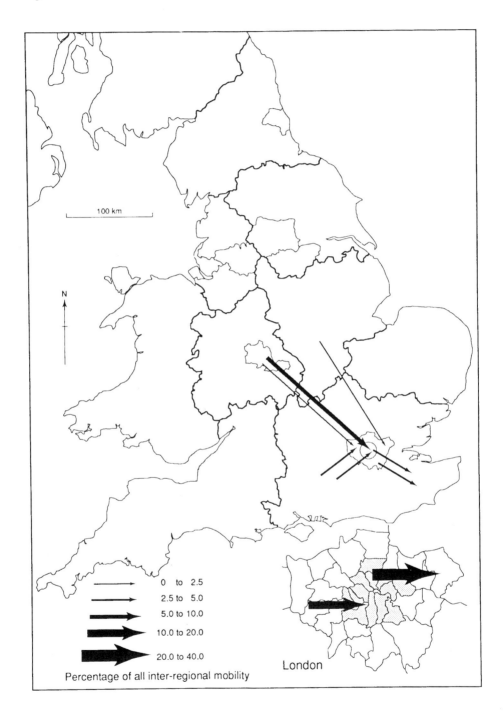

100 km

N

0   to   2.5

2.5 to   5.0

5.0 to 10.0

10.0 to 20.0

20.0 to 40.0

Percentage of all inter-regional mobility

London

Figure 5.9 *Immigrant Pakistani flows*

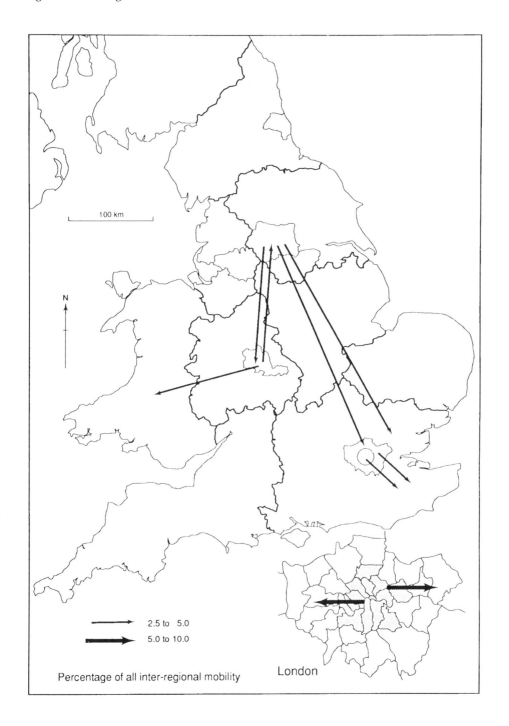

100 km

N

2.5 to 5.0
5.0 to 10.0

Percentage of all inter-regional mobility

London

Figure 5.10 *British Pakistani flows*

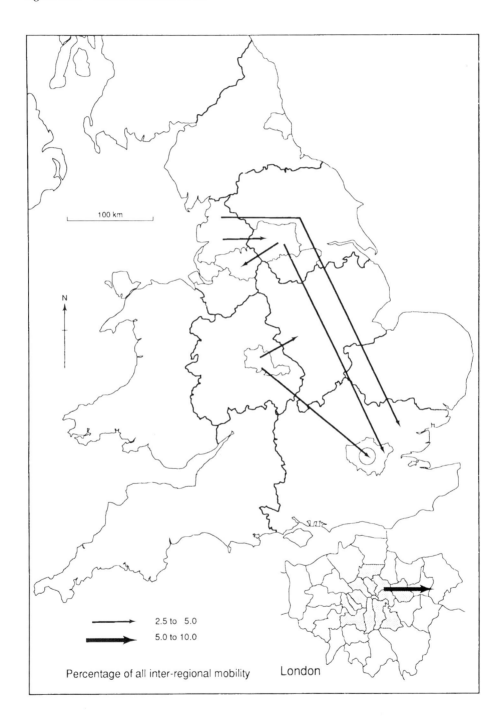

100 km

N

2.5 to 5.0

5.0 to 10.0

Percentage of all inter-regional mobility   London

of both fractions of each minority. Again, the LS permits such an analysis, although it is important to note that a respondent living in the same region in 1991 and 1981 could have moved out of, and then returned to, that region in the intervening years but still be recorded by the LS as immobile. The LS provided samples of between 911 individuals (British-born Pakistanis) and 3,616 individuals (Indian-born Indians). The data, which are presented in Figures 5.5 to 5.10, reveal the following:-

Indians

Comparison of the maps for British-born and immigrant Indians demonstrates that several key flows are shared. In both cases, there are significant flows from inner to outer London, from outer London to the South East, and from the West Midlands conurbation to outer London. Other shared flows include smaller movements from the West Midlands to the East Midlands and from the West Midlands to the South East. Differences are less significant, but include the existence of flows of British-born from the West Midlands and West Yorkshire to inner London, the loss of British-born from West Yorkshire contrasted with the loss of immigrants from the North West, the movement of British-born from the South East to the West Midlands, and flows of British-born direct from inner London to the South East.

Black–Caribbeans

Comparison of the maps for British-born and immigrant Black–Caribbeans reveals greater contrasts. For immigrants, the flows are dominated by the movement from inner to outer London and from both to the South East. While the British-born are also decentralising within London, there is much less evidence of movement out of London to the South East, and far more evidence of London attracting migrants from the West Midlands, the East Midlands and the South East.

Pakistanis

For immigrant Pakistanis, trends are relatively straightforward, albeit made up of a variety of very small flows. There has been an exchange of Pakistanis between two of the main core areas of settlement, namely the West Midlands and West Yorkshire, and a movement from the latter to outer London and the South East. Within London, there has been an exchange between the inner and outer parts of the conurbation and a loss from both to the South East. The pattern of flows of British-born Pakistanis is quite different. There is no decentralisation from London, no return flow from outer to inner London, no linkage between Yorkshire and the West Midlands, but withdrawal from the North West and a more general drift to London and the South East from the provinces.

Taken together, these two sets of data suggest that differences not only exist in the distribution of immigrants and their British-born counterparts but that the discrepancies appear to be widening, albeit at different rates for different groups. In greater detail they suggest that Black–Caribbean immigrants are rooted in their pre-existing areas of concentration and, in so far as there is evidence of mobility, the major component is a gradual shift of distribution within London and – to a lesser extent – out of London to the South East (c.f. Robinson (1991) for a discussion of trends in the previous decade).

It is hard to escape likening this pattern to that of incremental immigrant decentralisation driven by slow, lifetime, occupational mobility proposed in 1928 by Robert Park. The pattern for British-born Black–Caribbeans is rather different. They are somewhat more likely to have moved, and this mobility is directed from the provinces into London, and within London towards outer London. Here there are parallels with the migration patterns of young Whites; moving to London for work, greater opportunity and access to the unrivalled social facilities of the capital, prior to movement to outer London (following initial career success).

Within the Indian population, roles are reversed. Immigrant Indians are less rooted in the conurbations (other than London and the West Midlands), and there is evidence of an emerging new geography built upon more generalised decentralisation from inner to outer London and from outer London into the more attractive commuter settlements of the South East, as well as a movement into the nascent ethnic core of the East Midlands (see Robinson (1994; 1995) for a discussion of the significance of East African Asian origins, and Owen and Johnson (see Chapter 7 of this volume) for further analysis of settlement patterns in the East Midlands). Their British-born counterparts are also mobile, but their mobility tends to take the form of reciprocated circulation between and within existing areas of concentration rather than a clear progression into newly pioneered territory. There is, however, a flow into London from other centres of concentration, namely the West Midlands and West Yorkshire.

The Pakistani population is not as mobile as it once was, with the conurbations proving effective at retaining both immigrants and the British-born. Immigrants have been retained in West Yorkshire and the West Midlands and have engaged in reciprocated circulation between these cities and between inner and outer London. Migration has thus had little impact upon the geographical redistribution of this group, with migrants perhaps being 'workers in orbit'. The British-born have adopted different trajectories, with migrants leaving the major cores of concentration (West Midlands, West Yorkshire and the North West), and heading for London and the South East, albeit in small numbers. Within London, there has been outward gravitation but no evidence of exurbanisation.

5.5 Explanations for different geographical distributions

There are several possible explanations for differences in the geographical distribution of immigrant members of the minority ethnic population and their British-born counterparts. One of these would suggest that life in Britain, detachment from the frames of reference of the sending society, and adaptation have all combined to establish the British-born on different social trajectories to those of their immigrant parents; and these divergent trajectories are reflected in diverging geographical distributions. The position in 1991 would thus be a snapshot on a continuum of continual change and divergence. An alternative explanation is that differences in distribution and redistribution simply reflect a period effect, and that by comparing British-born and immigrants in 1991, we are comparing groups with dissimilar demographic and social characteristics which would, in themselves, produce different geographical distributions. We are thus recording a one-off step change brought about by the shift from an ageing immigrant to a youthful British-born minority ethnic population.

Before we are able to consider either of these possible explanations, we need therefore to establish whether the immigrant and British-born fractions of each group are different in their demography and social profile.

Figures 5.11 to 5.16 therefore provide a gendered age breakdown of each group. These reveal that the British-born and immigrant elements of each group do have very different age profiles. Not surprisingly, immigrants are older, with the modal age-group being 51–60 years of age for Black–Caribbeans, 41–50 for Indians and 31–40 for Pakistanis. Each wave has therefore aged *in situ*. Because of the different times of arrival, each group has also undergone family reunion or creation at different points in time. Peak fertility therefore occurred at different moments in time, and consequently the modal age for the British-born varies from 21–30 years for Black–Caribbeans to 11–20 years for Indians and 0–10 for Pakistanis. Simple comparisons of the settlement geography of British-born with immigrants are thus ignoring their very different age structures and the geographical differences which these are likely to produce.

Table 5.6 provides gendered LS data on social class profile (c.f. Robinson (1990) for data on the previous decade). Two generalisations are immediately apparent. First, the British-born fraction of each group is more prone to unemployment than their (older) immigrant counterparts and second, in all except one case, the British-born are more likely than immigrants to be white-collar workers. This reinforces the view expressed earlier that the British-born elements of the minority ethnic population are becoming polarised between those in work and gaining social, and perhaps spatial, mobility and those who are out of work and therefore likely to remain within known 'ethnic territory', with its protected economic opportunities.

On a different level, Table 5.6 also highlights differences between the social class profiles of the three principal minority ethnic groups. For Black–Caribbeans, the main distinction between those who are immigrants and those who are British-born is the extent to which the latter are relatively absent from unskilled and semi-skilled manual work and are found instead in junior white-collar work (especially women) or Social Class II (males). For the Indian and Pakistani ethnic groups the picture is rather different, with immigrant men and women having a higher penetration not only of the professions and Social Class II (men) but also of skilled and semi-skilled manual work, and the British-born having, instead, entered junior white-collar work.

Thus, in comparing the geographical distribution of immigrant and British-born fractions of each minority ethnic group we need to bear in mind that the fractions are dissimilar in age structure and social class composition. Moreover, these dissimilarities vary in size and direction between the three groups being considered

Figure 5.11
Immigrant Caribbean age structure

Figure 5.12
British-born Caribbean age structure

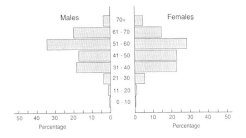

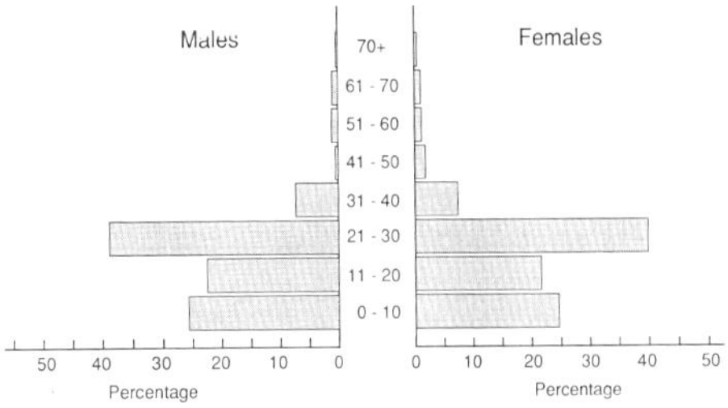

Figure 5.13
Immigrant Indian age structure

Figure 5.14
British-born Indian age structure

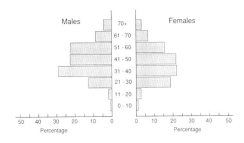

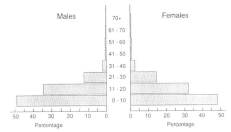

Figure 5.15
Immigrant Pakistani age structure

Figure 5.16
British-born Pakistani age structure

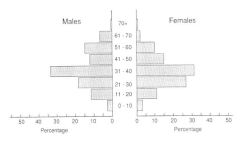

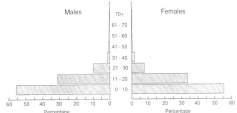

Table 5.6 *Social class profile of immigrant and British-born members of the minority ethnic population of England and Wales, 1991 (%)*

Group	I	II	IIIN	IIIM	IV	V	U	White-collar	Blue-collar
Black–Caribbeans									
British-born males	2.5	11.6	14.3	22.6	13.7	3.8	31.4	28.4	40.1
Immigrant males	1.5	7.4	4.6	36.9	23.5	8.5	17.5	13.5	68.9
British-born females	0.6	21.0	40.3	5.3	10.5	2.2	19.9	61.9	18.0
Immigrant females	0.4	32.7	14.0	7.5	22.9	14.2	16.7	54.6	44.6
Indians									
British-born males	7.0	16.7	13.3	19.0	14.6	4.2	25.3	37.0	37.8
Immigrant males	7.7	20.3	9.3	24.0	20.2	5.5	13.0	37.3	49.7
British-born females	1.2	18.0	41.1	3.0	11.5	0.3	24.9	60.3	14.8
Immigrant females	3.9	16.8	15.6	8.8	35.3	5.7	13.9	36.3	49.8
Pakistanis									
British-born males	1.0	12.1	12.6	17.4	13.7	1.6	41.6	25.7	32.7
Immigrant males	3.0	13.5	6.9	24.8	18.8	4.8	28.3	23.4	48.4
British-born females	2.2	8.1	29.6	3.0	14.1	0.7	42.2	39.9	17.8
Immigrant females	0.9	20.2	14.1	7.5	19.6	0.9	36.9	35.2	28.0

Note: Because the disaggregation of Longitudinal Study (LS) data can lead to small samples, these data should be used with caution.
Source: Calculated from LS data.

here. The British-born are younger (although the degree to which this is the case varies because of the different timings of the different waves of migration) and are simultaneously more likely to be either unemployed or junior white-collar workers. South Asian immigrants, however, are over-represented in more senior white-collar work, unlike their Black–Caribbean counterparts. Such discrepancies are likely to influence the willingness and ability of individuals to migrate within the UK and also the kinds of districts to which they are likely to be able to gain access. The literature on White British-born people clearly shows that migration propensities and distances vary according to age and social class, and it would be unusual were this not also the case for ethnic minorities.

Controlling for age

The section above thus tells us that the British-born from minority ethnic groups are both younger and have different social class profiles to their immigrant forebears. What it does not tell us is whether these two characteristics are associated, i.e. whether, given time, the social class profiles of immigrants and British-born would converge, as the latter gain lifetime social mobility. In other words, we cannot determine whether differences result from the groups being on divergent social trajectories or simply being at different points in time along the same trajectory.

The size of the ethnic samples included in datasets such as the LS, prevents their detailed decomposition into fractions defined by multiple criteria, such as social class and age. In order to progress the analysis, it was therefore decided to derive a

Table 5.7 *Social class profile of immigrant and British-born members of the minority ethnic population of England and Wales, 25–35-year-olds only, 1991 (%)*

Group	I	II	IIIN	IIIM	IV	V	U	White-collar	Blue-collar
Black–Caribbeans									
British-born	1.9	20.8	26.3	17.0	11.8	2.1	20.0	61.3	38.7
Immigrant	0.5	25.4	18.9	18.9	15.7	3.2	17.3	54.2	45.8
Indians									
British-born	8.4	30.2	19.3	10.9	12.6	0.8	17.6	70.4	29.6
Immigrant	5.0	21.0	13.7	14.2	28.1	5.0	13.2	45.6	54.4
Pakistanis									
British-born	0	17.4	21.7	26.1	8.7	0	26.1	52.9	47.1
Immigrant	5.1	21.3	11.1	24.0	13.5	2.4	22.8	48.4	51.6

Note: (1) % Blue/white collar relate only to those in work.
(2) Because the disaggregation of Longitudinal Study (LS) data can lead to small samples, these data should be used with caution.
Source: Calculated from LS data.

subsample of British-born and immigrants of approximately the same age, i.e. 25–35-year-olds, to see whether individuals at the same point in their life-courses had similar or different social characteristics.

Table 5.7 provides data on the social class profile of the matched samples of 25–35-year-olds. It demonstrates that, in each case where people of the same age are compared, the British-born have a greater presence in white-collar employment than the immigrants. The British-born also have a greater vulnerability to unemployment. The degree of over-representation in white-collar employment is most clearly shown within the Indian population, where the British-born are relatively more numerous in all three of the white-collar groups and considerably less numerous in all three of the manual classes. Differences between British-born and immigrant Black–Caribbeans are smaller, but follow a similar pattern, with the exception of Social Class II which has a greater representation of immigrants. The Pakistani analysis is made difficult by the small size of the British-born sample, but the latter are still over-represented in white-collar employment (especially junior white-collar work), and are more likely to be unemployed.

What this tells us is that the different social class profiles of British-born and immigrant elements of each minority ethnic group are not simply a product of comparing young British ethnics with older immigrant ethnics who have had much longer to acquire social mobility. Rather, the British-born are set on different social trajectories to their immigrant forebears. These will see the British-born gaining the lifetime social mobility into white-collar employment that a much smaller proportion of their immigrant counterparts achieved.

5.6 Conclusion

This chapter has considered the distribution and redistribution of three of Britain's minority ethnic populations. However, rather than defining the groups using criteria which are affective, proscribed and rooted in the society of origin, the analysis has focused upon disaggregation of the groups according to criteria which are both acquired and instrumental in nature, namely social class (defined as occupational status in the UK) and immigrant/British-born status.

The analysis has revealed that the immigrant and British-born fractions of each ethnic group do not share the same geographical distributions (regardless of the scale of measurement). Moreover, the British-born and immigrant fractions appear to have spatial distributions which are diverging over time, not converging. Two main explanations for difference have been considered. The first suggests that there is no underlying difference in the geography of settlement of the immigrants and the British-born, rather that differences visible in 1991 simply reflect the fact that the British-born are much younger and therefore at a much earlier stage in their social mobility life cycle. With time, the two geographies will converge, as the British-born acquire the social status and material wealth of their older immigrant counterparts.

The second suggests that the British-born and immigrants are not at different points on the same life trajectory, but are instead on entirely different trajectories, arising from the different backgrounds, human capital resources, values and aspirations possessed by first generation immigrants and Black and Asian Britons. These contrasting trajectories involve different likelihoods and forms of social mobility and consequently different spatial outcomes. Within the limits of the data available from the census, this chapter has argued that the second explanation for geographical difference is the more plausible. What is not yet clear is whether the different social trajectories will be fully reflected in different geographies of settlement.

In 1991, some of the differences in settlement patterns were still small and may even seem insignificant. In the future, however, differences at the macro- and micro-levels will probably increase, with growing contrasts between which cities and counties immigrants and the British-born reside in. What seems much less sure is whether the social mobility gained by the British-born will be fully translated into gains at the micro-level, and whether Britain's Black–Caribbeans, Indians and Pakistanis face the geographically constrained 'Black' future outlined by Massey and Mullen (1984) or whether one or all of these groups can overcome the deleterious effects of racism and follow Massey and Mullen's 'Hispanic' route in which social and geographical status are more equally matched.

Acknowledgements

I am grateful to OPCS for allowing use of the Longitudinal Study, and to Simon Gleave of the LS Support Programme, Social Statistics Research Unit at City University for accessing the data.

References

Boal, F. (1976) Ethnic residential segregation. In: Herbert, D. and Johnston, R. (eds), *Social Areas in Cities Volume 1. Spatial Processes and Form*. Chichester: Wiley, pp. 41–81.

Cater, J. and Jones, T. (1979) Ethnic residential space: the case of Asians in Bradford. *Tijdschrift voor Economische en Sociale Geografie*, 70, 86–98.

Glazer, N. and Moynihan, D. (1975) *Ethnicity: Theory and Experience*. Cambridge, MA: Harvard University Press.

Griffiths, A. (1960) *Coloured Immigrants in Britain*. London: Oxford University Press.

Hussain, M. (1975) The increase and distribution of New Commonwealth immigrants in Greater Nottingham. *East Midlands Geographer*, 5, 105–29.

Jones, P. (1970) Some aspects of the changing distribution of coloured immigrants in Birmingham 1961–66. *Transactions, Institute of British Geographers*, 50, 199–219.

Jones, P. (1978) The distribution and diffusion of the coloured population in England and Wales, 1961–71. *Transactions, Institute of British Geographers*, 3, 515–33.

Massey, D. and Mullen, B. (1984) Processes of Hispanic and black spatial assimilation. *American Journal of Sociology*, 89, 836–73.

Peach, C. (1968) *West Indian Migration to Britain: A Social Geography*. Oxford: Oxford University Press.

Peach, C. (1984) The force of West Indian island identities in Britain. In: Peach, C., Clarke, C. and Ley, D. (eds), *Geography and Ethnic Pluralism*. London: Allen and Unwin, pp. 214–30.

Peach, C. and Byron, M. (1993) Caribbean tenants in council housing: 'race', class and gender. *New Community*, 19(30), 407–23.

Peach, C., Winchester, S. and Woods, R. (1975) Distribution of coloured immigrants in Britain. *Urban Affairs Annual Review*, 395–419.

Robinson, V. (1979) *The Segregation of Immigrants in a British City*. School of Geography Research Paper 22, Oxford.

Robinson, V. (1986) *Transients, Settlers and Refugees: Asians in Britain*. Oxford: Clarendon Press.

Robinson, V. (1987) Race, space and place. The geographic contribution to the study of ethnic minorities in Britain 1957–87. *New Community*, 14, 186–97.

Robinson, V. (1990) Roots to mobility: the social mobility of Britain's black population, 1971–87. *Ethnic and Racial Studies*, 13, 27–86.

Robinson, V. (1991) Move on up; the mobility of Britain's ethnic population. In: Stilwell, J., Rees, P. and Boden, B. (eds), *Migration Patterns and Processes; Population Redistribution in the 1980s*. London: Belhaven, pp. 271–92.

Robinson, V. (1993) Making waves? The contribution of ethnic minorities to local demography. In: Champion, A. (ed.), *Population Matters: The Local Dimension*. London: Paul Chapman, pp. 150–69.

Robinson, V. (1994) Marching into the middle classes? The longterm resettlement of East African Asians in the UK. *Journal of Refugee Studies*, 6(3), 230–47.

Robinson, V. (1995) The migration of East African Asians to the UK. In: Cohen, R. (ed.), *The Cambridge World Migration History*. Cambridge: Cambridge University Press.

Chapter 6
London: a true cosmopolis

Marian Storkey and Rob Lewis

6.1   Introduction

This chapter uses new data from the 1991 Census to demonstrate London's unique position as a centre of minority ethnic population. It examines the size of the resident populations of the many different communities living in London, using data about people's ethnic origin as well as their country of birth. The heterogeneity and rich diversity are discussed, and each of the 10 main ethnic groups are examined in order to learn more about their composition. The chapter also illustrates the distribution of a number of the largest ethnic groups in London today, and describes how historical, social and economic factors have influenced the settlement patterns. Finally, the chapter looks at some of the main socio-economic variables from the census. Some of the variation exhibited by the different ethnic groups in London in the spheres of health, housing and labour market position are examined, and the results are set against comparable data for Great Britain as a whole.

In a volume which deals with the geographical spread and spatial concentration of minority ethnic populations, it would be unthinkable not to include a chapter on the city (a) which contains nearly half of Great Britain's minority ethnic population, (b) whose constituent districts occupy the first seven places (and 16 of the first 20 places) in the list of districts with the largest ethnic minority percentages, and (c) which has a strong claim to being the most cosmopolitan city in the world.

Since its foundation around 50 AD by people from Europe and mercenaries from most corners of the then-known world, London's development and growth have been fuelled by the talents and contributions of an enormous range of different peoples. After the Romans, there were settlers from the Germanic tribes, Scandinavians, and Normans. Irish and Jewish people followed; then medieval merchants from half of Europe; then Huguenots and other religious refugees, and Black servants, slaves and seamen. Trade, merchant sea power and the new colonies brought further migrants from beyond Europe; notably from India, China, Africa, the Americas and Australia. More recently, forces of globalisation, economic change and political turmoil in Britain's ex-colonies and elsewhere, have combined via migration since the 1950s to create an ever more cosmopolitan London.

6.2   The size of London's minority ethnic population

In the context of Great Britain

Greater London contains 12.2 per cent of the total population of Great Britain, but

Map 6.1   *Distribution of ethnic minorities in Great Britain, 1991*

Table 6.1 Ethnic groups in Greater London and Great Britain 1991

	Greater London Number	%	Great Britain Number	%
White	5,333,580	79.8	51,873,794	94.5
Born in Ireland	*256,470*	*3.8*	*837,464*	*1.5*
Black–Caribbean	290,968	4.4	499,964	0.9
Black–African	163,635	2.4	212,362	0.4
Black–Other	80,613	1.2	178,401	0.3
Indian	347,091	5.2	840,255	1.5
Pakistani	87,816	1.3	476,555	0.9
Bangladeshi	85,738	1.3	162,835	0.3
Chinese	56,579	0.8	156,938	0.3
Other–Asian	112,807	1.7	197,534	0.4
Other–Other	120,872	1.8	290,206	0.5
All ethnic minority groups	1,346,119	20.2	3,015,050	5.5
Total	6,679,699	100	54,888,844	100

Source: 1991 Census Local Base Statistics (LBS), Table 6.

nearly half (44.6 per cent) of Britain's minority ethnic population. As Map 6.1 shows, the large majority of the land area of Great Britain has a proportion of minorities below the national average of 5.49 per cent. Those of minority ethnic origin are concentrated in a handful of cities and towns, dominated by London. Of the 29 districts with a proportion of 15 per cent or more, 22 are in Greater London.

All the minority ethnic groups are strongly represented in London's population compared with Great Britain as a whole, as shown in Table 6.1. From the table it can be seen that the extent of the concentration in London varies for different groups. The proportions range from the Pakistani group, with 18.4 per cent of the Great Britain total living in London, to the Black–African group, with 77.1 per cent living in London.

Country of birth data allow us to identify numerous large groups of overseas-born communities living in Great Britain, and these also demonstrate a universal tendency towards concentration in London. The high figures for the Black–African ethnic group in Table 6.1 might lead us to anticipate some of the country of birth figures: for example, 82 per cent of Britain's Ghanaian-born population live in London, as well as 77 per cent of those born in Nigeria. The capital also contains 77 per cent of Britain's Turkish-born population, 72 per cent of those born in Guyana, 69 per cent of Moroccan-born people, 66 per cent of those born in Sri Lanka and Portugal, 65 per cent of the Cypriot-born population, and around 60 per cent of people born in Japan, the Philippines, Mauritius and Vietnam.

The size of the British-born population of minority ethnic origin

One of the important by-products of the introduction of the ethnic group question in the 1991 Census, is that for the first time analysts are able to assess the relative size of the UK-born component of the minority ethnic population. Over half a million

Table 6.2 *Ethnic group by countries of birth, 1991*

Born in (country)	Percentage	Born in (country)	Percentage
White		Bangladeshi	
UK	87	Bangladesh	64
Ireland	4	UK	35
Europe	3	Chinese	
Rest of World[1]	2	SE Asia (NC)	44
Cyprus	1	*Hong Kong*	26
Black–Caribbean		*Malaysia*	14
UK	53	*Singapore*	4
Caribbean (NC)	45	UK	26
Jamaica	25	China	10
Barbados	4	Vietnam	10
Guyana	3	Rest of World[1]	4
Trinidad & Tobago	2	*Mauritius*	2
West Indies	2	Taiwan	2
Rest of World[1]	1	Caribbean (NC)	1
Black–African		Other–Asia	
West Africa (NC)	39	Rest of World[1]	33
Nigeria	21	Japan	14
Ghana	16	*Philippines*	10
Sierra Leone	3	*Thailand*	2
UK	36	*Burma*	1
Rest of World[1]	14	UK	21
Africa (not NC)	14	Sri Lanka	19
East Africa (NC)	7	Mauritius	6
Uganda	5	East Africa (NC)	6
Zimbabwe	1	*Kenya*	3
Kenya	1	*Uganda*	1
Zambia	1	*Tanzania*	1
Southern Africa (NC)	1	Vietnam	5
Caribbean (NC)	1	SE Asia (NC)	3
Black–Other		*Malaysia*	3
UK	84	India	2
New Commonwealth	10	Caribbean (NC)	1
Africa (NC)	2	Other–Other	
Guyana	2	UK	54
Jamaica	1	Rest of World[1]	28
Cyprus	1	*Iran*	6
Mauritius	1	*Iraq*	3
Rest of World[1]	3	*Morocco*	2
USA	1	*Egypt*	2
Ireland	1	*Lebanon*	1
Indian		*Turkey*	1
UK	36	*Colombia*	1
India	35	India	6
East Africa (NC)	23	Caribbean (NC)	3
Kenya	13	*Guyana*	1
Uganda	5	East Africa (NC)	2
Tanzania	3	SE Asia (NC)	1
Rest of World[1]	2	Other EC[2]	1
SE Asia (NC)	1	Mauritius	1
Caribbean (NC)	1	USA	1
Mauritius	1		
Pakistani			
UK	45		
Pakistan	44		
India	6		
East Africa (NC)	3		
Kenya	2		
Rest of World[1]	1		

Notes NC = New Commonwealth; [1] Rest of World = all countries outside UK, Euro Commonwealth, USA, China and Vietnam; [2] Other EC = European Community excluding UK.
Source: LBS Table 51 and Special Table LRCT 14

(43 per cent) of London's minority population were born in the UK. There are also now three minority ethnic groups where over half have been born in the UK; those defined as Black–Other, Other–Other and Black–Caribbean. The proportion born in the UK in fact varies quite widely for the different ethnic groups as is discussed below (see also Table 6.2).

For each ethnic group, London had lower proportions of people born in the UK compared to all other areas of Great Britain. This is likely to be because London is often the place where people first arrive from abroad: indeed it has more temporary residents such as overseas students and diplomats than other areas of Great Britain. The biggest difference in the populations living inside and outside London was for the Other–Other group, but the Whites and the Indians also showed large differences. The White group in London had 87 per cent of people born in the UK, while areas outside London averaged 97 per cent. This indicates a greater variety within the White population in London as compared to areas outside the capital. Although London has 10.3 per cent of Great Britain's White population, it has a higher proportion of White groups born outside the UK, including, for example, people born in the Irish Republic, Cyprus and a number of other European countries.

Black British

Although coding schemes including the categories Black British and British Asian were tested, they did not appear in the final version of the census question. However, many Londoners took the opportunity to write in such a response – over 36,000 people actually wrote in 'Black British' on the census form, compared with 22,000 in the whole of the rest of Great Britain. In addition, nearly 7,000 people in London ticked the 'any other ethnic group' box and stated that they belonged to a British minority ethnic group (for example, British Indian).

Identifying the true size of country of birth categories

The country of birth data in the census are useful for many areas of analysis, but using them to estimate the size of minority ethnic communities can lead to serious underestimates of their true size as the figures exclude, amongst others, the British-born members of those groups. This has particular significance for those groups for which only country of birth data is available, and those with particular needs in terms of the provision of services. In London this includes the large Cypriot, Turkish and Irish populations. However, there are a number of steps which can be taken to augment the figures from the census. For the Cypriot group, for example, using 1981 data, we can estimate the number of young Cypriots who were born in the UK and who by 1991 had set up their own homes. Using births data, we can also estimate the number of children that Cypriot people not born in Cyprus might have had. The calculations show that the Cypriot population in London is likely to be around double the number actually born in Cyprus (Storkey, 1993a). The complications implicit in doing this kind of analysis highlight the benefit gained from having data from the ethnic group question to estimate the true size of communities rather than relying on the country of birth data.

Using the census as a base for population projections

Despite the important caveats outlined by Rees and Phillips in Chapter 2 (relating to the problems of under-enumeration and data imputation), researchers now have access to data on minority populations of an unprecedented quality. This in turn enables them to give much better estimates of future numbers.

Comparisons were made between the age structures of the population of London and Great Britain as a whole, after the figures had been adjusted for under-enumeration. Any differences, particularly in the numbers of women in the fertile age ranges, may have significant implications for the future numbers in each area. The results showed that the White, Black–Other, Pakistani and Other–Other groups had higher proportions (by about 3 percentage points) of women aged 15–44 in their populations in London compared to Great Britain. This would mean that, assuming similar fertility rates, there would be proportionately more births to the populations in these ethnic groups in London. The other groups had very similar proportions of women in these age-groups both inside and outside London. In order to project these starting populations, we would need to add the births to each ethnic group, reduce the populations by the deaths which occur, and adjust for net migration by ethnic group. Unfortunately, although migration data by ethnicity is available from the census, the task of producing accurate projections is greatly limited by the fact that births and deaths are only recorded by country of birth and not by ethnic origin.

6.3 The ethnic diversity of London's population

The cultural diversity of London is self-evident. If evidence were needed, then the census amply attests to London's cosmopolitan nature; in addition to the groups specified in the ethnic group question, we can identify a number of communities using the country of birth question. The 33 communities of over 10,000 people who were born outside Great Britain and Ireland and now live in London, are shown on Map 6.2.

It is important when looking at this data that birthplace is not confused with nationality or ethnicity; a prime example being those 'born in Germany'. A number of children have been born to British families stationed with the army in Germany. In the census these children will show up as 'born in Germany', although they may not be German by nationality and will almost certainly not be 'ethnically' German. (See also the discussion in Chapter 1 of the general issues underlying this debate.)

The largest of London's minority ethnic groups, that of Indian origin, contains its own internal diversity in terms of origin. It numbers some 347,000 people, of whom significant proportions were born in each of the UK, India and East Africa (see Table 6.2). Some 89 per cent of the Pakistani group, about 88,000 strong, were either UK- or Pakistan-born, and the Bangladeshi group, at nearly 86,000, is even more geographically homogeneous, with 99 per cent born either in Bangladesh or the UK.

The Black–Caribbean ethnic group is London's second largest, at 291,000 persons. In terms of geographic origin, it is relatively homogeneous, with 98 per cent born in

Map 6.2 *Communities over 10,000 who were born outside the British Isles living in London, 1991*

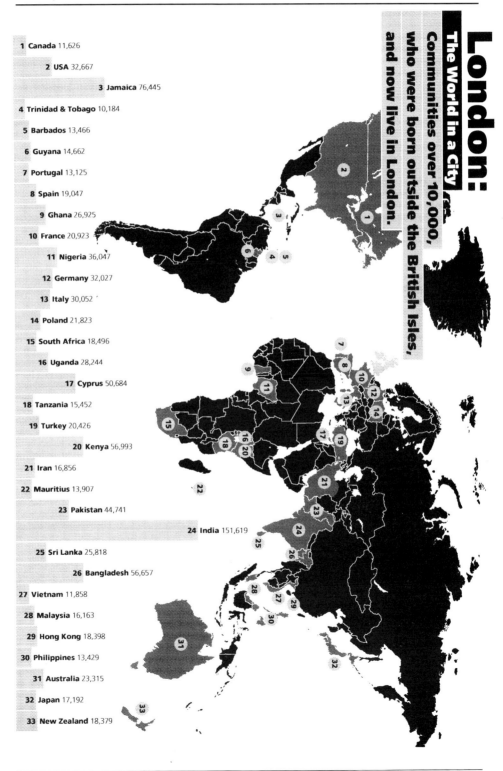

1 **Canada** 11,626

2 **USA** 32,667

3 **Jamaica** 76,445

4 **Trinidad & Tobago** 10,184

5 **Barbados** 13,466

6 **Guyana** 14,662

7 **Portugal** 13,125

8 **Spain** 19,047

9 **Ghana** 26,925

10 **France** 20,923

11 **Nigeria** 36,047

12 **Germany** 32,027

13 **Italy** 30,052

14 **Poland** 21,823

15 **South Africa** 18,496

16 **Uganda** 28,244

17 **Cyprus** 50,684

18 **Tanzania** 15,452

19 **Turkey** 20,426

20 **Kenya** 56,993

21 **Iran** 16,856

22 **Mauritius** 13,907

23 **Pakistan** 44,741

24 **India** 151,619

25 **Sri Lanka** 25,818

26 **Bangladesh** 56,657

27 **Vietnam** 11,858

28 **Malaysia** 16,163

29 **Hong Kong** 18,398

30 **Philippines** 13,429

31 **Australia** 23,315

32 **Japan** 17,192

33 **New Zealand** 18,379

London: The World in a City

Communities over 10,000, who were born outside the British Isles, and now live in London.

the UK or the Caribbean. The majority of the Caribbean-born originate in Jamaica, but there are also significant numbers from Barbados, Trinidad and Tobago, and Guyana.

The Black–African group comprises 164,000. Some 36 per cent are UK-born, with almost all the remainder born in Africa, predominantly in Commonwealth countries. Over 68,000 Londoners were born in West Africa alone, including 36,000 from Nigeria and 27,000 from Ghana, this representing nearly 80 per cent of Great Britain's entire West African-born population. A further 24,000 were born in a catch-all category of 'non-Commonwealth African countries', amongst which Ethiopia, Sudan and Somalia are probably the most significant.

Although the census did not include an Irish category in the ethnic group question, it is possible to identify some 256,000 Londoners born in Ireland using the country of birth data. The 214,000 born in the Irish Republic represent the largest migrant community from any country. As well as 42,000 people born in Northern Ireland, London is home to 113,000 born in Scotland and 71,000 born in Wales.

The Chinese group, with some 57,000 members, is the smallest of those defined by the census, but demonstrates a wide range of geographical origin (see Table 6.2). Those answering Chinese to the ethnic group question seem to have accepted the concept of Chinese ethnicity, since only 10 per cent were actually born in China. The UK-born account for 26 per cent of the group, 26 per cent were Hong Kong-born, 14 per cent born in Malaysia, 10 per cent in Vietnam, and 4 per cent in Singapore.

The remaining minority groups – Black–Other, Other–Asian and Other–Other – might by definition be expected to be disparate. The Black–Other group, however, is in fact closely identified with UK-born Black people, or those of mixed heritage, and therefore with the other two Black groups, particularly the Black–Caribbeans. Black–Others number 81,000 in London, and no less than 84 per cent were born in the UK (compared for example with 87 per cent of the White group). A further 4 per cent were born in the Caribbean, with the remainder spread throughout the world.

The Other–Asian group, totalling nearly 113,000, is less strongly identified with UK-born Asians, containing only 21 per cent born in the UK, alongside a number of interesting migrant component groups. There are about 26,000 Sri Lankan-born people, 17,000 from Japan and 13,000 from the Philippines, with the latter group displaying a uniquely biased gender balance for such a large group – 29 per cent male and 71 per cent female. This is clearly consistent with the common stereotype of Filipino women coming to London to fill domestic roles, though testing the assertion is difficult. Other smaller groups under this overall heading, tend to represent areas of the world typified by an ethnic mix – there are some 7,000 Other–Asians born in Mauritius, as well as 6,000 originating in the East African Commonwealth, 6,000 in Vietnam and 4,000 in South East Asia (mainly Malaysia). Mauritius is a good exemplar of ethnic diversity, and illustrates the possibilities for one small island in responding to the ethnic groups used in the census: 49 per cent were Other–Asian, 21 per cent Indian, 8 per cent White, 8 per cent Chinese, 7 per cent Other–Other, 4 per cent Black–Other and 3 per cent Black–Caribbean.

The Other–Other group numbers 121,000 people. Much of this group is hard to identify, containing many persons of mixed origin, and many who may have found it difficult (or invidious) to categorise themselves. Country of birth data indicate that there are some 17,000 Iranian-born Londoners, 8,000 from Iraq, 7,000 from Israel and 6,000 from Lebanon, all part of a total of 51,000 born in the Middle East, and a further 20,000 born in Northern Africa (e.g. Morocco, Algeria, Tunisia, Libya and Egypt).

Within the White group of 5,334,000, we can identify a number of immigrant Londoners from the country of birth data, in addition to the Irish already discussed. Those categorising themselves as White form the greater part of the following groups: the 51,000 people born in Cyprus, the 33,000 from the USA, the 32,000 people born in Germany, the 30,000 people from Italy, the 23,000 from Australia, 22,000 from Poland, 21,000 from France, 20,000 from Turkey, 19,000 from New Zealand, 19,000 from Spain, 16,000 from South America and 13,000 from Portugal. Interestingly, many of the European-born populations demonstrate a significant gender bias, similar to that seen in the Filipino population above. Examples of these are people born in Finland (78 per cent female) and Austria (71 per cent female).

6.4 Understanding the geographical distribution of London's ethnic groups

It is possible to quantify the spatial patterns associated with different ethnic groups by calculating indices of dissimilarity and segregation, as discussed by Peach in Chapter 3 of this volume. The indices, which he has calculated for minority ethnic groups in London, show consistently lower levels of segregation than those found in many American cities (at least in the case of African Americans), but there are significant differences between the groups. At ward level in London, the Bangladeshi group has by far the highest levels of segregation, followed by the Pakistani and Indian groups, and then by the three Black groups. The Chinese and Other groups have low levels of segregation at ward level. The indices are higher for all groups at enumeration district level, with the Chinese group showing much higher levels of segregation at enumeration district level than at ward level. This suggests that the Chinese are well distributed across the city, but in a series of small clusters.

Where people from different ethnic groups live is determined by a number of factors – economic, social and political. The following section aims to describe these patterns and to outline the historical factors influencing where people settled. The indices Peach has calculated confirm a number of the patterns of distribution described below (and shown in the accompanying maps), and the history of settlement in turn helps to explain a number of the differences between groups highlighted in Chapter 3. The maps have been designed to show the main concentrations of settlement, and it is important to note that the scales vary from map to map, reflecting the large differences in the overall sizes of, for example, the Indian community compared with that of the Chinese.

Map 6.3　*The percentage of Indians in London's wards, 1991*

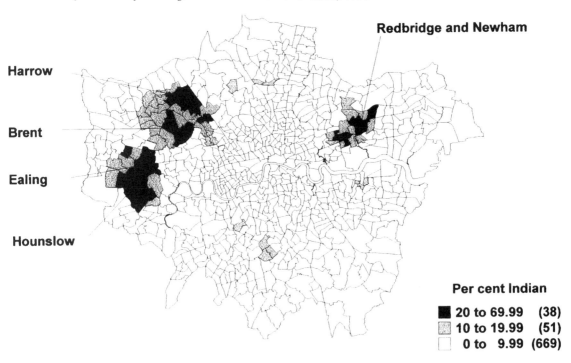

Redbridge and Newham

Harrow

Brent

Ealing

Hounslow

Per cent Indian

■ 20 to 69.99　(38)
▨ 10 to 19.99　(51)
□ 0 to 9.99　(669)

Map 6.4　*The percentage of Pakistanis in London's wards, 1991*

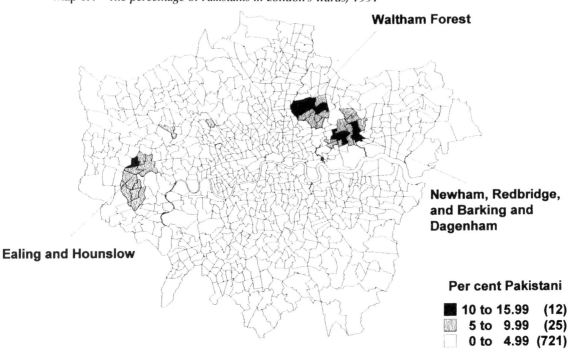

Waltham Forest

**Newham, Redbridge,
and Barking and
Dagenham**

Ealing and Hounslow

Per cent Pakistani

■ 10 to 15.99　(12)
▨ 5 to 9.99　(25)
□ 0 to 4.99　(721)

Map 6.5 *The percentage of Bangladeshis in London's wards, 1991*

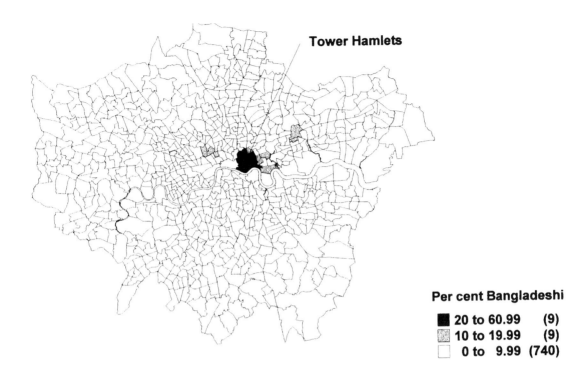

Tower Hamlets

Per cent Bangladeshi

■ 20 to 60.99   (9)
▨ 10 to 19.99   (9)
□ 0 to 9.99 (740)

The three South Asian groups

Each of the three South Asian groups has a long history of migration to London, dating back to the establishment of the East India Company in 1600. Some came as servants or 'ayahs', others as 'lascar' seamen, recruited from the Punjab, Bengal or the west coast of India. (In fact, the docks have historically played an important role in the migrant settlement process, providing cheap, if poor quality, accommodation, jobs and convenient location.)

Asian professionals such as doctors and lawyers began to arrive from the middle of the 19th century. In the 1920s and 1930s, Sikhs from the Punjab settled in the East End. Political upheaval following the partition of India in 1947 provoked further migration in the immediate post-war period, but net migration only really started to increase in the 1950s and 1960s, attracted by a flourishing economy and a labour shortage associated with post-war reconstruction. West London offered jobs in plastics, food-processing and other expanding industries, many servicing Heathrow airport (Merriman et al., 1993). In Tower Hamlets, the Bangladeshis, who arrived in the UK more recently, on average, than the other South Asian groups, at first tended to take jobs in local factories, then subsequently moved in greater numbers into the rag trade.

Initially most (South Asian) migrants were working-age men, but the late 1960s and 1970s, with restrictive legislation which brought a virtual end to primary immigration, saw the arrival of dependents, as families reunited. The late 1960s were notable for the entry of British passport-holding East African Asians as refugees, largely from Kenya, and the early 1970s witnessed another wave fleeing from the Obote and Amin regimes in Uganda (Robinson, 1986).

The South Asian community is extremely varied not only in terms of culture, language and social class (containing within it both some of the most affluent and some of the most deprived of Londoners), but also in terms of religion. The PSI study, *Black and White Britain* (Brown, 1984), indicates that the Pakistani and Bangladeshi groups are predominantly (96 per cent) Muslim, but that the Indian group demonstrates considerable religious diversity – for Indians originating from the subcontinent there are 43 per cent Sikhs, 31 per cent Hindus, 16 per cent Muslims and 7 per cent Christians, while for those from East Africa, the proportions are 60 per cent Hindus, 11 per cent Sikhs and 24 per cent Muslims.

Variations in religion and geographical origin are closely linked with area of settlement within London. There are three main areas of Indian settlement see Map 6.3): one around Southall (Ealing) and extending into Hounslow, where the population is largely Punjabi and mainly Sikh; North West London (Harrow and the Wembley half of Brent), where many East African Asians of Gujerati origin settled; and east London (Newham and parts of Redbridge), where there are significant Sikh, Hindu and Muslim populations, with a considerable number of Gujerati speakers. In three Ealing wards, over half the population is of Indian origin (peaking in Northcote ward at 67.2 per cent), and there are several more wards in these areas where the proportion is 30 per cent or higher.

London's Pakistani community (see Map 6.4) is mainly located in east London, with a concentration around Walthamstow and Leyton (Waltham Forest). The proportion of the total ward population formed by the Pakistani group is around the 10–15 per cent level here. Other communities can be found in the areas where Newham borders the boroughs of Redbridge and Barking and Dagenham, and in Southall. The Bangladeshi community (see Map 6.5), predominantly Sylheti, is uniquely concentrated in the borough of Tower Hamlets, accounting for over 60 per cent of the total population in Spitalfields ward, and for over 30 per cent in four other wards in the western half of the borough.

Chinese

Members of the Chinese group speak many different dialects but are linked by the written Chinese language (Shang, 1991). Chinese settlement in London dates back perhaps 200 years, and in 1814 legislation was enacted to force the East India Company to provide lodgings for Chinese and other migrant sailors. The growth of the Chinese population in London and Great Britain was linked to the growth of the Chinese catering trade, originated by ex-seamen. Subsequent migration by family dependants, the development of business activity surrounding catering, and the resettlement of the Vietnamese 'boat people' – at least half of them ethnic Chinese – have all helped to shape the development of the community. In terms of settlement, the Chinese (see Map 6.6) are spread very thinly across London, partly because of

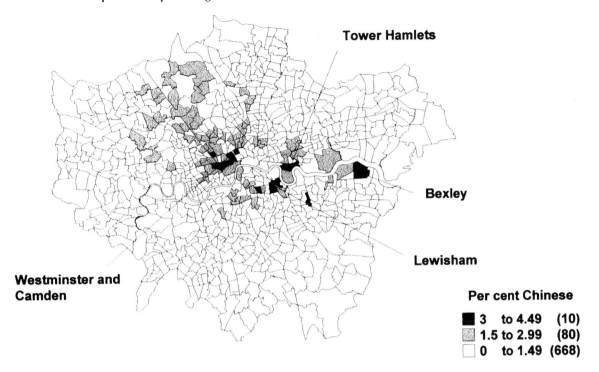

Map 6.6   *The percentage of Chinese in London's wards, 1991*

Tower Hamlets

Bexley

Lewisham

Westminster and Camden

Per cent Chinese

■ 3   to 4.49   (10)
▨ 1.5 to 2.99   (80)
□ 0   to 1.49   (668)

Map 6.7   *The percentage of Black–Caribbeans in London's wards, 1991*

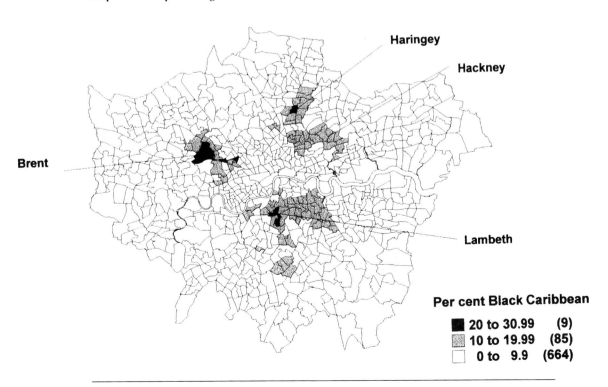

Haringey

Hackney

Brent

Lambeth

Per cent Black Caribbean

■ 20 to 30.99   (9)
▨ 10 to 19.99   (85)
□ 0 to 9.9   (664)

Map 6.8 *The percentage of Black–Africans in London's wards, 1991*

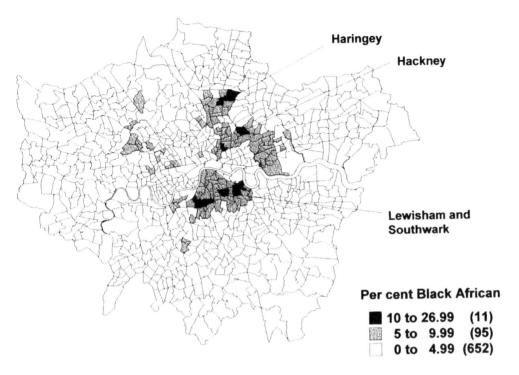

Haringey

Hackney

Lewisham and
Southwark

Per cent Black African

■ 10 to 26.99   (11)
▨ 5 to   9.99   (95)
□ 0 to   4.99 (652)

Map 6.9 *The percentage of Black–Others in London's wards, 1991*

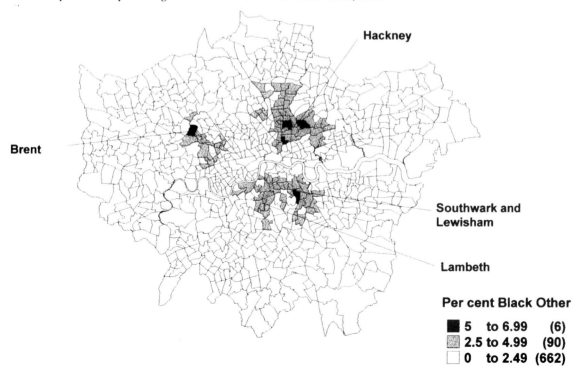

Hackney

Brent

Southwark and
Lewisham

Lambeth

Per cent Black Other

■ 5   to 6.99   (6)
▨ 2.5 to 4.99   (90)
□ 0   to 2.49 (662)

the demands of the catering trade. There are only two wards in London where the community amounts to more than 4 per cent of the total population. Two small concentrations emerge: one is the area from Soho north to Kings Cross, and the other is an area around Deptford and north of New Cross (Lewisham).

The three Black groups

There were Black Londoners during Roman times, but there has been a continuous presence since at least the mid-16th century (Faizi, 1986). This was very much associated with the English slave trade and the plantations of the English Caribbean. Although both Africans and Caribbeans originate from an enormous range of cultural and linguistic backgrounds, slavery and the subsequent persistence of racism, race prejudice and discriminatory practices has to a point bound them together. After the effective end of slavery in Britain around 1800, most migrants from Africa and from the Caribbean were students and sailors. The 20th century saw a continuation of this pattern, along with settlement by a number of servicemen and women from the two world wars.

The major period of Caribbean immigration took place during the 1950s, starting symbolically in 1948 with the arrival of almost 500 migrants on the *Empire Windrush*. The settlement patterns of this period – many immigrants were initially housed in former air-raid shelters in Clapham – had a substantial effect on the development of the south London Black community (Lambeth Council, 1988). Migration peaked in 1961, and declined following the 1962 Commonwealth Immigrants Act. The main reasons for this wave of migration were economic (unemployment at home, the post-war economic expansion in the UK), and a tightening of US immigration controls. However, some migration, especially that from Guyana in the 1960s, was mainly political in origin. By the early 1970s, net emigration was very low: the Black–Caribbean group was, and has remained, notably a youthful group. This is only now beginning to change.

Post-war emigration from Africa was driven more by the effects of independence in a number of Commonwealth countries and the ensuing political and economic uncertainties. Many migrants came as students, and study has remained a major factor to the present day. This is reflected in a number of census characteristics, particularly age structure, qualifications and housing position.

The main Black–Caribbean communities (see Map 6.7) are around Harlesden and Kensal Rise at the southern end of Brent, where the group accounts for over 25 per cent of the total population in two wards; around Brixton (Lambeth) and extending across a large area of south London in Lambeth, Southwark and Lewisham; and in Hackney and Haringey north of the river. The Black–African community is located in similar areas (see Map 6.8), particularly around Southwark and Lewisham, stretching across to Lambeth; and in parts of Hackney and Haringey.

Map 6.10 *The percentage of Irish-born in London's wards, 1991*

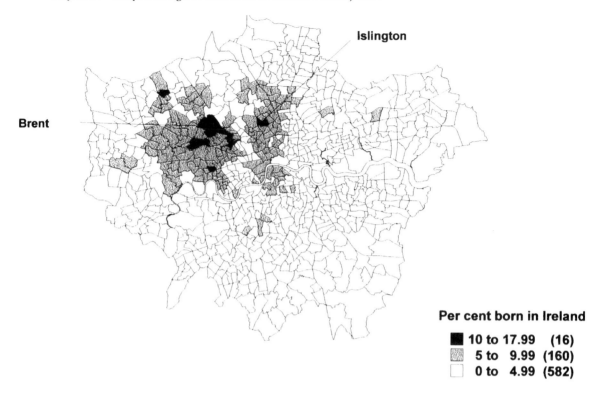

Per cent born in Ireland

■	10 to 17.99	(16)
▨	5 to 9.99	(160)
□	0 to 4.99	(582)

The Black–Other group, as Map 6.9 shows, is in spatial terms closely associated with the two larger Black groups, particularly the Black–Caribbean. Several wards in Hackney form a particular concentration, and there are also significant communities in Brent, Haringey, and in the Lambeth/Lewisham/Southwark area.

Irish

People born in Ireland are spread across London (see Map 6.10), but are represented in far higher numbers north of the river than south, and in particular in two large clusters. The larger of these is in Brent, spreading across to Camden, which takes in Kilburn, Cricklewood and Brondesbury, with their concentration of light industry and construction companies. The second, smaller, cluster is in the north of Islington, around Upper Holloway. In these areas the maximum density reached is around 10–18 per cent of the total population.

6.5   Migration and social mobility

Although we have thus far concentrated on the original settlement patterns of a number of groups, there is also a continuous process of migration to, from and within the capital. As groups became established, many moved into different areas of London (typically outwards) in search of better housing or to be nearer new jobs.

Many of these flows are identified in Chapter 4 of this volume. The census question dealing with residence one year earlier, allows us to examine the direction of those flows, and also provides a measure of social mobility.

The data reveal that 11 per cent of White residents in London had moved in the previous year. The Indian and Black–Caribbean groups – the two largest minority ethnic groups – had the lowest rates (with 8 per cent and 9 per cent respectively), while the Other–Asian (21 per cent) and Black–African (25 per cent) groups showed very high rates of mobility. The high mobility of the Black–African group may be linked to the high proportion of students in this population. The relative immobility of the two largest minority ethnic groups could be taken to indicate that they do not want to move to other areas, but is also consistent with the hypothesis that they do wish to move but suffer disproportionately from problems which prevent them from so doing.

6.6   Characteristics of London's minority ethnic population

Examining the diversity, size and distribution of London's minority ethnic population confirms London's status as a world city. However, we are also interested in evidence of differentials in the quality of life experienced by people from the various ethnic groupings. It is particularly important to highlight areas where some communities (or specific internal social fractions thereof) may be subjected to relative material disadvantage. Given the necessary political will, this will help service providers to target resources to those groups, and the highlighting of clearly documented and quantified disadvantage could provide the catalyst for further investigation into whether or not this disadvantage is being caused, or at least exacerbated, by 'racial' discrimination.

The census contains a number of variables which enable us to undertake a broad analysis of socio-economic conditions for each of the minority ethnic groups. Of course, a survey of the size of the census cannot ask questions in as much detail as would be needed to produce a comprehensive analysis, but broad differences can be established.

Health

Illness is often used as an indicator of disadvantage as it usually correlates strongly with lower incomes, unemployment, lower levels of education, poor diet and poor housing conditions. Together these indicators also correlate very highly with social class. In this analysis, therefore, it is not surprising that the same boroughs tend to come out with the highest rates of limiting long-term illness (llti) for each ethnic group, or that these are areas with the highest rates of deprivation. It is important that these locations are identified, and relative deprivation quantified. However, it is also important to recognise that within these boroughs there are often further differences by ethnic group. We are unable to tell from this analysis whether these differences are again due to socio-economic differentials between the different ethnic groups or to something intrinsic to the ethnic groups themselves (such as physiological differences affecting health). However the information can still be

Table 6.3 *Percentage of the population with a long-term limiting illness in Greater London and Great Britain by age, 1991*

| | Age (years) | | | | | |
| | 0–17 | | 30–34 | | 65–69 | |
	Greater London	Great Britain	Greater London	Great Britain	Greater London	Great Britain
White	2.4	2.3	4.2	4.6	27.8	30.3
Born in Ireland	*3.5*	*3.2*	*4.5*	*4.2*	*29.0*	*30.0*
Black–Caribbean	3.5	3.6	5.1	5.1	37.5	38.2
Black–African	3.2	5.2	3.8	4.6	34.0	37.7
Black–Other	3.6	3.6	6.4	6.1	37.9	37.1
Indian	2.1	2.1	4.0	4.2	39.7	40.0
Pakistani	2.8	3.1	5.7	6.7	45.1	42.3
Bangladeshi	2.9	2.8	7.5	7.0	39.2	38.6
Chinese	1.5	1.4	1.9	1.9	24.0	24.2
Other–Asian	2.2	2.1	2.8	2.7	31.9	33.2
Other–Other	3.0	3.0	5.9	5.1	32.9	32.9
Total	2.5	2.4	4.2	4.6	28.5	30.4

Source: 1991 Census Ethnic Group and Country of Birth Topic Report, and Special Table LRCT1.

used as an extremely good source of base data to assist in the effective targeting of resources.

In London, 11.3 per cent of residents in households had a llti (a little lower than the overall Great Britain figure of 12.4 per cent). The range was narrow in London, with a low of 9.3 per cent in Kensington and Chelsea, and a high of 14.1 per cent in Hackney. The rates varied quite significantly across the different ethnic groups, however. The Irish-born group and the White group were the only ones to have higher than average rates of llti. This finding is not unduly surprising given that rates of llti tend to increase with age (Jones, C., 1993); we would therefore expect these groups, with by far the oldest age structures, to have high rates of llti.

Table 6.3 allows investigation of these relationships by presenting llti rates for specific age-groups. In order to limit the effects of age structure, the three groups have been chosen to represent the experiences of young people (0–17-year-olds), young adults (30–34-year-olds) and older people (65–69-year-olds).

The main points to note from the table are:

1   A confirmation of the expected pattern of rising rates of llti with age for all ethnic groups
2   The overall rates for London and Great Britain are quite similar
3   The rates of llti for those aged 0–17 who are Black, or who were born in Ireland, are high. These rates highlight an area of some concern. The London boroughs with the highest numbers of young people in the three Black groups with a llti are Lambeth and Hackney with both boroughs having over 500 young Black people with health problems of this severity
4   Rates of llti for Bangladeshi adults and the South Asian elderly are exceptionally high.

Housing

Housing London's population in suitable accommodation poses a huge challenge to all those involved in housing provision. The type, quality and location of accommodation occupied by a household will depend on many disparate factors such as social class, income, wealth, place of birth, and number and age of children. Ethnicity only enters this equation if provision is actually influenced in some way by 'ethnicity' in and of itself, rather than (say) by factors (such as household size and structure) which vary with ethnic origin. It may be, for example, that 'ethnicity' might influence housing choice via a household's preference to live near a place of worship or community centre. Alternatively, discrimination on the part of housing providers/facilitators may result in the location of particular minority ethnic groups in different quality housing from their White counterparts (see also Chapter 10 in Volume 4 of this series).

The census provides a great deal of information about the housing situation of London's minority ethnic groups. It covers the key issues of household size, overcrowding, tenure and amenities (though, admittedly, it does not tell us anything about the quality of either the housing or the amenities). A number of these factors are examined here but it is important to bear in mind that all the factors are interlinked, and that many of the differences seen in the analysis will not be a function of 'ethnicity' as such, but will be influenced by a number of socio-economic factors, such as income and social class, which vary with ethnicity.

Much of the analysis here is for London as a whole, but it is at borough level that the data can really be useful as base data for people working within housing. The variables which have been examined are those that may reflect disadvantage, namely, overcrowding and lack of amenities .

Overcrowding

There were large differences across the ethnic groups in the levels of overcrowding in London (Table 6.4). Using the conventional measure of persons per room, it was clear that Bangladeshi- and Pakistani-headed households experienced by far the most overcrowding, with the former having three times the level of most of the other ethnic groups. Figures ranged from the Whites with only 2.5 per cent of households living at a density of over one person per room, to the Bangladeshi group with over half its population in this category.

There was a marked difference between the three Black groups – Black–Africans having high levels of overcrowding, while the Black–Caribbean and Black–Other groups lived on average at much lower densities. These levels of overcrowding correlate with differences in family size between the ethnic groups. Although in theory there should be no reason why larger households should not be adequately accommodated, the differences do appear to reflect the difficulties encountered in the housing of larger families. Overcrowding often results either when suitably sized properties are unavailable, or when they are available but cannot be afforded by the family. The London Research Centre's Census Housing Report (Barelli and

Table 6.4 *Percentage of the population living at 1+, 1–1.5 and 1.5+ per room in Greater London, 1991*

Ethnic group of head of household	1–1.5 people per room	1.5+ people per room	Total over 1 person per room
White	1.6	0.9	2.5
Born in Ireland	*2.7*	*1.6*	*4.3*
Black–Caribbean	3.9	1.8	5.7
Black–Other	4.3	3.0	7.3
Other–Other	5.7	3.5	9.2
Chinese	7.2	4.1	11.3
Other–Asian	8.0	4.4	12.4
Indian	10.0	3.2	13.2
Black–African	10.0	6.9	16.9
Pakistani	16.7	6.1	22.8
Bangladeshi	29.9	23.9	53.8

Source: 1991 Census LBS, Table 49.

Howes, 1995) highlights the relatively small size of dwellings in London, and this is likely to affect in particular the Bangladeshi and Pakistani groups which have the largest average household sizes.

Amongst the boroughs, Hackney stood out as having very high levels of overcrowding, with some of the highest densities for all ethnic groups. Other boroughs with high rates included Kensington and Chelsea, and Westminster, with particularly high rates for their (very large) Other – Other groups and their Black communities. Tower Hamlets was striking in that it had by far the largest community of Bangladeshis and by far the highest levels of overcrowding of any ethnic group in any borough. The census shows that almost 70 per cent of Bangladeshis in Tower Hamlets live in households with more than one person per room.

Table 6.5 *Percentage of households with five or more people in Greater London and Great Britain, 1991*

Ethnic group of head of household	Greater London	Great Britain
White	6.0	7.0
Born in Ireland	*8.3*	*8.8*
Black–Caribbean	9.0	9.3
Black–African	16.2	16.2
Black–Other	7.3	8.8
Indian	27.9	31.6
Pakistani	42.5	54.5
Bangladeshi	62.6	61.6
Chinese	17.0	20.3
Other–Asian	17.2	18.5
Other–Other	12.7	13.3

Source: 1991 Census Group and Country of Birth Topic Report, and Special Table LRCT11.

Household size

Overcrowding, as has been argued, tends to be related to household size; ethnic groups with larger average households sizes tending to exhibit higher levels of overcrowding. When looking at the percentage of larger households (those with five or more people) in London and Great Britain (see Table 6.5), London emerged as having slightly smaller proportions of larger households for all ethnic groups apart from two. The exceptions were the Black–African group, where the figures were the same inside and outside London, and the Pakistani group, which had significantly fewer of these larger households in London.

Tenure

A lower proportion of the minority ethnic population owned or were buying their properties in London than the average for Great Britain. From Table 6.6 it can be seen that this was particularly true for the Bangladeshis, where the proportion of households owning (or buying) their homes in London was little more than half the figure for Great Britain as a whole. The other ethnic groups with large London–GB differentials were the Whites, Pakistanis and the Irish-born.

All ethnic groups in London were more likely to rent accommodation privately or from a housing association than in Britain as a whole (see Table 6.7). This was particularly true for the White, Irish-born and Pakistani groups.

Table 6.8 gives the proportions of households in local authority housing. Bangladeshis were 20 percentage points more likely to be in local authority housing if they lived in London, than if they lived outside London, whereas all the other ethnic groups were only slightly more likely to be in local authority housing in London.

Bathroom amenities

Although the percentage of households lacking or sharing bathroom facilities was universally low (with all ethnic groups having 5 per cent or fewer households in this category), compared with Britain as a whole London had slightly higher proportions without exclusive access to these facilities, for every ethnic group. The differences were greatest for the White and Pakistani groups where London had almost twice as many households who lacked, or shared the use of, a bath, shower or WC.

Employment

The 1991 Census enables us to gain some insight into the relative labour market position of the various ethnic groups. Again, the measures are fairly rudimentary and no details about skills or training are available, but the large sample allows us to make fairly precise assessments of economic activity and unemployment rates,

Table 6.6 *Percentage of households owning or buying their homes in Greater London and Great Britain, 1991*

Ethnic group of head of household	Greater London	Great Britain
White	58.3	66.6
Born in Ireland	*44.0*	*55.4*
Black–Caribbean	44.2	48.1
Black–African	24.1	28.0
Black–Other	33.4	36.7
Indian	78.8	81.7
Pakistani	67.0	76.7
Bangladeshi	26.3	44.5
Chinese	55.0	62.2
Other–Asian	50.3	53.9
Other–Other	49.2	54.0

Source: 1991 Census LBS, Table 49.

Table 6.7 *Percentage of households in privately rented and housing association accommodation in Greater London and Great Britain 1991*

Ethnic group of head of housedhol	Renting privately Greater London	Great Britain	Housing Association Greater London	Great Britain
White	14.0	7.0	5.2	3.0
Born in Ireland	*19.2*	*10.9*	*8.0*	*5.1*
Black–Caribbean	6.3	5.6	10.5	9.7
Black–African	18.0	17.8	11.7	10.8
Black–Other	13.1	13.6	13.6	11.2
Indian	9.0	6.5	2.6	2.2
Pakistani	12.5	9.6	3.5	2.2
Bangladeshi	7.7	9.6	8.3	6.1
Chinese	22.0	17.0	4.4	3.5
Other–Asian	28.7	24.5	4.8	4.4
Other–Other	19.7	18.2	7.9	6.2

Source: 1991 Census LBS, Table 49.

Table 6.8 **Percentage of households in local authority housing in Greater London and Great Britain, 1991**

Ethnic group of head of household	Greater London	Great Britain
White	22.4	21.1
Born in Ireland	*28.8*	*26.0*
Black–Caribbean	39.0	35.7
Black–African	46.1	41.1
Black–Other	39.9	34.4
Indian	9.6	7.8
Pakistani	16.9	10.4
Bangladeshi	57.6	37.0
Chinese	18.5	13.1
Other–Asian	16.1	13.6
Other–Other	22.5	19.3

Source: 1991 Census LBS, Table 49.

occupations and (broad) qualification levels. These figures allow us to gain a better understanding of the dynamics of the labour market and therefore allow us to assess the degree to which future changes may affect different ethnic groups to varying extents.

Participation in the labour force

The economic activity rate is taken as all people working or available for work, divided by all people aged 16 and over. As there are proportionately many more elderly people in the White group, we would expect all minority ethnic groups to have higher rates of economic activity (than Whites). In fact, the Bangladeshi and Pakistani groups have lower rates (Storkey, 1993b). There are also marked differences in the rates for men and women (see Table 6.9). Men have higher rates than women for every ethnic group, with the average figure for men being 75 per cent, and that for women 53 per cent. The Black–Caribbean group has the highest economic activity rates both among men (81 per cent) and women (67 per cent). The Bangladeshi and Pakistani groups are notable for the low economic activity rates among women. The reasons for this are complicated but have been attributed to their cultural traditions and family responsibilities (Jones, T., 1993), to a lack of appropriate childcare and to participation in family businesses which is often not recorded in surveys as economic activity (Bhavnani, 1994).

Unemployment

The unemployment rates for men and women in London and in Great Britain as a whole are presented in Table 6.10. This shows that men in most groups had between one and five percentage points higher unemployment rates in London compared with Great Britain as a whole. The exceptions were the Black–Caribbean group which had the same rates inside and outside London, and the Indian and Pakistani

Table 6.9 *Percentage economically active by sex: London 1991*

	Females	Males
Bangladeshi	22	71
Pakistani	33	74
White	52	75
Chinese	54	72
Other–Other	55	76
Born in Ireland	*56*	*75*
Indian	56	78
Other–Asian	57	76
Black–African	61	71
Black–Other	65	80
Black–Caribbean	67	81

Source: 1991 Census LBS, Table 9.

Table 6.10 *Unemployment as a proportion of economically active people aged 16 and over, 1991*

	Males		Females	
	Greater London	Great Britain	Greater London	Great Britain
Bangladeshi	36	31	35	35
Black–African	32	29	27	25
Black–Other	28	25	20	18
Pakistani	24	28	23	30
Black–Caribbean	24	24	14	14
Other–Other	22	20	16	15
Other–Asian	16	14	13	12
Chinese	15	10	10	8
Indian	12	13	12	13
White	12	11	8	6

Source: 1991 Census LBS, Table 9.

groups where the rates were respectively one and four percentage points higher in Great Britain than in London.

The women in each ethnic group followed almost exactly the same pattern as the men, except the geographical differences widened for Pakistani women, with those in London having unemployment rates seven percentage points lower than for Great Britain as a whole. The key point about the rates for minority groups, however, is that they are almost *universally high* (*relative to Whites*). In fact, but for the Indian, Chinese and Other–Asian groups, unemployment levels for minorities (for both London and GB, male and female) stood at around two to four times those for Whites.

These rates mask large differences between boroughs. As with limiting long term illness, unemployment is often used as an indicator of social stress, reflecting the relative well-being or deprivation of groups of people. Not surprisingly, therefore, the borough analysis tends to suggest a correlation between these factors (e.g. the same boroughs having high rates of both). What is useful is to see the *relative* unemployment rates for the different ethnic groups within boroughs.

The four boroughs in London with over 7,000 unemployed people from minority groups were Hackney, Newham, Lambeth and Brent. These boroughs have been estimated by the Department of the Environment as being among the most deprived districts in England, with Newham being the district with the highest level of deprivation in England, Hackney third, Lambeth eighth and Brent 29th (Department of the Environment, 1994). It is not surprising therefore that these boroughs do show high levels of unemployment, but it is particularly disturbing as these boroughs are also notable for having among the highest proportions of residents from minority ethnic groups.

6.7   Conclusions

There is much to celebrate: this chapter has been able to highlight the remarkable diversity of London's population, the fact that different ethnic groups are not segregated within the city to the same extent as has happened in the USA and the low rates of illness for some groups. The census provides evidence of the successes of some minority ethnic groups, with significant proportions of qualified people and high numbers in professional occupations.

However, the analysis does also give cause for concern, with high levels of illness in Black children, children born in Ireland, and Bangladeshi and Pakistani adults; high unemployment rates for all minority ethnic groups; and problems of overcrowding particularly in the Bangladeshi group. The results need to be investigated further, with local analyses standardising the data as much as possible for differences in age structure and social class. This could also identify communities where a number of factors are working to compound social problems. Only then can we really begin to pinpoint areas of need and, at a policy level, produce a framework which enables the development of social and economic policies targeted towards those in most need.

Finally, London would not be London without the contribution made, throughout its history, by immigrants and their descendants. The 1991 Census of Population, and in particular data from the new question on ethnic group, provide an unparalleled source of information on London's multifarious population. The information helps to illustrate the way in which people with different ethnic identities have helped create a city which has an exciting future. It also gives credibility to the status of London as one of the most, if not *the* most, cosmopolitan city in the world.

References

1991 Census data from the LBS, Topic Report on Ethnic Group and Country of Birth, and Special Tabulations commissioned from OPCS.

Barelli, J. and Howes, E. (1995) *Housing data for the London boroughs*. London: London Research Centre.

Bhavnani, R. (1994) *Black Women in the Labour Market: A Research Review*. Manchester: Equal Opportunities Commission.

Brown, C. (1984) *Black and White Britain*. London: Policy Studies Institute/Heinemann.

Department of the Environment (1994) *Index of Local Conditions — An Analysis Based on 1991 Census Data*. London: HMSO.

Faizi, G. (1986) *A History of the Black Presence in London*. London: The Greater London Council.

Jones, C. (1993) *Limiting Long Term Illness in London*. London: London Research Centre.

Jones, T. (1993) *Britain's Ethnic Minorities*. London: Policy Studies Institute.

Lambeth Council (1988) *Forty Winters On. Memories of Britain's Post-War Caribbean Immigrants*. London: Lambeth Council.

Merriman, N., et al. (1993) *The Peopling of London*. London: Museum of London.

Robinson, V. (1986) *Transients, Settlers and Refugees — Asians in Britain*. Oxford: Clarendon Press.

Shang, A. (1991) *Seeds of Chinatown: the Chinese in Britain*. In: Coombe and Little (eds), Race and Social Work, A Guide to Training. London: Tavistock.

Storkey, M. (1993a) *Identifying the Cypriot Community from the 1991 Census*. London: London Research Centre.

Storkey, M. (1993b) *Ethnic Group Data*. London: London Research Centre.

Storkey, M. (1994) *London's Ethnic Minorities — One City, Many Communities*. London: London Research Centre.

Chapter 7
Ethnic minorities in the Midlands

David Owen and Mark Johnson

7.1 Introduction

The Midland counties of England contain the largest concentrations of people from minority ethnic groups outside London. The Midlands are conventionally defined as the two standard regions used for statistical purposes: the West and East Midlands, which together stretch from the eastern border of Wales to the North Sea, and from their southern extreme just north of the Forest of Dean to the Peak District and Humber estuary in the north. The axis of greatest urbanisation in Britain, running from London to Leeds, passes through the central parts of the Midlands. This is an extremely large and diverse region containing a wide range of local environments ranging from Birmingham, Britain's 'second city' lying at the heart of an urban region containing almost as many people as Wales, to small, rural and peripheral localities on the Lincolnshire coast.

This region has long enjoyed relative prosperity. The West Midlands conurbation had the most rapid population growth of any urban area in Britain between 1911 and 1951 (Rugman and Green, 1977) and experienced high rates of economic growth until the early 1970s, mainly driven by the expansion of the engineering and car industries. The East Midlands was one of the most rapidly growing regions in the 1970s and 1980s, when it benefited from the relative 'urban–rural shift' of employment, which acted to the detriment of the West Midlands. The East Midlands gained economic activity and population not only from the West Midlands but also from the South East. Economic growth has acted as a magnet for migrants in the East and West Midlands, both internally and externally. The largest single destination for 'emigrants' from Birmingham between 1966 and 1971 was the overspill estate of working class tenants from inner city clearances formed at Chelmsley Wood near Birmingham (International) Airport (Rugman & Green, 1977).

The period of greatest post-war economic prosperity coincided with a time of mass in-migration of people from minority ethnic groups, many of whom were specifically recruited to work in the region's industries. This period saw the inner areas of the West Midlands conurbation begin to lose population, but the extent of the decline in White residents was masked by the growth of a replacement population largely composed of migrants from the New Commonwealth and Ireland, attracted to jobs in the growing industries of the region. These migrants settled in the inner parts of the conurbation, frequently referred to as the 'zone in transition' by urban sociologists (Rosing and Wood, 1971; Rex and Moore 1967), which were being abandoned by the more mobile sections of the White population.

The continuing post-war trend towards the counterurbanisation of population, from larger cities and inner urban areas to smaller towns and more rural localities, resulted in people from minority ethnic groups becoming increasingly concentrated (relative to the White population) in a few local authority districts of the Midlands, and indeed into certain wards and streets within these. With the transformation of the economies of the Midlands over the post-war period, the overall demand for labour has declined in the traditional industries and places of employment and new types of job have developed, in new locations well away from the areas where most people from minority ethnic groups reside.

This chapter begins by reviewing the growth of minority ethnic groups in the region since the second world war. It goes on to demonstrate how the ethnic composition of the population varies over space and across different types of local environment in the Midlands. It also considers the social and economic conditions experienced by people from minority ethnic groups living in the region and shows how these vary between groups according to where they live. In addition, the patterns revealed by the 1991 Census will be placed in the context of previous research into minority ethnic groups in the Midlands, to demonstrate how their experience has evolved over time.

7.2   The development of minority ethnic group populations in the Midlands

Minority ethnic group populations developed earlier and grew larger in the Midlands than in most other parts of Britain. In 1961, 5.7 per cent of the minority ethnic group population of Great Britain lived in the West Midlands. By 1966, of 852,750 New Commonwealth-born residents in Britain, 13.7 per cent lived in the West Midlands, compared to 44.9 per cent in Greater London. The 1971 Census showed that of the 1,486,000 people in Britain estimated to be of New Commonwealth origin, 6.2 per cent lived in Birmingham and 12.4 per cent in the metropolitan county – of which they formed 6.6 per cent of the total. At the wider scale, 16.2 per cent of the national population of New Commonwealth descent lived in the West Midlands region with a further 84,000 (5.7 per cent) in the East Midlands. The same pattern was repeated in 1981, when 13 per cent of the estimated minority ethnic population lived in the West Midlands metropolitan county. By 1991, the 600,000 people from minority ethnic groups living in the two regions still represented 20.3 per cent of all those resident in Great Britain.

As a consequence, academic interest in the questions of minority ethnic group settlement patterns and experience in this region has a long history. The availability of the 1966 Census data coincided with the growth of academic interest in race relations and the adoption of techniques of Social Area Analysis. Edwards et al (1970) found that the distribution of New Commonwealth immigrants in Birmingham in 1966 described a 'broken ring' around the city centre, and coincided with areas of relative economic and housing deprivation as measured by households living at high density (more than 1.5 persons per room), shared dwellings (houses in multiple occupation (HMOs), males employed in Social Class V and privately rented housing. At the same time, very few people in those areas were in local authority tenure or dwellings with exclusive use of all amenities. The spatial distribution of minority ethnic groups was very similar to the areas of greatest concentration of those born in Ireland. Minority ethnic groups tended to work in 'the prosperous (sic) manufacturing industries that have been generally short of labour in recent years' (Rosing and Wood, 1971).

Rosing and Wood (1971) conducted a similar analysis to that of Edwards et al, for a wider geographical area, showing at the same time what a significant role Birmingham played in the concentration of ethnic minorities (of both New Commonwealth and Irish origin) *within* the conurbation. They also noted that immigrant communities were characterised by unequal sex ratios and tended to work in manufacturing industry. While associated with areas characterised by poor housing (but not exclusively, nor *consistently* with the presence of HMOs), their distribution was highly skewed, so that 102 out of 161 wards had 'virtually no immigrants'.

While minority ethnic groups have had a distinctive geography in comparison to that of White populations, there has also been a variation in the distribution of minority ethnic origins between areas and localities within the region, and within individual cities. Thus, using 1971 Census data, early analysts were able to remark that 'Indians and Pakistanis were more concentrated in Coventry, Sandwell and Walsall, with West Indians (sic) more so in Birmingham' (Rugman and Green, 1977). Within Birmingham there was further sorting, so that according to city statistics the 'non-White' population of Ladywood ward was 90 per cent 'West Indian', but that of Sparkhill 80 per cent South Asian (City of Birmingham Statistical Office, unpublished report, 1980).

Nor is the minority population only distinguishable between those of South Asian and Black–Caribbean origin. For example, it is a commonplace that Leicester's population owes more to East African Asian origins following the expulsions triggered by Idi Amin (Marrett, 1989), while Coventry's Asians are largely of Punjabi origin (Winchester, 1974) and Saltley in East Birmingham is noteworthy for its Kashmiri communities. The minority ethnic group population of the Midlands has increased substantially due to the considerable growth in the British-born Black–Caribbean and Asian populations. The responses to the ethnic group question in the census demonstrate that the British-born still largely retain their national identities. Hence, the marked geographical differences in the distribution of these national ethnic groups was preserved in 1991. These geographical contrasts also reflect contrasts in the geographical distribution of religious communities (although the data can give no direct evidence on religion, or the stability or homogeneity of such populations).

The 1971 Census data provided greater detail on the nature and distribution of the population and hence enabled much more sophisticated analyses to be undertaken. It illustrated the rapid growth of the minority ethnic group populations in the region. Among the research based on 1971 Census data, Wallis (1974) reported a study of those born in Pakistan (which at that time included both Pakistan and Bangladesh and may have excluded some born in India before partition). She noted that the West Midlands (conurbation) showed distinctive differences from both the Greater London and West Yorkshire areas, with the population of Pakistani origin being distinctively younger than that resident in Greater London, with most people in the age ranges 16–20 and 31–45. While men in the West Midlands outnumbered women by three and a half to one, there were twice as many girls (aged 10 or less) as boys. Evidently this population structure had implications for the provision of services (and housing need), and was then regarded as being an unstable basis for the development of community. With hindsight, this can be seen to have been a temporary imbalance, which was subsequently corrected by family completion migration.

A detailed multivariate analysis of the 1971 Census data was conducted by Winchester, examining the various 'immigrant' communities of Coventry. This stemmed from a concern that concentrations might be undesirable 'because of the American experience of race riots ... and the co-variation of immigrant concentrations and multi-deprivation' (Winchester, 1974), but he equally made the point that 'the forces behind segregation are complex and ... the net outcome of positive and negative forces'. Within the city population, those identified as Pakistani (about 10 per cent of the minority total) were the most segregated, while West Indians (16 per cent of the total) exhibited a low and falling level of segregation.

A further division between Pakistani- and Indian- or African-born groups seemed to be emerging. As found elsewhere, there was a clear association between the presence of minority ethnic groups and other indices of deprivation such as lack of basic amenities. However, distinctions could be drawn between Asian, West Indian and Irish dominated areas, with the non-European groups notably absent from areas of local authority housing and the Irish (and to a lesser extent at that time, the 'West Indian') found in both publicly and privately rented housing and as households *sharing* amenities. Unusually for such studies, Winchester also looked briefly at other (European) minorities, who also tended to live in areas of immigrant settlement but in larger houses.

Lomas and Monck (1975) were able to draw upon both published and specially commissioned tabulations from the 1971 Census in a study of Leicester, Wolverhampton, Bradford and Manchester; the four places with the greatest numbers of New Commonwealth immigrants after London and Birmingham. There were, in their view, significant differences between these cities in terms of immigration history and demography, although all four had been reliant upon immigration to maintain their labour force. Minority ethnic groups in the two Midlands towns were characterised by 'family' populations (a high proportion of children) while that of Manchester contained significant numbers of lone parents and pensioners, as well as a greater percentage of households sharing accommodation.

As found by other studies (e.g. Ratcliffe, 1981; Davies and Newton, 1972) those wards with the highest proportions of households of New Commonwealth origin were consistently those with the poorest housing condition index – although they note that this adverse relationship did not always hold true at the enumeration district level (Lomas and Monck, 1975). Despite significant growth in the minority populations of each city since the 1966 (sample) Census, they observed that, while there had been some slight extension of settlement from the core areas, there was very little redistribution: hence the remark that 'the evidence for any real dispersal is fairly small' (Lomas and Monck, 1975). The observation of patterns of intercensal movement led them to conclude that there was in fact more evidence of greater localisation, although the *international* movement into Leicester following the expulsions from East Africa had slightly confounded this analysis. As a result of discrimination, 'the normal pattern of suburbanisation among households with young children is being frustrated (for 'coloured' households)' (Lomas and Monck, 1975).

Jones (1978), once again using unpublished 1971 Census data to identify 'coloured immigrants' (defined as those with one or two parents born in the New Commonwealth and Pakistan (NCWP)), analysed their national distribution patterns. This demonstrated that the major urban centres of the West Midlands conurbation combined with Leicester and Nottingham represented the second most important area of minority ethnic group settlement in Britain, after London and before the Pennine conurbations (South and West Yorkshire and Greater Manchester). Jones also noted contrasts in geographical distribution between ethnic groups. For example, South Asians of Pakistani origin were mostly in the West Midlands, while those of African descent mainly lived in the East Midlands. Hence a typology could be drawn up to distinguish such towns as Birmingham and Huddersfield (where Indians, Pakistanis and West Indians were in balance), towns dominated by two groups to the virtual absence of others (e.g. High Wycombe (West Indian and Pakistani) or Halifax (Indians and Pakistanis)), and those in which virtually all ethnic minorities came from one group (such as Gravesend (Indians)). The urban areas of the Midlands, it should be observed, were characterised by balance or diversity of origins at this level of analysis.

Ratcliffe (1981), reporting further statistical analysis of the survey data collected for Rex and Tomlinson's classic study *Colonial Immigrants in a British City* (1979), refers to and builds upon census data for Birmingham in 1951, 1961 and 1971, using ward and enumeration district data to illustrate both the temporal and geographical patterns of settlement of West Indian and Asian groups. This study reinforces the description of a pattern of settlement in the 'middle ring' areas, which is somewhat different between those two groupings. Moreover, the use of social indicators clearly demonstrates the association between minority ethnic group settlement and areas of deprivation; in particular, areas in which the incidence of privately rented housing, the sharing of amenities, and overcrowding were high, and rates of car ownership were low. Ratcliffe further drew attention to the age and gender imbalance of the (then) immigrant communities and predicted a relatively rapid convergence towards the demographic structure of the majority, but a slower transition to geographical equivalence (Ratcliffe, 1981; Woods, 1979).

Cross and Johnson (1982) presented a complementary analysis of data from the 1977/78 National Dwelling and Household Survey, which was conducted in part as a replacement for the cancelled mid-term census of 1976. In this, they characterised the location of minority ethnic groups as being 'still concentrated in the ring of largely Victorian terraced housing built to accommodate the burgeoning proletariat of the Industrial Revolution', and found that the minority communities were at that time twice as likely as White people to live in an area statutorily defined as in need of 'inner area' regeneration assistance. Furthermore, '74 per cent of the West Indian and Asian population of Birmingham lived within this area of particular stress'. Even when some people had been able to move out of the 'inner areas', they remained significantly more likely to live in 'industrial, commercial and poor residential' areas (as defined by the Inland Revenue), and also to gain less economic or environmental advantage from owner–occupation or local authority tenancy than White people.

Academic analyses of the 1981 Census data were much less common, possibly because of the clear inadequacies of data based on the country of birth of individuals or household heads as an indicator of ethnicity, in the context of rapid growth in the British-born minority ethnic group population. The work of Vaughan Robinson was most prominent among such studies. Robinson's (1986) thesis was to argue that, as proposed by Jones (1978, using 1971 data), the minority ethnic group population of Britain had developed its own distinctive urban hierarchy, arising from segmented employment opportunities. While the local government reorganisation caused some loss of continuity with the 1981 Census data, he argued that 'at a broad scale the 1981 (ethnic minority) urban hierarchy appears very similar to the 1971' picture (Robinson, 1986). While Robinson's main analysis was concerned with survey data from Blackburn, he also discussed the national picture in some detail, noting that (in 1981) a mere 69 urban centres contained 81 per cent of the estimated minority population, which he argued was still engaged in declining industries which were otherwise shedding (or losing) labour. In passing, it should be noted that while poorly paid minorities may have been propping up such industries in the 1970s, they were badly affected by the radical shake-out of labour which manufacturing industry experienced in the 1980s, resulting in local concentrations of high unemployment.

Table 7.1 *South Asian groups in the Midlands as a proportion of their population in Great Britain, 1991*

	Indian	Pakistani	Bangladeshi	East African
1961 (Midlands)	12%	25%	n/a	n/a
1971 (West Midlands)	19%	20%	n/a	n/a
(East Midlands)	7%	3%	n/a	n/a
1981 (West Midlands)	19%	19%	n/a	9%
(East Midlands)	9%	4%	n/a	13%
1991 (West Midlands)	19%	21%	12%	n/a
(East Midlands)	12%	4%	3%	n/a

n/a = Data not available (Bangladesh subsumed in Pakistan).
(After Robinson (1986, pp. 37–45); Owen (1994).

The pattern of change in geographical distribution differed slightly between minority ethnic groups. The Indian-born population became more geographically concentrated between 1961 and 1971 while the Pakistani-born population became more diffused, but for both, Warwickshire (i.e. Birmingham) retained its primacy (Robinson, 1986). The 1981 Census showed no loss of this concentration even with the advent of East African Asian groups, who were highly concentrated in Leicester, and elsewhere in the East Midlands. Both Robinson's breakdown of the data for Asian groups and 1991 Census data confirm this pattern (Table 7.1). It is quite striking that such consistent results are shown over 30 years, and that so little evidence is available of a diffusion of the minority ethnic populations from their original points of settlement (but see Chapter 4 of this volume). For Bangladeshis, the most recently migrated group, there appears to be a repetition of earlier patterns. While the primary locus for this group is in London (mainly Tower Hamlets), there are significant numbers in the Midlands, who also should command attention.

The East Midlands

The data for East Midlands towns have not been as closely studied as those for the West, although there have been several seminal studies of race relations conducted within this region (e.g. Katznelson, 1973). These have, however, largely relied on ethnographic methods and local surveys, including the major survey of Leicester undertaken by the City and County Councils in 1983. Marrett made some use of census data in her discussion of the history of Leicester, remarking, however, that 'a comprehensive history of the post war settlement of New Commonwealth people in the City has yet to be written' (Marrett, 1989). Her analysis showed that the 700 Asians in the city in 1951 were mostly Punjabi Sikhs from Jullundur and Hoshiarpur. The 1960s saw the arrival of people from Pakistan and Gujerat, taking the New Commonwealth population to 10,750, while the start of the East African Asian settlement more than doubled this to 23,280 (out of a total resident population of 284,210) in 1971. The 1983 survey recorded 63,200 people 'of Asian origin' – 22 per cent of the city total, but, as in other cities, heavily clustered geographically, in this case in Highfields and the Belgrave and Melton Road areas.

Phillips (1981) also made (sparse) use of the census, relying more on electoral roll and survey data, but makes the useful point that significant numbers of Asians, such as Gujeratis from Birmingham and Coventry, had moved (within the UK) to Leicester during the early 1970s to take advantage of the later arrival of the recession in that town, and subsequently because of the 'rapidly growing Asian sub-economy'. Both social and economic links, and this internal migration, served to reinforce the degree of spatial separation of Asian communities, and indeed accentuate it locally.

Similarly Lawrence (1974) (followed by Husain, 1975), writing about Nottingham, dated New Commonwealth settlement from the 1950s, and notes that the 1966 Census showed an NCWP population of less than 3 per cent of the total (some 8,500 people), arguing that the city's 'coloured population' at that time was unlikely to exceed 5 per cent. The working population of NCWP origin was found to be heavily concentrated in certain industrial and occupational sectors. He used the census data mostly to identify the appropriate areas for his survey fieldwork, but

Table 7.2   The ethnic composition of the Midlands and Great Britain, 1991

Ethnic group	The Midlands (000s)	(%)	West Midlands (000s)	(%)	East Midlands (000s)	(%)	Great Britain (%)
White	8,491.2	93.3	4,725.8	91.8	3,765.4	95.2	94.5
Minority ethnic groups	612.3	6.7	424.4	8.2	188.0	4.8	5.5
Black	140.8	1.5	102.2	2.0	38.6	1.0	1.6
Black–Caribbean	102.5	1.1	78.1	1.5	24.4	0.6	0.9
Black–African	8.8	0.1	5.3	0.1	3.5	0.1	0.4
Black–Other	29.5	0.3	18.8	0.4	10.7	0.3	0.3
South Asian	397.2	4.4	276.8	5.4	120.4	3.0	2.7
Indian	257.6	2.8	158.7	3.1	98.9	2.5	1.5
Pakistani	116.0	1.3	98.6	1.9	17.4	0.4	0.9
Bangladeshi	23.6	0.3	19.4	0.4	4.2	0.1	0.3
Chinese and Others	74.4	0.8	45.4	0.9	29.0	0.7	1.2
Chinese	17.2	0.2	9.6	0.2	7.6	0.2	0.3
Other–Asian	18.7	0.2	11.5	0.2	7.2	0.2	0.4
Other–Other	38.5	0.4	24.3	0.5	14.2	0.4	0.5
All ethnic groups	**9,103.6**	**100**	**5,150.2**	**100**	**3,953.4**	**100**	**100**

Source: 1991 Census Local Base Statistics.

in the process found that, while the minority population was largely concentrated in areas with the highest proportion of substandard housing, even in these central wards proportions of the population of NCWP origin at enumeration district level ranged from 0 to 26 per cent. In other words, despite concentration at ward level, there was concentration or segregation of the population even at a more micro-scale. It is also significant that while his survey confirmed that their tenure patterns and housing circumstances were distinctive from White patterns, it also uncovered a complexity which could not be predicted from, or reflected in, census data, since the associations (for example between social class and material circumstances) did not necessarily follow a consistent pattern.

7.3   The ethnic composition of the Midlands in 1991

The two Midland regions together contained 9.1 million people in 1991, representing about a sixth of all people living in Great Britain. The share of the population from minority ethnic groups was 6.7 per cent, somewhat higher than the British average of 5.5 per cent (Table 7.2). This overall average obscures the contrast between the West Midlands, where minority ethnic groups comprised 8.2 per cent of the population, and the East Midlands, where this percentage was below the British average, at 4.8 per cent. This largely reflects the relative concentration of the population of the West Midlands into the major conurbations of the region, while the East Midlands has a more decentralised population distribution.

The ethnic composition of the two Midland regions taken together is presented graphically in Figure 7.1. This reveals that Indians were the largest single minority ethnic group in the Midlands in 1991, followed by the Pakistanis and Black–Caribbeans, these three together accounting for over three quarters of the 612,000 people from minority ethnic groups resident in the region. The share of these three minority ethnic groups in the population was greater than the corresponding percentages for Great Britain as a whole (the percentage is nearly twice the British average for Indians), but the percentages of the population in the Black–African, Chinese, Other–Asian and Other–Other ethnic groups was smaller than for Britain as a whole. However, there is a marked contrast in ethnic composition between the two standard regions. The share of the population from the Black–Caribbean, Black–Other and South Asian groups is above the British average in the West Midlands, but in the East Midlands, only the percentage of the population from the Indian group exceeds the average for Great Britain.

Table 7.3 contrasts the composition of the Other ethnic groups in the Midlands and Great Britain, making use of the full 35-fold classification of answers to the ethnic group question devised by OPCS. This shows that people in the Midlands who wrote in answers to the ethnic group question (i.e. those who implicitly rejected the fixed choice categories) were more likely to be of mixed parentage than in Britain as a whole, though those of mixed Asian and White parentage were a little less common. Those identified as British formed a higher percentage of the Black–Others than in Britain as a whole (Owen, 1995a), while East African Asians were slightly more common than average in the Other–Asian ethnic group; a reflection of the settlement of East African Asians in Leicester. The Other–Asian component of this ethnic group mainly contains South East Asians, and the higher percentage (than the British average) may be a result of the location of the Vietnamese in cities such as Birmingham and Nottingham.

Figure 7.1 *Ethnic composition of the Midlands, 1991*

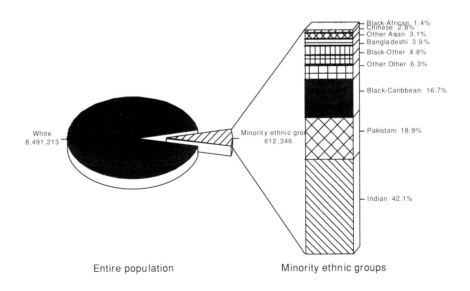

Entire population   Minority ethnic groups

Table 7.3 *Detailed composition of the 'Other' ethnic groups in the Midlands and Great Britain, 1991*

Ethnic group	The Midlands (000s)	(%)	West Midlands (000s)	(%)	East Midlands (000s)	(%)	Great Britain (%)
Black–Other	29.5	100	18.8	100	10.7	100	0.3
British	7.2	24.6	5.2	27.4	2.1	19.6	32.6
Other answers	5.4	18.2	3.0	16.2	2.3	21.9	25.2
Mixed Black/White	5.2	17.5	3.3	17.4	1.9	17.7	13.8
Other mixed	11.7	39.7	7.4	39.1	4.4	40.7	28.4
Other–Asian	18.7	100	11.5	100	7.2	100	0.4
E. African Asian/ Indo-Caribbean	0.9	4.6	0.5	4.7	0.3	4.7	3.7
Indian subcontinent	2.5	14.3	1.6	13.7	1.1	15.2	22.9
Other Asian	15.2	81.0	9.4	81.7	5.8	80.1	73.3
Other–Other	38.5	100	24.3	100	14.2	100	0.5
North African/Arab/Iranian	5.7	14.8	4.2	17.1	1.5	10.7	20.2
British – no ethnic	2.7	7.1	2.0	8.3	0.7	5.0	4.8
minority stated	1.9	4.9	1.2	5.0	0.7	4.7	20.2
Other answers	4.6	12.1	2.0	8.0	2.7	19.0	14.4
Mixed Black/White	6.1	15.9	4.1	17.0	2.0	14.0	10.3
Mixed Asian/White	7.2	18.8	4.2	17.1	3.1	21.8	21.3
Other mixed	10.2	26.5	6.7	27.6	3.5	24.8	21.2

Source: OPCS/GRO(S) (1993) 1991 Census Country of birth and ethnic group report

Table 7.4 *Demographic summary of minority ethnic groups in the Midlands, 1991*

Ethnic group	Percent of population aged 0–15	aged 16–24	of pens -ionable age	Male Median age (yrs)	Female Median age (yrs)	Males per 1000 females
White	16.1	12.7	19.2	36.3	39.0	953
Minority ethnic groups	29.6	16.9	4.8	23.6	24.0	1,010
Black	24.8	16.1	6.8	26.5	26.3	981
Black–Caribbean	18.7	15.2	8.8	30.3	29.3	971
Black–African	24.1	17.2	3.0	27.0	26.1	1,173
Black–Other	46.4	18.6	0.9	12.3	12.9	962
South Asian	30.7	17.3	4.4	23.0	23.3	1,020
Indian	26.6	16.8	5.3	26.1	26.2	1,007
Pakistani	37.7	18.2	2.9	18.4	18.8	1,046
Bangladeshi	41.0	17.7	1.8	16.5	16.5	1,044
Chinese and others	32.5	16.7	3.3	21.1	21.8	1,015
Chinese	20.8	20.1	4.3	26.3	28.6	1,036
Other–Asian	25.2	16.8	3.3	25.6	27.6	904
Other–Other	41.2	15.1	2.8	15.1	14.8	1,064
Born in Ireland	2.8	4.0	29.5	53.5	53.7	966
All ethnic groups	**17.0**	**12.9**	**18.3**	**35.2**	**37.7**	**956**

Source: 1991 Census Local Base Statistics.

Table 7.4 presents some of the key demographic features of the ethnic groups resident in the Midlands in 1991. Two key contrasts between White people and those from minority ethnic groups stand out. First, White people were considerably older on average; and second, while females were in the majority among White people, the majority of people from minority ethnic groups were male. The excess of males over females was greatest for Black–African people, due to the presence of many male African students at higher education establishments in the Midlands. Sex ratios were lower than the Great Britain average in other ethnic groups where males were in the majority (Owen, 1995b). In the other Black groups, females were very much in the majority, but only in the Other–Asian group was the ratio of males to females less than that for White people.

The minority ethnic groups with the oldest populations on average were the Black–Caribbeans, followed by the Black–Africans, Chinese, Indians and Other–Asians. The median age for Black–Caribbean people was around 30 years, with the difference in median age relative to White people being six years for men and 10 years for women. The contrast with those born in Ireland was even greater, since their median age was about 53 years. On average, Indian and Chinese people were, in 1991, around four years younger than the Black–Caribbeans. The youngest minority ethnic groups of all were the Black–Others, Other–Others and Bangladeshis. The median age of Other–Other people was about 15 years, and only half of all Bangladeshis were of school-leaving age or above. The Black–Other group was even younger, with nearly half of the population not yet old enough to attend secondary school.

The Black–Caribbean group contains some of the earlier post-war migrants from minority ethnic groups, who had reached middle age in 1991. The South Asian groups tend to be younger both as a result of higher birth rates within Britain and due to the migration of wives and families to join household heads (see also Chapter 2). Family reunification occurred later for Pakistani than for Indian people, and latest of all for the Bangladeshis.

Contrasts in age structure are revealed even more sharply if the percentage of the population in key age-groups is compared across ethnic groups. Almost a fifth of White people were of pensionable age, compared to 4.8 per cent for minority ethnic groups as a whole. Among the minority ethnic groups, the share of older people in the population was largest in the Black–Caribbean, Indian and Chinese groups. At the other end of the age range, children formed more than a quarter of the minority ethnic group population, exceeding 40 per cent in the Black–Other, Bangladeshi and Other–Other groups, and representing more than a third of Pakistani people. Younger adults formed a larger share of the minority ethnic group population than of the White population, with the percentage of 16–24-year-olds highest in the most youthful ethnic groups. This contrast is set to increase as those who were children in 1991 enter the labour market in the late 1990s and early 21st century.

Figures 7.2 (a) to (d) present the population pyramids for the three largest minority ethnic groups and for White people. The pyramid for *Whites* displays the shape typical of an ageing population, broadly rectangular with a relatively wide apex.

Figure 7.2 *Population pyramids for ethnic groups resident in the Midlands, 1991*

Age group

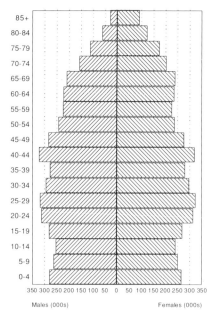

a) White

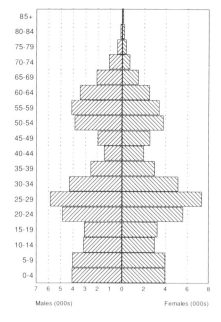

b) Black–Caribbean

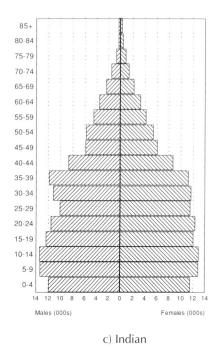

c) Indian

d) Pakistani

There are 'bulges' for people aged 40–44 and 20–29, representing the 'baby boom' of the mid-to-late 1940s, and the increase in birth rate of the early 1960s, when many of the baby boomers had their own children. A third increase in the birth rate in the late 1980s is evident in the slightly larger number of 0–4-year-olds than 5–9-year-olds. Males were in the majority in the younger age-groups, but women formed an increasing majority of those of retirement age and over, reflecting their greater life expectancy.

The pyramid for the *Black–Caribbean* group was very distinctive, being dominated by two marked bulges; for people aged from 50 to retirement age and for people aged 20–34. These appear to comprise the first generation of migrants and their children, respectively. Men were in the majority among those aged 50 and over, who would have migrated to Great Britain in the 1950s. Women formed the majority of Black–Caribbean people in their twenties and early thirties, but this was the age range in which the impact of census under-enumeration was most severe across all ethnic groups, mainly due to the failure to enumerate young men (Dorling and Simpson, 1993). The age structure and geographical distribution of minority ethnic groups were such that data for these groups are subject to a higher degree of undercount than the White population (OPCS/GRO(Scotland), 1994; Chapter 2 of this volume). The widening base of the pyramid indicates the growth of the third generation of Black–Caribbeans, though this understates the number of British-born children of Black–Caribbean origin, since many will have been coded as Black–Other (which contains the offspring of parents from different ethnic groups, and those consciously recording themselves on the census form merely as British) during census processing.

The population pyramid for the *Indian* group indicates a relatively youthful population in which rates of population growth are stabilising, with most of the five-year age-groups being of similar size. Most of the population was aged under 45 in 1991, but there was a growing number of older people in the population. The smaller numbers of 0–4-year-olds compared to 5–9-year-olds indicate that birth rates were falling in the late 1980s, after having been relatively high in the late 1970s and early 1980s. Males were in the majority in most age-groups, but women again outnumbered men in the 20–34 age-group.

The pyramid for *Pakistanis* is typical of a youthful population experiencing high rates of growth, since the base of the pyramid is much broader than the upper parts. The bulk of the population was aged under 25, but there was a small bulge in the pyramid for people of later middle age and in their thirties. Males were in the majority in all parts of the age range except for 20–34-year-olds. As is the case for Indian people, the smaller size of the 0–4 age-group compared to the 5–9 age-group may indicate a decline in fertility rates in the late 1980s.

7.4 The social and economic circumstances of minority ethnic groups in the Midlands

A wide range of social and economic phenomena can be analysed for minority ethnic groups using data from the 1991 Census. In this section, contrasts between

Table 7.5   Minority ethnic groups in the Midlands and the labour market, 1991

Ethnic group	Economic activity rate		Unemploym't rate		% of workers self-employed	Entrepreneur-shiprate*	% of workforce female	% of employed part-time
	Male	female	Male	female				
White people	89.5	72.0	10.1	6.0	11.7	3.7	42.3	41.3
Minority ethnic groups	80.4	56.0	21.8	17.0	14.7	5.1	41.8	24.9
Black	85.7	72.7	25.7	15.4	5.2	1.2	46.1	25.8
Black–Caribbean	87.1	75.2	25.6	14.8	4.8	1.0	46.7	25.9
Black–African	71.7	61.4	21.5	15.9	8.6	3.0	41.3	25.6
Black–Other	85.8	63.5	28.0	18.7	6.2	1.5	44.8	25.2
South Asian	79.5	50.1	21.1	18.5	17.5	6.3	37.8	23.2
Indian	81.7	61.0	15.8	14.8	17.2	6.9	42.1	22.9
Pakistani	75.4	25.8	33.8	39.3	19.0	3.9	24.4	26.2
Bangladeshi	71.5	23.0	35.0	38.2	17.8	9.0	23.6	23.1
Chinese and Others	74.5	53.4	17.1	14.1	18.0	7.9	41.0	31.1
Chinese	67.8	52.5	9.6	8.0	33.2	17.7	41.8	34.2
Other–Asian	74.3	50.8	19.2	16.9	12.2	4.9	43.5	30.3
Other–Other	79.2	56.3	20.2	16.0	11.2	3.8	38.8	29.7
Born in Ireland	85.8	74.4	17.2	7.3	13.0	3.9	42.4	47.0
All ethnic groups	**88.9**	**70.9**	**10.8**	**6.6**	**11.8**	**3.8**	**42.2**	**40.6**

* Defined as self-employed with employees as a percentage of the economically active.
Source: 1991 Census Local Base Statistics.

ethnic groups on three groups of socio-economic indicators will be described; the labour market, housing conditions, and social class and educational achievement.

The labour market

Table 7.5 compares the position of men and women in the 10 ethnic groups of the census classification, on a number of key dimensions of labour market performance. Men from minority ethnic groups had lower levels of labour market participation than White men, and there was also a marked differential between Black and Asian groups. The participation rates of Black males (except for Black–African men) were similar to those of White men and Indians. However, under three quarters of Pakistani and Bangladeshi men and just over two thirds of Chinese men of working age were economically active. Economic activity rates were much lower for women than men in all ethnic groups, but the Black–Caribbean rate was higher than that for Whites. Asian participation rates were again much lower than those of Black women, but there was also a major difference between Indian women, among whom 61 per cent of those of working age were economically active, and Pakistani and Bangladeshi women, where participation rates for those aged 16–59 were a quarter or less.

There were also marked ethnic group and gender contrasts in unemployment rates. The overall unemployment rate for minority ethnic groups was well above that for

White people, but there were notable contrasts among the minorities. At one extreme, Black unemployment rates for both men and women were 2.5 times greater than those for Whites, while more than a third of economically active Pakistanis and Bangladeshis were unemployed. At the other extreme, Indians experienced lower unemployment rates than all other minority ethnic groups except the Chinese, whose male unemployment rate was below that for White men. In most ethnic groups, female unemployment rates were considerably lower than those for males, but this pattern was reversed for Pakistanis and Bangladeshis, among whom nearly 40 per cent of economically active women were unemployed.

Self-employment has become an increasingly important component of employment over time, growing particularly rapidly during the economic boom years of the later 1980s. In 1991 nearly 12 per cent of all persons in work were self-employed, and self-employment was more common for people from minority ethnic groups than for White people. However this global point conceals major variations. Black people were less likely, and Asians far more likely, to be self-employed than Whites. Nearly a fifth of South Asian workers and a third of Chinese people in work were self-employed.

Self-employment is often a consequence of changing employment relations, however, rather than the result of a worker's decision to start up in business. One indicator of this is whether or not they employ other people. Column 6 of Table 7.5 presents an 'entrepreneurship rate', defined as 'persons self-employed with employees as a percentage of all economically active persons'. This reveals a similar pattern of much greater entrepreneurship in the Asian groups compared with White or Black people; the Chinese being the most likely to be running their own businesses, and Bangladeshis more likely than other South Asians to be doing so.

Other major trends in the labour market over the last few decades include the increasing participation of women, driven by the rapid growth of part-time employment. Over 42 per cent of the Midlands workforce in 1991 was female, and this percentage was even higher for the Black-Caribbean, Black-Other, Indian, Chinese and Other-Asian groups. However, less than a quarter of the Pakistani and Bangladeshi work-force were women. The influence of part-time working upon female economic activity was stronger for White women than for women from minority ethnic groups; though two fifths of women worked part-time in 1991, this was much more typical of White women than of minority women. Only about a quarter of Black and South Asian women employees held part-time jobs, but the figure rose to over a third for Chinese women. This may well reflect the importance of the distribution sector (retailing and catering) as a source of work for Chinese people, while more South Asian women work in the manufacturing industry.

Housing and households

The average household size of each minority ethnic group was equal to or greater than that for White-headed households in 1991, but there were considerable differences between ethnic groups (Table 7.6). At the smaller end, Black–Africans had slightly larger households than Black–Caribbean and Black–Other people, but

Table 7.6 *Housing and household characteristics of minority ethnic groups in the Midlands*

Ethnic group	Mean household size	Percent of households							Mean number ill per household
		Lone parents	> One person per room	No exclusive bathroom /WC	Owner occupiers	With no car	With long-term ill person	
White people	2.5	3.6	1.5	1.1	69.0	31.1	25.3	1.3
Minority ethnic groups	3.7	8.6	12.9	1.1	68.9	39.2	9.3	1.4
Black people	2.5	16.9	3.8	1.1	48.5	55.6	2.3	1.4
Black–Caribbean	2.5	16.2	3.7	0.9	49.8	56.1	7.9	1.2
Black–African	2.7	11.5	6.5	2.4	45.7	48.4	3.1	3.1
Black–Other	2.5	26.1	3.9	1.5	37.9	55.6	2.3	2.3
South Asian	4.4	3.7	19.1	1.0	82.7	31.1	5.0	1.4
Indian	4.1	3.1	13.2	0.8	85.4	25.0	3.5	1.4
Pakistani	5.1	5.1	31.3	1.6	78.4	41.9	1.5	1.5
Bangladeshi	5.6	5.2	41.0	1.5	64.5	63.1	1.3	1.5
Chinese and Others	3.2	8.7	8.3	1.9	58.3	32.5	0.7	1.6
Chinese	3.3	4.2	9.8	2.1	63.7	23.4	3.3	1.4
Other–Asian	3.6	5.7	9.6	1.2	61.9	28.3	2.1	1.4
Other–Other	2.9	13.1	6.7	2.1	52.9	40.6	5.1	1.8
Born in Ireland	2.5	3.2	2.4	1.6	60.1	46.0	13.2	1.2
All ethnic groups	**2.5**	**3.9**	**2.0**	**1.1**	**ʹ69.0**	**31.5**	**24.4**	**1.3**

Source: 1991 Census Local Base Statistics.

these were still much smaller than Asian-headed households. South Asians had by far the largest households, with more than four persons per household on average for Indians and over five persons per household for Pakistanis and Bangladeshis. This is reflected in differences between ethnic groups in the percentage of households living at a density greater than one person per room. This percentage was negligible for White households, but over an eighth of minority ethnic group households lived in overcrowded conditions. In 1991, just under 4 per cent of Black and nearly a tenth of Chinese and Other–Asian households lived at a density of more than one person per room, but the problem of overcrowding was particularly serious in the case of South Asians, with figures of 31.3 per cent for Pakistani and 41 per cent for Bangladeshi households.

Though minority households were larger on average than White households, lone parent families accounted for a higher percentage of minority-headed households than of White-headed households. The incidence of lone-parent households was higher than for Whites in all Asian groups except the Indians, but the most marked contrast was between Black people (and to a lesser extent the Other–Other group) and all other ethnic groups. Over a quarter of Black–Other households, 16.2 per cent of Black–Caribbean households and 13.1 per cent of Other–Other households fell into the category.

There were also considerable differences between ethnic groups in housing tenure and housing conditions. There was little difference between the percentage of White and minority ethnic group households as a whole, owning their own homes in 1991, but this obscures the fact that Indians and Pakistanis were much more likely to be home-owners than Whites, while Bangladeshi, Chinese and Black people were less likely than Whites to live in owner-occupied accommodation. Those ethnic groups in which rates of home-ownership were lowest also tended to include the highest percentages of households without the exclusive use of basic amenities (bathroom and WC), usually resulting from living in shared accommodation. However, this percentage was also relatively high for Pakistani-headed households, a very high percentage of whom were owner-occupiers.

The lack of physical amenities is an indicator of the ability to afford higher quality accommodation, while a household's possession of a motor vehicle is also often used as an indicator of relative wealth (though it must be noted that many people from minority ethnic groups live in urban areas where public transport is better and hence the need for a car is less). The higher percentage of minority ethnic households without a car (compared to Whites) was not unexpected, but this global figure conceals major contrasts. Half or more of Black households were without a car, but only a quarter or less of Indian and Chinese households were in this position. Within the South Asian groups, the percentage of Pakistani households without a car was much higher than for White households and well below the corresponding percentage for Black households. Nearly two thirds of Bangladeshi households did not have access to a car, highlighting their material disadvantage relative to other ethnic groups, already evident from the high degree of overcrowding which they experienced.

The census provides some information on the general health of the population through the question on the experience of limiting long-term illness (which does not mention specific illnesses or disabilities). This reveals major contrasts in overall levels of health between ethnic groups in the Midlands (Table 7.6). Nearly a quarter of White households contained a person with a limiting long-term illness in 1991, compared with 9.3 per cent of minority ethnic households. Among the latter, the incidence of illness was highest in those with older median ages, such as the Black–Caribbeans, Indians and Chinese, and lowest in the youngest ethnic groups, such as the Black–Others, Pakistanis and Bangladeshis. However, the pattern is somewhat different if the average number of persons per household containing a long-term ill person is compared across ethnic groups. This average was much higher (than for White people) in the Black–African and Black–Other ethnic groups, and slightly higher in the Other–Other, Pakistani and Bangladeshi groups. This possibly indicates poorer levels of health, which the youthful age structures of these ethnic groups mask (since health tends to worsen with increasing age).

Education and social class

Overall, the percentage of people aged 18 and over from minority ethnic groups holding degrees, diplomas, HNCs, HNDs, teaching, nursing or other professional qualifications as their highest educational qualification in 1991, was slightly lower

Table 7.7 Education and social class characteristics of minority ethnic groups in the Midlands

Ethnic group	Full-time students aged 16 and over (%)	All highly qualified (%)	Highly qualified aged 18–29 (%)	Highly qualified economic activity rate	Highly qualified unemployment rate	Class I (%)	Class IV (%)
White	3.8	11.4	20.2	89.6	3.4	4.1	17.2
Minority ethnic groups	4.1	9.7	34.1	85.4	9.7	5.0	23.7
Black people	6.8	9.6	31.3	87.7	7.0	2.2	23.7
Black–Caribbean	5.0	8.1	30.4	91.9	6.5	1.3	24.6
Black–African	19.6	28.4	27.6	70.8	11.8	14.7	16.2
Black–Other	11.6	10.5	42.1	90.3	4.5	2.6	20.9
South Asian	10.5	7.7	36.8	89.2	9.8	5.2	28.9
Indian	10.4	9.2	36.7	89.6	9.1	5.5	30.1
Pakistani	10.7	4.1	37.8	86.8	13.8	5.2	27.6
Bangladeshi	12.0	2.9	33.3	90.0	12.5	4.4	31.8
Chinese and Others	17.7	21.6	31.4	75.4	13.0	11.6	16.2
Chinese	24.0	21.8	43.0	68.2	11.9	12.4	10.6
Other–Asian	16.0	21.0	22.8	78.0	10.8	13.4	20.0
Other–Other	14.4	22.1	28.8	79.0	15.4	9.9	17.9
Born in Ireland	1.0	10.0	15.2	88.2	3.0	3.8	22.3
All ethnic groups	4.1	11.3	20.8	89.4	3.7	4.2	17.7

Source: 1991 Census Local Base Statistics.

than that for White people (Table 7.7). However, marked contrasts exist between minority ethnic groups. Over a fifth in the Chinese and Other groups held such qualifications, while the Black–Africans were the most highly qualified of all, with 28.4 per cent over 17 years of age having an educational qualification better than A-level standard. This percentage was nearly three times the average for the other Black groups and those of Indian origin, and probably reflects the number of African overseas students resident in the Midlands. At the other extreme, only 2.9 per cent of Bangladeshis and 4.1 per cent of Pakistanis held such qualifications.

The percentage of people aged 16 and over who were full-time students in 1991 was higher for minority ethnic groups than White people, and was highest of all for people from the Chinese, Black–African and Other–Asian groups. Full-time students represented about a tenth of South Asian people aged 16 and over. Differences in age structure strongly influence the pattern of qualifications, with the younger ethnic groups having had less opportunity to obtain educational qualifications, but a higher percentage still in full-time education. Thus, if the percentage of 16–29 year-olds with higher level educational qualifications is examined, it can be seen that the percentage for minority ethnic groups as a whole was larger than that for White people by a factor of two thirds (34:20). The ethnic group with the highest percentage qualified was the Chinese, closely followed by the Black–Others, and more than a third of people in all three South Asian groups possessed such qualifications. The Other–Asian and Black–African groups displayed the lowest percentages qualified, but this was still well above the figure for 16 to 29-year-old White people.

The possession of higher education qualifications tends to improve performance in the labour market within a given ethnic group. In most ethnic groups, the economic activity rate of the highly qualified was higher than that of the ethnic group as a whole, the effect being strongest for the Pakistanis and Bangladeshis. However, in ethnic groups where the percentage of students was high, such as the Black–Africans and Chinese, the economic activity rate was relatively low. Unemployment rates for the highly qualified were lower than those for the population as a whole in all ethnic groups, but a differential between Whites and the minority ethnic groups remained. The average unemployment rate for the minority ethnic groups was nearly three times that for Whites, and was only below 10 per cent for the Black–Caribbean, Black–Other and Indian groups. Pakistanis and Bangladeshis again experienced some of the highest unemployment rates for highly qualified people, as did the Other–Other group.

Table 7.7 reveals that the percentages of people in professional occupations (Social Class I) and semi-skilled occupations (Social Class IV) were both higher for minority ethnic groups than for White people in 1991. Black–Africans again stood out from the other minority ethnic groups because of the high percentage of workers who were professionals, and the smaller than average percentage of semi-skilled workers; in the other Black groups, the pattern was reversed. In the South Asian groups, the percentage of semi-skilled workers was well above the corresponding figure for White people. A higher than average percentage of Chinese and Other–Asian people were professionals, but a much smaller percentage of Chinese were semi-skilled; this may result from a relatively high percentage being in managerial and technical occupations, resulting from a high rate of self-employment. Overall, the occupational specialisation of individual ethnic groups is clearly influenced by their educational qualifications and employment structures, and reflects contrasts in prosperity between ethnic groups.

7.5 The geographical distribution of minority ethnic groups in the Midlands

Thus far, the discussion has focused on what selected social indicators can tell us about the overall characteristics of people from minority ethnic groups living in the Midlands, as compared with the White population. However, despite the convenience of the regional scale for summarising socio-economic phenomena across the range of ethnic groups, its diversity is such as to make analysis of the Midlands as a whole misleading.

This is emphasised by Figure 7.3, which maps the percentage of the resident population from minority ethnic groups for the 76 local authority districts in the East and West Midlands at the time of the 1991 Census. The map demonstrates that minority ethnic groups were concentrated in the central part of the region and were largely absent from the rural west and east. Within the central area, the share of the population from minority ethnic groups was greatest in the larger cities, accounting for 21.5 per cent of the population of Birmingham and 28.5 per cent of Leicester's population. Geographical contrasts in the ethnic composition of local authority districts are presented in Figure 7.4. The area of each circle is proportional to the

Figure 7.3   Per cent of resident population from minority ethnic groups, 1991

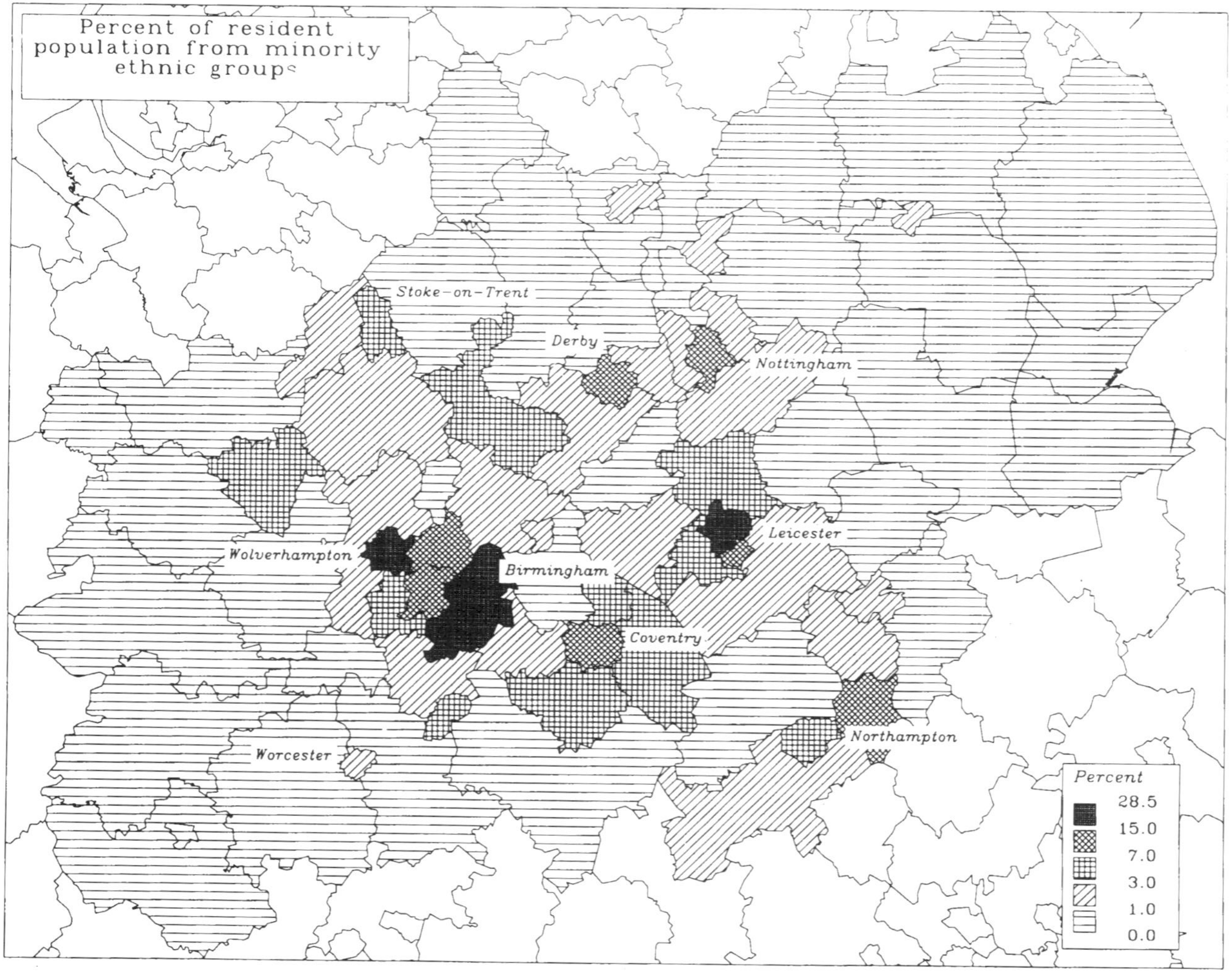

Percent of resident
population from minority
ethnic groups

Percent
28.5
15.0
7.0
3.0
1.0
0.0

Nottingham

Leicester

Northampton

Derby

Coventry

Stoke-on-Trent

Birmingham

Wolverhampton

Worcester

Figure 7.4 *Ethnic composition of resident population, 1991*

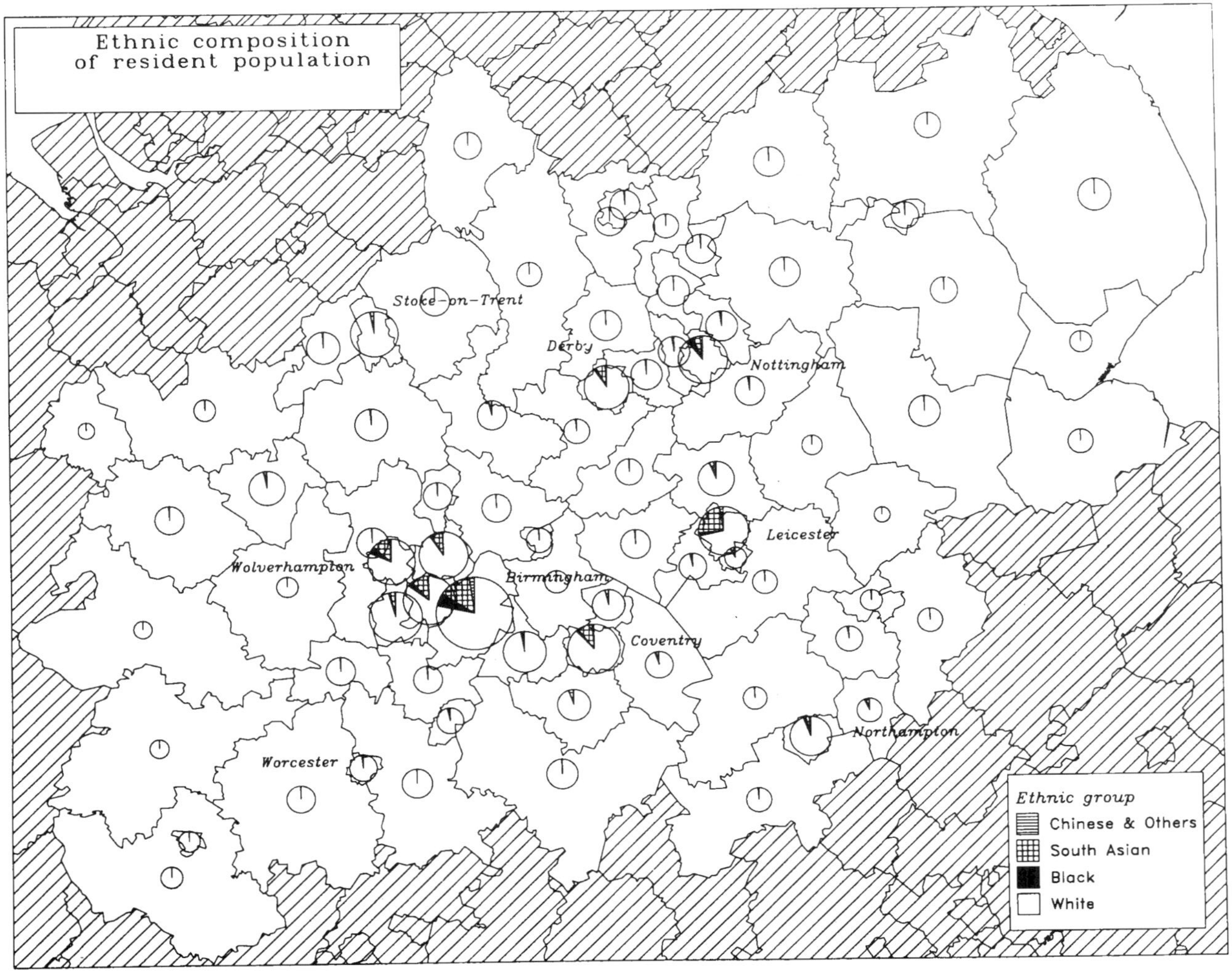

Ethnic composition
of resident population

Ethnic group
Chinese & Others
South Asian
Black
White

Northampton

Leicester

Nottingham

Coventry

Derby

Birmingham

Stoke–on–Trent

Wolverhampton

Worcester

Table 7.8 *Midlands districts with largest local concentrations of people from minority ethnic groups, 1991*

	Population (000s)	Percent of district population					% of ethnic group in Midlands			
		Minority groups	All minorities	Black	South Asian	Chinese and Other	All minorities	Black	South Asian	Chinese and other
Leicester	270.5	77.0	28.5	2.4	23.7	2.4	12.6	4.7	16.1	8.6
Birmingham	961.0	206.8	21.5	5.9	13.5	2.1	33.8	40.0	32.7	27.5
Wolverhampton	242.2	45.0	18.6	5.1	12.3	1.1	7.4	8.8	7.5	3.6
Sandwell	290.1	42.6	14.7	3.3	10.5	0.8	7.0	6.8	7.7	3.2
Coventry	294.4	34.9	11.8	1.6	9.0	1.2	5.7	3.4	6.7	4.6
Nottingham	263.5	28.3	10.8	4.6	4.5	1.6	4.6	8.6	3.0	5.7
Derby	218.8	21.1	9.7	2.1	6.4	1.1	3.5	3.3	3.5	3.3
Walsall	259.5	24.8	9.6	1.3	7.6	0.7	4.0	2.4	5.0	2.3
Oadby and Wigston	51.5	4.5	8.7	0.7	6.8	1.3	0.7	0.2	0.9	0.9
Wellingborough	67.8	4.9	7.2	2.6	3.8	0.8	0.8	1.2	0.6	0.8
Charnwood	141.8	8.8	6.2	0.4	4.7	1.1	1.4	0.4	1.7	2.2
Northampton	180.6	10.7	5.9	2.3	2.4	1.3	1.7	2.9	1.1	3.1
Warwick	116.3	6.6	5.6	0.6	4.3	0.8	1.1	0.5	1.2	1.3
Rugby	84.6	4.3	5.0	1.4	2.9	0.8	0.7	0.8	0.6	0.9
Top 14 districts	3,442.6	520.3	15.1				85.0	84.0	88.3	68.0

Source: 1991 Census Local Base Statistics.

population of each district, again emphasising that minority ethnic groups tended to live in the main population concentrations. South Asians were the largest minority group in most districts. Only in Nottingham and Northampton among the larger cities did the Black groups match the South Asian groups in size.

The degree of geographical concentration of minority ethnic groups is reinforced by Table 7.8, which shows that there were only 10 local authority districts in which the percentage of the population from minority ethnic groups exceeded the regional average of 6.7 per cent. Moreover, the 14 districts in which minorities formed at least 5 per cent of the population together accounted for 85 per cent of all people from minority ethnic groups resident in the Midlands in 1991, and 88.3 per cent of South Asians. People from the Chinese and Other groups had a more geographically dispersed distribution, but even so, just over two thirds lived in these districts.

Differences in the spatial distribution of the three broad categories of minority ethnic groups can be identified, repeating the findings of earlier census-based studies. For all three groups, Birmingham was the main population centre, but for South Asians, the other main centres were Leicester and the smaller West Midlands cities, while Wolverhampton and Nottingham were secondary centres of population for Black people. The most important additional centres for the Chinese and Other groups were Leicester and Nottingham.

There is a marked urban–rural divide in ethnic composition, with minority ethnic groups most prominent in the major cities and almost absent from the smaller towns and rural areas, with the exception of the commuting hinterlands of the larger cities

Table 7.9 *Distribution of minority ethnic groups by type of urban area, 1991*

	Total popu-lation (000s)	Minority popu-lation (000s)	% Of total popu-lation	% Of minority popu-lation	Percent of population			
					Minority ethnic groups	Black	South Asian	Chinese and Other
Principal cities	961.0	206.8	10.6	33.8	21.5	5.9	13.5	2.1
Other metropolitan	1,590.6	166.8	17.5	27.2	10.5	2.2	7.4	0.8
Large non-metropolitan	997.5	134.1	11.0	21.9	13.4	2.5	9.5	1.4
Small non-metropolitan	163.7	2.8	1.8	0.5	1.7	0.3	0.9	0.5
Industrial districts	2,406.6	37.3	26.4	6.1	1.5	0.4	0.8	0.4
New Towns	451.2	19.0	5.0	3.1	4.2	1.4	1.9	0.9
Mixed urban and rural	1,479.3	39.2	16.2	6.4	2.6	0.4	1.6	0.6
Remoter, largely rural	1,053.6	6.5	11.6	1.1	0.6	0.2	0.2	0.3

Source: 1991 Census Local Base Statistics.

(examples include Warwick, Loughborough, and the Oadby and Wigston district near Leicester). This is explored further in Table 7.9, which presents the ethnic composition of different types of local authority district, using the OPCS urban size classification (only eight of the 11 classes are present in the Midlands). Over nine million people lived in the Midlands in 1991, a tenth of them in Birmingham (the only principal city in the Midlands) alone. A further quarter lived in industrial districts (reflecting the importance of the manufacturing industry for the region), but a slightly larger percentage lived in mixed urban and rural and remoter rural districts. The distribution of minority ethnic groups varied greatly around this average. Overall, 82.9 per cent lived in Birmingham, the other boroughs of the West Midlands (former) metropolitan county and larger non-metropolitan districts, such as Leicester and Nottingham, a degree of concentration more than twice as great as that of the population as a whole.

The spatial separation of the White population from minority ethnic groups is emphasised by a comparison of the share of the region's population living in industrial districts and the more rural districts. These accounted for 54.2 per cent of the entire population, but only 13.6 per cent of people from minority ethnic groups. Industrial districts suffered major employment losses during the 1980s, while the mixed urban and rural areas are those which have benefited most from the urban–rural shift in employment opportunities. Moreover, these and the remoter, largely rural areas, have also experienced some of the most rapid rates of population growth due to the operation of the counterurbanisation process (Champion, 1991) through the 1970s and 1980s. The picture revealed is therefore one of the concentration of minority ethnic groups in the larger cities and towns in the most heavily urbanised parts of the region, while both the areas of traditional industrial development and those in which new types of economic growth are emerging have not attracted significant numbers of people from minority ethnic groups.

The former set of districts specialised in industries (such as coal mining) which did not recruit migrant workers in the early post-war decades, and which have been in economic decline in more recent decades. The latter types of district are located well away from the older urbanised areas in which minority ethnic groups are concentrated, and the high cost of obtaining housing has acted as a constraint upon their migration to these areas. Moreover, much of the 'footloose' industry located in these areas has been attracted by the availability of a local work-force more willing to adopt flexible working practices, and these areas have seen considerable increases in both part-time employment and female (especially married female) economic activity rates in recent years.

The relative geographical concentration of minority ethnic groups is emphasised by Figures 7.5 to 7.8, which map the percentage of the resident population in 1991 from minority ethnic groups as a whole, the Black groups, the South Asian groups and those from the Chinese and Other category for each of the 1,750 census wards in the East and West Midlands. In each map, the area of the circle is proportional to the percentage of the population in the ethnic group concerned. Figure 7.5 shows that while the overall spatial spread of minority ethnic groups corresponds well with the district level map (Figure 7.3), in most districts, minorities tended to be concentrated in the central parts of the urban area. This can be seen clearly in cities such as Derby, Nottingham, Northampton and Coventry.

The same pattern is apparent but on a larger scale in the West Midlands former metropolitan county, in which the percentage of the population from minority ethnic groups was greatest along the central axis of the conurbation, stretching from south west Birmingham to northern Wolverhampton. There is little evidence of outward spread into the more suburban areas, such as Sutton Coldfield or Solihull district, and indeed, the county boundary seems to act as a barrier, with a very small share of minority ethnic groups in the population of the semi-rural wards surrounding the county. Leicester represents a rather different pattern, with minority ethnic groups having a wider distribution (though also comprising the dominant share of the population of many central wards), and tending to spread into areas of Leicestershire neighbouring the city. Figure 7.5 also reveals that some urban areas, in districts with relatively low minority ethnic group shares of the population, had higher percentages of their population from minority ethnic groups; examples of such local concentrations are Telford in Shropshire, Leamington in Warwick district and Loughborough in Charnwood district.

The degree of concentration of Black people into urban and inner city areas was much greater than for minority ethnic groups as a whole (Figure 7.6). Black people were largely confined to the major cities of the region, and demonstrated an even stronger tendency than other minority ethnic groups to reside in the central parts of those cities. South Asian people had a more widespread distribution, both between and within districts (Figure 7.7). People from the Chinese and Other ethnic groups do not represent as large a share of the resident population as the other two broad ethnic groupings, and display a more even distribution in those districts in which they live: their tendency to concentrate in the central parts of urban areas was much weaker (Figure 7.8).

7.6   The classification of residential areas

Minority ethnic groups are thus highly geographically concentrated within the

Figure 7.5 *Per cent of ward population from minority ethnic groups, 1991*

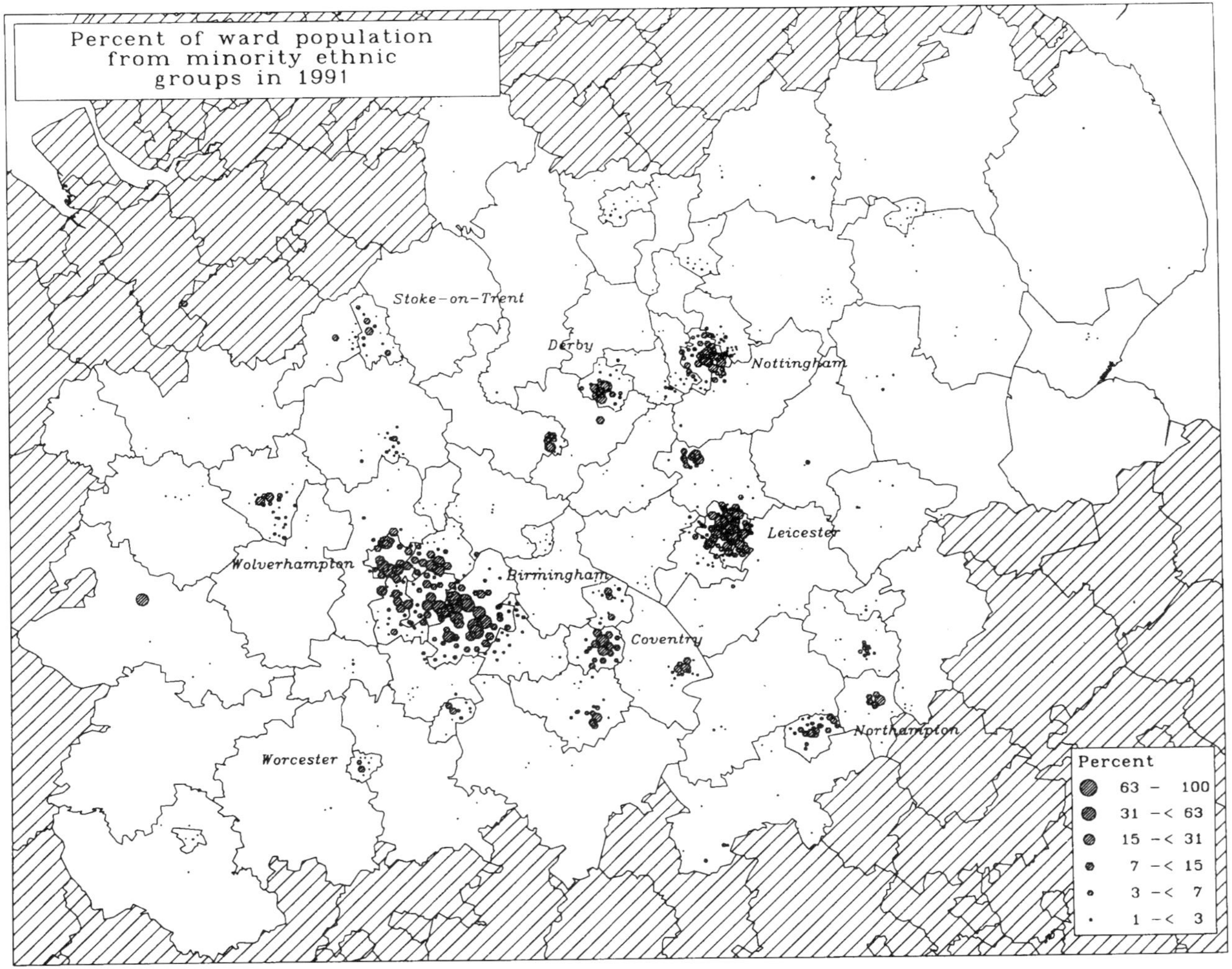

Percent of ward population
from minority ethnic
groups in 1991

Percent

63 – 100
31 – < 63
15 – < 31
7 – < 15
3 – < 7
1 – < 3

Northampton

Leicester

Nottingham

Coventry

Derby

Birmingham

Stoke–on–Trent

Wolverhampton

Worcester

Figure 7.6 *Per cent of ward population from Black ethnic groups, 1991*

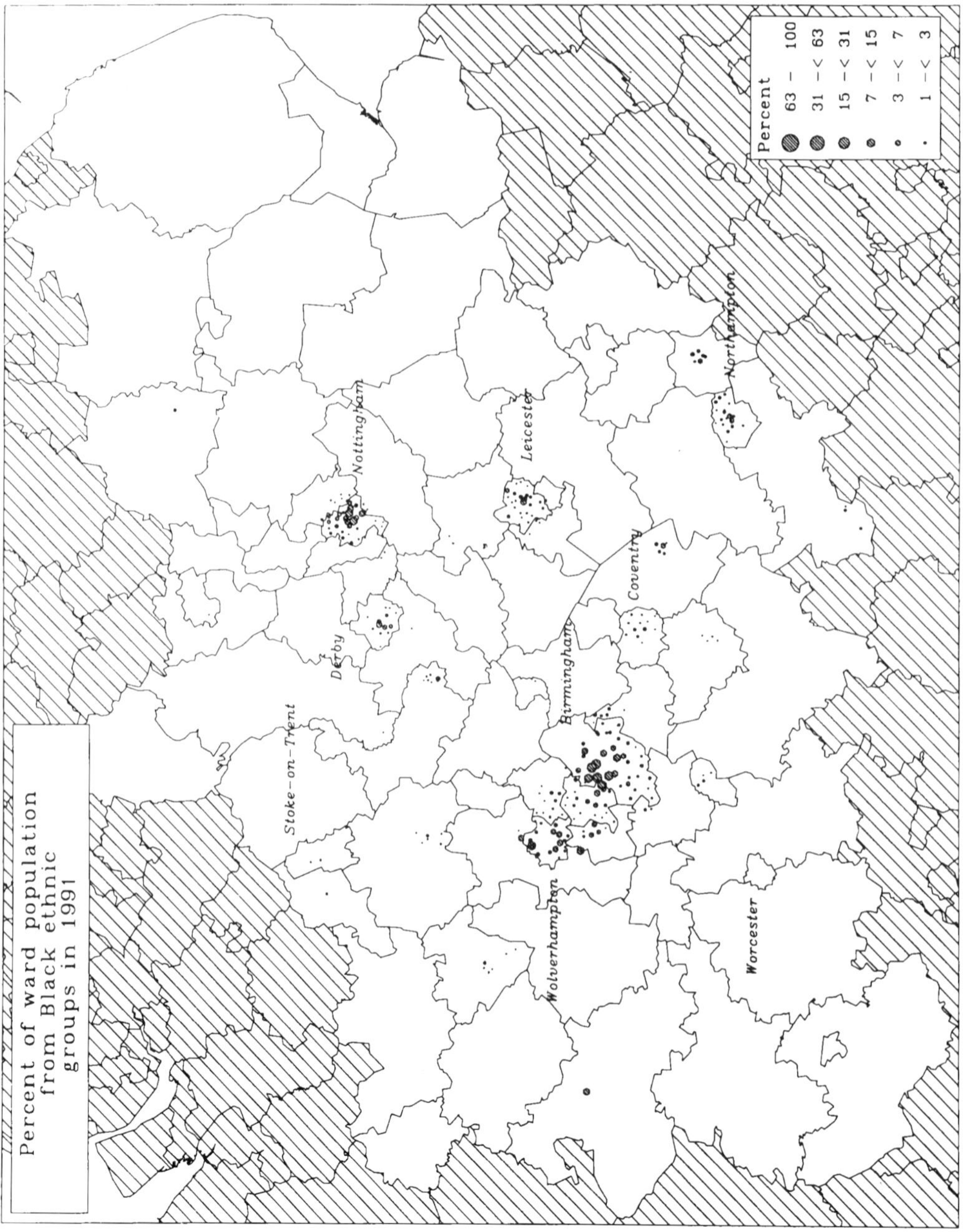

Percent of ward population
from Black ethnic
groups in 1991

Percent

63 — 100
31 — < 63
15 — < 31
7 — < 15
3 — < 7
1 — < 3

Nottingham

Leicester

Northampton

Derby

Coventry

Stoke-on-Trent

Birmingham

Wolverhampton

Worcester

Figure 7.7 Per cent of ward population from South Asian ethnic groups, 1991

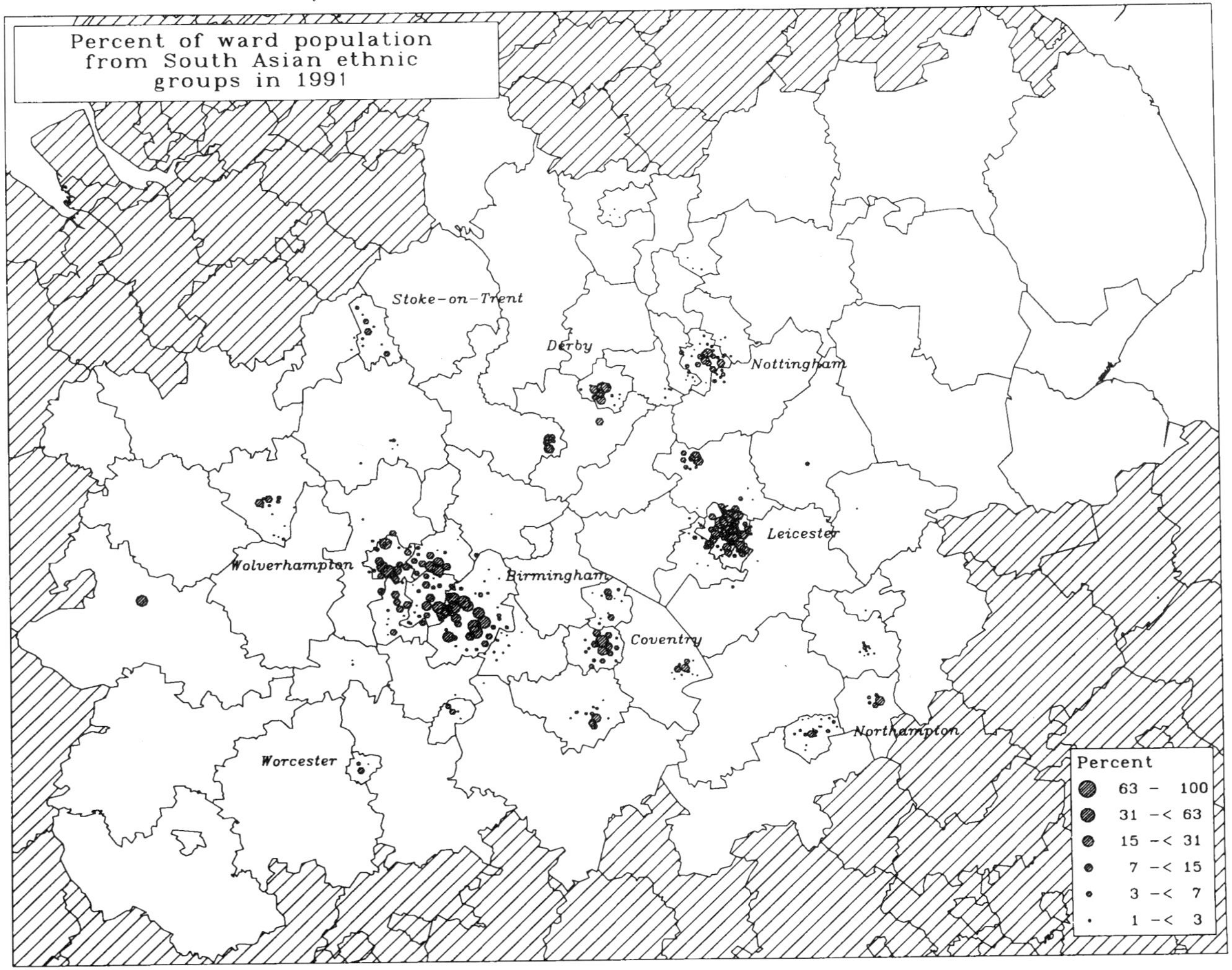

Percent of ward population
from South Asian ethnic
groups in 1991

Figure 7.8 *Per cent of ward population from Chinese and Other ethnic groups, 1991*

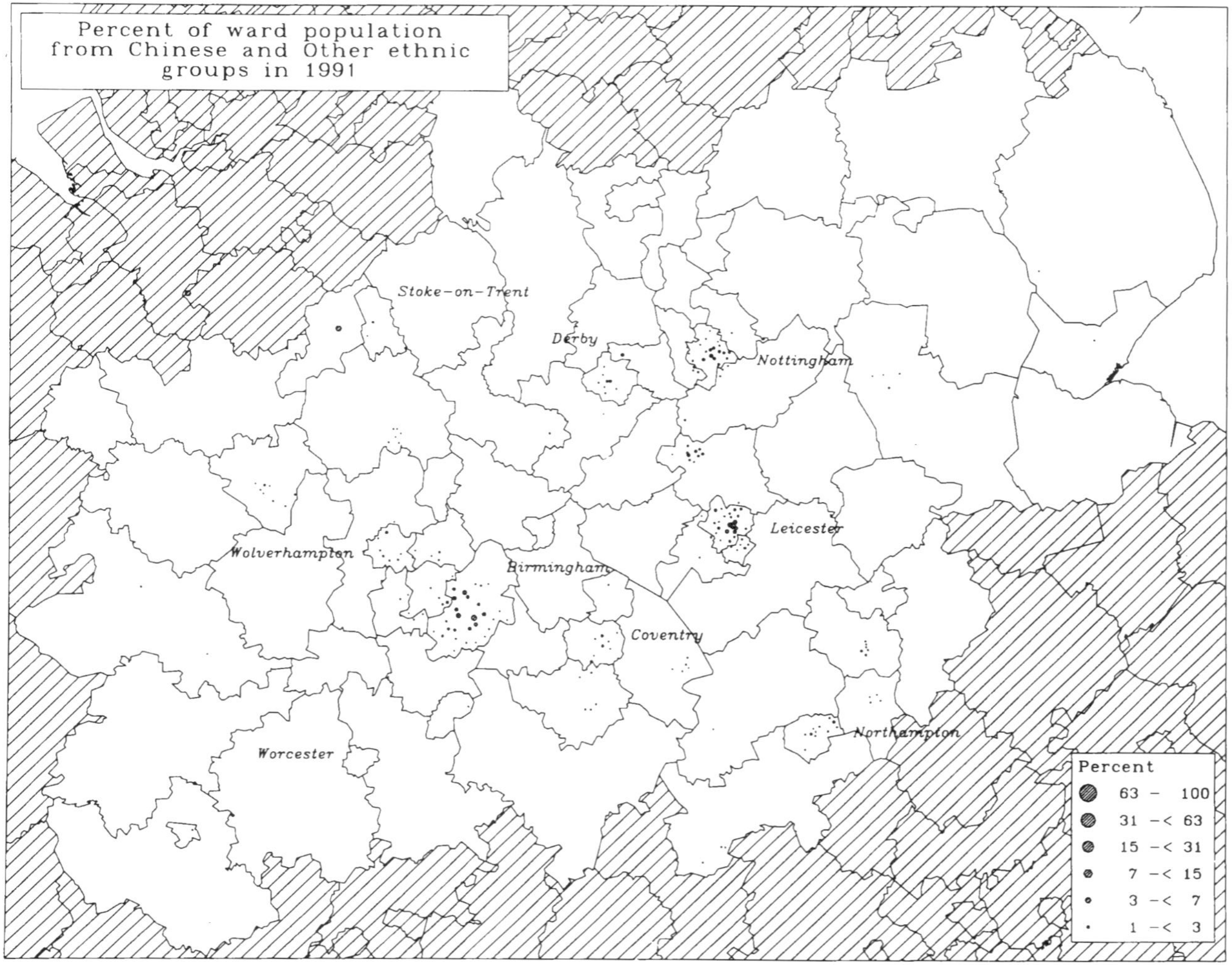

Box 7.1 *The classification method*

The first stage in the classification process is to identify the common dimensions of variation underlying the values for each variable in each area, through performing a principal components analysis on the original variables. This technique reallocates the variance in the original variables to a new set of variables or principal components, which are uncorrelated with each other. It was found that eight of these components together accounted for 90.3 per cent of the variance in the original dataset. These components can be interpreted by examination of their correlations with the original variables (see Appendix 7.2).

The first component, which accounted for nearly 40 per cent of the variance within the dataset, represents relative deprivation in inner city areas with high percentages of young people, since it is positively correlated with population density, the percentage of households living in flats, the unemployment rate and the percentage of the population aged 16–29 and negatively correlated with measures of wealth such as the percentage of households with cars, owner-occupation and the percentage of white-collar workers. The second component represents a dimension of young populations, with high economic activity rates, the third component represents high levels of educational qualifications, a high degree of flat-dwelling and employment in the service sector, the fourth represents retired persons living in urban areas with a relatively high percentage of employment in the service sector, and the fifth represents a dimension of older housing and poorer amenities, but older populations and lower unemployment rates. The remaining components individually account for a small part of the variance and are less easy to label.

The wards were then grouped together on the basis of their scores on these eight components, using an iterative relocation technique, yielding eight clusters. The nature of each cluster can be determined from the average values for each of the classificatory variables (see Table 7.10).

Midland regions, and different ethnic groups tend to live in different types of urban area. The factors underlying this pattern of concentration can be investigated in greater depth by creating a classification of areas on the basis of their social and economic characteristics, and determining whether there are systematic differences between ethnic groups located in the various types of residential environment.

Accordingly, the (1,750) census wards were grouped into 'clusters' of wards sharing similar social and economic characteristics, as measured by the set of census variables presented in Appendix 7.1. These cover a range of phenomena including population structure, economic activity, unemployment, social class, educational qualifications and physical urban structure (the details of the classification methodology are presented in Box 7.1). The classification process identified eight broad types of area (Table 7.10).

Cluster 1 (affluent suburbs) consists of largely suburban and relatively affluent areas in which a high percentage of the population were people of prime working age. The unemployment rate was low, the rates of house and car ownership were high,

Table 7.10 *Characteristics of cluster types*

Variable	Overall mean	Affluent suburbs	De-prived urban areas	Less prosp-erous semi urban	Dyna-mic rural areas	Inner city Leicester	Older housing older people	De-pressed council estates	Pros-perous rural areas
Population density	14.7	15.5	32.5	10.8	1.8	173.0	29.0	29.7	1.1
% Aged 0-15	19.3	19.9	26.5	18.4	20.9	33.0	19.1	19.2	18.6
% Aged 16-29	19.1	19.1	23.7	18.4	28.5	26.6	22.9	21.8	16.7
% Aged 30-59/64	41.4	44.0	36.7	40.6	37.9	33.1	38.0	38.7	45.5
% Pensionable age	18.5	17.0	13.2	22.6	12.7	7.3	20.0	20.3	19.2
% Highly qualified	12.6	14.7	6.3	8.9	13.8	6.8	9.0	10.7	17.2
% Households in flats	7.4	5.7	11.2	6.7	3.9	3.2	9.5	22.5	2.2
% Households in semi-detached	34.1	40.9	27.5	41.6	35.5	0.5	27.1	32.0	27.0
% Households in terraced houses	21.0	15.5	47.2	18.4	21.2	86.8	48.2	27.8	11.4
% Households owner-occupied	70.6	82.0	54.0	68.1	55.7	63.1	69.7	56.9	73.3
% Households without amenities	16.0	11.1	16.7	13.0	12.8	16.0	29.2	23.1	17.8
Cars per household	1.1	1.2	0.8	1.0	1.2	0.5	0.8	0.8	1.4
Male economic activity rate	72.8	76.7	75.7	68.6	81.9	73.0	73.6	72.5	74.5
Married female economic activityrate	52.9	58.6	51.2	48.9	56.5	34.8	53.7	52.2	52.1
% Working in manufacturing	22.0	23.7	30.6	21.5	9.8	48.3	25.9	25.8	16.6
% Working in services	58.7	61.7	55.1	58.2	78.0	47.5	59.0	61.3	57.4
% White-collar	32.2	34.9	20.2	26.8	30.9	18.4	25.1	28.1	42.8
Unemployment rate	7.4	5.5	15.1	8.7	4.6	23.8	9.4	11.3	5.2
Number of wards	1,750	558	104	293	24	1	156	183	402

Source: 1991 Census Local Base Statistics.

economic activity rates for married women were high, the percentage with higher education qualifications was high and most employment was in white-collar jobs and the service sector. *Cluster 2* (deprived inner urban areas) includes older urban areas with a younger population structure than cluster 1, a much lower rate of owner-occupation, nearly half of all households living in terraced accommodation, a much lower rate of car ownership, low percentages with higher education qualifications, a higher percentage working in manufacturing, a smaller percentage of white-collar workers and a very high unemployment rate. *Cluster 3* (less prosperous semi-urban areas) includes areas on the urban fringes with older populations, lower rates of car and home ownership, low economic activity rates and relatively low unemployment rates. The percentages working in manufacturing and services were both relatively low, indicating greater employment in the primary sector. *Cluster 4* (dynamic rural areas) contains rural areas with relatively high percentages of young adults, a very high percentage of the population with higher education qualifications, high economic activity rates, very high percentages working in the service sector and very low unemployment rates.

Cluster 5 (inner city Leicester) contains only one ward, located in Leicester. This is an inner city area with a very youthful population, mainly living in terraced houses, having a high percentage of households without exclusive use of amenities, a low married female economic activity rate, a high percentage working in manufacturing and an extremely high unemployment rate. *Cluster 6* (older housing and older people) also contains urban areas that had a high percentage of pensioners, an older housing stock, a low percentage of the population holding higher education qualifications, a low rate of car ownership, a relatively high percentage working in the service sector and a relatively high unemployment rate.

Wards in *cluster 7* (depressed council estates) are also found in urbanised areas, and have older populations, but flats comprise a higher percentage of the housing stock, the rate of owner-occupation is lower, economic activity rates are lower and the unemployment rate is relatively high. Finally, *cluster 8* (prosperous rural areas) contains sparsely populated rural wards (just over one person per hectare), with a lack of children and young people, a high rate of owner-occupation, a very high percentage of the population with higher education qualifications, a very high rate of car ownership, a higher percentage working in white-collar occupations than any other cluster and a very low unemployment rate.

To summarise, clusters 1 and 8 (and to a lesser extent cluster 4) represent the most affluent neighbourhoods; the former is suburban and the latter highly rural. Clusters 2 and 5 contain areas of inner city deprivation (most extreme in the case of cluster 5), cluster 3 contains semi-rural areas where primary industry is more significant, and clusters 6 and 7 contain higher density suburbs in urban areas, the latter containing more local authority estates.

7.7 Geography of living conditions for minority ethnic groups

This classification can be used to identify the types of area in which people from minority ethnic groups tend to live and to identify the ethnic composition of particular types of residential environment (Table 7.11). Overall, more than a third of the White population of the Midlands lived in wards in cluster 1 (the affluent suburbs), nearly 10 per cent lived in the prosperous rural areas (cluster 8), and clusters 6 (older housing and older people) and 7 (depressed council estates) together contained a further third of the White population. In marked contrast, 37.2 per cent of people from minority ethnic groups lived in the deprived inner urban areas contained in cluster 2, a further quarter lived in the depressed council estates of cluster 7, and they were also under-represented relative to Whites in cluster 3 (less prosperous semi-urban areas). However, this is not a simple dichotomy, since 15 per cent of people from minority ethnic groups lived in the affluent suburbs, and nearly 9 per cent of White people lived in the most deprived inner city wards of cluster 2.

There were marked contrasts in the types of residential environment in which individual minority ethnic groups lived. Just over a third of Black people and two fifths of South Asian people, but only a quarter of the Chinese and Other group, lived in deprived inner urban areas. Within these broad ethnic categories there were also marked contrasts. Among Black groups, a higher percentage of Black–Caribbean than other Black people lived in deprived inner urban areas. However, Blacks were almost as likely to live in depressed council estates, possibly reflecting

Table 7.11 Distribution of ethnic groups across cluster types

Table 7.11 Distribution of ethnic groups across cluster types   percentages

Ethnic group	Population	Affluent suburbs	Deprived inner urban areas	Less prosperous semi-urban rural areas	Dynamic rural areas	Inner city Leicester	Older housing older people	Depressed council estates	Prosperous rural areas
Entire population	9,103,511	34.1	10.7	14.2	0.6	0.1	12.8	18.4	8.8
White people	8,490,987	35.5	8.7	15.0	0.7	0.0	12.6	17.8	9.4
Minority ethnic groups	612,524	15.2	37.2	3.3	0.1	1.4	15.7	26.0	1.2
Black	141,003	11.7	34.9	4.4	0.2	0.4	15.7	31.1	1.6
Black–Caribbean	102,677	10.2	36.9	3.6	0.1	0.3	15.7	32.0	1.3
Black–African	8,770	18.5	28.2	5.9	0.3	0.8	15.6	27.4	3.2
Black–Other	29,556	15.0	30.3	6.6	0.3	0.3	16.1	29.2	2.2
South Asian	397,393	14.7	40.3	2.3	0.0	1.8	15.9	24.2	0.8
Indian	257,750	20.0	32.8	2.8	0.0	2.4	14.1	27.2	0.7
Pakistani	116,090	5.1	52.9	1.3	0.0	0.5	20.5	18.4	1.2
Bangladeshi	23,553	4.0	59.9	1.1	0.0	1.6	12.9	20.2	0.3
Chinese and others	74,128	24.5	25.1	6.5	0.3	0.9	14.5	25.5	2.6
Chinese	17,095	32.2	16.0	8.6	0.2	0.1	16.8	23.6	2.4
Other–Asian	18,654	22.7	32.3	4.9	0.1	1.8	13.1	22.9	2.2
Other–Other	38,379	21.9	25.7	6.3	0.5	0.9	14.1	27.6	3.0
Born in Ireland	133,767	24.7	16.3	8.1	0.6	0.1	20.7	25.3	4.0

Source: 1991 Census Local Base Statistics.

the greater availability of council housing in these areas. A higher percentage of Black African people than other Black people lived in the affluent suburbs, and the percentage living in the prosperous rural wards of cluster 8 was higher than for any other minority ethnic group. This may partly be a reflection of their high educational qualifications (already noted), and partly the fact that this is a small group overall.

In the South Asian groups, over half of all Pakistanis and nearly 60 per cent of Bangladeshis lived in the deprived inner urban areas, but less than a third of Indians lived in such wards. A further fifth of Pakistanis lived in the less prosperous suburban and council estate areas contained in each of clusters 6 and 7, while a fifth of Bangladeshis lived in wards in depressed council estates. In marked contrast, 20 per cent of Indians lived in the affluent suburbs, though 27.2 per cent lived in wards in cluster 7.

The contrast with the stereotype of minority ethnic group disadvantage is most marked for the Chinese and Other ethnic groups. Nearly a third of Chinese people, slightly less than the corresponding percentage for White people, lived in the affluent suburbs, and only 16 per cent lived in the deprived inner urban wards of cluster 2. Chinese and Others were more likely than South Asians to live in clusters 3 and 7, and were also more likely to live in the prosperous rural areas of cluster 8. Other–Asians and people from the Other–Other group were more likely than the Chinese to live in deprived inner city areas.

Use of the cluster analysis therefore reinforces the evidence of a strongly urban focused distribution of most minority ethnic groups. Furthermore, it shows that

Figure 7.9   *Variations in unemployment rates by ethnic group across cluster types*

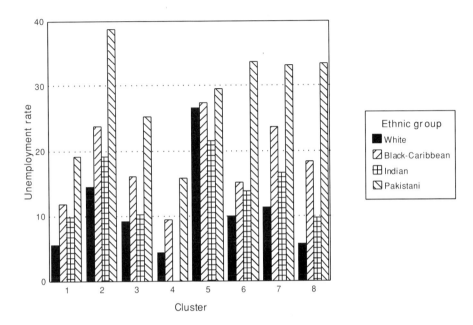

Figure 7.10   *Variations in the percentage of people with higher education qualifications by ethnic group across cluster types*

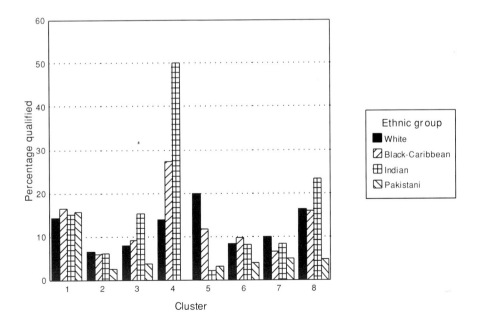

even the more successful minority ethnic groups such as the Indians and Chinese were over-represented in the disadvantaged areas of the urban system and under-represented in affluent and rural areas.

Figures 7.9 and 7.10 illustrate, using the unemployment rate and the percentage of the population aged 18 and over holding post-school educational qualifications, how individual minority ethnic groups fared in different types of residential environment, compared with Whites. The ranking of unemployment rates by ethnic group (Figure 7.9) was preserved across nearly all types of residential environment. Thus White people had the lowest unemployment rates, levels rose for the Indian and Black-Caribbean groups and reached a maximum for Pakistanis. For Whites, Black–Caribbeans and Indians, the unemployment rate tended to reflect the cluster average, but Pakistanis experienced unemployment rates of over 30 per cent in clusters 6, 7 and 8 (the prosperous rural areas) in addition to the most deprived areas of cluster 2.

The pattern of advantage and disadvantage represented by the percentage with higher education qualifications (Figure 7.10) was rather different. In the most affluent clusters (1 and 8), there was little difference between White people and those from minority ethnic groups. If anything there was a tendency for the latter to do better (though this affects small numbers of people). However, in the more deprived areas (clusters 2, 5, 6 and 7), the percentage of Whites with qualifications was higher than for the three minority ethnic groups. For the latter three groups favourable differentials tended to be magnified in the more affluent areas, while their position in the more deprived areas was even worse than would be implied by the average characteristics of these areas.

7.8 Population change and the changing geographical segregation patterns of ethnic groups 1981–91

Section 7.2 showed that most minority ethnic groups in the Midlands have youthful population structures, resulting both from relatively high birth rates in Britain and the continued in-migration of family members, many of whom have been women of child-bearing age. Unfortunately, as the 1991 Census was the first to collect data on the ethnic group of individuals, it is not possible to use it to directly measure change in the population of individual ethnic groups over time. Even worse, the Labour Force Survey (LFS), which reveals that the total number of people in Great Britain from minority ethnic groups grew by about a quarter between 1981 and 1991, cannot (because of the nature of the sampling procedure) provide reliable information on the changing ethnic mix of the population at the regional or sub-regional scales (see Chapter 2 of this volume). The LFS data for the Midlands yields particularly odd results: the percentage of the population from minority ethnic groups in the West Midlands metropolitan county is estimated to have hardly changed between 1981–83 and 1989–91, while this percentage is estimated to have declined in both the remainder of the West Midlands and the East Midlands over the same period (Owen, 1995c).

Thus, the calculation of trends over time in minority ethnic group populations is limited to using the data which are available from the census (derived from the country of birth of individuals or household heads), making the assumption that the majority of people were either born in the New Commonwealth or live in households headed by a person born in the New Commonwealth. Table 7.12 presents estimates of population change between 1981 and 1991 for the local authority districts in which the share of minority ethnic groups is greatest. Focusing upon the areas of largest minority populations, the number of people born in the New Commonwealth increased at only a modest rate in Leicester and Birmingham, and declined in Wolverhampton, Sandwell, Coventry and Derby. Rapid increases occurred in Northampton (where the total population also grew rapidly because of its status as a New Town and its location close to Milton Keynes, the most rapidly growing New Town in Britain) and the commuter areas of Leicestershire, which may indicate a tendency for more economically successful persons to move out of Leicester into the higher status commuter villages and small towns surrounding the city.

These results may be unexpected, but slow growth and decline can be explained as being a result of the considerable slowing in primary immigration from the New Commonwealth, the ageing of the earliest migrants and hence increasing numbers of deaths amongst the first generation, and the growth in return migration. The

Table 7.12 *Indicators of change in minority ethnic group populations, 1981–91*

Local authority district	NCW-born persons		Persons living in NCW headed households		% of ethnic minorities 1991	
	Change	(%)	Change	(%)	NCW born	In NCW headed households
Leicester	1,252	3.0	11,040	18.7	56.7	90.9
Birmingham	4,522	5.2	16,376	11.0	44.3	80.1
Wolverhampton	−1,611	−7.7	−1,879	−4.8	42.6	82.1
Sandwell	−661	−3.4	668	1.9	44.0	83.6
Coventry	−604	−3.4	353	1.2	49.1	85.6
Nottingham	103	0.9	−845	−4.0	42.3	72.0
Derby	−533	−5.1	37	0.2	46.6	85.1
Walsall	551	5.1	2,765	14.6	45.8	87.6
Oadby and Wigston	1,222	88.0	2,446	127.0	58.2	97.4
Wellingborough	−232	−7.7	−283	−6.4	57.0	85.0
Charnwood	1,225	28.5	2,657	47.7	62.5	93.0
Northampton	884	18.1	1,686	22.9	53.8	84.5
Warwick	−285	−7.2	−53	−0.8	55.9	95.0
Rugby	−185	−7.0	−29	−0.7	58.2	94.4

NCW = New Commonwealth
Source: 1991 Census Small Area Statistics and 1991 Census Local Base Statistics.

number of persons born in the New Commonwealth is now a poor surrogate for the size of the minority ethnic group population, as the percentage born in the UK has been steadily growing over time. Indeed, half or more of the minority ethnic population in the districts presented in the table were born in the UK, with the minimum 42.6 per cent in Wolverhampton and the maximum 62.5 per cent in Charnwood.

A better indicator is the number of people living in households headed by a person born in the New Commonwealth; the measure adopted by the 1981 Census when plans to include a question on ethnic group were abandoned (see Chapter 1 of this volume). This yields a more exaggerated pattern of change, with the numbers in this category more than doubling in Oadby and Wigston, increasing by nearly half in Charnwood and growing by around a fifth in Leicester and Northampton. However, this estimate yields a decline in Wolverhampton and Nottingham; both districts in which Black groups comprise a large part of the total minority ethnic group population. Part of the explanation of this pattern is provided by the final column in Table 7.12. This demonstrates that as minority ethnic groups become more firmly established in Britain, the share of persons living in households headed by a person born in the New Commonwealth declines from a value which would have been near 100 per cent in the early post-war years, the time at which these minority ethnic groups began to enter the UK in substantial numbers.

This percentage is lowest in Nottingham and Wolverhampton, indicating that in these cities, the number of people from minority ethnic groups in households with British-born heads is increasing, as the children and grandchildren of first generation immigrants move out of the parental home or start their own families. However, this estimate of the minority ethnic group population also fell marginally in districts such as Rugby and Warwick, where the percentage of people from minority ethnic groups living in a household headed by a person born in the New Commonwealth is relatively high. A possible explanation might be a decline in declared household size between 1981 and 1991 resulting from fear of the poll tax. The main conclusion that can be drawn from this exercise is that minority ethnic group populations appear to be growing fastest in the areas of largest minority populations and also in areas of rapid overall population change.

An important dimension of the experience of minority ethnic groups in Great Britain has been their tendency to concentrate in certain neighbourhoods and hence to be relatively isolated from White people. A number of authors, such as Lieberson (1980), have interpreted the degree of geographical segregation experienced by an ethnic group as an indicator of the degree of its (social) integration and assimilation. The more segregated an ethnic group, the less well integrated it is into the population as a whole. Conversely, the argument runs, levels of segregation would decline over time if minority ethnic groups were becoming increasingly well integrated (or even assimilated) into society as a whole.

The degree of geographical segregation of individual ethnic groups can be calculated by application of an appropriate statistical measure of segregation to data on the ethnic composition of enumeration districts. These areas, which contained on average 150 households in 1981 and 200 households in 1991, are used for fieldwork

Box 7.2   *Measuring isolation*

The P* index was originally devised by Bell and has been extensively used by Lieberson. It measures the degree of exposure of ethnic group x to ethnic group y:

$$_xP_y^* = \sum_{i=1}^{k} \frac{x_i}{X} \cdot \frac{y_i}{t_i}$$

where X is the total population of ethnic group X in the area over which the statistic is being calculated (in this instance, a local authority district), x_i is the population of the ethnic group x in the areal subunit i, y_i is the population of the ethnic group y in areal subunit i, t_i is the total population of areal subunit i, and there are k subunits. In this application, the areal subunits are 1991 Census enumeration districts. The value resulting from this calculation represents the probability for an average member of ethnic group x that he or she will have a neighbour from ethnic group y. An ethnic group can also be compared with itself, to yield an estimate of its isolation from others; in other words the probability that it will have neighbours of the same ethnic group. Clearly the probability of having a neighbour from a given ethnic group will be related to the relative size of that ethnic group in a city's population, but this can be taken into account by subtracting the population share of ethnic group y from the value of the $_xP_y^*$ index. Positive values then indicate a tendency for ethnic group x to concentrate in areas where the percentage of the population from ethnic group y is relatively high, and negative values thus indicate a negative association between the spatial distribution of the two ethnic groups.

Table 7.13   *Patterns of geographical segregation by ethnic group, 1991*

Local authority district	Isolation index for White people	P* segregation indices minus ethnic group population share $_xP_y^*$							
		All minorities/ White	Black Caribbean/ White	Indian/ White	Pakistani/ White	Bangla-deshi/ White	Chinese/ White	South/ Asian	Asian/ Other
Leicester	11.5	−29.0	−9.9	−32.5	−30.7	−35.0	3.7	4.0	1.1
Birmingham	8.7	−31.8	−21.0	−30.8	−44.2	−46.9	−10.3	9.2	1.8
Wolverhampton	4.4	−20.5	−12.3	−24.4	−32.0	−12.3	−7.6	5.1	0.7
Sandwell	4.0	−24.5	−17.0	−26.0	−33.2	−39.0	−4.1	8.7	0.7
Coventry	2.5	−19.5	−5.7	−19.7	−38.1	−38.0	−1.4	3.4	0.8
Nottingham	1.2	−11.3	−8.5	−8.9	−19.8	−19.3	−10.6	2.0	1.2
Derby	2.5	−25.8	−17.0	−23.9	−44.6	−30.2	−1.3	10.8	1.1
Walsall	2.4	−25.0	−12.9	−22.9	−35.3	−45.3	−7.3	8.7	0.8
Oadby & Wigston	0.0	−9.0	−3.9	−10.1	−12.3	−10.5	−2.7	3.1	0.5
Wellingborough	0.4	−13.1	−6.8	−19.6	−15.1	−20.6	0.5	2.9	0.5
Charnwood	0.6	−15.5	−3.6	−15.4	−4.8	−37.0	−5.1	5.3	1.2
Northampton	0.0	−4.8	−3.8	−3.5	−6.8	−12.4	−4.2	1.2	0.5
Warwick	0.6	−12.8	−6.6	−16.3	−3.5	−7.9	−3.0	3.4	0.1
Rugby	0.4	−14.3	−14.6	−16.5	−24.2	−8.8	−3.8	7.9	0.5

Source: 1991 Census Local Base Statistics.

planning and data collection: they could be seen as approximating to the concept of neighbourhoods. A number of segregation measures have been devised, most of which are based on the index of dissimilarity (see Jackson and Smith, 1981; Chapters 2 and 3 of this volume). However, the P* index, devised by Bell and used extensively by Lieberson, is an appealing alternative. This measures the degree to which two ethnic groups come into contact; a factor which is assumed to be a function of the ethnic mix of the areas in which the ethnic group is concentrated (the details of how P* is calculated are presented in Box 7.2).

The results of calculating the P* index (standardised for population shares) for a number of ethnic groups in Midlands districts in 1991 are presented in Table 7.13. They indicate the degree of isolation of White people from other ethnic groups, the segregation of Black–Caribbean, Indian, Pakistani, Bangladeshi and Chinese people from White people, the segregation of Black people relative to South Asians and the segregation of South Asians relative to Chinese and other ethnic groups.

Whites are most isolated from other ethnic groups in those districts where the minority ethnic group share of the population is greatest, and the degree of isolation declines as the minority share of the population declines. However, the likelihood of a White person in Leicester or Birmingham having White neighbours is still smaller than in districts with smaller minority ethnic group populations. The degree of spatial segregation, of minority ethnic groups as a whole from White people, is substantial, with the chance of a person from a minority ethnic group in Leicester or Birmingham having a White neighbour being about 30 per cent less than would be implied by the population structure of these cities. The degree of segregation is also substantial in the other large Midlands cities, and is least in the smaller districts with smaller minority ethnic group populations.

There are marked differences between minority ethnic groups in their degree of spatial segregation from White people. The Chinese display the smallest degree of segregation in most districts, except in Birmingham, Wolverhampton and Nottingham, which contain the largest concentrations of Chinese people in the Midlands. A similar pattern of greater segregation in areas of greatest concentration is displayed by the Black–Caribbean group, for whom Black–Caribbean people account for 21 per cent more of their neighbours than would be predicted from the population structure. The greatest degrees of segregation from Whites across all Midlands districts are displayed by the three South Asian groups. Indians experience their greatest degree of segregation in Leicester, Birmingham, Derby and the other districts of the West Midlands metropolitan county. The degree of segregation of Pakistanis and Bangladeshis is even greater than that of Indians, being greatest in Birmingham and Derby for Pakistanis and greatest in Birmingham and neighbouring districts for Bangladeshis. The Black groups tend to live in similar areas to the South Asians, with the association between their geographical distributions closest in Derby, Birmingham, Sandwell and Walsall, and weakest in Northampton. South Asian and Chinese people exhibit a weaker tendency to live in similar areas, with their spatial association again closest in Birmingham.

It is possible to use census data on the country of birth of individuals to assess the manner in which these patterns of residential segregation have changed over the

Table 7.14: *Changing patterns of geographical segregation by country of birth, 1981–91*

Local authority district	East Africa		Caribbean		India		South East Asia		Pakistan	
	1981	1991	1981	1991	1981	1991	1981	1991	1981	1991
Leicester	−23.6	−18.5	−10.2	−6.5	−23.9	−19.6	−7.3	0.0	−23.5	−16.4
Birmingham	−20.0	−12.5	−13.5	−10.0	−20.5	−14.1	−12.4	−9.0	−26.1	−22.0
Wolverhampton	−14.7	−8.6	−7.4	−5.9	−17.8	−11.8	−9.2	−6.4	−20.9	−15.0
Sandwell	−13.1	−9.1	−10.3	−7.9	−17.9	−12.6	−11.3	−4.6	−17.2	−17.2
Coventry	−11.7	−8.3	−5.0	−3.5	−14.9	−9.7	−7.6	−15.3	−22.5	−17.7
Nottingham	−7.4	−4.4	−6.8	−4.2	−10.1	−5.3	−8.1	−6.0	−15.2	−11.1
Derby	−10.6	−5.5	−12.1	−9.3	−18.5	−11.4	−5.8	−2.8	−28.7	−22.3
Walsall	−20.1	−9.8	−8.4	−6.5	−17.2	−11.1	−8.6	−3.3	−20.3	−16.9
Oadby and Wigston	−2.0	−5.5	−1.4	−2.1	−2.6	−6.7	−2.5	−2.1	−6.8	−4.5
Wellingborough	−12.9	−11.6	−5.7	−3.8	−15.1	−13.8	−0.9	−0.2	−10.5	−10.5
Charnwood	−12.9	−9.4	−1.6	−2.1	−14.6	−9.4	−9.9	−9.8	−7.6	−9.8
Northampton	−3.9	−2.6	−3.9	−2.7	−2.6	−2.0	−3.4	−1.7	−6.9	−5.4
Warwick	−8.1	−4.6	−8.5	−4.1	−11.0	−7.9	−4.2	−4.0	−7.9	−6.7
Rugby	−17.9	−9.9	−16.7	−10.1	−12.8	−8.5	−7.2	−2.4	−19.2	−13.0

Source: 1981 Census Small Area Statistics and 1991 Census Local Base Statistics

period 1981–91. In Table 7.14, the standardised P* indices representing the geographical segregation of persons born in East Africa, the Caribbean, India, South East Asia and Pakistan in 1981 and 1991, calculated at the enumeration district scale, are presented for the same set of 14 local authority districts.

There are some similarities with the segregation patterns calculated from ethnic group data. The degree of segregation tends to be greater for East Africans and South Asians than for Caribbeans and South East Asians. The degree of segregation again tends to be greater in the districts with larger percentages of their population from minority ethnic groups, especially in 1981. Overall, the geographical segregation of people born in countries of the New Commonwealth from persons born in the UK declined over the decade (possibly a reflection of the growing percentage of the minority ethnic group population born in the UK, rather than declining segregation relative to White people). The decline in segregation was greatest in most districts for people born in India and the Caribbean, and least for Pakistanis. While the segregation of South East Asians declined greatly in Leicester and Birmingham, their segregation increased greatly in Coventry and changed little in some of the smaller districts.

7.8   Conclusions

This chapter has addressed the complex task of providing an overview of the characteristics of people from different ethnic groups living in the Midlands. It has also attempted to review these against the patterns observed by studies based on previous census data. The region is large and diverse, and there are a range of aspects of life which should ideally be covered for all 10 ethnic groups. Given the constraints of space, this chapter has focused on the areas in which minority ethnic groups are concentrated and upon those ethnic groups which are most strongly represented in the region.

There are marked differences in living conditions between the region's White population and its minority ethnic groups, many of which mirror differences already explored at the national scale in other chapters in these four volumes. Minority ethnic groups are more youthful than the White population, and the younger ethnic groups are even younger in the Midlands than the British average; for example, only half of people from the Black–Other group are of secondary school age and above. The Other ethnic groups are also more likely to have parents from different ethnic groups than people in Britain as a whole. Males are more common in most ethnic groups than in the British population as a whole. Overall, while minority ethnic groups are disadvantaged relative to Whites, not all are disadvantaged to the same degree. Chinese and Indian people experience unemployment rates closest to those for Whites, and have better material living conditions than the other minority ethnic groups. The Black–Africans and Chinese have the highest levels of educational qualifications. In contrast, the Bangladeshi and Pakistani groups suffer the highest unemployment rates, lowest levels of qualifications and poorest physical housing conditions.

The analysis has demonstrated the considerable degree of geographical concentration which still exists in the location patterns of minority ethnic groups. The geographical distribution is still strongly oriented towards large urban areas and the older, central parts of these cities and towns. This parallels a socio-economic divide: White people are more likely to live in the relatively affluent residential environments, while people from minority ethnic groups are more likely to live in the most deprived environments. However, this is not a neat dichotomy; White people also live in deprived areas and members of some minority ethnic groups (notably the Black–African, Indian and Chinese ethnic groups) are also found in more affluent areas. The Pakistani and Bangladeshi groups are most likely to live near people of the same ethnic group (usually in more deprived areas with older housing), while the Chinese have the most dispersed geographical distribution. The degree of geographical segregation between White people and people from minority ethnic groups is still substantial, though it appears to have declined over the decade 1981–91. Overall, the pattern is one of continuity and surprisingly little change. That which has occurred over time is much as might be expected from the natural processes of demographic transition, but it has not demonstrated the same breadth and depth as has been found among the White populations.

The early studies found an association between the presence of immigrant groups and economies of relative prosperity and growth (though individuals were often located in the older sectors of manufacturing industry, with harsh working conditions). The communities had a specific location within zones in transition, and were largely seen as replacement populations. Over time, however, increasing levels of concentration and frustrated attempts at suburbanisation could be discerned. Research showed a concern with segregation and ethnic sorting, but was rarely able to draw comparisons with other populations either local (White) or elsewhere. The analysis of 1991 data repeats and continues that association with the larger urban cores and housing deprivation. While the demographic ratios indicate that they are not yet a fully settled or mature population, there is little evidence that ethnic sorting is decreasing, suggesting that minority ethnic groups are still in some senses a replacement population.

It may be asked what would have been the fate of these areas had this population not been available. Further, the analysis by area types gives depressing confirmation of the continuing links with discrimination and exclusion, despite within- and between-group contrasts, and of the lack of return for such economic or educational success as has been achieved. The earlier studies reviewed belonged to a very different political and social climate, and reflected attitudes and practices which would not nowadays be regarded as acceptable (or indeed legal). That the patterns have remained as recognisable as they have, demonstrates the problems for the second and third (or later) generation of descendants of the original migrants in escaping the patterns of history.

References

Champion, A. G. (1991) *Counterurbanisation*. London: Edward Arnold.

Cross, M. and Johnson, M. R. D. (1982) Migration, settlement and inner city policy: the British case. In: Solomos, J. (ed.), *Migrant Workers in Metropolitan Cities*. Strasbourg: European Science Foundation, pp.117–34.

Davies, P. and Newton, K. (1972) The social patterns of immigrant areas. *Race*, 14(1), 43–57.

Dorling, D. and Simpson, S. (1993) Those missing millions: implications for social statistics of undercount in the 1991 Census. *Radical Statistics*, 55, 14–35.

Edwards, J., Leigh, E. and Marshall, T. (1970) *Social Patterns in Birmingham 1966*. Occasional Paper 13. Centre for Urban and Regional Studies, University of Birmingham.

Husain, M. S. (1975) The increase and distribution of New Commonwealth immigrants in Greater Nottingham. *East Midlands Geographer*, 6, 105–29.

Jackson, P. and Smith, S. (1981) *Social Interaction and Ethnic Segregation*. Institute of British Geographers Special Publication 12. London: Academic Press.

Jones, P. N. (1967) *The Segregation of Immigrant Communities in the City of Birmingham 1961*. Occasional Papers in Geography 7. University of Hull.

Jones, P. N. (1978) The distribution and diffusion of the coloured population in England and Wales 1961-71. *Transactions*, Institute of British Geographers, 3(4), 515–32.

Joyce, F. (1977) *Metropolitan Development and Change – the West Midlands: A Policy Review*. London: British Association for the Advancement of Science.

Katznelson, I. (1973) *Black Men, White Cities*. London: IRR/Oxford University Press.

Lawrence, D. (1974) *Black migrants, White natives: A study of race relations in Nottingham*. Cambridge: Cambridge University Press.

Lieberson, S. (1980) *A Piece of the Pie: Blacks and White Immigrants Since 1880*. Berkeley: University of California Press.

Lomas, G. B. G. and Monck, E. M. (1975) *The Coloured Population of Great Britain*. London: Runnymede Trust.

Marrett, V. (1989) *Immigrants Settling in the City*. Leicester: Leicester University Press.

OPCS/GRO(Scotland) (1993) *1991 Census, Ethnic Group and Country of Birth, Great Britain*. Two volumes. CEN91 EGCB. London: HMSO.

Owen, D. W. (1994) *South Asian People in Great Britain: Social and economic circumstances*. 1991 Census Statistical Paper No. 7, National Ethnic Minority Data Archive. Coventry: University of Warwick Centre for Research in Ethnic Relations.

Owen, D. W. (1996a) Black–Other: the melting pot. In: Peach, G. C. K. (ed.), *The Ethnic Minority Populations of Great Britain*. Ethnicity in the 1991 Census series, Volume 2. London: HMSO.

Owen, D. W. (1996b) Size, structure and growth of the ethnic minority populations. In: Coleman, D. and Salt, J. (eds), *Demographic Characteristics of the Ethnic Minority Populations*. Ethnicity in the 1991 Census series, Volume 1. London: OPCS.

Owen, D.W. (1995c) *Integrating survey and Census data in estimating minority ethnic group populations*. Paper presented to the Annual Conference of the Institute of British Geographers, University of Northumbria, Newcastle-upon-Tyne, January 1995.

Phillips, D. (1981) The social and spatial segregation of Asians in Leicester. In: Jackson, P. and Smith, S. (eds), *Social Interaction and Ethnic Segregation*. Institute of British Geographers Special Publication 12. London: Academic Press, pp. 101–22.

Ratcliffe, P. (1981) Racism and Reaction: *A Profile of Handsworth*. London: Routledge and Kegan Paul.

Rex, J. and Moore, R. (1967) *Race, Community and Conflict*. London: Oxford University Press.

Rex, J. and Tomlinson, S. (1979) *Colonial Immigrants in a British City*. London: Routledge Keagan Paul.

Rosing, K.E. and Wood, P.A. (1971) *Character of a Conurbation*. London: University of London Press.

Rugman, A. J. and Green, M.D. (1977) Demographic and Social Change. In: Joyce, F. (ed.), *Metropolitan Development and Change – The West Midlands: A Policy Review*. London: British Association for the Advancement of Science, pp. 50–74.

Solomos, J. (ed.) (1982) *Migrant Workers in Metropolitan Cities*. Strasbourg: European Science Foundation.

Survey of Leicester 1983. Leicester: Leicester City Council/Leicestershire County Council, 1984. Robinson, V. (1986) *Transients, Settlers and Refugees*. Oxford: Clarendon Press.

Wallis, S. (1974) Pakistanis in Britain. *New Community*, 4(1), 105–15.

Winchester, S. (1974) Immigrant areas in Coventry. *New Community*, 4, 97–104.

Woods, R.I. (1979) Ethnic segregation in Birmingham in the 1960s and 1970s. *Ethnic and Racial Studies*, 2(4), 455–75.

Appendix 7.1

Variables used in the cluster analysis of electoral wards

Variable	Mean	Standard deviation
Population density	14.7	17.4
Per cent aged 0–5	19.3	3.9
Per cent aged 16–29	19.1	4.4
Per cent aged 30–59/64	41.4	6.7
Per cent pensionable age	18.5	5.0
Per cent highly qualified	12.6	7.2
Per cent households in flats	7.4	7.4
Per cent households in semi-detached houses	34.1	14.7
Per cent households in terraced houses	21.0	16.1
Per cent households owner-occupied	70.6	11.5
Per cent householdw without amenities	16.0	9.9
Cars per household	1.1	0.3
Male economic activity rate	72.8	10.6
Married female economic activity rate	52.9	9.1
Per cent working in manufacturing	22.0	8.6
Per cent working in services	58.7	11.5
Per cent white-collar	32.2	12.6
Unemployment rate	7.4	4.3

Source: 1991 Census Local Base Statistics

Appendix 7.2

Loadings (correlations) of classificatory variables on principal components

Variable	Component number							
	1	2	3	4	5	6	7	8
Population density	-0.521	0.527	0.077	0.012	-0.288	0.129	0.458	-0.189
Per cent aged 0–15	0.007	0.804	-0.187	-0.263	0.111	-0.240	0.030	0.228
Per cent aged 16–29	-0.206	0.839	0.040	-0.179	-0.025	-0.121	-0.152	-0.159
Per cent 30–59/64	0.818	0.443	-0.064	0.137	0.125	-0.020	-0.013	0.138
Per cent pensionable age	0.245	0.116	0.488	0.749	0.046	0.132	-0.237	0.044
Per cent highly qualified	0.782	-0.098	0.380	-0.192	-0.127	0.066	0.232	0.055
Per cent households in flats	-0.496	0.426	0.440	0.052	-0.364	0.108	0.014	0.238
Per cent households in semi-detached houses	0.058	0.332	-0.626	0.534	-0.257	-0.239	0.099	-0.079
Per cent households in terraced houses	-0.548	0.528	0.268	-0.266	0.174	0.206	-0.240	-0.227
Per cent households owner-occupied	0.806	0.279	-0.143	0.091	-0.001	0.267	0.017	-0.168
Per cent households without amenities	-0.359	0.357	0.320	0.284	0.593	-0.129	0.324	-0.187
Cars per household	0.945	0.010	-0.071	-0.061	0.190	-0.046	0.044	0.100
Male economic activity rate	0.498	0.822	-0.103	-0.070	0.109	-0.054	-0.061	0.015
Married female economic activity rate	0.588	0.705	-0.152	-0.098	-0.098	0.131	-0.062	-0.133
Per cent working in manufacturing	-0.316	0.632	-0.331	0.111	0.091	0.491	0.062	0.253
Per cent working in services	0.558	0.478	0.434	0.044	-0.309	-0.240	-0.096	-0.167
Per cent white-collar	0.839	-0.066	0.379	-0.115	0.020	0.035	0.193	0.136
Unemployment rate	-0.650	0.512	0.215	0.062	0.031	-0.229	-0.004	0.306

Chapter 8
Geographical patterns in a cluster of Pennine cities

Philip Rees and Deborah Phillips

8.1 Introduction

Previous chapters in this volume have described the national distribution of minority ethnic groups at the time of the 1991 Census, revealing intense concentrations in the largest cities of the United Kingdom and in particular in the London metropolitan region (Chapter 6) and in the West Midlands metropolitan area (Chapter 7). This chapter examines the geographical pattern of ethnic minorities in the northern third of England which contains another significant set of minority ethnic communities in its larger cities and towns.

Northern England is here defined as the standard regions of the North, North West, and Yorkshire and Humberside (Figure 8.1). The North contains the counties of Cleveland, Cumbria, Durham and Northumberland, and the former metropolitan county of Tyne and Wear, with the largest urban districts being Newcastle, Middlesbrough and Sunderland (Figure 8.2). The North West contains the counties of Cheshire and Lancashire together with the heavily populated former metropolitan counties of Greater Manchester and Merseyside. Yorkshire and Humberside contains the counties of Humberside and North Yorkshire and the former metropolitan counties of South and West Yorkshire. These counties and former metropolitan counties contain a total of 84 districts, ranging in population size from just over 700,000 in the largest city district (Leeds) to just over 23,000 in the smallest rural district (Teesdale).

The whole area is unified by the presence (running north to south through the region) of the Pennine Hills; the valleys penetrating these hills contain towns and cities whose original economic activities were dominated by the textile, and associated textile machinery, industries. These towns and cities had, in the late 1950s and 1960s, a strong demand for labour to work in the cotton and woollen textile mills (Robinson, 1986; Smith, 1989). This demand was in part met by the attraction of immigrant workers from the Indian subcontinent. These workers, their dependants and offspring give the region the particular character of its minority ethnic populations.

Table 8.1 compares the ethnic composition of northern England's population with that of Great Britain as a whole. Minority ethnic groups make up only 3.7 per cent of the area's population compared with 5.5 per cent for the country as a whole. Only one of the principal minority ethnic groups has a larger presence in the region than in Britain as a whole. Pakistanis constitute 1.4 per cent of northern England's population compared with only 0.9 per cent of the Great Britain population. The

Figure 8.1 Northern England: standard regions, counties and districts

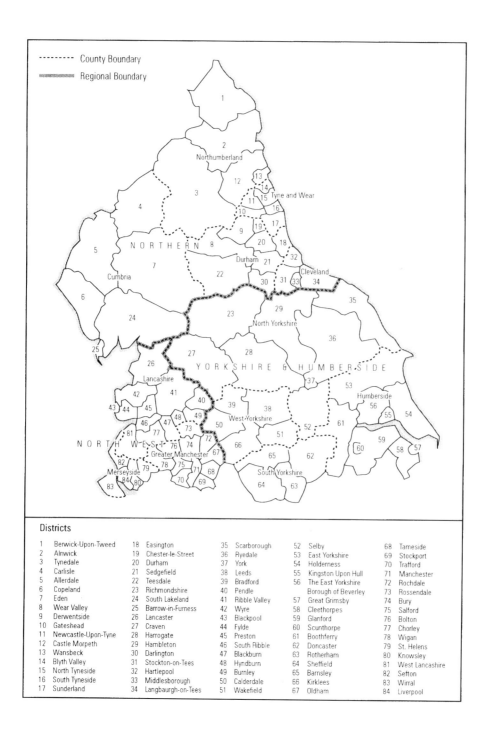

Districts

1	Berwick-Upon-Tweed	18	Easington	35	Scarborough	52	Selby	68	Tameside
2	Alnwick	19	Chester-le-Street	36	Ryedale	53	East Yorkshire	69	Stockport
3	Tynedale	20	Durham	37	York	54	Holderness	70	Trafford
4	Carlisle	21	Sedgefield	38	Leeds	55	Kingston Upon Hull	71	Manchester
5	Allerdale	22	Teesdale	39	Bradford	56	The East Yorkshire	72	Rochdale
6	Copeland	23	Richmondshire	40	Pendle		Borough of Beverley	73	Rossendale
7	Eden	24	South Lakeland	41	Ribble Valley	57	Great Grimsby	74	Bury
8	Wear Valley	25	Barrow-in-Furness	42	Wyre	58	Cleethorpes	75	Salford
9	Derwentside	26	Lancaster	43	Blackpool	59	Glanford	76	Bolton
10	Gateshead	27	Craven	44	Fylde	60	Scunthorpe	77	Chorley
11	Newcastle-Upon-Tyne	28	Harrogate	45	Preston	61	Boothferry	78	Wigan
12	Castle Morpeth	29	Hambleton	46	South Ribble	62	Doncaster	79	St. Helens
13	Wansbeck	30	Darlington	47	Blackburn	63	Rotherham	80	Knowsley
14	Blyth Valley	31	Stockton-on-Tees	48	Hyndburn	64	Sheffield	81	West Lancashire
15	North Tyneside	32	Hartlepool	49	Burnley	65	Barnsley	82	Sefton
16	South Tyneside	33	Middlesborough	50	Calderdale	66	Kirklees	83	Wirral
17	Sunderland	34	Langbaurgh-on-Tees	51	Wakefield	67	Oldham	84	Liverpool

Figure 8.2 *Concentration of minority ethnic populations in the districts of Northern England (minority ethnic population as a percentage of the district total population)*

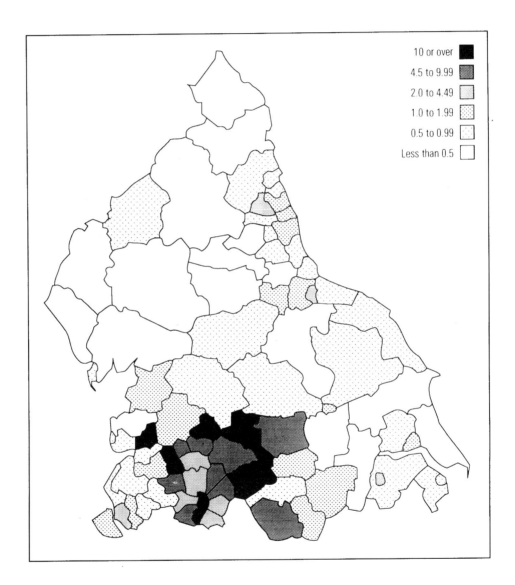

Table 8.1 *The ethnic composition of northern England's population compared with Great Britain, 1991*

Ethnic group	Great Britain per cent	Northern England per cent
White	94.5	96.3
Black	1.6	0.7
Indian	1.5	0.8
Pakistani	0.9	1.4
Bangladeshi	0.3	0.2
Other	1.1	0.7
Total ethnic minorities	5.5	3.7

Source: Author's computations from 1991 Census, Local Base Statistics. Crown copyright. ESRC/JISC purchase.

Black groups are under-represented in the region with only 41 per cent of their national percentage, while Indians have 52 per cent and the Other groups and Bangladeshis 64 and 67 per cent of their national representation respectively.

8.2 The district pattern

The general pattern

These regional statistics, of course, conceal profound differences in the ethnic composition of individual districts. Figure 8.2 classifies districts into groups according to the percentage of the population made up of ethnic minority groups.

Some 10 per cent or more of the population of six districts belongs to ethnic minorities. These districts are the woollen textile cities of Bradford and Kirklees, the north east Lancashire cotton textile towns of Blackburn, Pendle and Preston, and the metropolitan district of Manchester.

The second category, in which 4.5 to 9.9 per cent of the district's population are drawn from minority ethnic groups, includes most of the other cotton textile districts (Oldham, Bolton, Rochdale, Hyndburn, Burnley, Trafford) together with the large metropolitan districts of Leeds and Sheffield.

The third category, in which between 2 and 4.4 per cent of the district population is from a minority ethnic group, includes other textile districts (Bury, Rossendale) and larger metropolitan/urban districts across the region (Middlesbrough, Tameside, Newcastle upon Tyne, Stockport, Salford, Liverpool).

The fourth category with between 1 and 2 per cent from minority ethnic groups comprises 15 smaller industrial and mining districts (e.g. Doncaster). The fifth category, where minorities make up between half and one per cent of the population consists of 28 districts; the seaside resorts, smaller urban districts and more accessible rural districts of the region. The sixth, and final, category with less than half a percent of the population being of minority origin consists of 17 remoter rural districts.

Table 8.2 *Minority ethnic communities of 1,000 persons or more in northern England: Blacks, 1991*

District	Black total	Black–Caribbean	Black–Other	Black–African
Manchester	18,672	10,329	5,015	3,328
Leeds	10,630	6,475	2,887	1,268
Sheffield	7,892	4,965	1,866	1,061
Liverpool	7,052	1,448	3,230	2,374
Kirklees	6,544	4,428	1,743	373
Bradford	5,272	3,299	1,392	581
Trafford	4,040	2,878	952	210
Oldham	1,789	1,051	596	142
Bolton	1,523	680	476	367
Preston	1,505	890	501	114
Doncaster	1,248	771	379	98
Stockport	1,096	487	388	221
Total	67,263	37,701	19,425	10,137
Northern England	84,622	42,959	27,034	14,629
% of Northern England	79.5	87.8	71.9	69.3

Source: 1991 Census, Local Base Statistics. Crown Copyright. ESRC/JISC purchase.

Table 8.3 *Minority ethnic communities of 1,000 persons or more in Northern England: Indians, Pakistanis, Bangladeshis, 1991*

District	Indians	District	Pakistanis	District	Bangladesh
Bolton	13,329	Bradford	45,227	Oldham	5,130
Kirklees	11,885	Kirklees	17,456	Bradford	3,651
Bradford	11,676	Manchester	15,314	Manchester	1,993
Blackburn	10,470	Rochdale	11,035	Leeds	1,751
Leeds	9,871	Leeds	9,292	Rochdale	1,641
Preston	8,188	Oldham	8,914	Tameside	1,599
Manchester	4,339	Sheffield	8,855	Newcastle	1,300
Tameside	3,327	Blackburn	8,030	Sheffield	1,081
Trafford	2,678	Pendle	8,008		
Oldham	1,552	Calderdale	6,271		
Sheffield	1,393	Bolton	4,235		
Stockport	1,372	Hyndurn	3,778		
Liverpool	1,247	Middlesbrough	3,636		
Doncaster	1,177	Rotherham	3,241		
		Bury	3,239		
		Burnley	3,138		
		Newcastle	2,913		
		Wakefield	2,170		
		Trafford	2,082		
		Tameside	1,888		
		Preston	1,717		
		Stockport	1,575		
		Stockton	1,218		
		Doncaster	1,017		
Total	82,514		174,249		18,146
Northern England	101,406		179,955		26,320
% of Northern England	81.4		96.8		68.9

Table 8.4 *Minority ethnic communities of 1,000 persons or more in northern England: Chinese, Other–Asians and Other–Others, 1991*

District	Chinese	District	Other–Asian	District	Other–Others
Liverpool	3,246	Manchester	1,788	Manchester	5,432
Manchester	2,885	Bradford	1,579	Leeds	4,242
Leeds	2,021	Leeds	1,527	Sheffield	3,540
Sheffield	1,295			Liverpool	3,386
Newcastle	1,114			Bradford	2,993
Wirral	1,013			Kirklees	2,068
				Trafford	1,201
				Stockport	1,085
Total	11,574		4,874		23,947
Northern England	28,070		17,872		44,662
% of Northern England	41.2		27.4		53.6

The distribution of individual minority ethnic groups

The general pattern of Figure 8.2 is replicated to a degree for the individual minority ethnic groups, but each has its own unique geographical mosaic. Tables 8.2, 8.3 and 8.4 list the districts with minority communities containing at least 1,000 people. Table 8.2 lists those districts with communities of 1,000 or more Black residents. Black represents a conflation of the closely linked Black–Caribbean and Black–Other populations (which in part represent the different generations of West Indian origin) with people of Black–African origin. For all groups it is the larger, more diversified metropolitan and industrial districts which house the larger communities: cities such as Manchester, Leeds, Sheffield and Liverpool. In general, Black–Caribbeans are the largest group followed by the Black–Other group, with Black–Africans found in large numbers only in large cities, linked to higher education institutions. The only exception is the port city of Liverpool in which the Black–Other group is the largest; this represents a temporally well-established group of mixed heritage, descended from African seamen serving on Liverpool-based shipping (Gifford, et al., 1989; Small, 1991). This long-standing Black population is now characterised by a high level of mixed marriages and cohabitation compared with other Black communities in Britain (Small, 1991).

With the exception of the older Liverpool community, the settlement of the Black population in the North in 1991 still largely reflects the early pattern of post-war migration from the West Indies (especially Jamaica) and Africa; a pattern which, according to Peach (1986), was established by 1961. Black–Caribbeans in particular played an important economic role in the early post-war years, providing cheap labour to support key services (e.g. hospitals and transport) and to bolster other labour intensive industries. The timing and pattern of their migration reflected market forces, both in Britain and their homeland (poverty was a push factor), although the flow of Black–Caribbeans was channelled by the direct recruitment strategies of key employers such as London Transport and the National Health

Service (Peach, 1968; Rose et al., 1969). This recruitment strategy was chiefly responsible for the settlement of Black–Caribbeans in the South East and Midlands, where they acted as a replacement population, rather than in northern England.

The groups of South Asian origin have a strong representation in the large, economically diversified cities of the North, but of greater importance are the textile towns of West Yorkshire, Lancashire and Greater Manchester (Table 8.3). Bradford's Pakistani population is the largest ethnic community in any northern England district, making up just over 10 per cent of the district's population. This is the second largest Pakistani community in the country (after Birmingham), although large Pakistani communities figure in most of cotton and woollen textile towns. The communities originate in the demand for shift labour in the textile mills in the late 1950s and 1960s. The attraction of primarily South Asian migrants rather than Black–Caribbean groups to these northern jobs, reflects a change in the spatial distribution of employment opportunities for cheap labour, at a time when migration from the West Indies was slowing and South Asian migration was growing (Castles, 1984; Robinson, 1986).

Immigrants from the Indian subcontinent were recruited on to the night shifts that were increasingly unpopular with the native White population. It is important to note that these South Asians constituted a supplementary rather than a replacement work-force (as had been the case for the Black–Caribbeans), securing undesirable, poorly paid jobs in a vulnerable industry. Asian men on the night shift were often performing tasks undertaken by White female workers during the day, but with fewer opportunities for advancement (Harris, 1987). This resulted in a segmented labour force based on a racialised (and gendered) division of labour, setting up inequalities which came to the fore in later years of contraction in the textile industry (Castles and Kosack, 1973; Fevre, 1984).

The migration histories of several of the larger South Asian communities have been extensively studied (Ballard and Ballard, 1977; Khan, 1977; Anwar, 1979; Robinson, 1986). Their origin areas within either Pakistan or India were extremely localised. Pakistanis in Bradford, for example, predominantly originate from the Mirpur region of northern Pakistan, while smaller communities come from the North West Frontier (Pathans) or Pakistani Kashmir. Similarly, Pakistanis in Rochdale come from specific locations in the Punjab and Mirpur. Indians in Bradford come from either the Doaba region of the Punjab or the coastal areas of Gujarat (Ram, 1986). The Punjabi population is either Sikh or Hindu in religious affiliation, while the Gujaratis are primarily Hindus. The Pakistani population is almost exclusively Muslim. The Bangladeshi group is much smaller in numbers and concentrated in only a handful of districts, with the Oldham and Bradford communities being among the largest outside east London (Table 8.3).

The final three minority ethnic groups (Table 8.4) have a much wider dispersion. Only 41 per cent of the Chinese population of northern England is found in the 1,000-plus communities. As in the case of the African population, the Chinese minority groups have roots in a seafaring (Cantonese) population, which stretch back several generations (Jones, 1979). These origins have given rise to a significant Chinese population in Liverpool (3,246 in 1991) and later Manchester (2,885). The

Table 8.5 *Minority ethnic segregation from Whites in northern England, at district scale, 1991*

Ethnic group	Index of dissimilarity with Whites	Exposure index to White	Exposure index to own group
White	0.0	96.5	96.5
Black–Caribbean	58.5	91.7	1.2
Black–African	43.7	93.4	0.3
Black–Other	42.8	93.2	0.5
Indian	54.5	91.3	3.1
Pakistani	58.1	90.1	5.2
Bangladeshi	54.8	92.5	0.9
Chinese	26.0	95.4	0.3
Other–Asian	31.8	93.5	0.2
Other–Other	32.8	93.8	0.6

numbers of Chinese resident in Britain were boosted in the late 1950s and the 1960s as economic pressures in rural Hong Kong encouraged farmers from the New Territories to emigrate to Britain (Watson, 1977).

The current pattern of geographical dispersal among those of Chinese origin reflects a transformation in the economic base of the community over time, from seafaring and menial service employment (e.g. laundries) into self-employment in the restaurant and take-away trade (Jones, 1979). This employment shift was linked to a strategy of wide dispersion to maximise market share. By contrast Indian and Pakistani restaurant enterprises cluster in favoured city centre or inner city locations and draw clientele on a comparison 'eating-out' basis, an agglomerative strategy typified by the concentration of restaurants in Manchester's inner suburb of Rusholme.

Comparison with the White population

These general observations on the geography of ethnic minorities across northern England's districts can be made more precise by the computation of standard indices, which compare the distribution of a minority ethnic group across northern England's districts with that of the White majority. Two sets of indices are reported in Table 8.5.

The index of dissimilarity (ID) is half the sum of absolute differences between the percentage of northern England's Whites in a district and the percentage of the northern England population of the minority group. IDs vary between a minimum of 0, indicating no difference between the relative distributions of the two groups, and a maximum of 100, where the two groups show no overlap in their distribution.

The first exposure index is the average percentage of Whites experienced by a particular minority ethnic group, the district White percentages being weighted by the proportion of the relevant minority's northern England population who live in the district. The second exposure index applies the same calculation, but to the percentage of the group itself that it experiences; in other words, it is a measure of exposure to those who share the same ethnic background.

The IDs confirm that Black–Caribbeans, Pakistanis, Bangladeshis and Indians are most segregated from Whites, with IDs above 50. More than half of each of these groups would need to move residence in order to produce a district distribution parallel to that of the White population. They are followed by the Black–African and Black–Other groups, with IDs in the mid-40s, and the Other–Asian and (even more heterogeneous) Other–Other groups in the lower 30s. The Chinese have the lowest index value. The exposure indices show the inverse of the ID pattern with Pakistanis, Indians, Black–Caribbeans and Bangladeshis having the lowest exposures to Whites. However, even the lowest value is over 90 per cent, which underlines the fact that in northern England all minority ethnic groups live in districts thoroughly dominated by the 'ethnic majority', namely Whites.

8.3 The geographical patterns within districts

Just as ethnic minorities are distributed very unevenly across districts in northern England, so they are geographically concentrated within the districts. Ideally the patterns of geographical concentration should be studied for every district and at several spatial scales. However, here attention is confined to the 24 districts falling in the top three concentration categories in Figure 8.2 because these contain the significant minority ethnic populations, and the spatial resolution is confined to ward scale. Statistics are available at the smaller enumeration district scale but only for four groups (Whites, Blacks, Indians/Pakistanis/Bangladeshis, and Chinese and Others). Such groupings are too crude to provide much additional insight.

Wards are electoral areas revised between censuses in order to ensure rough equality in electorate size within local government districts. Wards decline in population size from the largest district, Leeds, where about 20,000 live in a ward, to the smallest districts which contain wards with around 4,000 inhabitants. While not an ideal spatial filter for studying ethnic geography, the associated data from the 1991 Census Local Base Statistics are easily accessed and comparable in nature. A word of caution needs to be added in the case of IDs for those minority groups that are small numerically, however, in that they may be unable to achieve an even distribution because there are not enough households to go around (Jones and McEvoy, 1978). This may result, for example, in exaggerating the ID of the small Bangladeshi population.

Table 8.6 presents the IDs (as before, on a scale 0 to 100) between each minority ethnic group and the White majority. At the bottom of the table are the summary statistics for the 24 (out of 84) districts in northern England which house the vast majority of the region's minority ethnic population. The general pattern resembles that at the district scale but there are significant differences. The Black–Caribbean group was the most concentrated in relation to Whites at district scale but drops to sixth position when intra-district segregation is examined. The Bangladeshi and Pakistani groups exhibit quite high degrees of spatial segregation from Whites and are significantly more segregated than Indians, any of the Black Groups and the Other – Asian group. The Chinese exhibit the lowest index of segregation followed by the Other – Other and Black–Other groups.

Table 8.6 *Minority ethnic segregation from Whites (IDs) in 24 Pennine districts at ward scale, 1991*

District	Black–Caribbean	Black–African	Black–Other	Indian	Pakistani	Bangla-deshi	Chinese	Other–Asian	Other–Other
Greater Manchester									
Bolton	38	43	31	65	68	54	20	47	30
Bury	26	25	29	26	57	46	23	20	23
Manchester	44	41	30	29	42	49	23	38	26
Oldham	43	37	32	53	76	79	20	47	30
Rochdale	22	36	33	45	69	88	26	43	19
Salford	33	39	28	27	45	55	18	34	27
Stockport	28	28	20	40	47	46	22	30	20
Tameside	27	32	22	56	59	70	21	38	21
Trafford	73	41	55	55	67	45	26	45	27
Merseyside									
Liverpool	46	51	46	31	43	62	29	36	31
South Yorkshire									
Sheffield	44	51	36	33	64	65	39	41	33
Tyne and Wear									
Newcastle-upon-Tyne	40	44	33	32	59	66	30	50	32
West Yorkshire									
Bradford	40	33	30	44	47	55	23	42	27
Calderdale	28	35	28	31	71	77	31	45	23
Kirklees	64	41	52	58	54	76	35	44	33
Leeds	53	35	42	36	53	72	29	32	29
Cleveland									
Middlesborough	33	50	39	40	69	79	40	46	33
Humberside									
Scunthorpe	55	57	44	38	59	75	43	47	39
Lancashire									
Blackburn	35	48	44	62	61	57	21	52	51
Burnley	30	34	43	31	69	89	36	50	35
Hynburn	58	61	43	36	67	67	40	64	33
Pendle	47	54	46	36	62	88	44	49	40
Preston	39	33	36	57	62	59	40	39	34
Rossendale	17	51	39	29	55	62	35	48	34
Statistics									
mean	40	42	37	41	59	66	30	43	30
minimum	17	25	20	26	42	45	18	20	19
maximum	73	61	55	65	76	89	44	64	51
standard deviation	14	10	9	12	10	14	8	9	7

Source: Computed from 1991 Census Local Base Statistics. Crown copyright. ESRC/JISC purchase supplied by CDU on Midas system.

How might we account for this variation in degree of segregation from Whites? Several hypotheses can be put forward. Although their evaluation is beyond the scope of this chapter in that it would imply a detailed study of individual cities, they should provide a useful basis for future research:

1   The position of a minority ethnic group on the socio-economic status scale undoubtedly plays a role (see section 8.4 for a more detailed picture). That is not to say that we can predict the residential locations of a group from its social and economic characteristics. Most groups only occupy some of the residential areas in a city that their income levels make accessible. However, it is clear that the Bangladeshi and Pakistani groups have long been, and still are, severely disadvantaged in socio-economic terms compared with Whites, and can only afford to live in the cheaper housing areas of northern cities. The widening unemployment gap between minority ethnic and White groups since 1991 can only serve to fossilise this pattern (Runnymede Bulletin, 1995). The Chinese and Indian groups are quite similar in socio-economic terms to Whites, enabling some members of these groups to gain access to more expensive housing areas, which are also closer to Whites.

2   A second set of factors involves the recency of arrival in the country. The Bangladeshi group was the latest to arrive (Peach, 1990) and they have had little time to advance in socio-economic terms and to spread geographically.

3   A third set of factors relates to a group's distinctiveness, cultural cohesion and desire to live among others who share their ethnic background. This is particularly relevant to our understanding of clustering amongst the culturally distinct Pakistani and Bangladeshi groups, whose Muslim faith provides a strong bond for group cohesion. Studies of the early period of Pakistani settlement in places such as Rochdale (Anwar, 1979), Manchester (Werbner, 1979) and Bradford (Dahya, 1974) clearly illustrated the power of ethnic affiliations to produce social and spatial segregation. Once established, cultural institutions together with social networks based around the group help to anchor the ethnic population in areas of initial settlement (usually poor inner city areas), although early attempts to relocate among the Pakistan community have been documented (Werbner, 1979). Indians display similar tendencies towards clustering for cultural reasons, although regional and religious divisions within this group provide a basis for social and spatial sorting between group members as well as between Indians and other ethnic groups (Robinson, 1981; Ram and Phillips, 1985).

4   Fourthly, the role of the indigenous population (Whites) in excluding minority ethnic groups from access to better areas of housing (in both public and private sectors) must be acknowledged. Past accounts of the search for housing in these northern towns and cities indicate that discrimination has been as widespread here as elsewhere (Khan, 1977; Dahya, 1974; Fenton 1984; Anwar, 1979). Although ethnic minority housing access has improved over the decades, discrimination is not a thing of the past. In recent years, the Commission for Racial Equality (CRE) has uncovered racial discrimination in public housing allocation in Oldham (CRE, 1993) and Liverpool (CRE, 1989), and in the private rental sector in Manchester

(CRE, 1990a). It is also a feature of the allocation of mortgages in the owner-occupied sector and in the way in which estate agents direct the housing searches of minority ethnic households, as exemplified in investigations into mortgage lending in Rochdale (CRE, 1985) and estate agency practice in Oldham (CRE, 1990b). However, these discriminatory influences should not be seen as a determinant of ethnic patterns. Minority households with sufficient capital and income are easily able to establish residences in pleasant suburban neighbourhoods. Rees et al. (1995), for example, show that Indians in Leeds and Bradford have suburbanised rapidly in the 1981–91 decade to suburbs such as Pudsey, Moortown and the North ward (Alwoodley). Research elsewhere, however, suggests that the process of relocation is often more costly and difficult for minority households compared with Whites (Sarre et al., 1989).

Table 8.6 shows that there is a wide variety of experience across the 24 districts. Although the average ordering of the groups is followed in most districts, there are some exceptions. The textile districts of Lancashire have the highest IDs, with Hyndburn and Pendle topping the list with average IDs across all groups of 52. Kirklees and Scunthorpe also have IDs above 50. Districts with low average segregation of minority groups from Whites are predominantly located in Greater Manchester: districts with IDs below 40 are, in descending order, Tameside (38), Bradford (38), Manchester (36), Salford (34), Stockport (31) and Bury (30). The other 14 districts have average IDs in the 40 to 49 range. No definitive explanation can be offered for the inter-district variation in level of ethnic segregation. It is not related to the size of the minority ethnic population *per se*. Both Bradford and Pendle fall in the group with more than 10 per cent of their population belonging to ethnic minorities but they appear at opposite ends of the ID scale. The same is true of Manchester and Kirklees. The explanation for these differences is most likely to lie in the pattern of employment and housing opportunities open to the minority ethnic groups in the smaller textile towns as opposed to the larger metropolitan areas.

8.4   Socio-economic structure

Although much more detailed coverage of the demographic and social character of Britain's ethnic minorities is provided in other volumes in this series, it is useful to take a brief look at these issues in the specific context of northern England. We first examine the district pattern (for each of the 24 districts with significant minority concentrations), looking at three variables diagnostic of the socio-economic position of an ethnic group. Then the interrelationships between these variables are examined in more detail, drawing on information in the 2% Individual Sample of Anonymised Records for northern England as a whole.

Socio-economic levels for six ethnic groups across the 24 districts

In their analysis of the socio-economic position of ethnic minorities in Leeds and Bradford, Rees et al. (1995) identify three principal contrasts between groups:

1   Varying age structures, with Whites in particular having much older age distributions, and the South Asian groups having particularly youthful age structures.
2   Varying degrees of socio-economic disadvantage assessed in terms of unemployment and economic activity in the various minority groups, ranging from near equality with Whites for the Chinese and Indians, severe disadvantage for Pakistanis and very severe disadvantage for Bangladeshis.
3   In some ways surprisingly favourable positions vis a vis Whites for consumption variables such as central heating and car availability (except for the very deprived Bangladeshi group).

The key questions are whether or not these findings are replicated across all Pennine cities, and whether any explanation can be offered for the apparently conflicting evidence provided by the employment-based as against the consumption-based indicators (of disadvantage).

The 1991 Census Local Base Statistics were used to compute key socio-economic indicators for ethnic groups, and the results are shown in Table 8.7 for the age structure domain, using the percentage of children (defined as persons aged 0–15) in an ethnic group; in Table 8.8 for the employment domain, using the percentage of the economically active population unemployed; and in Table 8.9 for the consumption domain, using the percentage of households without access to a car. The number of ethnic categories has been reduced to six by amalgamating the Black groups, and likewise the Chinese, Other – Asian and Other – Other groups.

The differences in age structure between the groups is clear, and uniform across all districts (Table 8.7). Children make up only 20 per cent of the White group's population, with a standard deviation over the 24 districts of only 1 per cent. In contrast, between 31 and 46 per cent of the populations of minority ethnic groups are children. The Bangladeshi group is the most youthful, reflecting its high level of recent fertility, followed by the Pakistanis, both with over 40 per cent of their population under 16 in 1991. Then follow the broad Other category and the Black grouping with percentages between 35 and 39. The minority with the smallest proportion of children is the Indian group, though their proportion under 16 is still 50 per cent greater than that of Whites. These differences clearly have implications for the ethnic composition of age cohorts moving into the local labour market at particular points in time, and for patterns of new household formation.

Moving on to consider the world of work, Table 8.8 demonstrates how unsuccessful minority·ethnic groups have been in achieving employment, by reporting the percentage of the economically active population which was unemployed in the week preceding the 1991 Census for each of the six groups in the 24 districts. (It should be noted that 1991 witnessed a downswing in economic activity and relatively high levels of unemployment, though the bottom of the recession was

Table 8.7 *Percentages in childhood ages in six ethnic groups for 24 Pennine districts, 1991*

District	Per cent aged under 16						
	Total	White	Black	Indian	Pakistani	Bangladeshi	Other
Greater Manchester							
Bolton	22	20	31	36	48	44	39
Bury	21	20	35	29	46	47	36
Manchester	23	21	33	29	41	44	37
Oldham	22	20	35	36	51	55	43
Rochdale	23	21	34	35	45	50	43
Salford	21	20	34	30	35	48	31
Stockport	20	20	34	25	39	31	33
Tameside	21	20	35	26	44	51	35
Trafford	20	20	28	36	36	45	35
Merseyside							
Liverpool	21	21	37	24	31	46	30
South Yorkshire							
Sheffield	18	17	33	24	44	44	35
Tyne and Wear							
Newcastle	20	19	29	28	41	48	29
West Yorkshire							
Bradford	24	20	31	31	47	51	46
Calderdale	21	20	37	29	48	53	42
Kirklees	21	19	28	37	46	53	46
Leeds	20	19	30	30	44	51	38
Cleveland							
Middlesbrough	24	23	44	32	43	24	41
Humberside							
Scunthorpe	22	22	39	30	39	49	35
Lancashire							
Blackburn	24	21	42	42	49	47	43
Burnley	23	21	40	28	48	58	42
Hyndburn	22	20	41	29	51	43	43
Pendle	23	20	42	29	49	20	42
Preston	22	20	31	36	44	48	45
Rossendale	22	21	35	24	46	53	41
Totals	21	20	32	34	46	50	37
Statistics							
Mean	22	20	35	31	44	46	39
Minimum	18	17	28	24	31	20	29
Maximum	24	23	44	42	51	58	46
Standard deviation	1	1	5	5	5	9	5

Note: The mean figure for per cent children refers to the total population of the 24 districts rather than to the average of the districts in the table.

Source: Computed from 1991 Census Local Base Statistics. Crown copyright. ESRC/JISC purchase supplied by CDU on Midas system.

Table 8.8 *Percentage unemployed in six ethnic groups for 24 Pennine districts, 1991*

District	Total	White	Black	Indian	Pakistani	Bangladeshi	Other
			% Unemployed				
Greater Manchester							
Bolton	10	9	21	24	31	30	17
Bury	7	7	13	6	23	7	7
Manchester	19	18	30	18	31	29	24
Oldham	11	10	18	12	34	44	17
Rochdale	12	11	25	12	26	35	15
Salford	13	13	23	10	23	17	16
Stockport	7	7	9	8	18	11	10
Tameside	10	10	16	11	25	34	11
Trafford	8	8	18	19	23	10	16
Merseyside							
Liverpool	21	21	35	14	25	25	22
South Yorkshire							
Sheffield	12	12	26	14	40	39	22
Tyne and Wear							
Newcastle	15	15	23	11	27	31	17
West Yorkshire							
Bradford	11	9	21	15	36	36	22
Calderdale	9	8	19	5	44	64	15
Kirklees	9	7	18	21	29	28	19
Leeds	9	9	21	12	30	38	17
Cleveland							
Middlesbrough	17	17	37	11	34	11	25
Humberside							
Scunthorpe	13	13	35	11	15	32	5
Lancashire							
Blackburn	12	10	19	28	34	28	20
Burnley	9	9	15	6	32	39	12
Hyndburn	8	7	13	19	31	29	14
Pendle	8	7	20	9	24	0	11
Preston	11	10	21	23	30	16	17
Rossendale	7	7	18	2	22	38	12
Mean	12	11	24	18	32	35	19
Minimum	7	7	9	2	15	0	5
Maximum	21	21	37	28	44	64	25
Standard deviation	4	4	7	7	7	14	5

Source: Computed from 1991 Census Local Base Statistics. Crown copyright. ESRC/JISC purchase supplied by CDU on Midas system.

not reached until 1992. These conditions are reflected in the 11.6 per cent level of unemployment.)

The general pattern is for Whites to have the lowest levels of unemployment, followed by Indians, the Other group and the Black group; with Pakistanis and Bangladeshis having by far the worst experience. This pattern is not universal across all of the districts, however. For example, Indians have lower unemployment rates than Whites in Bury, Calderdale, Middlesbrough, Burnley and Rossendale. Bangladeshis actually experience very low unemployment rates in a few districts (e.g. Bury, Trafford, Pendle) but not too much attention should be paid to these as the numbers involved are very small. The level of Black unemployment falls between that of Indians on the one hand and Pakistanis on the other, but is very high in the largest community, Manchester, at 30 per cent.

These differences between the groups cannot be directly interpreted as evidence of discrimination in the labour market, although this undoubtedly plays a role. Studies by Penn and Scattergood (1992) in Rochdale and by Aldrich et al. (1981) in Bradford and Huddersfield show how culturally influenced aspirations intertwine with racial barriers in the job market to shape South Asian employment patterns. Meanwhile, Small (1991) draws on a wide range of studies in Liverpool (e.g. Gifford et al., 1989; Manpower Services Commission, 1985) to argue that systematic racialised discrimination has structured the patterns of employment and unemployment for the Black population in the city. However, background factors such as the age distribution of the economically active population, the level of qualifications attained and the industry/occupational skills mix of the labour force must also be taken into consideration.

Here we make the general observation that the substantial decline of operator jobs in the textile industry which the Pakistani immigrants of the 1950s and 1960s came to fill has radically affected their employment chances. However, as the study by Penn et al. (1990) of South Asians' employment trajectories in Rochdale shows, the deliberate exclusion of Pakistanis from the skilled and technical jobs in the textile industry in the past has served to decrease their alternative employment prospects. Indians and Blacks, with a lesser concentration in such a declining industry, have suffered less in the restructuring of the economy and Indians, in particular, have made good use of their relatively high levels of educational qualifications to move into professional and white-collar work (Jones, 1993).

The final diagnostic indicator relates to household consumption, namely, the availability of a car in the household. Not having a car available is generally considered a deprivation in modern society (making it harder to transport household goods and increasing substantially the time and monetary cost of travel), and it is also a reflection of income levels in the household; a reasonable income level is needed to purchase and maintain such an expensive consumer durable. Table 8.9 sets out the results for our 24 districts with populations of 2 per cent or more from minority ethnic groups. In the light of the disadvantage revealed in the unemployment table, the results are quite surprising. Whites are not the group with the lowest percentage of households without access to a car: Indians, the Other group and Pakistanis are more favourably placed, the first group substantially, the second and third groups marginally. Both Bangladeshis and Blacks are quite severely

Table 8.9 *Percentage with no car available in six ethnic groups for 24 Pennine districts, 1991*

District	% Households with no car available						
	Total	White	Black	Indian	Pakistani	Bangladeshi	Other
Greater Manchester							
Bolton	38	38	52	36	34	57	31
Bury	32	32	33	8	32	12	18
Manchester	57	57	68	33	33	55	46
Oldham	43	42	57	26	48	78	28
Rochdale	42	42	48	20	41	77	29
Salford	48	48	51	18	31	38	38
Stockport	29	29	26	8	13	18	13
Tameside	41	41	40	22	30	64	27
Trafford	31	31	47	27	20	24	23
Merseyside							
Liverpool	57	57	72	31	34	58	51
South Yorkshire							
Sheffield	45	45	63	27	45	71	50
Tyne and Wear							
Newcastle	54	55	64	26	32	66	38
West Yorkshire							
Bradford	41	40	61	30	47	74	41
Calderdale	39	39	48	14	49	84	32
Kirklees	37	37	58	32	42	63	37
Leeds	41	41	63	21	40	75	42
Cleveland							
Middlesbrough	48	48	61	26	38	40	42
Humberside							
Scunthorpe	41	41	59	15	34	73	30
Lancashire							
Blackburn	41	41	44	39	41	55	31
Burnley	41	41	37	15	41	73	31
Hyndburn	36	36	18	22	38	63	28
Pendle	36	36	43	21	45	67	36
Preston	39	39	57	34	40	41	40
Rossendale	33	33	36	3	39	70	14
mean	43	43	61	29	41	68	40
minimum	29	29	18	3	13	12	13
maximum	57	57	72	39	49	84	51
standard dev	8	8	14	9	9	20	10

Source: Computed from 1991 Census local base statistics.
Crown copyright. ESRC/JISC purchase supplied by CDU on Midas system.

disadvantaged in comparison with the average. This pattern is repeated across the districts: in no district do Whites exhibit the lowest value on this index, the Indian figure always being lower. And usually, other groups also exhibit lower values.

How can we account for this incongruity between the unemployment and car availability results? We must, of course, look at intermediate variables for some explanation. We note first that car availability is a household-based indicator whereas unemployment is an individual-based measure. Minority groups have larger households (by far) than Whites and hence the greater probability of more than one income source through work or benefits. Pooled resources may enable minority households to afford a car while smaller White households cannot. The second factor at work may be the age distribution. The White distribution contains a high proportion of elderly persons, who not only have less income than the average but may also lack the ability to drive a car, or are prevented from doing so by infirmity.

Table 8.10 *The relationship between ethnicity, age and unemployment in northern England, 1991*

Age	Ethnic group	Employed	Government scheme	Unemployed
16–29	White	81	4	15
	Black	66	5	29
	Indian	66	5	29
	Pakistani	58	5	36
	Bangladeshi	68	12	20
	Chinese–Other	77	5	18
30–39	White	91	1	8
	Black	79	6	15
	Indian	81	3	15
	Pakistani	74	2	24
	Bangladeshi	54	4	42
	Chinese–Other	84	1	15
40–49	White	93	1	6
	Black	85	0	15
	Indian	90	2	8
	Pakistani	72	2	26
	Bangladeshi	47	0	53
	Chinese–Other	91	5	5
50–64	White	89	0	10
	Black	80	1	19
	Indian	73	3	24
	Pakistani	56	1	43
	Bangladeshi	36	4	61
	Chinese–Others	78	1	21

Source: Computed from 1991 Census Sample of Anonymised Records (2%).
Crown Copyright. ESRC/JISC purchase, supplied by CMU, University of Manchester via Midas service of Manchester Computing.
Note:
The figures are row percentages and add to 100 across each row.

To look in part at the validity of these suggestions, we construct tables that cross-classify the population by age, ethnicity and unemployment, and age, ethnicity and car availability.

The relationship between ethnicity and socio-economic level, controlling for age

The Individual Sample of Anonymised Records from the 1991 Census gives us a large sample of observations for northern England (the combination of the North, North West, and Yorkshire and Humberside standard regions), from which we can construct cross-tabulations that control for the influence of background variables that may intervene between ethnicity and socio-economic level. The analysis carried out here is very simple in nature: we look at whether the ethnic differences observed in the previous subsection persist when a control for age is introduced.

Table 8.10 reports, for broad age-groups, the percentage unemployed in each ethnic group. At all ages, Whites fare best in percentage employed and have the lowest percentages unemployed, with one exception (the unemployment rate of the Chinese and Others grouping at ages 40–49 is lower than that of Whites). The differences are particularly pronounced between Whites, on the one hand, and Pakistanis and Bangladeshis on the other. The level of unemployment varies by age: it is highest in the youngest age-group, declines in the next two (30–39, 40–49) and then increases in the last age-group (50–64). The minority ethnic groups face severe disadvantage in the labour market at all ages (Ohri and Faruqi, 1988), so the differences in age distribution between ethnicities does not play a role in explaining the overall differences reported in section 8.3. The disproportionately high level of youth unemployment among the Black and South Asian minorities does nevertheless have implications for capital accumulation and household formation among this younger cohort.

The relationship between ethnicity, age and car availability is reported in Table 8.11 for northern England. Here we obtain a rather different picture when controlling for age than we did using the aggregate statistics (reported in Table 8.9). In the 0–19, 20–39 and 40–59 age-groups, Whites have a lower percentage (than the other ethnic groupings) in the 'no car' category. They also have much higher percentages in the 'two cars' and 'three cars or more' categories than the other groups. The picture is a little different in the final age-group, where the White percentage with no car is higher than that for Indians and Pakistanis. This probably reflects the greater probability of living in a multi-generation household in the latter two groups than the former. If you are an elderly person in an Indian or Pakistani household, you are more likely to have access to a car, owned and driven by your cohabiting offspring, than are Whites, who are much more likely to be living as independent households, a large proportion of them single person households.

Table 8.11 also shows that Indian and Chinese and Other households maintain a car availability, allowing for age, comparable to that of Whites; that Pakistanis still fare better than Blacks; and Bangladeshis remain worst off. It was suggested by

Table 8.11: *The relationship between ethnicity, age and car availability in Northern England*

Age	Ethnic group	Cars				
		0	1	2	3+	NA
0–19	White	27	45	23	4	1
	Black	55	34	8	1	2
	Indian	26	51	19	2	1
	Pakistani	36	54	8	2	0
	Bangladeshi	71	24	4	1	0
	Chinese–Other	29	50	15	2	4
20–39	White	24	46	23	5	2
	Black	47	36	9	3	6
	Indian	22	54	18	2	3
	Pakistani	34	49	13	3	2
	Bangladeshi	62	27	8	2	1
	Chinese–Other	30	46	16	2	6
40–59	White	20	45	27	7	1
	Black	44	38	13	2	3
	Indian	21	46	28	4	0
	Pakistani	37	50	10	3	1
	Bangladeshi	68	19	12	0	1
	Chinese–Other	21	50	20	4	5
60+	White	50	37	7	1	6
	Black	66	29	3	1	1
	Indian	37	44	12	3	3
	Pakistani	40	43	8	7	2
	Bangladeshi	63	19	19	0	0
	Chinese–Other	51	37	6	2	4

Source: Computed from 1991 Census Sample of Anonymised Records (2%).
Crown Copyright. ESRC/JISC purchase, supplied by CMU, University of Manchester via Midas service of Manchester Computing.
Note: The figures are row percentages and add to 100 across each row.
NA = Not applicable. This refers to persons not in private households.

Rees et al. (1995) that the better position of Pakistanis in terms of car availability (than their employment position would indicate) was in part due, in Leeds and Bradford, to their occupational concentration in taxi driving, a hypothesis in need of further investigation.

These two cross-tabulations derived from 1991 Census microdata show how important it is to control for intermediary variables in interpreting the differences in socio-economic level between ethnic groups.

8.5 Conclusions

The cities of northern England have not developed the sizeable minority ethnic communities seen in the large cities of southern England (in London, Birmingham, and Leicester, in particular) and, as a result, the proportion of the area's population drawn from minority groups is lower than the national average. Nevertheless, some towns and cities do house minority communities that are important both in absolute size and as a proportion of the district population they belong to. The largest cities in northern England, such as Manchester, Leeds, Sheffield and Newcastle, house large or moderate sized communities of each of the nine minority ethnic groups distinguishable in the 1991 Census. Another group of cities, closer to the Pennines and associated with the textile industry, have more specialised ethnic compositions with high concentrations (relative to the region average) of one or more of the Indian subcontinent groups. The minority ethnic community of Pendle district, for example, is almost exclusively of Pakistani ethnicity, while the minority community in Preston is largely Indian by origin. Other Pennine cities such as Bradford and Kirklees have large Pakistani and Indian communities. The corollary of these urban concentrations is that there is a majority of districts of lower density and rural character which have fewer than 2 per cent of their populations who are 'non-White'.

An analysis of segregation from Whites was carried out at both district and ward scale. There are some commonalities but also some contrasts. Bangladeshis and Pakistanis tend to be highly segregated from Whites at both district and ward scale. The Chinese and Other – Other groups are widely dispersed relative to Whites at both district and ward scale. However, both the Indian and Black–Caribbean groups are quite highly segregated at district scale but only moderately segregated at ward scale in districts with higher levels of minority concentration. Black–Africans and Black–Others show the same intermediate level of segregation at both spatial levels, while Other – Asians have relatively low segregation at district scale but somewhat higher levels at ward scale, akin to those of Indians.

One important ingredient, though only a very minor one, in explaining these degrees of geographical segregation from Whites are the socio-economic profiles of the groups. The demographic and household structures of Whites, on the one hand, and all other ethnic groups on the other, are very different in all districts studied. These demographic differences do not play much part in differentiating the groups in terms of employment chances: the latter are better for Whites at all ages, though Chinese and Indian experiences are quite close to those of Whites. Pakistanis and Bangladeshis on the other hand, tend to fare rather worse than the White population.

When a major household consumption variable, namely the car, was examined, Whites appeared to be the disadvantaged group. This is largely due to the relationship of car availability to age and household structure: Whites are much more concentrated in the car-poor older ages in smaller, more isolated households. If you want to enjoy the benefits of a car in old age, be a member of a multi-generation minority household and be driven around by your son/son-in-law/daughter/ daughter-in-law. If you are White, lobby very hard for good public transport!

Acknowledgements

All the statistics are derived from the 1991 Census of Population and are Crown copyright. The data are supplied through the ESRC/JISC Census Programme purchase and are made available by the Census Dissemination Unit and Census Microdata Unit, University of Manchester on the MIDAS service of Manchester Computing.

References

Aldrich, H., Cater, J., Jones, T. and McCroy, D. (1981) Business development and self-segregation: Asian enterprise in three cities. In Peach, C., Robinson, V. and Smith, S. (eds), *Ethnic Segregation in Cities*. London: Croom Helm.

Anwar, M. (1979) *The Myth of Return: Pakistanis in Britain*. London: Heinemann.

Ballard, R. and Ballard, C. (1977) The Sikhs: the development of South Asian settlement in Britain. In Watson, J. (ed.), *Between Two Cultures*. Oxford: Blackwell.

Castles, S. (1984) *Here for Good. Western Europe's New Ethnic Minorities*. London: Pluto Press.

Castles, S. and Kosack, G. (1973) *Immigrant Workers and Class Structure in Western Europe*. Oxford: Oxford University Press.

Commission for Racial Equality (1985) *Race and Mortgage Lending*. London: CRE.

Commission for Racial Equality (1989) *Racial Discrimination in Liverpool City Council: Report of a Formal Investigation into the Housing Department*. London: CRE.

Commission for Racial Equality (1990a) *Sorry its Gone; Testing for Racial Discrimination in the Private Rented Housing Sector*. London: CRE.

Commission for Racial Equality (1990b) *Racial Discrimination in an Oldham Estate Agency*. London: CRE.

Commission for Racial Equality (1993) *Housing Allocations in Oldham*. London: CRE.

Dahya, B. (1974) The nature of Pakistani ethnicity in industrial cities in Britain. In Cohen, A. (ed.), *Urban Ethnicity*. London: Tavistock.

Fenton, S. (1984) Costs of discrimination in the owner occupied sector. In Ward, R. (ed.), *Race and Residence in Britain: Approaches to Differential Treatment in Housing*. Birmingham, SSRC Research Unit on Ethnic Relations.

Fevre, R. (1984) *Cheap Labour and Racial Discrimination*. Aldershot: Gower.

Gifford, A., Brown, W. and Bunday, R. (1989) *Loosen the Shackles: First Report of the Liverpool 8 Inquiry into Race Relations in Liverpool*. London: Karia Press.

Harris, C. (1987) British capitalism, migration and relative surplus population: a synopsis. *Migration*, 1, 47–96.

Jones, D. (1979) The Chinese in Britain; origins and development of a community. *New Community*, 12, 397–402.

Jones, T. (1993) *Britain's Ethnic Minorities*. London: PSI.

Jones, T. and McEvoy, D. (1978) Race and space in cloud-cuckoo land. *Area*, 10(3), 162–6.

Khan, V. S. (1977) The Pakistanis: Mirpuri villagers at home and in the city of Bradford. In Watson, J. L. (ed.), *Between Two Cultures: Migrants and Minorities in Britain*. Oxford: Blackwell.

Manpower Services Commission (1985) *Ethnic Minorities in Liverpool: Problems faced in their Search for Work*. Merseyside Area Services Board.

Ohri, S. and Faruqi, S. (1988) Racism, employment and unemployment. In Bhat, A., et al. (eds), *Britain's Black Population*. Aldershot: Gower.

Peach, C. (1968) *West Indian Migration to Britain: a Social Geography*. London: Oxford University Press.

Peach, C. (1986) Patterns of Afro-Caribbean migration and settlement in Great Britain; 1945–1981. In Brock, C. (ed.), *The Caribbean in Europe*. London: Frank Cass.

Peach, C. (1990) Estimating the growth of the Bangladeshi population of Great Britain. *New Community*, 16(4), 481–91.

Penn, R. and Scattergood, H. (1992) Ethnicity and career aspirations in contemporary Britain. *New Community*, 19, 75–98.

Penn, R., Scattergood, H. and Martin, A. (1990) The dialectics of ethnic incorporation and exclusion: employment trajectories of Asian migrants in Rochdale. *New Community*, 16(2), 175–98.

Ram, S. (1986) *Indian immigrants in Great Britain*. New Delhi: Mittal.

Ram, S. and Phillips, D. (1985) *Indians in Bradford. Socio-economic Profile and Housing Characteristics, 1971–84*. University of Leeds, School of Geography Working Paper No. 433.

Rees, P., Phillips, D. and Medway, D. (1995) The socio-economic geography of ethnic groups in two northern British cities. *Environment and Planning A*, 27, 557–91.

Robinson, V. (1981) The development of South Asian settlement in Britain and the myth of return. In Peach, C., et al. (eds) *Ethnic Segregation in Cities*. London: Croom Helm.

Robinson, V. (1986) *Transients, Settlers and Refugees*. Oxford: Clarendon Press.

Rose, E. J. B., Deakin, N. and Abrams, M. (1969) *Colour and Citizenship: a Report on British Race Relations*. London: Oxford University Press.

Runnymede Bulletin (1995) *Ethnic minorities in the labour market*. Runnymede Bulletin, June, 7.

Sarre, P., Phillips, D. and Skellington, R. (1989) *Ethnic Minority Housing: Explanations and Policies*. Aldershot: Avebury.

Small, S. (1991) Racialised relations in Liverpool; a contemporary anomaly. *New Community*, 17(4), 511–38.

Smith, S. J. (1989) *The Politics of 'Race' and Residence*. Cambridge: Polity Press.

Watson, J. (1977) The Chinese: Hong Kong villagers in the British catering trade. In Watson, J. (ed.), *Between Two Cultures*. London: Blackwell.

Werbner, P. (1979) Avoiding the ghetto: Pakistani migrants and settlement shifts in Manchester. *New Community*, 7, 376–89.

Chapter 9
Methodological refinement, policy formulation and the future research agenda: some brief reflections

Peter Ratcliffe

9.1 Introduction

As previous chapters will have made abundantly clear, the study of issues such as concentration and segregation is not merely an abstract academic exercise. It is undertaken, at least partially, because the findings provide insights into the nature and direction of social change, and thereby have implications for social policy formulation. The volume has also highlighted a whole variety of methodological problems for which solutions remain to be found. Until they are, our results will always have to reflect a degree of uncertainty.

This concluding chapter tackles each of these issues in turn. First, there is the question of how, by further improving our research methodology we can enhance our knowledge of the social geography of ethnicity in Britain. Second, there is the crucial question of policy development; namely, that of how policy should respond to the changing, and in some cases static, ethnic geography of Britain's towns and cities. Third, and finally, the analyses reported in this book raise a number of issues the exploration of which could provide the basis of a substantive research agenda, not only for urban geographers but also for sociologists and social scientists in general.

9.2 The enhancement of research methodology

Perhaps the key developments in the area of methodology have to do with the definition and measurement of ethnicity/ethnic group. What we have at the moment is an 'ethnic group' categorisation which could be said to work 'best' in its least detailed, and therefore in some ways least informative, version. It is also the form in which ascriptive rather than self-defined identity arguably plays the major role. In this four-fold system, as argued in Chapter 1, 'Black' is seen essentially to imply African (ultimate) origin, hence the coding as Other–Asian of those who define themselves as (say) Black–Asian, and is implicitly underpinned by the idea that these individuals share characteristics of a phenotypic nature. The same goes for the broad 'Asian' grouping. Rather than listing ethnic groups then, this coding scheme effectively reifies pseudo-racial categories. The sense in which it might 'work' is in cases where differential treatment of individuals or groups is correctly perceived as grounded in a crude form of racialisation.

What our analyses show quite clearly, however, is that the term 'Asian' (or 'South

Asian') conflates a number of disparate groups whose positions in material terms were/are radically at variance. It may also be useful to take on board the views of commentators such as Modood (1992, 1994) who frequently berate social scientists for excluding the possibility, for example, of an 'anti-Islamic' factor in discriminatory processes. An effective ethnic geography of Britain, therefore, has to be based on a much more sophisticated allocation system; one which balances a sense of belonging (self-identity) with exogenous ascriptive processes. This is clearly not provided by the current ethnic group question, given that a substantively important group such as the 'East African Asians' are not directly discernible from the data, and nor are the 'Indo–Caribbeans', the 'Black–British' (given the temptation to opt for one of the listed categories), the 'Irish', and many others. The outcome of current discussions (taking place between the Office for National Statistics, CRE and other interested parties) geared to finding a new question for the 2001 Census, is therefore crucial (see, in particular, Aspinall, 1995).

However 'good' the replacement question is, of course, there will potentially be a problem with data comparability. As was stressed by a number of authors in this volume, 1981–1991 comparisons were made difficult not so much by changes in geographical boundaries but by the lack of ethnic group data in 1981. Any shift in the format of the 2001 question, in wording or coding, clearly has to be done in such a way that comparability problems (vis-a-vis the 1991 data) are minimised. This argues in effect for an expansion of categories which can be collapsed to the 1991 list where necessary; though, given the ambiguity in coding of groups such as the 'East African Asians' in 1991, any change analysis based on the revised categorisation will inevitably have to be grounded in a certain degree of pragmatism. (The 1991–2001 LS will, of course, eventually permit some interesting reflections on the two alternative measures of ethnic group.)

However good the new question is in tapping into the salient features of ethnic differentiation, its benefits will be lost unless levels of under-enumeration and undercount are kept to a minimum. Although in comparison with professional (non State sponsored) surveys, 'non-response' and non-contact levels in the decennial Census are extremely low, their possible differential impact on the data for urban areas with mobile populations, and in particular areas with large concentrations of minority residents, is a matter of some concern. Insofar as the Poll Tax probably induced a one-off reaction in 1991, the problem of missing data may lessen in 2001. Much clearly depends on the relations between the government of the day and the currently alienated and disaffected residents of many inner urban areas. In terms of matters which are within the sphere of influence of the body conducting the 2001 exercise, much reliance will need to be placed on public relations and 'selling the census' to the general populous.

The third methodological issue relates to the context within which the ethnic group question is set. Much has been made throughout this volume of data which are not currently collected. Those who specialise in housing research, for example, will bemoan the lack of effective 'quality' measures beyond the rather weak section on amenities, and data on the presence or absence of central heating. Educationalists would clearly like to see much more detail on lower level qualifications than those currently targeted. Much more could be asked of respondents' working life and labour market problems (especially those of women). Many whose work focuses on the salience of race and ethnicity in Britain's social structure would wish to delve far beyond the existing question which simply aims to allocate people to an ethnic category. In particular, data on religion would go a long way to meeting the requirements of those, such as Modood, who see this as crucial to the notion of ethnic identity.

As noted in Chapter 1, however, the current research technique (the self-completion questionnaire) necessarily imposes constraints on both the amount and nature of data which can be collected. Costs are central to the equation on all counts; hence the existing limits on the number of questions which are coded 100 per cent. All of this means that the resulting census form is inevitably a compromise. Those researching labour market issues at least have the LFS and occasional *ad-hoc* projects such as the 'Working Lives Survey 1993'. Housing researchers have to lean heavily on data from the General Household Survey (GHS), the LFS and the periodic 'House Condition Surveys', but the latter suffers from a paucity of detail on residents (as distinct from their dwellings) and, for the analyst interested in the position of minorities, it suffers from extremely small sample sizes in the case of some groups. A relatively straightforward question on 'housing needs and conditions' would therefore be a welcome addition to the census agenda, as would a question on lower level (i.e. school/college leaving) qualifications.

A fourth, and final, issue which needs to be addressed here was raised in particular by Tony Champion in Chapter 4. All researchers, one would imagine, welcomed the introduction in 1991 of the SARs. Those same researchers would also accept as paramount the need to preserve the confidentiality of data and the anonymity of individual respondents and their households. Many, however, (particularly geographers) understandably feel that the spatial scale limitation imposed on the 1 per cent (Household) SAR in particular is overly restrictive, and that boundaries which permit a 'finer grain' analysis could be introduced without damaging the commitments rightly given to respondents in relation to personal data held on file. Attempting to map social change (say, via one-year migrants) in an urban context is extremely difficult with the present dataset. This may be one issue which could usefully be debated prior to the 2001 Census.

9.3 Developing a research agenda

The key thing to bear in mind when considering the lessons of the current volume is that what we have called 'ethnic geography' is an abstraction; in that the patterns we have described only acquire meaning when set in a substantive context. As demonstrated in particular by Chapters 6 to 8, spatial location is a function of class, wealth, employment and housing opportunities, as well as factors which relate directly to 'ethnicity' (i.e. nearness to kin, places of worship, and so on). Specifically on the external constraints side, as pointed out by a number of our authors, are the issues of 'racial'/ethnic discrimination and racism. Insofar as these are key elements of the twin (but related) processes of exclusion and marginalisation, these influence both current settlement patterns and the likelihood, and nature, of any future relocation.

The immediate agenda for the social geographer is to develop and refine the measurement and analysis of changing spatial patterns, and to see how these relate to social indicators such as class, ethnicity and life-cycle stage. Current research being undertaken by David Owen and the present author, and funded by the Economic and Social Research Council, aims to initiate these debates by focusing on changes over the decade 1981–91. In some respects it represents a further elaboration of the analysis of spatial redistribution performed by Philip Rees and Deborah Phillips in Chapter 2, and the inter-generational analysis of spatial patterns and internal migration by Vaughan Robinson in Chapter 5. But it also aims to explore different ways of measuring segregation in the British context, principally by attempting to make progress on a problem recognised by geographers for at least the last twenty years; namely, the rigid and arbitrary nature of given spatial units. It has long been recognised, as noted by Ceri Peach and David Rossiter in Chapter 3, that both spatial scale and the nature of the underlying areal units have a critical influence on computed segregation/isolation measures (not to mention the 'small population problem' discussed by Philip Rees and Deborah Phillips in Chapter 8).

The key issue for the future is, in many ways, population redistribution. As discussed in the next section, high spatial concentration is at the moment linked to the presence of urban deprivation and decay. Suburbanisation and exurbanisation, touched upon in the chapters by Tony Champion and Vaughan Robinson, may therefore hold the key to the future of ethnic differentiation in material terms. Much depends on the nature of any outward movement from the urban core associated with the 'traditional' settlement areas. If this generally represents little more than 'spillover' into contiguous districts (Phillips and Karn, 1992), gains in housing quality and environment may be more apparent than real, being essentially little more than a natural expansion of existing settlements. If suburban moves are over a longer distance, and are into areas which are at present largely White, and longer distance relocation is of a similar nature, we would be witnessing changes which were of much wider significance in terms of 'racial'/ethnic differentials. Indeed, one of the population shifts noted in the Phillips and Karn article (in relation to Birmingham) took the form of a reversal of the 'invasion-succession' hypothesis, with young White households moving into the renovated inner area housing originally bought by minorities in the period of 'White flight', essentially the 1960s and 1970s.

Whatever the nature of the future population trajectories, the analysis needs to shift to focus to a greater extent on the character of the 'movers'. Are they predominantly the second (and third) generation rather than the 'immigrant' cohort: are they middle class rather than working class and, are they (say) Indians and East African Asians of Hindu or Sikh background rather than Pakistani or Bangladeshi Muslims? How, then, do the new settlement patterns vary in terms of ethnicity, class and life-cycle stage?

In terms of the future sociological agenda, the task seems to me to rest on the explanation of change in a number of respects, most of which might seek to understand the underlying reasons for the sort of possible developments intimated in the previous paragraph. Because of the vast number of possible scenarios probably the best approach here is to take for illustrative purposes three quite distinct characterisations. Each is concerned with levels of mobility; distinguishing quite clearly between relocation beyond existing areas of settlement and that of a more localised form, and highlighting the significance of migration into areas formerly lacking a significant minority presence.

Low levels of ethnic mobility

In the event of universally low levels of minority ethnic mobility, the focus of attention will clearly be on the possible influence of exogenous factors such as unemployment, 'racial'/ethnic exclusion or marginalisation, and stagnation in the housing market. As internal factors are such issues as obligations to kin, the availability of places of worship, and so on. Many of these factors apply equally to the White population, and therefore a comparative analysis would be needed which controlled key variables such as class, employment status, age/life-cycle stage, household size and structure, family commitments, and so on. In other words, to perform this task effectively, the data required would go far beyond that which is routinely available via the census, GHS, LFS and other 'off-the-peg' sources.

Even then, a quantitative analysis of differential propensities to relocate, would leave many questions unanswered. It might tell us, for example, that the Indian middle class of a particular social background, a certain age, family size and structure, and so on is less likely to move in a given period than an ostensibly similar White group. What it would not tell us is why this is the case. The only solution here lies in ethnographic data; research geared to looking at the motives, aims and strategies of individuals and households and the external constraints on their behaviour. This might tell us, for example, that the Indian middle class are less likely to move because of a very different orientation to the housing market, in particular less of a commitment to local cultural norms such as the notion of a 'housing career'. Alternatively, it might reveal any number of other forces which produce much the same result; fewer employment options, fear of movement (based on perceived vulnerability to racist attacks), obligations to kin, and so on.

Differential ethnic mobility

In the (more likely) event of quantitative analyses showing evidence of differentials in the propensity of various groups to migrate, a whole series of interesting issues are raised. Once again the 'groups' which form the basis of the analysis will need to comprise not simply of monolithic blocks of 'ethnic groups' but age/gender/class subsets thereof. Migration itself can take a number of forms, of course. The analysis needs to differentiate between numerous types of movement (subject to data of sufficient spatial detail being available). Local, or within-district, moves from areas of minority settlement can clearly entail relocation to the same (or same 'type' of) area, to suburban settings with or without an existing minority presence, or (as is the case with exurbanisation – discussed in Chapters 4 and 5) to more rural areas, which are at present almost exclusively 'White'. Moves involving longer distances, whether between districts, between counties or between regions, involve further issues, in that they may mark a rather greater spatial redistribution of minority ethnic groups; and may be of even more significance in sociological terms.

Again, for reasons of lack of space, we cannot spell out the many interesting comparisons which are suggested by this analysis. What follows is a selection of the more obvious examples and questions by way of illustration:

(i) The data may reveal higher levels of (gross) mobility at a 'local' scale by those of Indian, rather than Pakistani or Bangladeshi, origin. If this were to be the case, the critical question would be whether nor this could be 'explained' by class differences. For example, the much higher levels of non-manual employment amongst the Indian group, and the association (which holds for the Great Britain population as a whole) between social class and migration propensity, may alone account for any observed differences.

The question would then arise as to whether mobility levels varied significantly across Britain and, crucially, whether the nature of the relocation patterns varied as between (say) middle class Indians and comparable groups of Whites, Pakistanis and Bangladeshis. Parallel analyses would then look at the manual groups. In many ways the key issue in relation to these changing location patterns remains the salience of 'race'/ethnicity; but implicit in the comparison of the various South Asian groups is the question of whether religion, and in particular the Muslim/non-Muslim divide is of significance (over and above the influence of the class factor). On the one hand, there is the suggestion that the ongoing greater spatial isolation of Muslim communities (and especially the Bangladeshis) is related to the village/kin networks of those who migrated to Britain, combined with the 'demands' of Islam as a way of life. On the other, there are the arguments of writers such as Tariq Modood who, as noted earlier, have insisted that the build up of anti-Islamic sentiment through the 1980s and early 1990s has added an extra, even more virulent, dimension to racism in Britain.

(ii) Case (i) may also hold in the event of longer distance movements. Again the key questions relate to the interplay of ethnic/religious/class differentials, but the issue raised here is the possibility of much greater levels of substantively significant population redistribution. Given the concluding remarks of the previous paragraph, an interesting focus for analysis here would be whether migration differentials widened for these longer distance moves. It might be that the predominantly Muslim groups, and even their British-born middle class, have lower propensities (than their Sikh and Hindu counterparts) to relocate in this way. But once again it should be remembered that significant levels of gross migration may simply lead to a circulation or 'reshuffling' of populations and not to redistribution in ethnic terms. Furthermore, a major focus has to be on the precise nature of the migration flows. Are the moves, for example, predominantly between what were described earlier in this volume as 'ethnic core' (primarily poor quality residential) areas, or are they (say) increasingly reflecting upward 'housing career' trajectories? And importantly, does the answer to this question depend on ethnicity, religion, generation, and social class?

(iii) For those of Black-African origin, higher levels of education (which are closely associated with their pattern of migration to the UK) may be linked to quite distinctive settlement patterns, at least in comparison with other Black groups. On the other hand, their concentration in London, as witnessed in Chapter 6, may, if associated with continuing employment in the metropolis, lead to lower levels of population redistribution than amongst (say) middle class Whites. On the other hand, outward relocation to the suburbs and/or to Essex, Kent and

Surrey is also a possibility (assuming financial considerations are the primary factor; outweighing the social and cultural implications of such a move).

(iv) Black–Caribbean patterns may show significant differences at generation level. In particular, inner urban densities may not decline for the British-born: relocation may be extremely localised, i.e. not showing any tendency towards suburbanisation or exurbanisation. But, assuming this were to be the case, is it a function of the development of a distinctive urban culture which rejects alternative housing/residential solutions, or (say) a reflection of a particular predicament in socio-economic terms, i.e. essentially a 'class' factor stemming from marginalisation in the educational system, and marginalisation within, and/or exclusion from, the labour market?

Universal ethnic mobility

Were universally significant levels of migration to be observed, i.e. irrespective of ethnicity and generation, this would potentially signal a major transformation in Britain's social geography, and would have wide-ranging implications in terms of what have often misleadingly been termed 'race relations'; or at least it would if it represented more than simply a circulation of population. As argued in Ratcliffe (1996, forthcoming), the 'race and housing' literature has consistently argued that the choices made by migrants and the constraints upon them have together conspired to deny them access to better quality housing outside minority settlement areas. The 'racialisation' of the housing market is therefore seen to compound class/wealth-based inequalities to produce existing levels of concentration, segregation and isolation.

Significant levels of both 'local' and longer distance migration would cause these already dubious forms of deterministic theorisation to be re-evaluated. This volume has already clearly demonstrated that some population redistribution has occurred during the 1980s. If this was to be followed in the current decade (say) by significant numbers of all South Asian groups, and perhaps the second or third generations in particular, moving into areas previously sparsely populated by minorities, this would herald changes of major sociological importance. On present evidence, however, this appears extremely unlikely. Whatever the case, however, researchers need to assess the policy implications of their findings, and it is to this set of concerns which we now move.

9.4 Concentration, segregation and migration: social and urban policy implications

Much debate about ethnic segregation begins from the premise that even moderate levels are *by definition* a 'bad thing'. The obvious question this invokes is whether this form of spatial patterning is any less desirable than the traditional segregation of White middle class and working class communities. To those whose preferred vision of the Britain of the future is based on the assimilationist ideal linking spatial integration with social integration, it clearly is. But this equally clearly fails to take into account the wishes of those whose origins happen to lie beyond these shores: democratic rights embodied in the notion of citizenship permit the retention of distinct 'ethnic group' identities which may evolve and/or be preserved more easily under conditions of spatial separation, i.e. the 'social pluralism' model in the work of the Jamaican sociologist M.G.Smith (cf. Kuper, 1974).

The 'problem' is not segregation *per se* but the extent to which both the fact of segregation and the location of the segregated areas are not in keeping with the desires of the groups who reside there. In short, physical separation is not the problem: poor housing is. Minorities may opt for concentration or segregation, but not in the poorest urban locations. It is also important to remember that ('forced') segregation has sometimes been used as a policy option. In the case of the Bangladeshi community in Tower Hamlets, for example, high levels of concentration were in part a direct result of the local authority's inability to deal effectively with racial attacks (Phillips, 1986). Rather than attempt to deal with the perpetrators they simply moved the victims; and indeed compounded their maltreatment by moving them into some of the worst (and, for them, most inappropriate) property in the borough – hard-to-let high rise flatted accommodation, thus effectively 'caging' them. Only later did policy shifts render racial harassment an offence leading to the possibility of the perpetrator (and his/her household) being evicted and treated thereafter as intentionally homeless.

Policy makers have often displayed a certain ambiguity in their response to concentrations of minorities. On the one hand, in the context of what have often been highly racialised debates, high levels of concentration have been seen as 'controlling the problem'; i.e. by 'protecting' White areas. On the other, high levels of concentration have been viewed as potentially dangerous, especially when they coincide with areas of poor housing and infrastructure (and especially when the dominant minority population is Black). Such was the view taken in Liverpool as far back as the early decades of this century (May and Cohen, 1974): similar arguments were heard throughout the 1980s and early 1990s in response to outbreaks of violence in Bristol, Brixton and Tottenham in London, Toxteth in Liverpool, and elsewhere. Birmingham's civic leaders, who had (in the 1960s) expressed some satisfaction at their control of the 'immigrant problem' (i.e. via their confinement to certain areas) ultimately changed tack, and attempted to implement a now notorious scheme aimed at dispersing minority tenants throughout their local authority stock. Their refusal to let any vacant property to a minority household if there was another 'coloured' household within a specified distance from it, was eventually deemed discriminatory under the 1968 Race Relations Act (Flett, 1981).

There is no space here to reflect on past policy strategies in the 'inner areas'. But it is important for us both to look at the implications for policy of current settlement patterns, and in particular to show how these intersect with the agenda taken up by Valerie Karn in volume 4 of the current series of 'ethnic analyses'. As we have already seen, it makes little sense to divorce the question of settlement patterns from such substantive concerns as education, employment, health and housing.

The first point to make, however, is that in many ways the inner area problems are not of the same scale, or for that matter of the same level of intractability, as those (say) in the United States. As Ceri Peach and David Rossiter pointed out in Chapter 3, segregation levels in Britain have never, even in the case of the Bangladeshis, reached the sort of levels regularly observed there (in the case of African Americans at least). Slavery on American soil created the sort of deeply entrenched divisions between Black and White which in reality have never been totally transcended; as *de jure* segregation via Jim Crow laws gave way (in most cities) to equally rigid *de facto* segregation (Allen, 1994). Although living in relatively high status areas, the Black middle class were, and are, often as segregated (from middle class Whites) as their blue collar counterparts are from working class Whites. There are no parallels in Britain, and it seems likely that segregation levels in general may well if anything decline as we approach the next millennium.

On the other hand, high levels of unemployment or underemployment combined with a decline in the overall quality of the built environment and, at times, less than sensitive policing strategies, have produced (and still produce) deep-seated resentment which has the potential to spill over into violence (Solomos, 1993). As recently as June 1995, anger amongst the Muslim community in Bradford over the apparent failure of the police to deal with prostitution in the residential areas where most had settled combined with insensitivity on the part of some local officers in dealing with second and third generation youths, sparked off two days of serious street disturbances. And in December, the death in police custody of a Black male under questioning concerning allegations of involvement in a robbery, led to protests and street violence in Brixton, in south London. As with earlier disturbances in the 1980s, underlying material inequalities were a key element of the causal network. So, what are the policy options?

The two most obvious are those which are in some sense ethnicity/race-specific and those which are 'colour-blind', relying in one way or another on the trickle-down effect, i.e. those which are targeted at poor urban communities in general. As Ratcliffe (1992) argued, the latter have generally failed in practice, as funds have tended to be channelled into projects which favoured Whites, and often not the poorest amongst even this group. Race-or ethnicity-specific policies would on past evidence, if adopted (and this is extremely unlikely under future administrations formed by either of the major political parties), be likely to favour those within the respective minority groups who have *some* measure of political representation.

It would seem that the appropriate strategies have to be those which correctly locate the core problem. The problem, as noted earlier, is not ethnic segregation or for that matter lack of mobility *per se*: it only is so when location is a function of external constraints and not of a wish to share residential space with those of a similar background in terms of ethnicity. The problem is one of material inequalities; inequalities rooted partly at least in a society which routinely treats (or implicitly sanctions the treatment of) minorities as inferior, and as not deserving equal citizenship rights to those of indigenous Whites. Research evidence suggests that discrimination, whether at an individual or an institutional level, remains more often than not the norm rather than the exception. An effective policy solution would therefore need to tackle the twin problems of material deprivation (which also, of course, affects poor Whites) and discrimination at all levels against minorities.

It appears somewhat trite to argue that the core of the problem is poverty stemming from unemployment. It appears equally trite to say that housing conditions are directly related to this urban poverty. But both are true, and at the same time neither is solely a function of class, and therefore amenable to conventional 'colour blind' solutions. Unemployment levels for manual workers, as we have seen in the chapters dealing specifically with particular urban locations, have been consistently higher for the non-White working class in general and far higher for the predominantly Muslim groups. Housing conditions display a similar ethnic gradient within classes, and these in turn have a major bearing on health differentials between minority groups and ostensibly comparable Whites.

It follows that urban policy will need to be 'ethnicity-sensitive' if not 'ethnicity-specific'. The one thing which has been conspicuously absent in the policy arena (outside the Commission for Racial Equality) has been a commitment to monitor the impact of policy (in all institutional domains) on different sectors of the population. A recently published report (CRE, 1994) amply demonstrates the widespread lack of monitoring in Britain's local authorities, in particular in the area of service delivery; and even then one has to ask precisely how (or even whether) monitoring is to be linked to remedial action where the evidence suggests this is necessary. Crucially, however, what this report also highlights is the CRE's general impotence to deal effectively with the global problem of unequal treatment and unequal outcomes. Much of this stems from the dual problem of underfunding and the fact that the existing legislation arguably needs to be considerably strengthened to cope with the scale, severity and complexity of the problems faced by Britain's minorities. The treatment of 'racial discrimination' as a civil rather than as a criminal matter was always seen as diminishing the importance and impact of the CRE's work (and that of the Community Relations Commission before it). But, in the era of decentralisation and 'internal markets' and of compulsory competitive tendering (CCT), where a local authority's recruitment policy is more complex, the monitoring-action framework needs to be both increasingly sophisticated and have the appropriate legislative support. The current Race Relations Act has been on the Statute Book for twenty years, and if there is one thing which unites the many and varied critical reviews of its operation it is the view that the time for consultation and gentle persuasion is past: what is needed is the political will to tackle the problems head-on.

The report noted in the previous paragraph demonstrated conclusively that local authorities all too often failed even to avail themselves of the basic census data which would have enabled them to assess the likely needs of their customers. Even in the 1981 Census, without both 'ethnic group' data and the SARs, there was much to assist enlightened policy making. With the advent of the 1991 Census, incorporating both of these refinements along with additional data on housing amenities and health, local authorities as well as central government have at their fingertips a considerably more powerful database. The 'best' authorities in the CRE survey (ibid.) spelt out the implications (for the different minority groups resident in their area) of various policy options and carefully monitored outcomes for those put into practice. But those which did so were rare: few authorities placed such a high priority on equality issues. This is especially unfortunate given that a key element of the OPCS's original case for inclusion of the ethnic group question was that it would help in an assessment of the effectiveness of the Race Relations Act (Sillitoe, 1978).

9.5 Concluding remarks

One of the key messages to emerge from this volume is that an understanding of social geography and changing spatial patterns are a central component of any sociological analysis which purports to assess the salience of race and ethnicity in urban Britain. The use of space interpreted both as a cultural entity and as an embodiment and focus of material experiences is vital to such a task. What is now needed in addition to a refinement in the methodology associated with the measurement of ethnicity, and the sophisticated quantitative analysis of differential redistribution of sub-populations defined by ethnicity, class, age, life-cycle stage, and so on, is an ethnographic study of the aspirations, expectations and motivations of the various groups.

Spatial patterns are also central to any attempt to assess policy options. Here it is important to recognise that minorities have quite distinctive locations not only spatially but in relation to the employment and housing markets. Although the specificity of particular geographical locations should feature in any serious analysis of ethnic differentials, given local variations in housing and labour markets, there is a certain commonality of experience in the 'ethnic core' areas. Ratcliffe (1996, forthcoming) shows, for example, in relation to housing that tenure, property type, amenity levels and the incidence and severity of overcrowding vary significantly both between Whites and non-Whites and amongst minority ethnic groups themselves according to social class, age/generation, household size and structure, and so on. Many, though not all, of the 'ethnic core' areas are those where the once sought-after skills of the migrants are no longer required, following years of recession and economic restructuring. But once again there are dramatic variations by ethnic group and specific fractions thereof. For many of the urban working class and particularly the first generation migrants, however, the fact remains that lack of education, unemployment and poverty inhibit migration: poverty is linked to poor housing which is in turn associated with greater levels of morbidity: and health problems inhibit future employment prospects. It is one of the central challenges of contemporary urban social policy to break this vicious spiral.

Data contained in this volume suggest that future policy should address these concerns, and not assume that with the passage of time, the British-born will escape the fate of many from the immigrant generation. Discriminatory behaviour, although rarely overt in the manner common in earlier decades, is far too entrenched within British 'custom and practice' to fade, at least without the type of interventionist policy noted in the previous section. The 2001 Census, especially if further refined in methodological terms and used much more widely by local authorities as part of their day-to-day policy assessment procedures, should prove indispensable as part of the push towards bringing the 'One Nation' concept so beloved of politicians of all hues, to fruition.

References

Allen, W.R. (1994) The dilemma persists: race, class and inequality in American life. In P.Ratcliffe (ed.) *'Race', Ethnicity and Nation: international perspectives on social conflict.* London: UCL Press. pp.48–67.

Aspinall, P. (1995) *Report on the findings of a consultation exercise carried out with members of the Working Group on the 2001 Census Ethnic Group Question, July-September 1995,* South East Institute of Public Health/United Medical and Dental Schools of Guy's and St. Thomas's Hospitals.

Commission for Racial Equality (1994) *Environmental Health and Racial Equality,* London: CRE.

Flett, H. (1981) *The politics of dispersal in Birmingham.* Working Papers on Ethnic Relations, No. 14, SSRC Research Unit on Ethnic Relations.

Kuper, L. (1974) *Race, Class and Power.* London: Duckworth.

May, R and Cohen, R. (1974) The interaction between race and colonialism: a case study of the Liverpool race riots of 1919. *Race and Class,* XVI(2), 111–26.

Modood, T. (1992) *Not Easy Being British: colour, culture and citizenship.* London: Runnymede Trust and Trentham Books.

Modood, T. (1994) Political blackness and British Asians. *Sociology,* 28(4), 859–876.

Phillips, D. (1986) *What Price Equality?: a report on the allocation of GLC housing in Tower Hamlets.* London: GLC.

Phillips, D. and Karn, V. (1992) Race and housing in a property owning democracy. *New Community,* 18(3), 355–369.

Ratcliffe, P. (1992) Renewal, regeneration and 'race': issues in urban policy. *New Community,* 18(3), 387–400.

Ratcliffe, P. (1996, forthcoming) 'Race', housing and the city. In N.Jewson and S.MacGregor (eds.) *Transforming Cities: Contested governance and new spatial divisions.* London: Routledge.

Sillitoe, K. (1978) Ethnic origins: the search for a question. *Population Trends,* 13, 25–30.

Solomos, J. (1993) *Race and Racism in Britain* Basingstoke/London: Macmillan.

INDEX

For consistency with the indexes of other
volumes in this series, 'minority ethnic groups'
has been indexed under the entry 'ethnic
minority groups'.

Italic page numbers refer to figures and **bold**
page numbers to tables.

Printed in the United Kingdom for HMSO
Dd 301922 8/96 65862